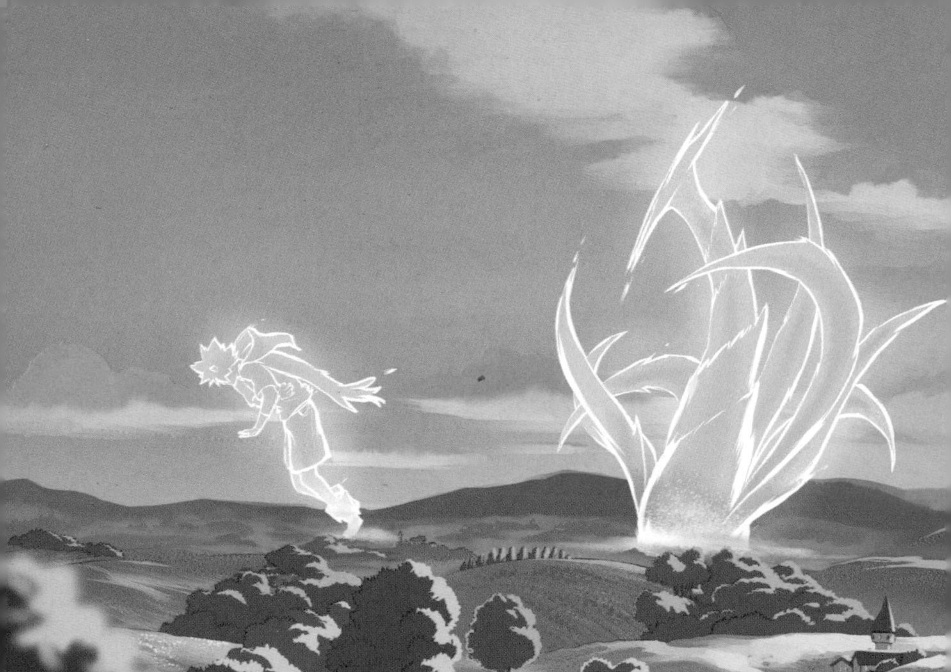
Chapter 37
The Spectrum Falls
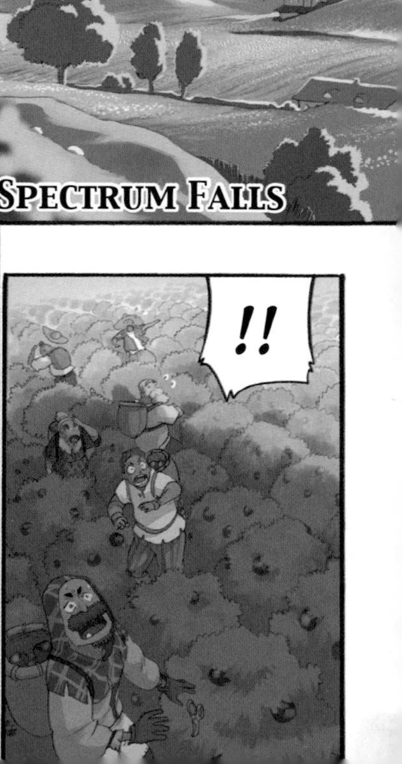
!!
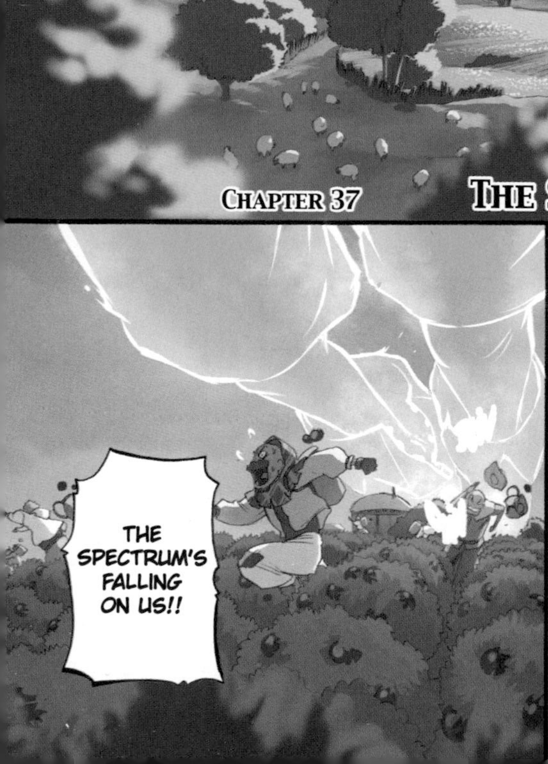
THE SPECTRUM'S FALLING ON US!!

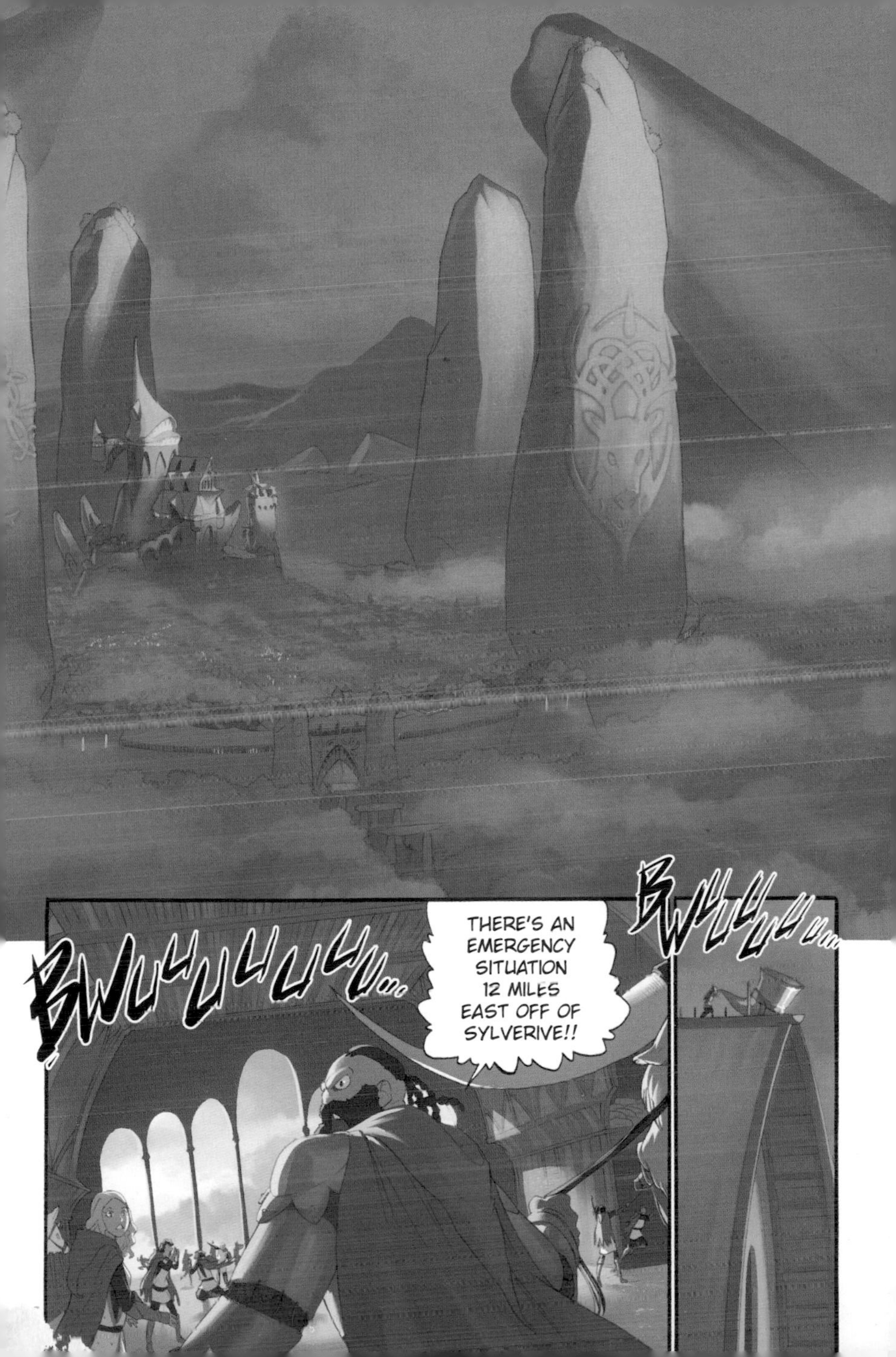

BWUUUUU...
THERE'S AN EMERGENCY SITUATION 12 MILES EAST OFF OF SYLVERIVE!!
BWUUUUUUUU...

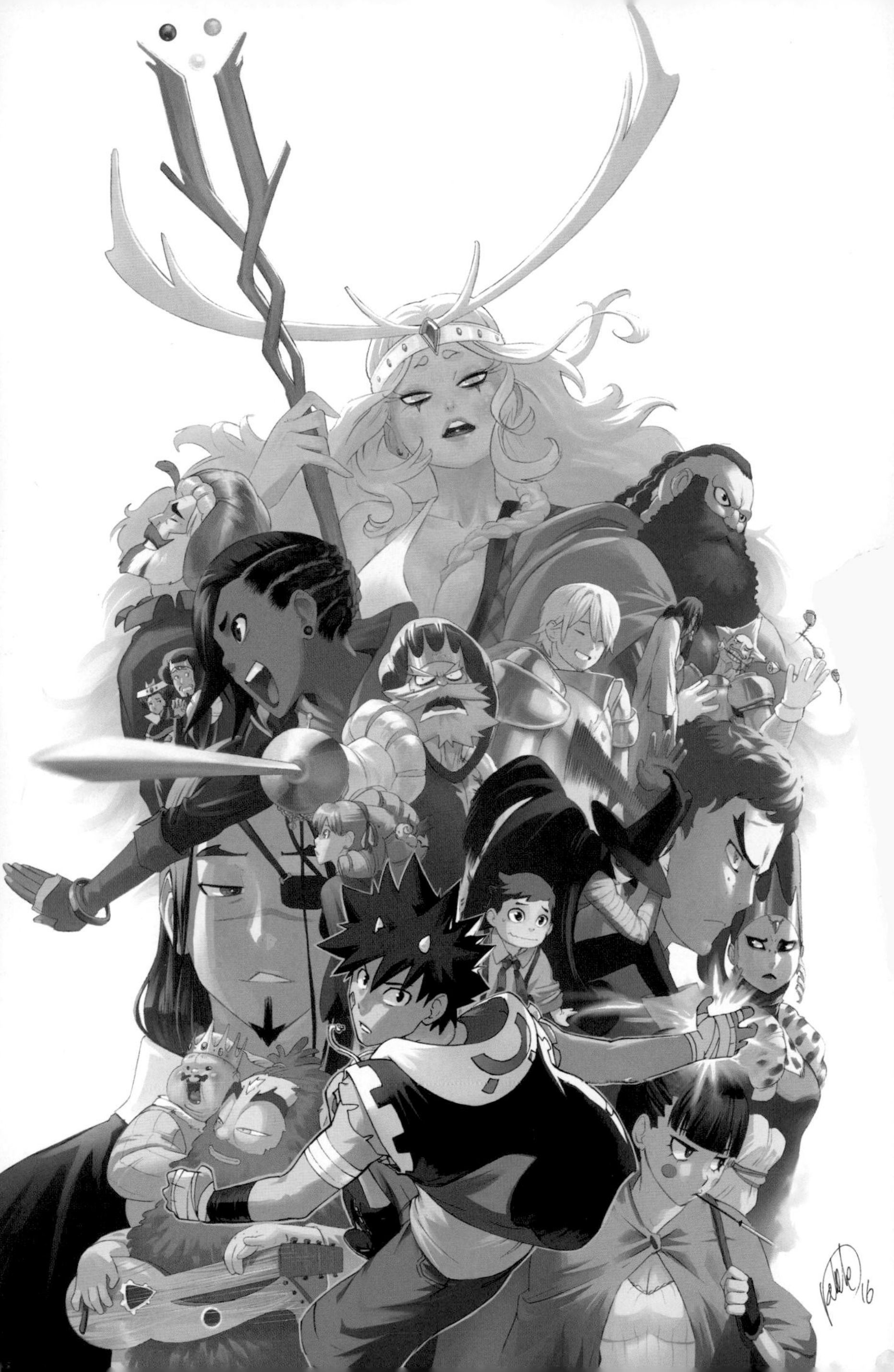

CONTENTS

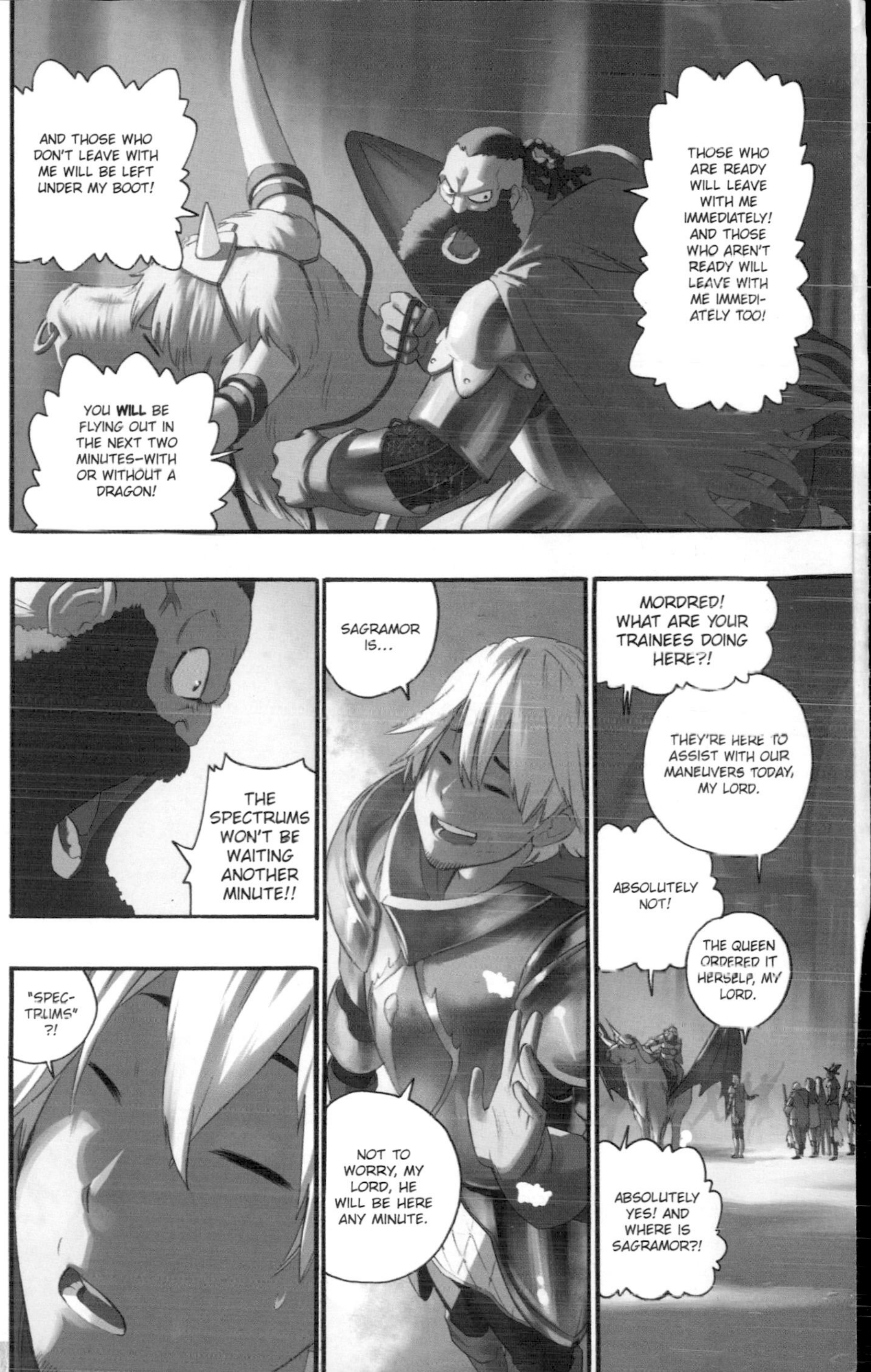
THOSE WHO ARE READY WILL LEAVE WITH ME IMMEDIATELY! AND THOSE WHO AREN'T READY WILL LEAVE WITH ME IMMEDI-ATELY TOO!
AND THOSE WHO DON'T LEAVE WITH ME WILL BE LEFT UNDER MY BOOT!
YOU **WILL** BE FLYING OUT IN THE NEXT TWO MINUTES–WITH OR WITHOUT A DRAGON!
MORDRED! WHAT ARE YOUR TRAINEES DOING HERE?!
THEY'RE HERE TO ASSIST WITH OUR MANEUVERS TODAY, MY LORD.
ABSOLUTELY NOT!
THE QUEEN ORDERED IT HERSELF, MY LORD.
ABSOLUTELY YES! AND WHERE IS SAGRAMOR?!
SAGRAMOR IS...
NOT TO WORRY, MY LORD, HE WILL BE HERE ANY MINUTE.
THE SPECTRUMS WON'T BE WAITING ANOTHER MINUTE!!
"SPEC-TRUMS" ?!

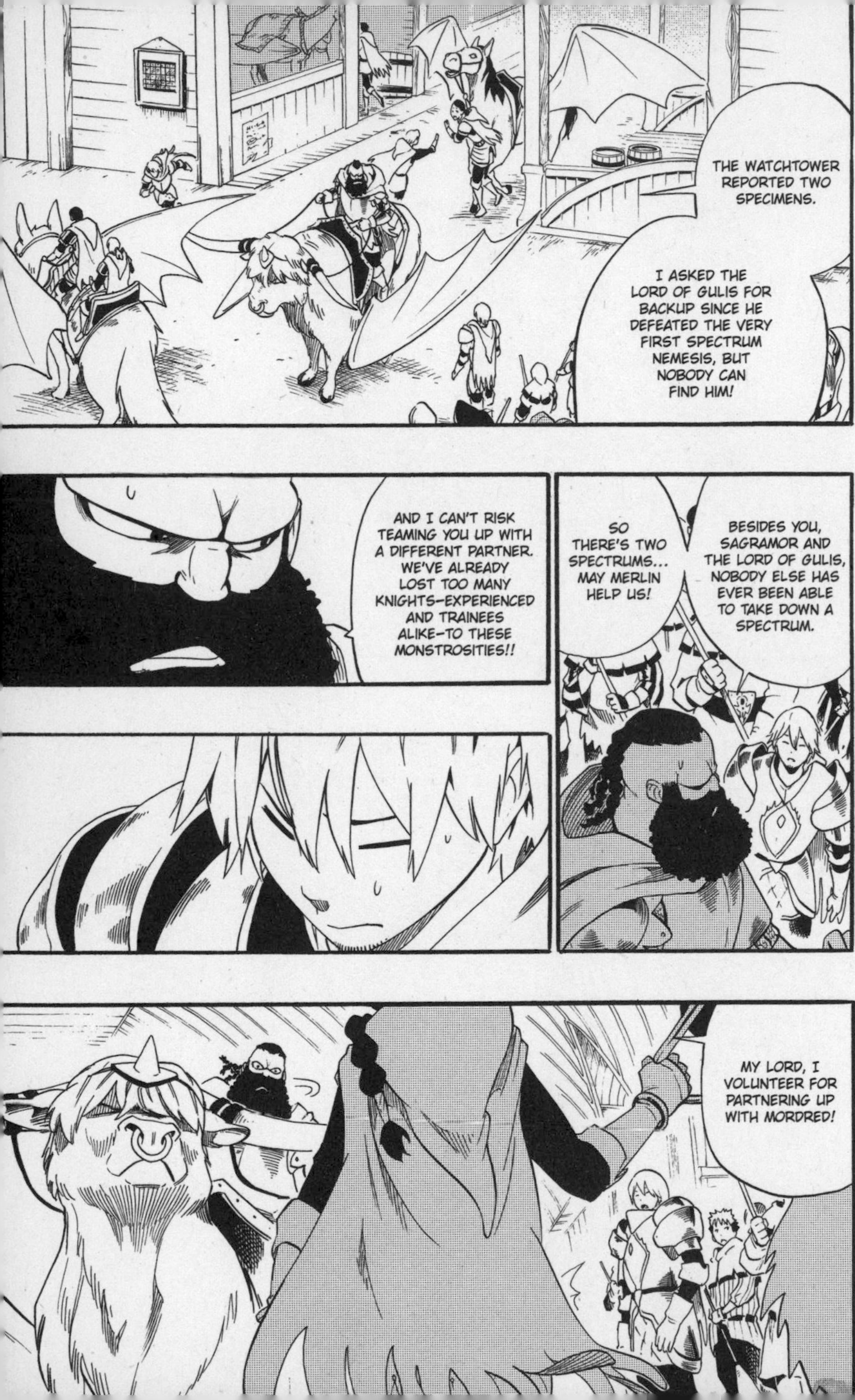
THE WATCHTOWER REPORTED TWO SPECIMENS.
I ASKED THE LORD OF GULIS FOR BACKUP SINCE HE DEFEATED THE VERY FIRST SPECTRUM NEMESIS, BUT NOBODY CAN FIND HIM!
BESIDES YOU, SAGRAMOR AND THE LORD OF GULIS, NOBODY ELSE HAS EVER BEEN ABLE TO TAKE DOWN A SPECTRUM.
SO THERE'S TWO SPECTRUMS... MAY MERLIN HELP US!
AND I CAN'T RISK TEAMING YOU UP WITH A DIFFERENT PARTNER. WE'VE ALREADY LOST TOO MANY KNIGHTS—EXPERIENCED AND TRAINEES ALIKE—TO THESE MONSTROSITIES!!
MY LORD, I VOLUNTEER FOR PARTNERING UP WITH MORDRED!

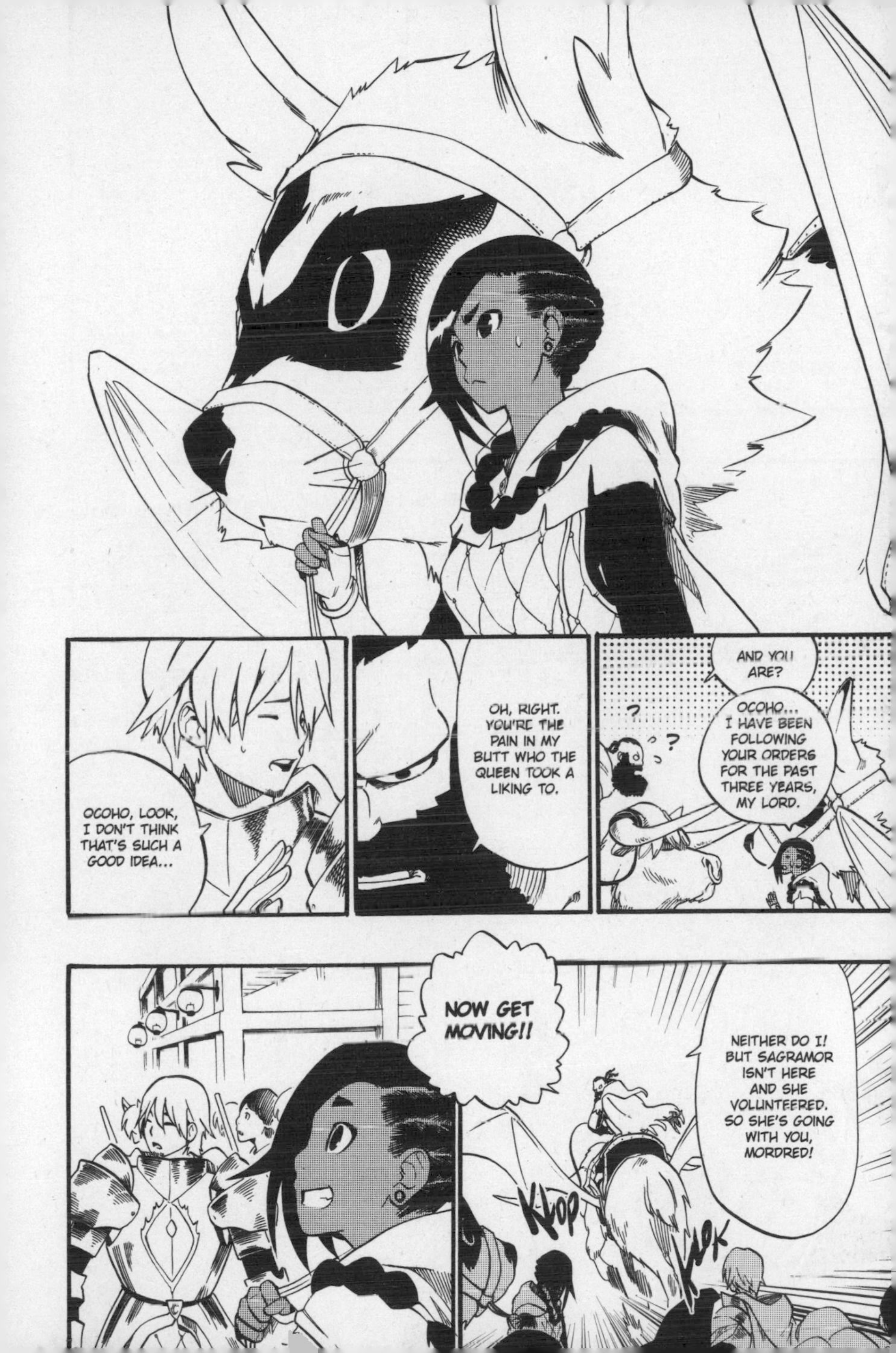
AND YOU ARE?
OCOHO... I HAVE BEEN FOLLOWING YOUR ORDERS FOR THE PAST THREE YEARS, MY LORD.
OH, RIGHT. YOU'RE THE PAIN IN MY BUTT WHO THE QUEEN TOOK A LIKING TO.
OCOHO, LOOK, I DON'T THINK THAT'S SUCH A GOOD IDEA...
NEITHER DO I! BUT SAGRAMOR ISN'T HERE AND SHE VOLUNTEERED. SO SHE'S GOING WITH YOU, MORDRED!
NOW GET MOVING!!
K-LOP

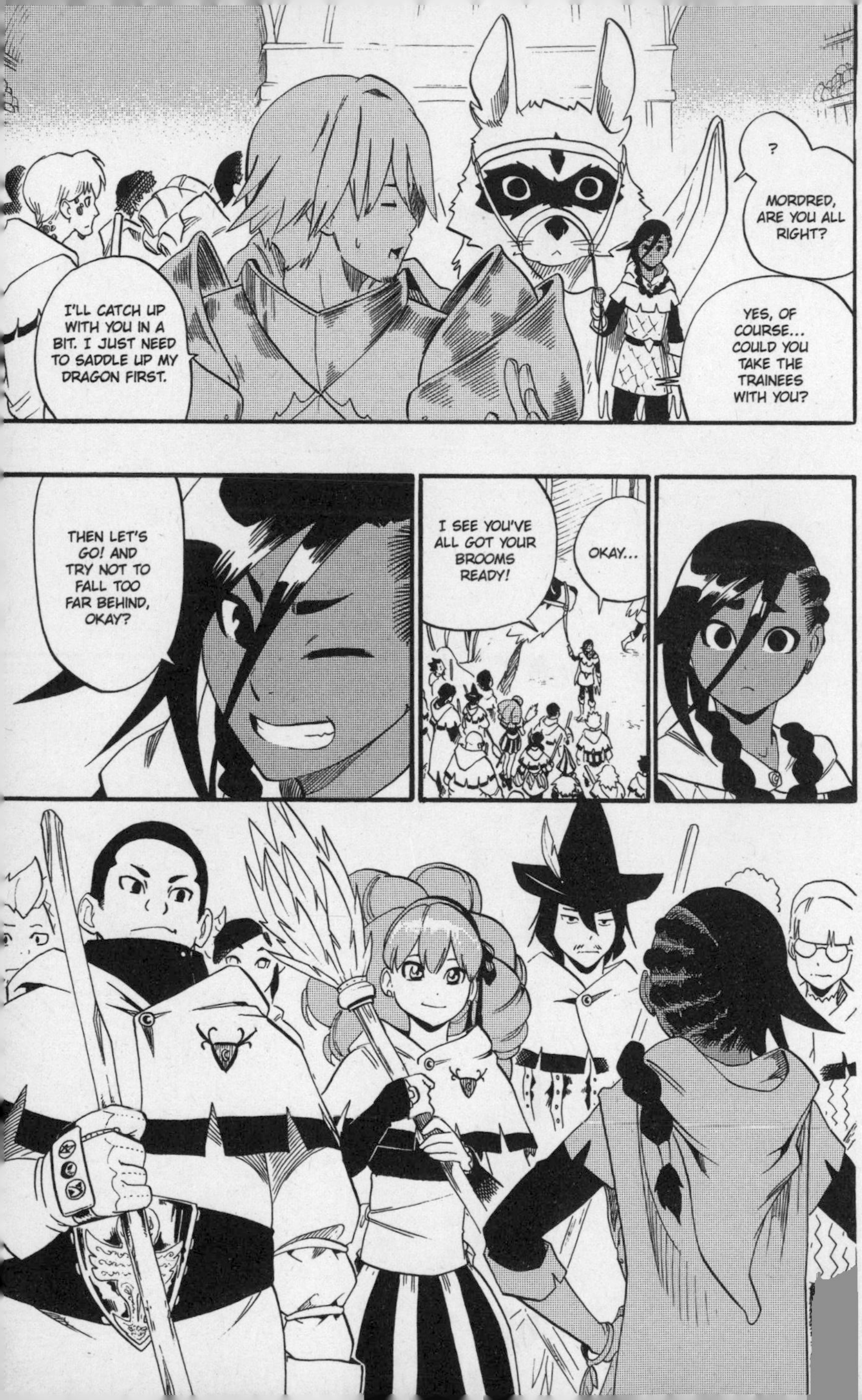
?
MORDRED, ARE YOU ALL RIGHT?
YES, OF COURSE... COULD YOU TAKE THE TRAINEES WITH YOU?
I'LL CATCH UP WITH YOU IN A BIT. I JUST NEED TO SADDLE UP MY DRAGON FIRST.
OKAY...
I SEE YOU'VE ALL GOT YOUR BROOMS READY!
THEN LET'S GO! AND TRY NOT TO FALL TOO FAR BEHIND, OKAY?

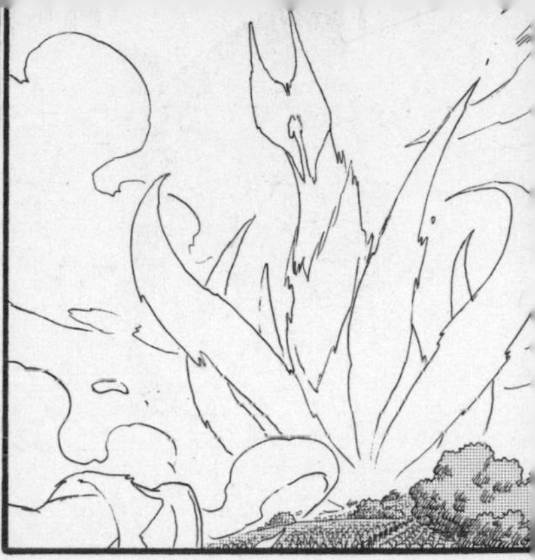

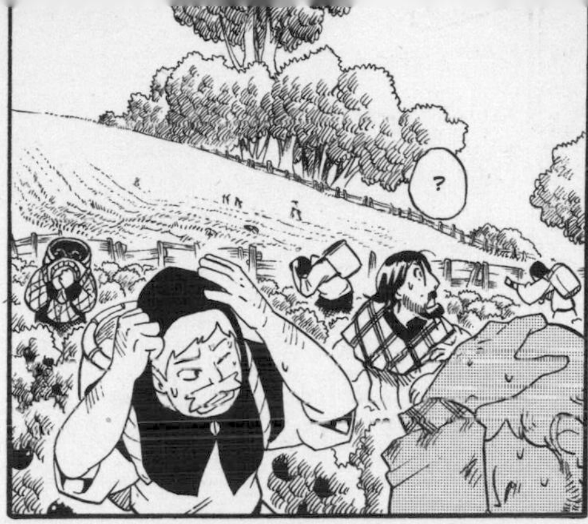
?

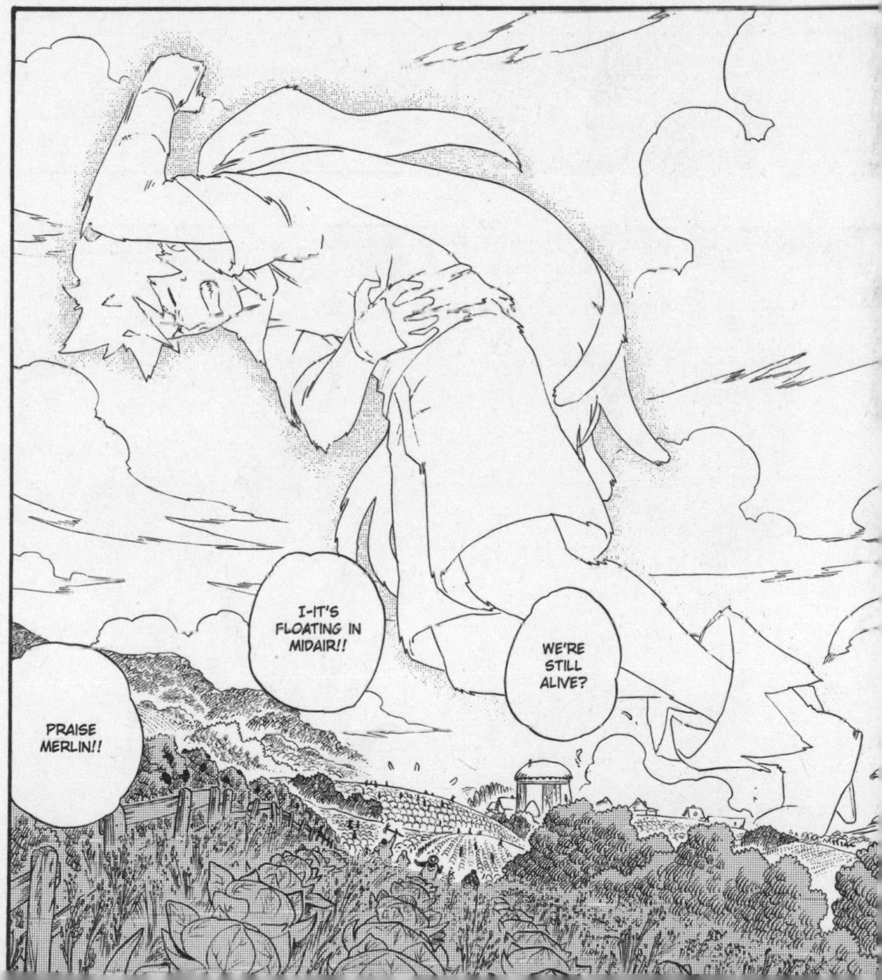
WE'RE STILL ALIVE?
I-IT'S FLOATING IN MIDAIR!!
PRAISE MERLIN!!

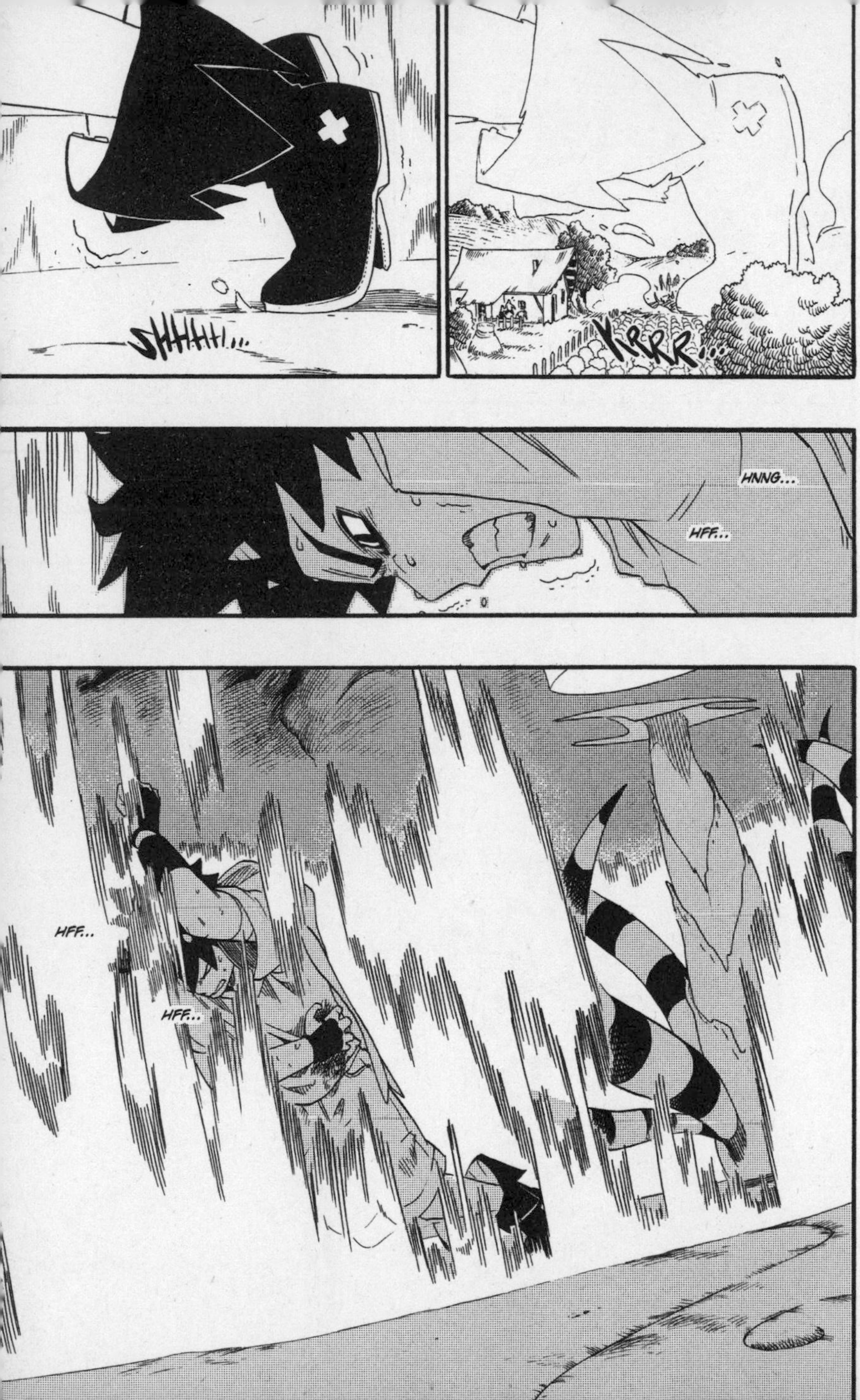
KRRR...
SHHHH...
HNNG...
HFF...
HFF...
HFF...

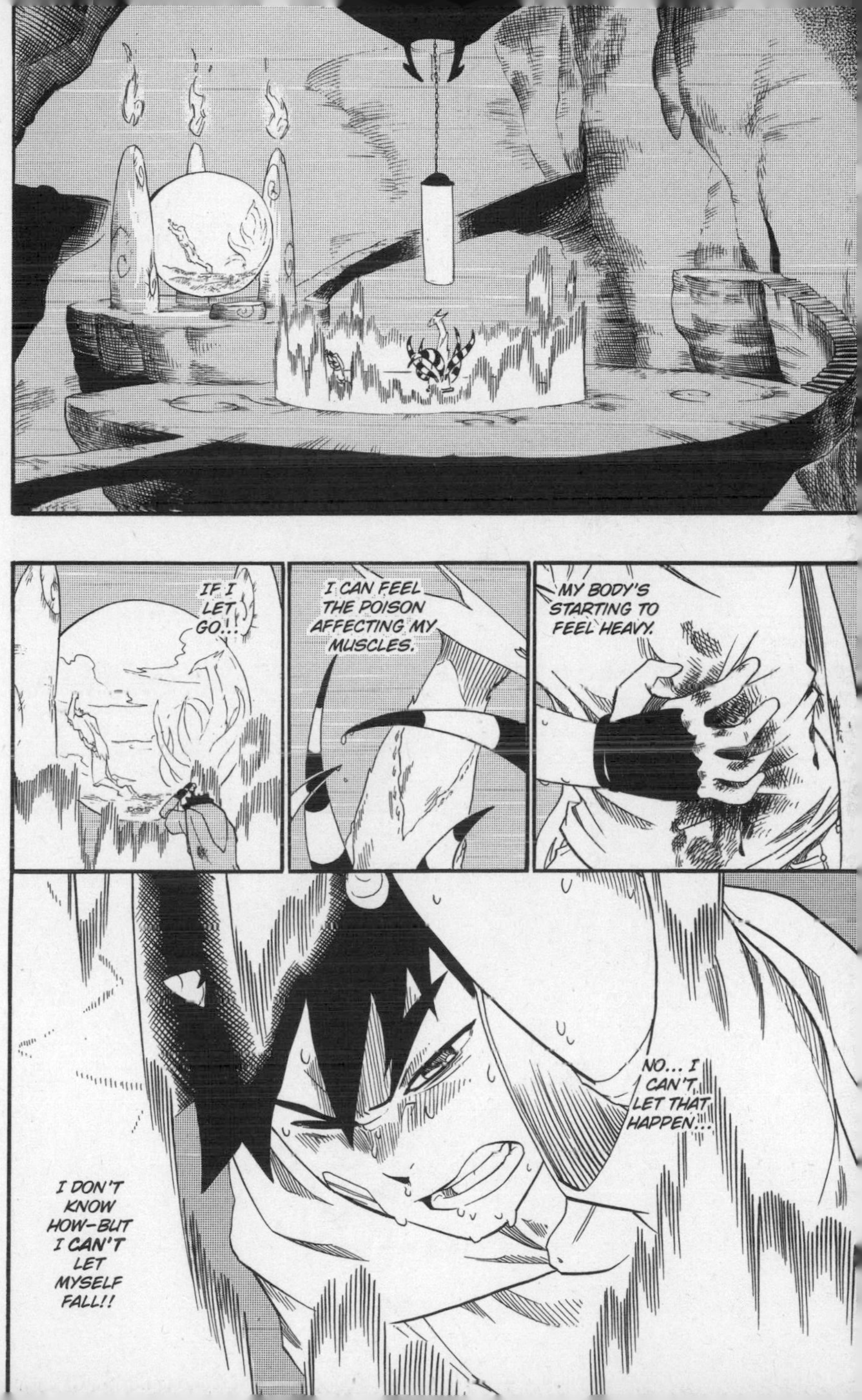
MY BODY'S STARTING TO FEEL HEAVY.
I CAN FEEL THE POISON AFFECTING MY MUSCLES.
IF I LET GO...!!
NO... I CAN'T LET THAT HAPPEN...
I DON'T KNOW HOW—BUT I CAN'T LET MYSELF FALL!!

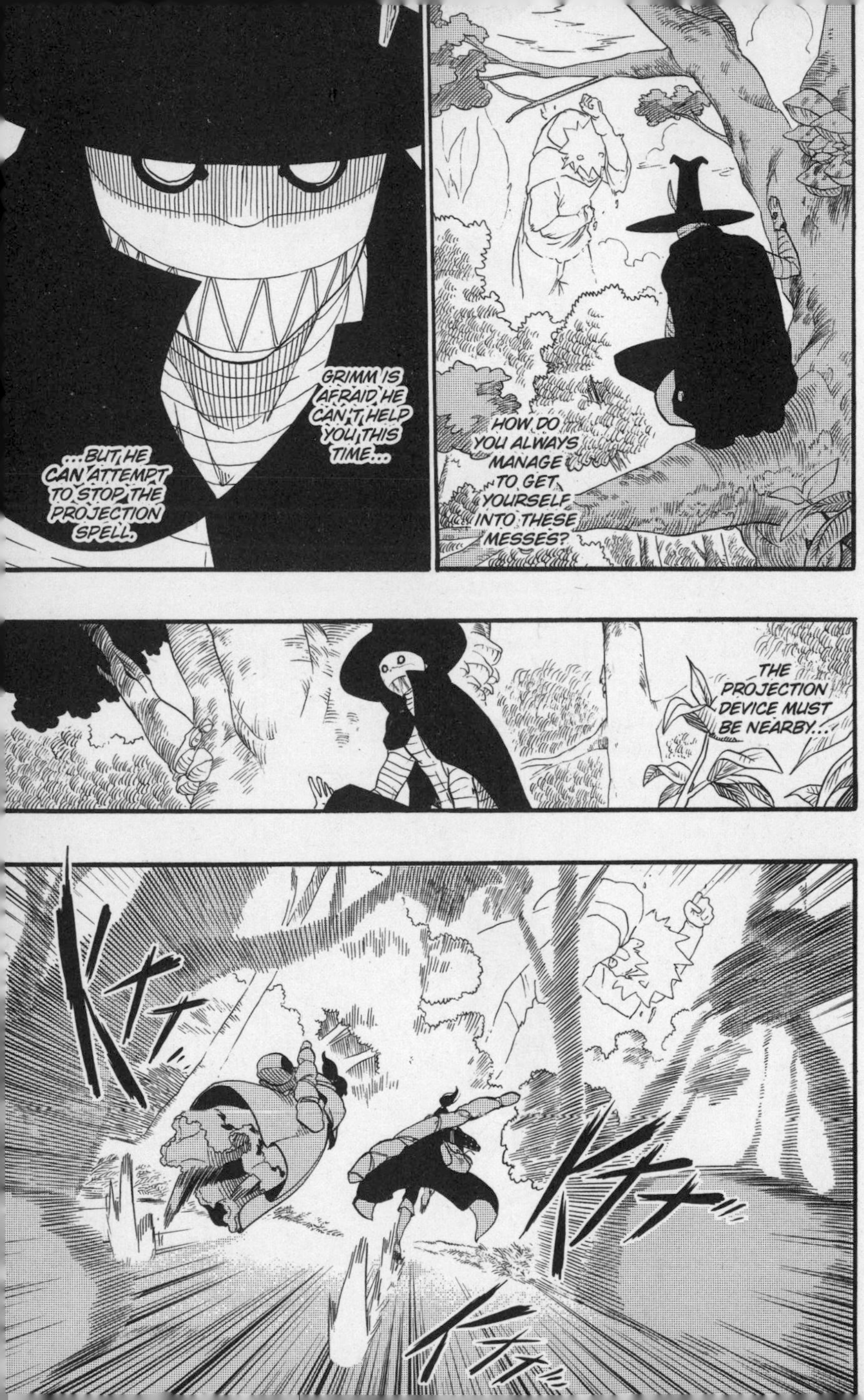
HOW DO YOU ALWAYS MANAGE TO GET YOURSELF INTO THESE MESSES?
GRIMM IS AFRAID HE CAN'T HELP YOU THIS TIME...
...BUT HE CAN ATTEMPT TO STOP THE PROJECTION SPELL.
THE PROJECTION DEVICE MUST BE NEARBY...

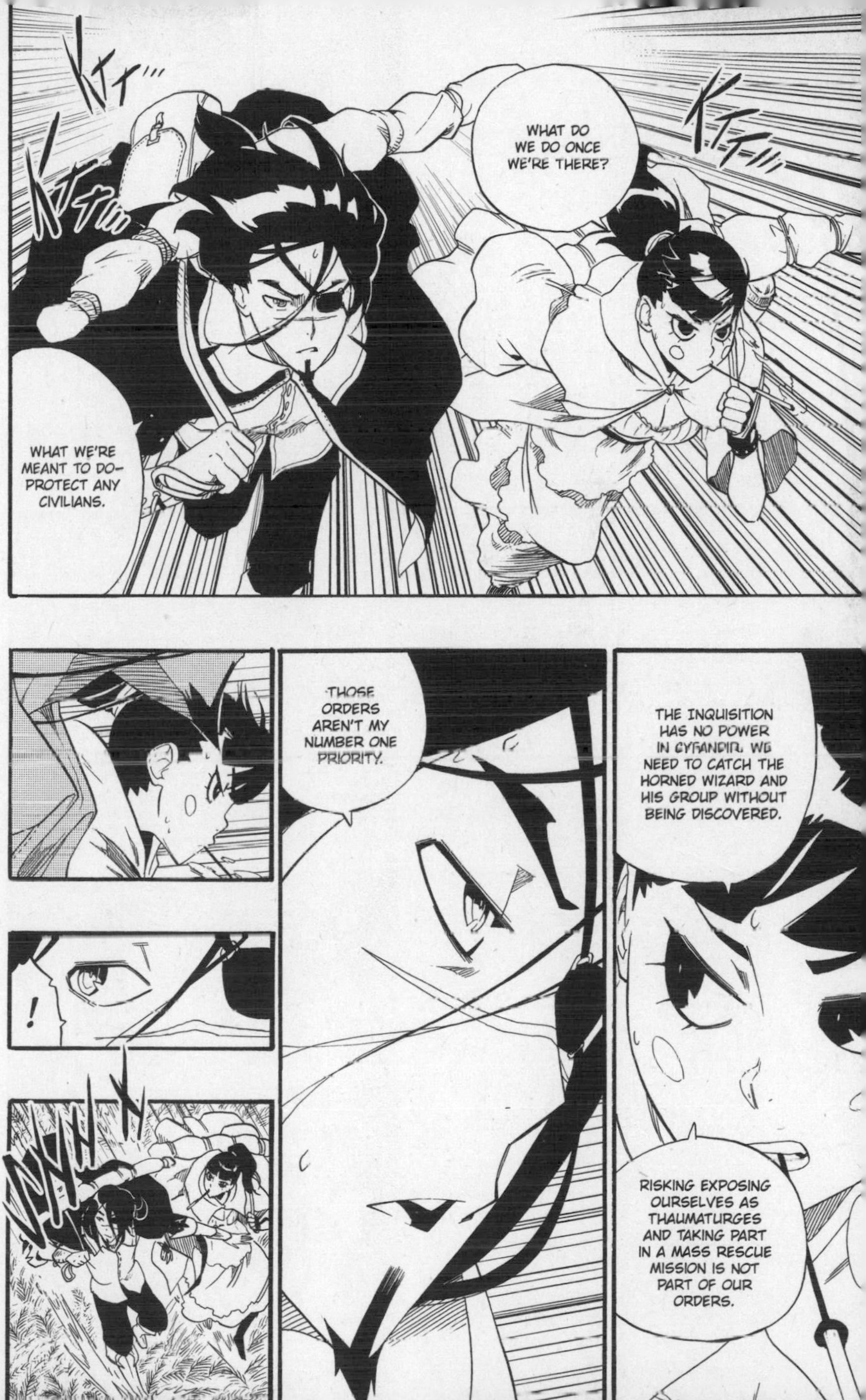
WHAT DO WE DO ONCE WE'RE THERE?
WHAT WE'RE MEANT TO DO—PROTECT ANY CIVILIANS.
THE INQUISITION HAS NO POWER IN CYFANDIR. WE NEED TO CATCH THE HORNED WIZARD AND HIS GROUP WITHOUT BEING DISCOVERED.
RISKING EXPOSING OURSELVES AS THAUMATURGES AND TAKING PART IN A MASS RESCUE MISSION IS NOT PART OF OUR ORDERS.
THOSE ORDERS AREN'T MY NUMBER ONE PRIORITY.
!

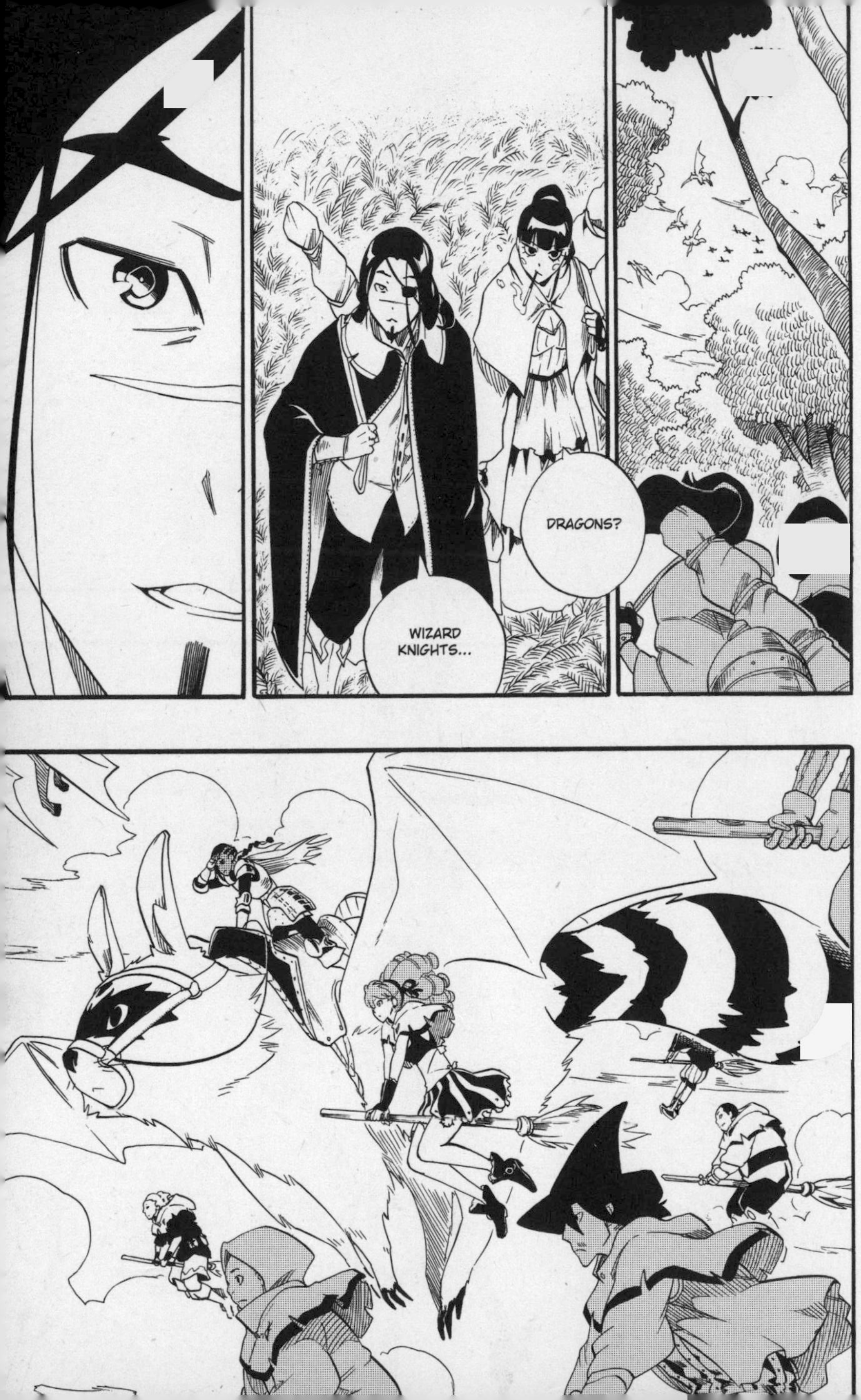
DRAGONS?
WIZARD KNIGHTS...

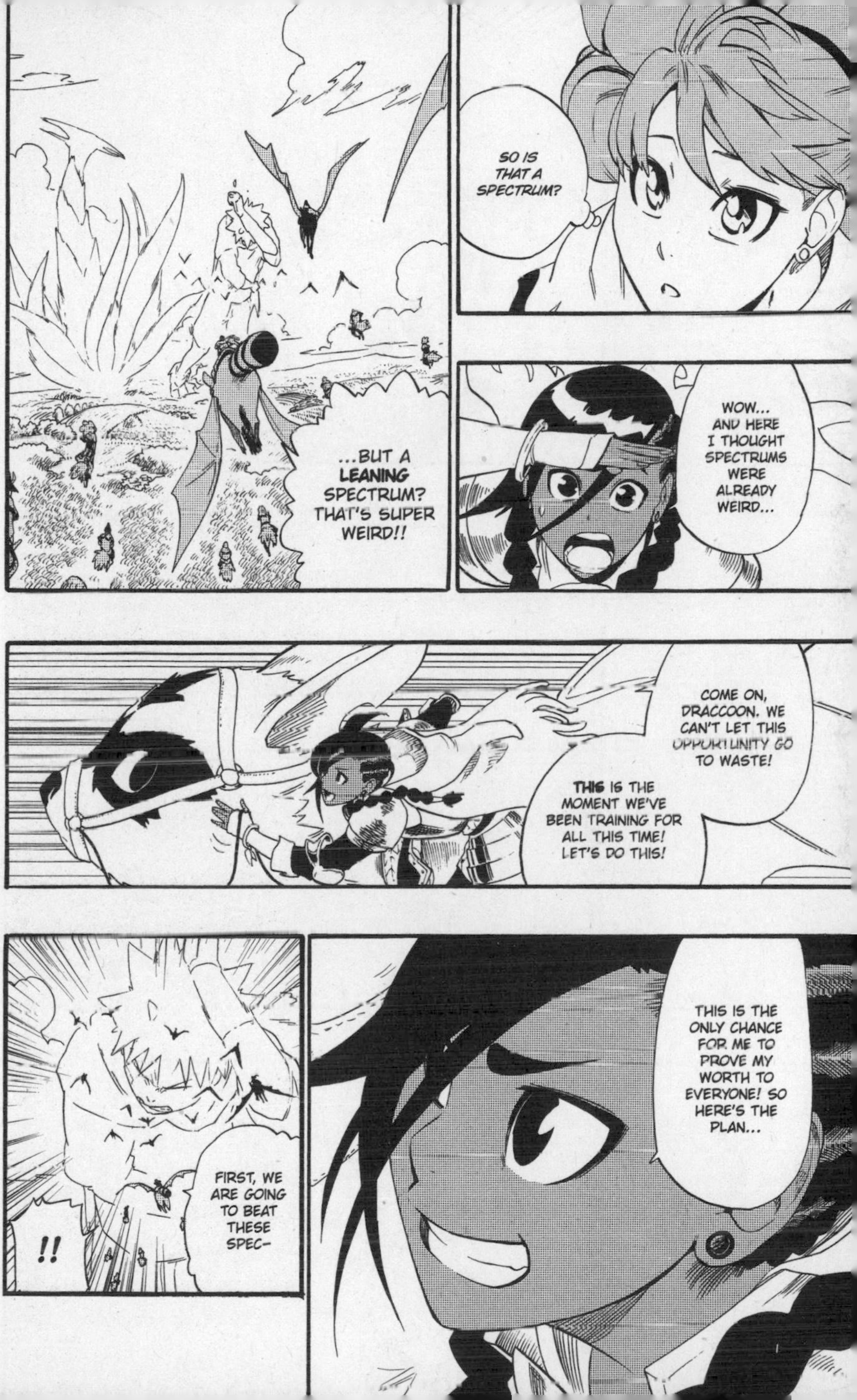
SO IS THAT A SPECTRUM?
WOW... AND HERE I THOUGHT SPECTRUMS WERE ALREADY WEIRD...
...BUT A **LEANING** SPECTRUM? THAT'S SUPER WEIRD!!
COME ON, DRACCOON. WE CAN'T LET THIS OPPORTUNITY GO TO WASTE!
THIS IS THE MOMENT WE'VE BEEN TRAINING FOR ALL THIS TIME! LET'S DO THIS!
THIS IS THE ONLY CHANCE FOR ME TO PROVE MY WORTH TO EVERYONE! SO HERE'S THE PLAN...
FIRST, WE ARE GOING TO BEAT THESE SPEC-
!!

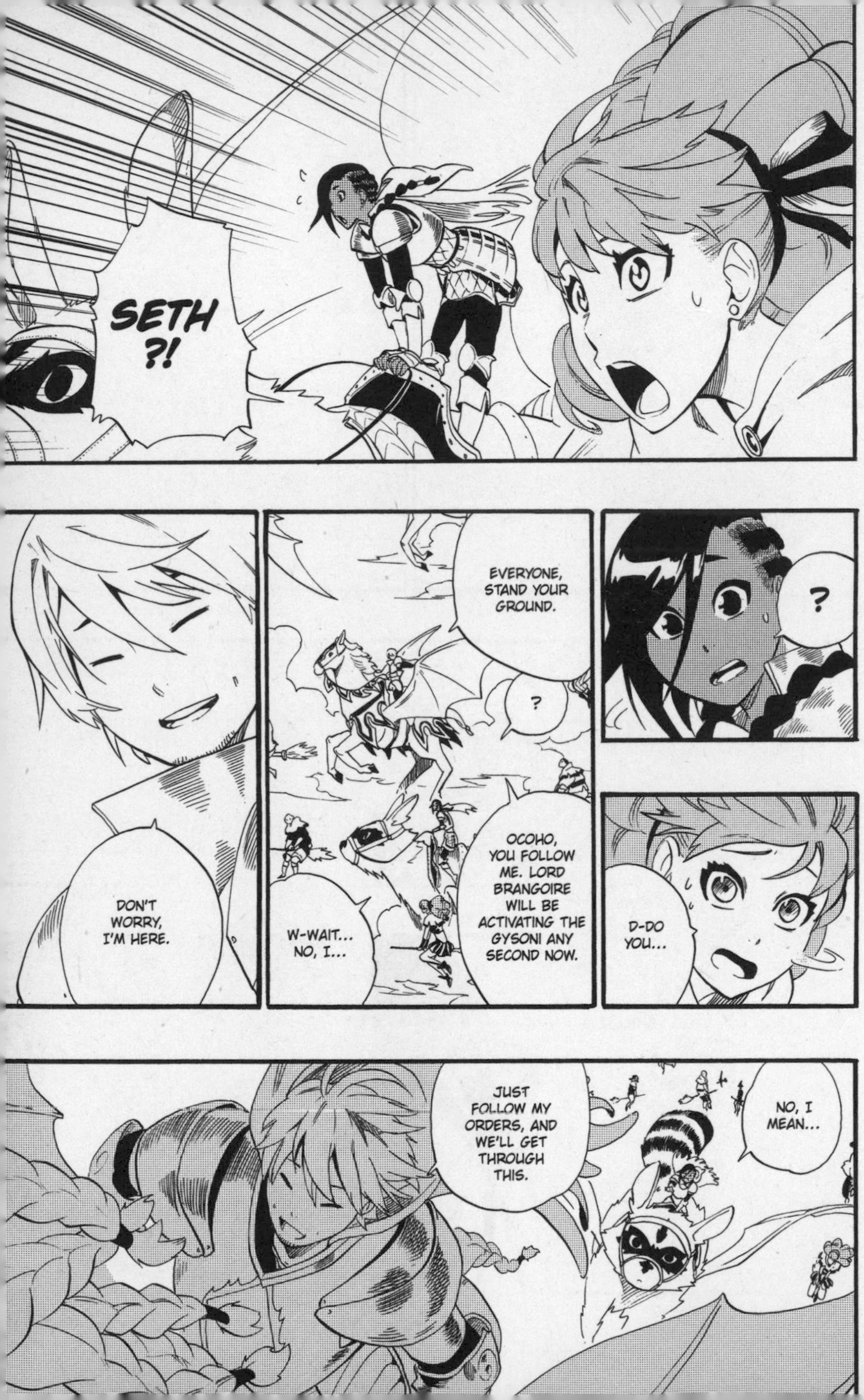
SETH ?!
?
D-DO YOU...
EVERYONE, STAND YOUR GROUND.
?
OCOHO, YOU FOLLOW ME. LORD BRANGOIRE WILL BE ACTIVATING THE GYSONI ANY SECOND NOW.
W-WAIT... NO, I...
DON'T WORRY, I'M HERE.
NO, I MEAN...
JUST FOLLOW MY ORDERS, AND WE'LL GET THROUGH THIS.

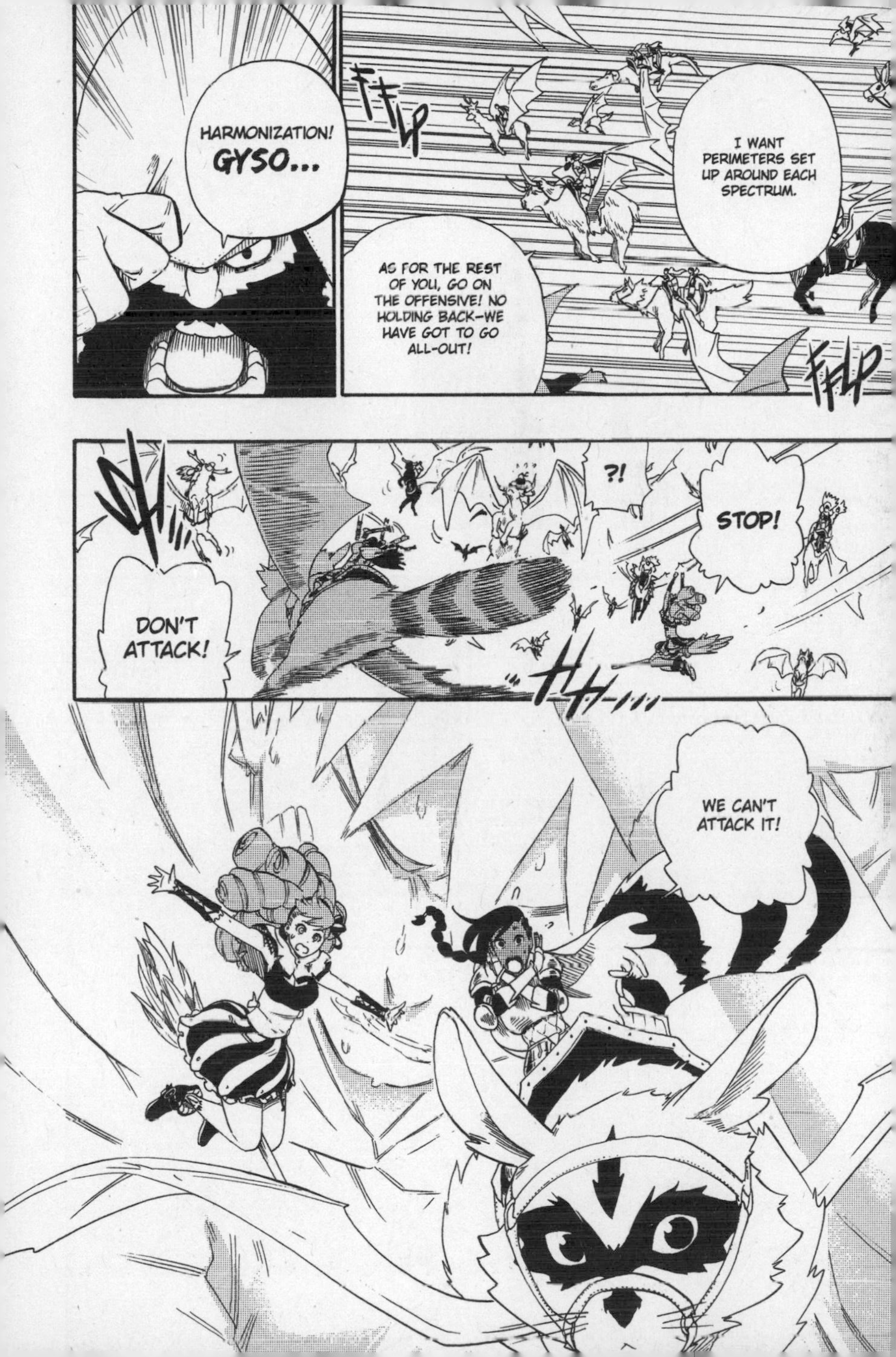
FFLP
I WANT PERIMETERS SET UP AROUND EACH SPECTRUM.
AS FOR THE REST OF YOU, GO ON THE OFFENSIVE! NO HOLDING BACK—WE HAVE GOT TO GO ALL-OUT!
FFLP
HARMONIZATION! GYSO...
STOP!
?!
DON'T ATTACK!
WE CAN'T ATTACK IT!

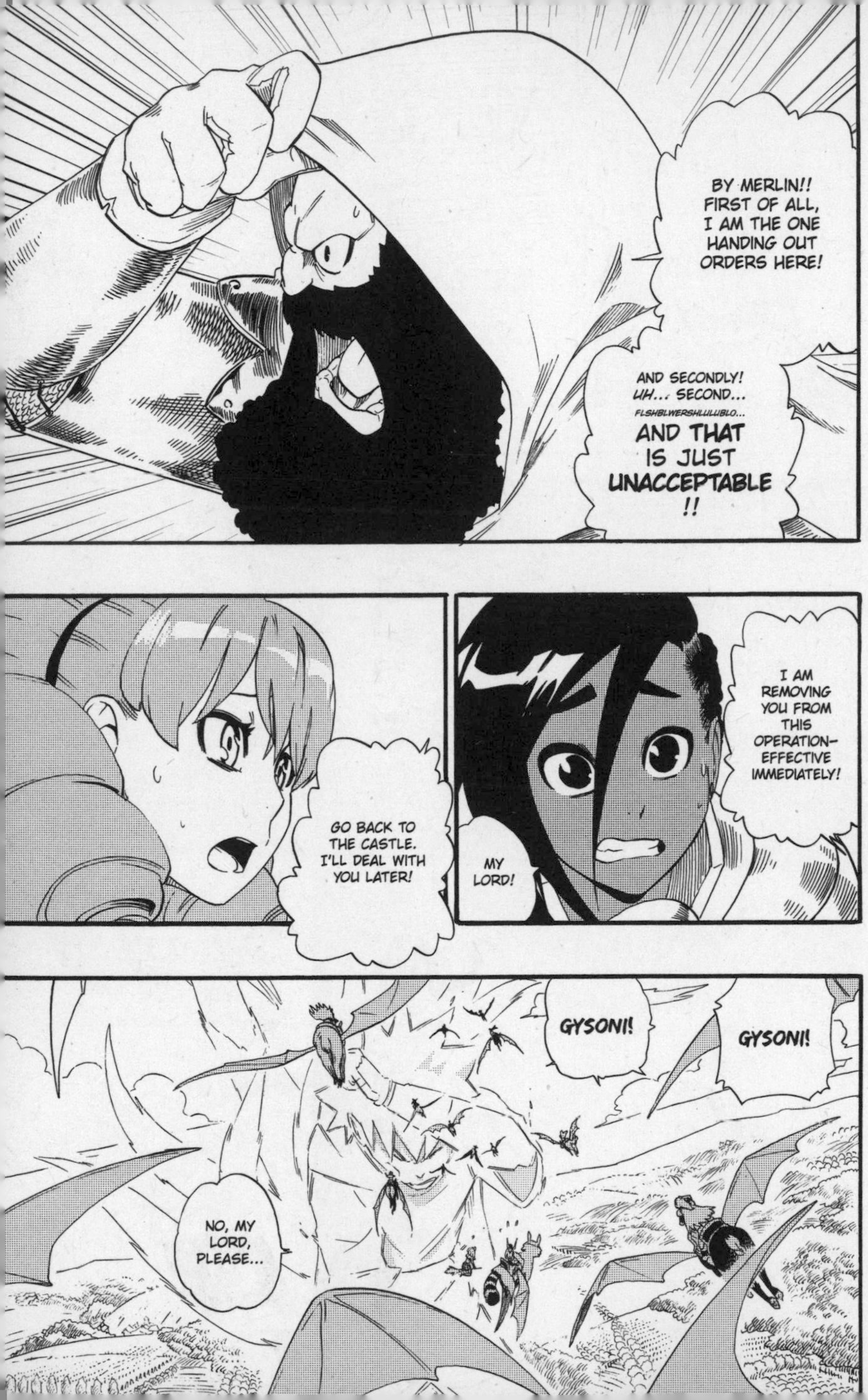
BY MERLIN!! FIRST OF ALL, I AM THE ONE HANDING OUT ORDERS HERE!
AND SECONDLY! UH... SECOND... FLSHBLWERSHLULUBLO... AND THAT IS JUST UNACCEPTABLE!!
I AM REMOVING YOU FROM THIS OPERATION—EFFECTIVE IMMEDIATELY!
MY LORD!
GO BACK TO THE CASTLE. I'LL DEAL WITH YOU LATER!
GYSONI!
GYSONI!
NO, MY LORD, PLEASE...

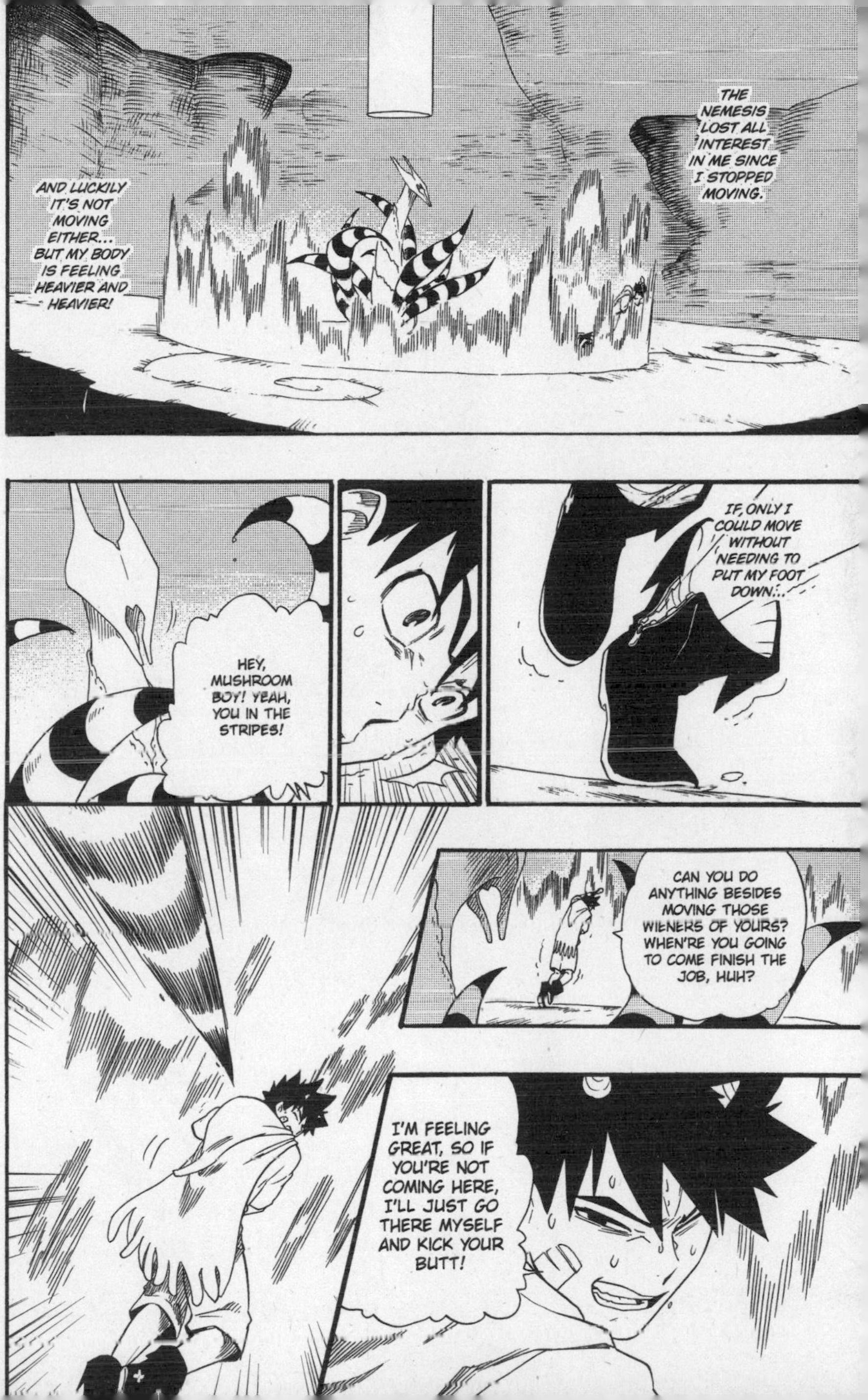
THE NEMESIS LOST ALL INTEREST IN ME SINCE I STOPPED MOVING.
AND LUCKILY IT'S NOT MOVING EITHER... BUT MY BODY IS FEELING HEAVIER AND HEAVIER!
IF ONLY I COULD MOVE WITHOUT NEEDING TO PUT MY FOOT DOWN...
HEY, MUSHROOM BOY! YEAH, YOU IN THE STRIPES!
CAN YOU DO ANYTHING BESIDES MOVING THOSE WIENERS OF YOURS? WHEN'RE YOU GOING TO COME FINISH THE JOB, HUH?
I'M FEELING GREAT, SO IF YOU'RE NOT COMING HERE, I'LL JUST GO THERE MYSELF AND KICK YOUR BUTT!

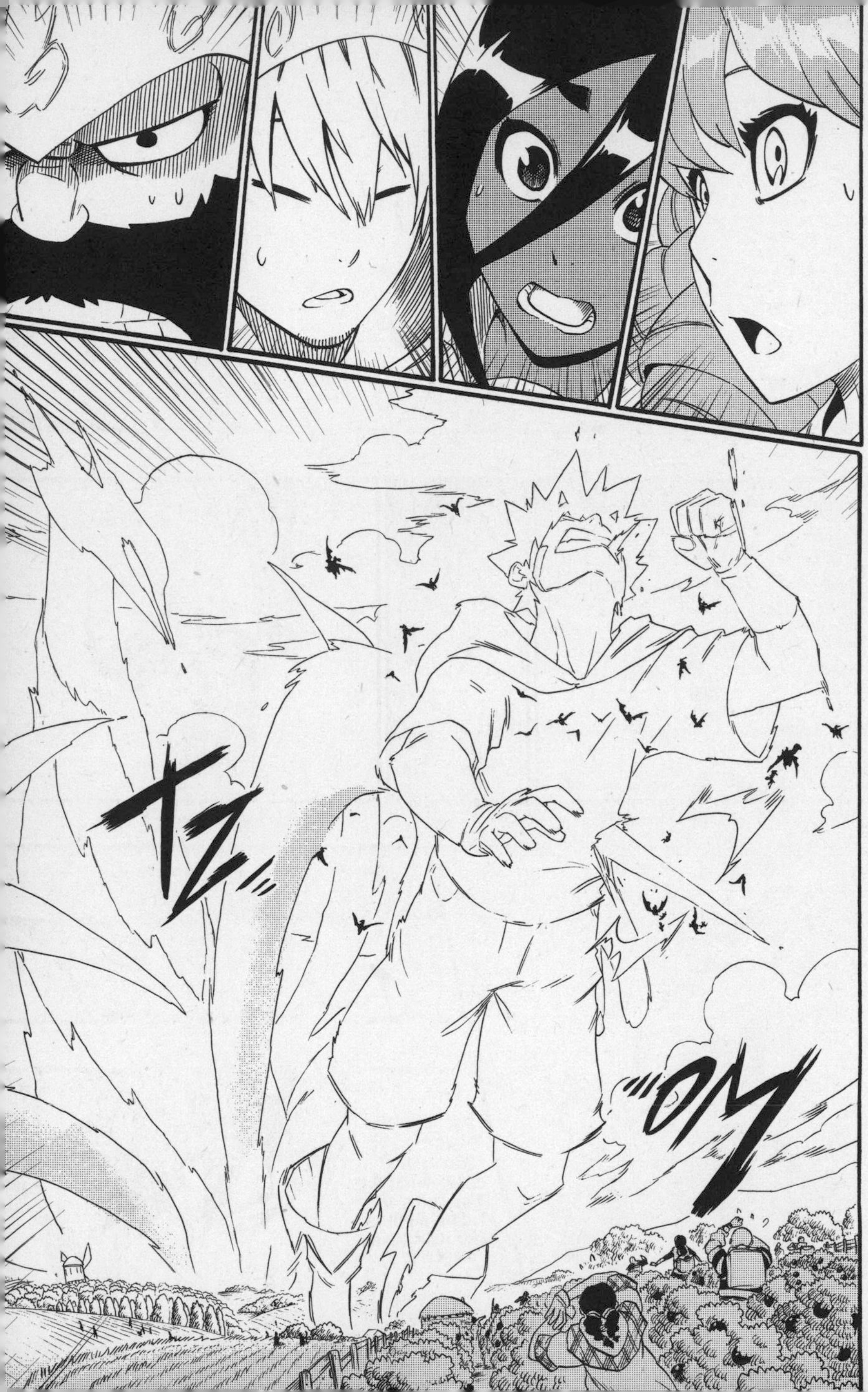
TZ
OM

"DRACOW"
THE NOBLE DRAGON-COW OF LORD BRANGOIRE...

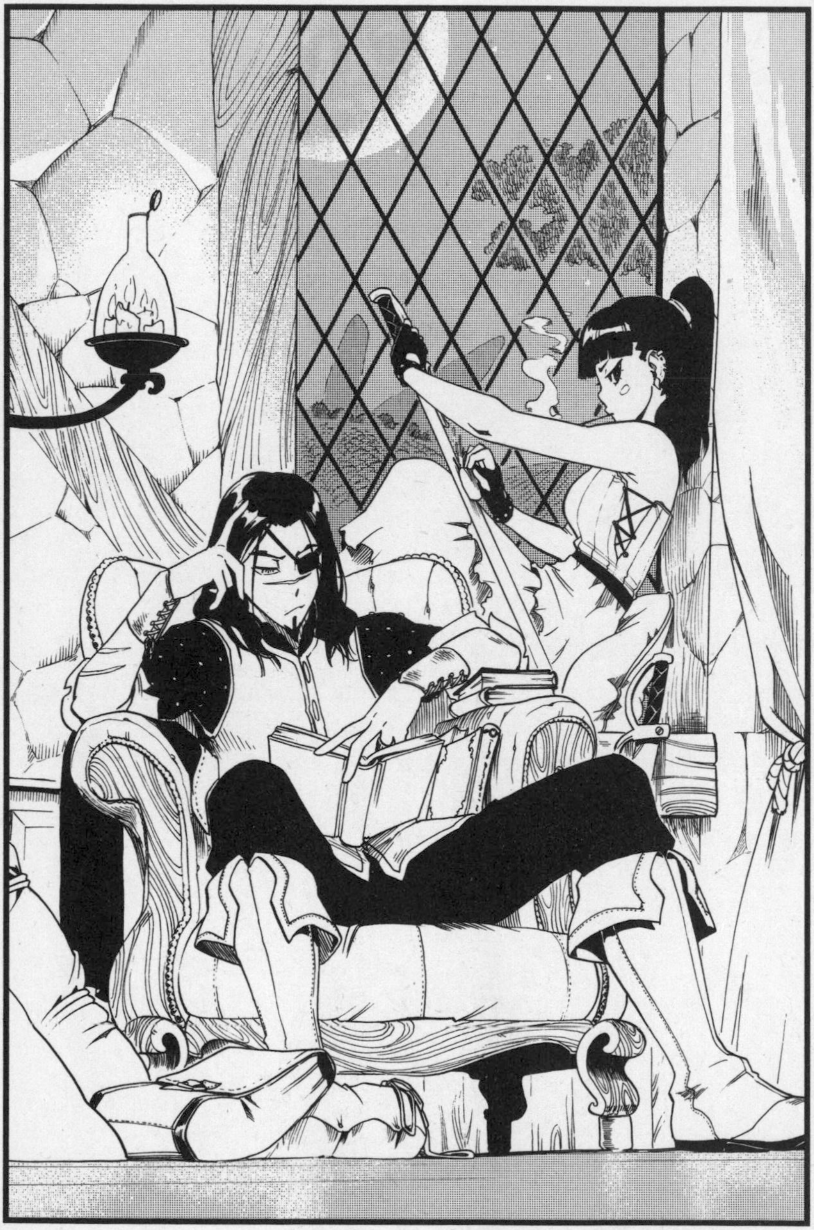

Chapter 38

Last Breath

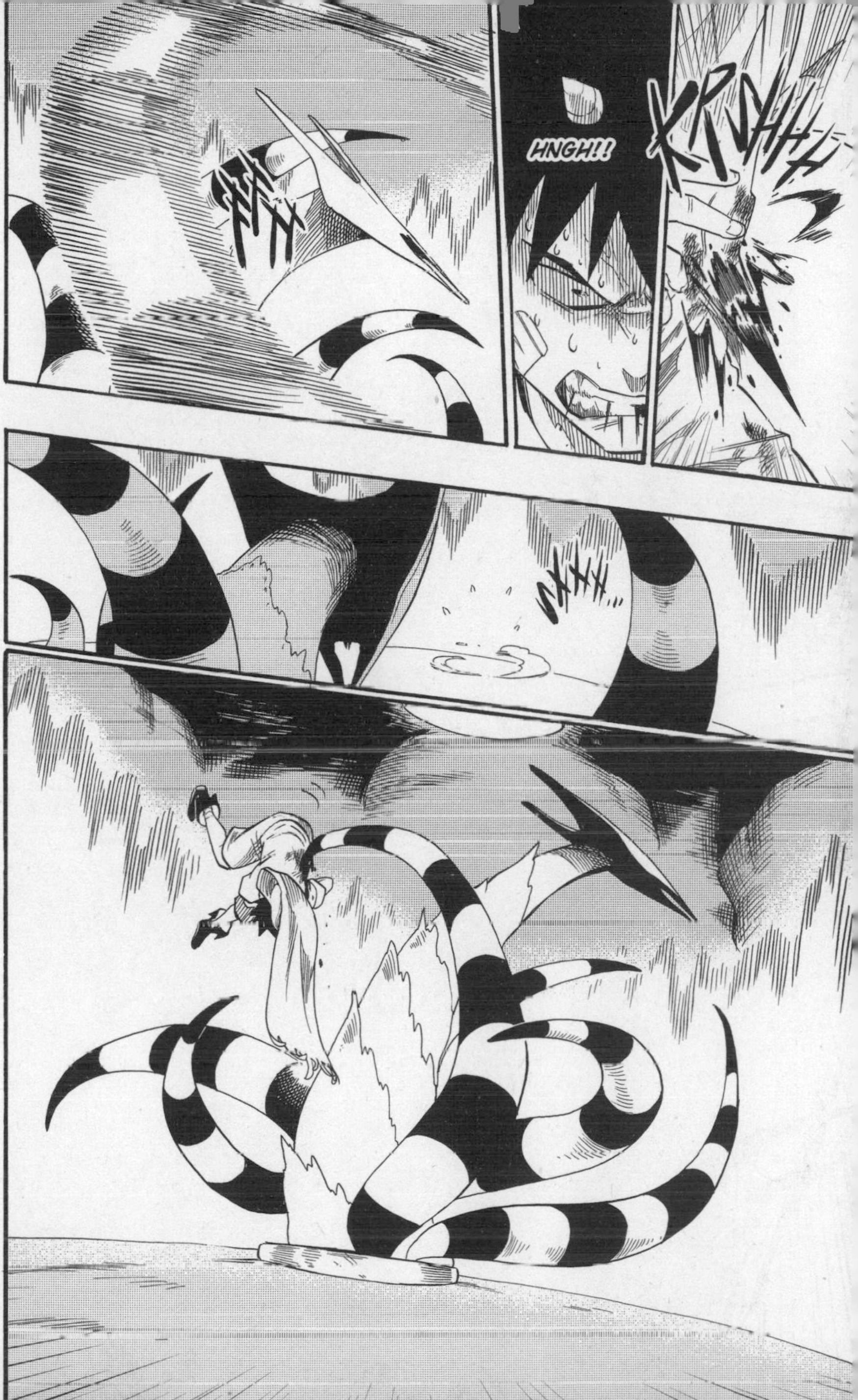
KRSHHH
HNGH!!
SHHH..

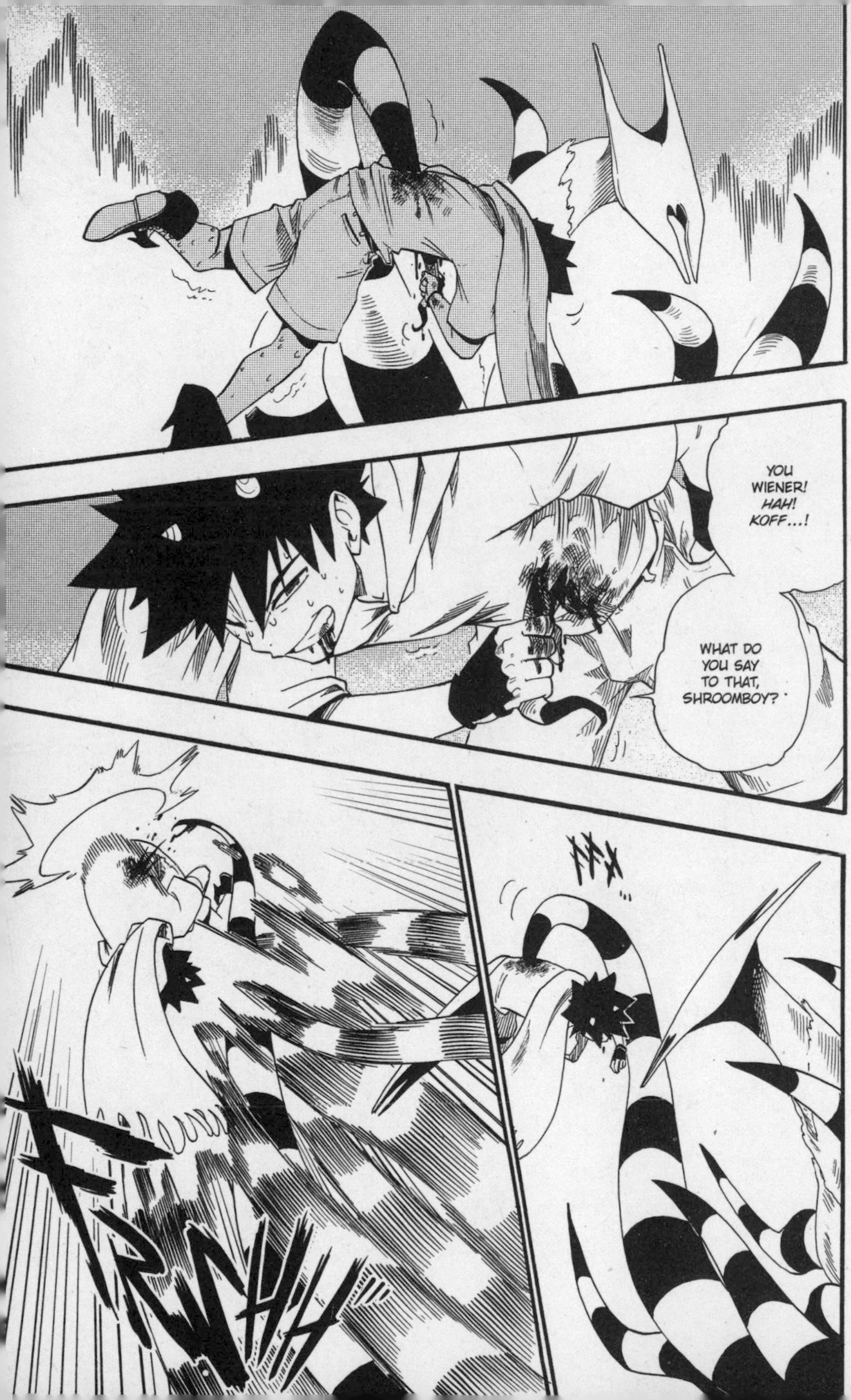
YOU WIENER! HAH! KOFF...!
WHAT DO YOU SAY TO THAT, SHROOMBOY?

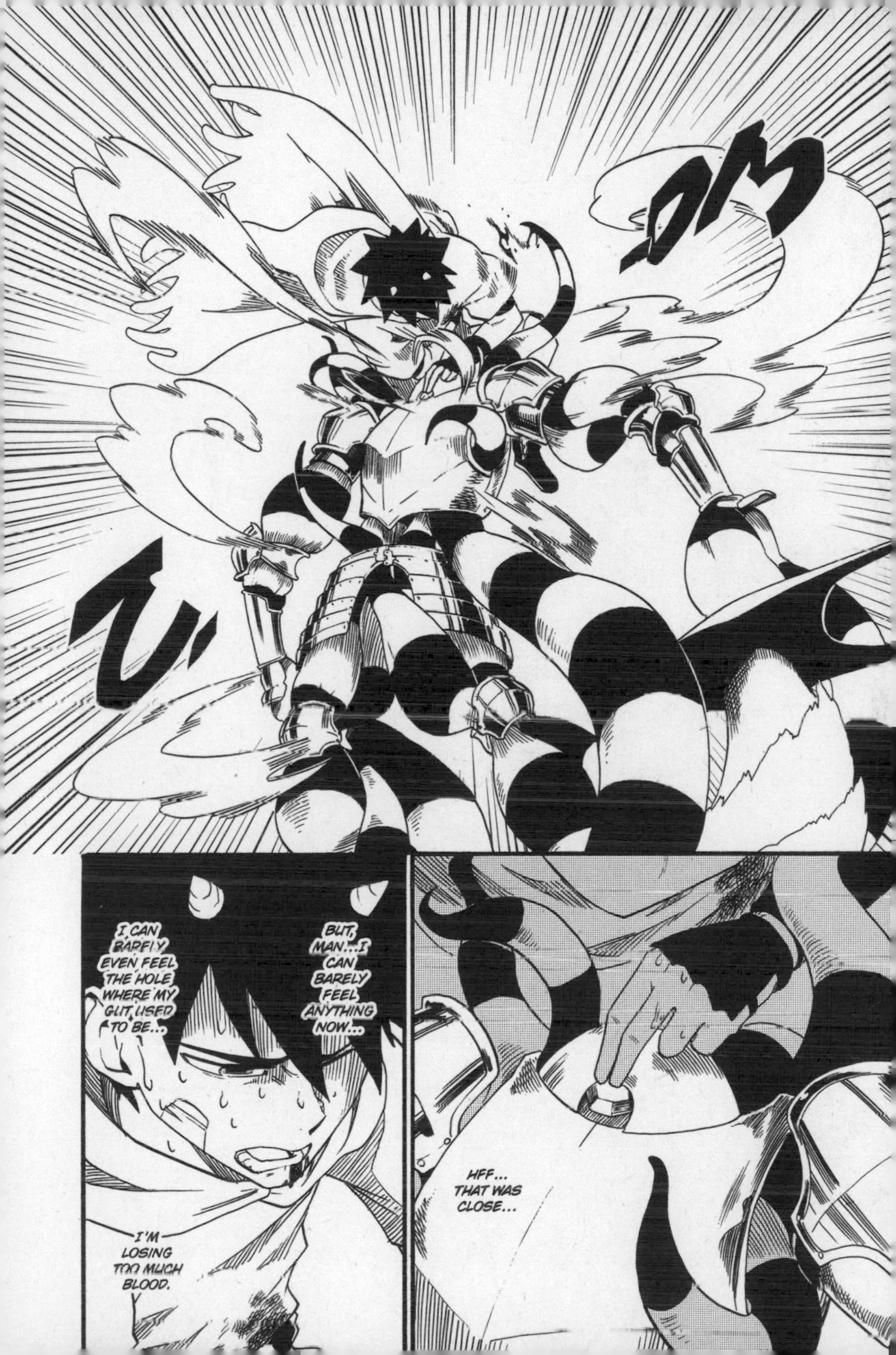
HFF... THAT WAS CLOSE...
BUT, MAN...I CAN BARELY FEEL ANYTHING NOW...
I CAN BARELY EVEN FEEL THE HOLE WHERE MY GUT USED TO BE...
I'M LOSING TOO MUCH BLOOD.

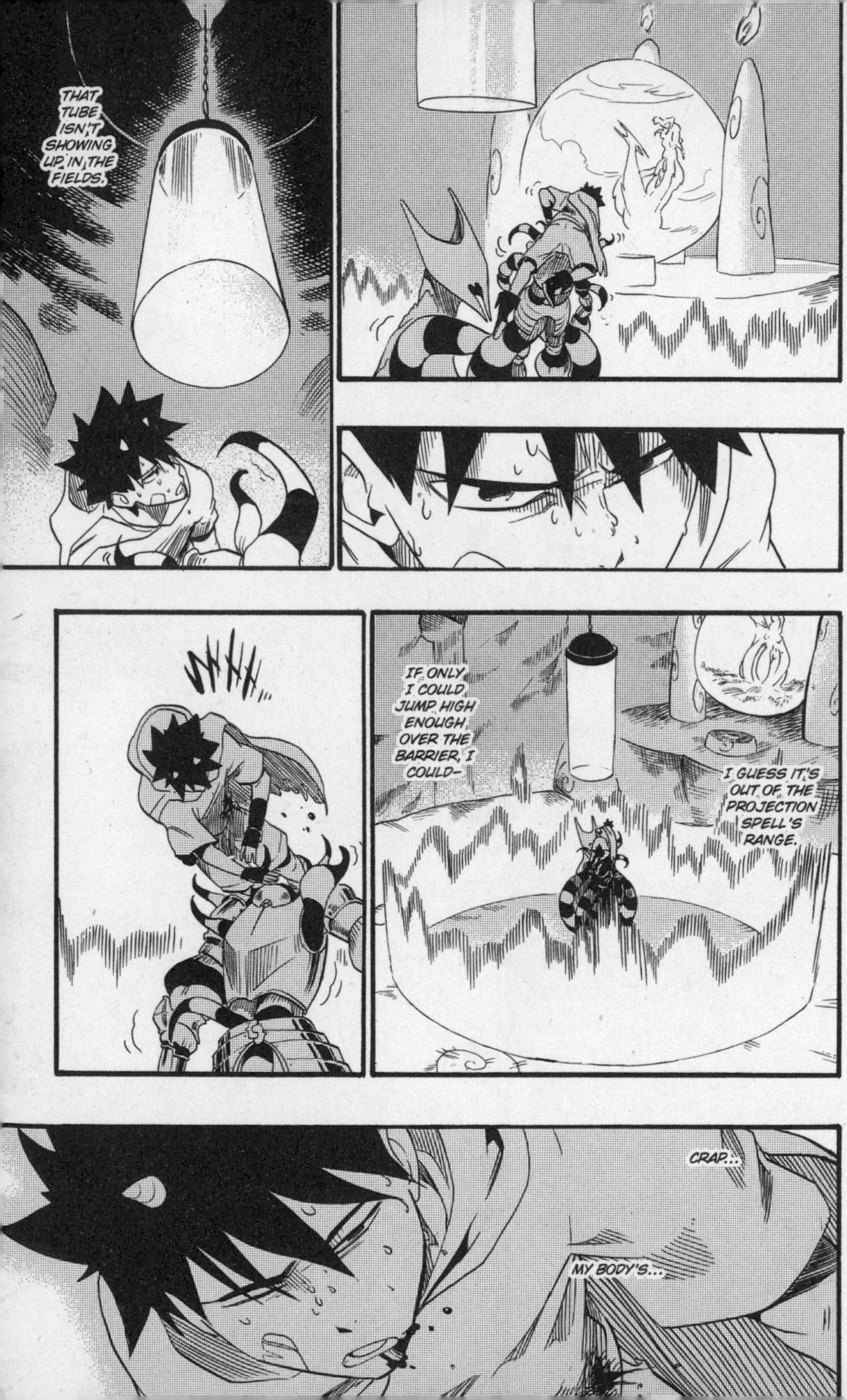
THAT TUBE ISN'T SHOWING UP IN THE FIELDS.
I GUESS IT'S OUT OF THE PROJECTION SPELL'S RANGE.
IF ONLY I COULD JUMP HIGH ENOUGH OVER THE BARRIER, I COULD-
SHHH...
CRAP...
MY BODY'S...

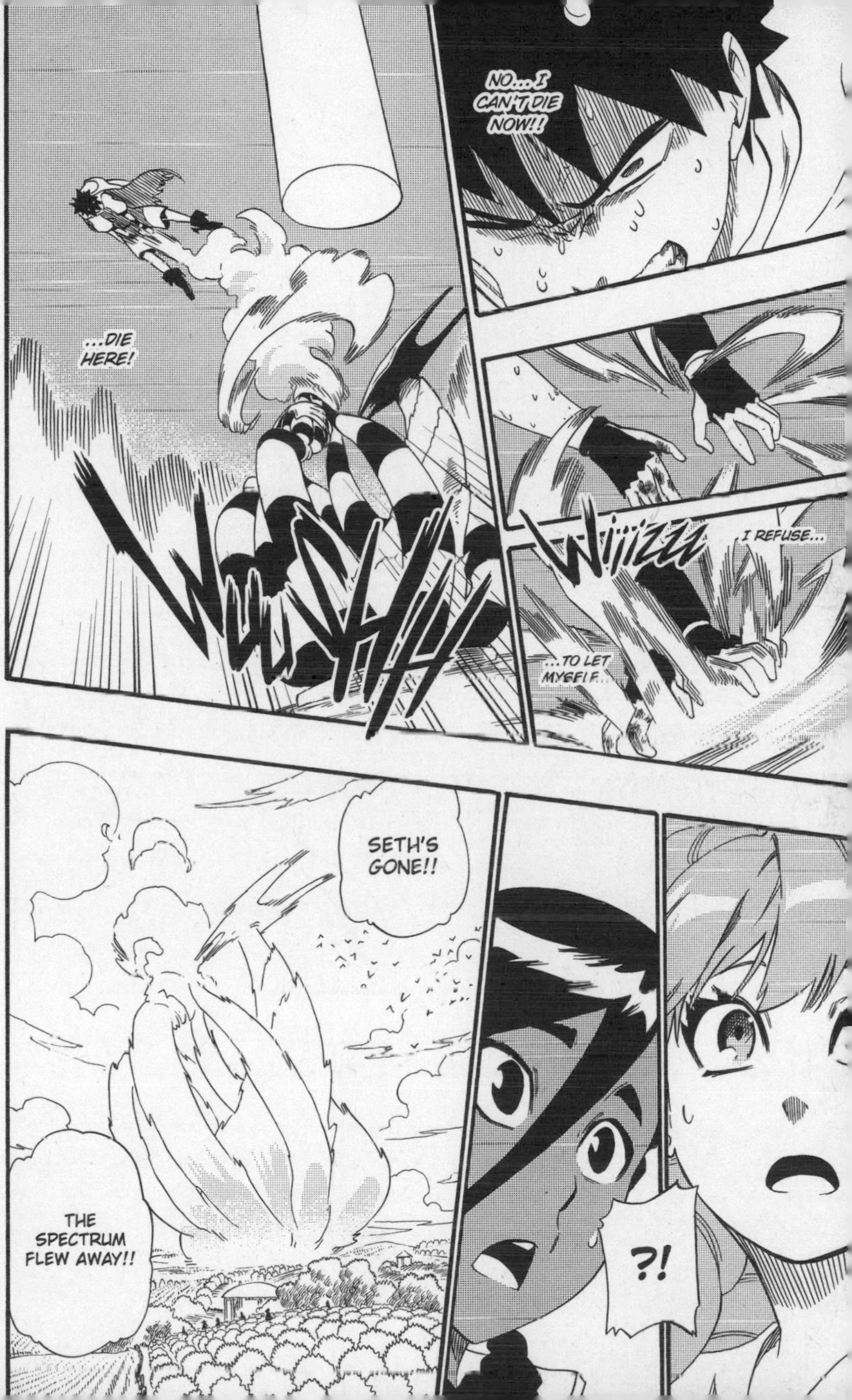
NO... I CAN'T DIE NOW!!
I REFUSE...
...TO LET MYSELF...
...DIE HERE!
?!
SETH'S GONE!!
THE SPECTRUM FLEW AWAY!!

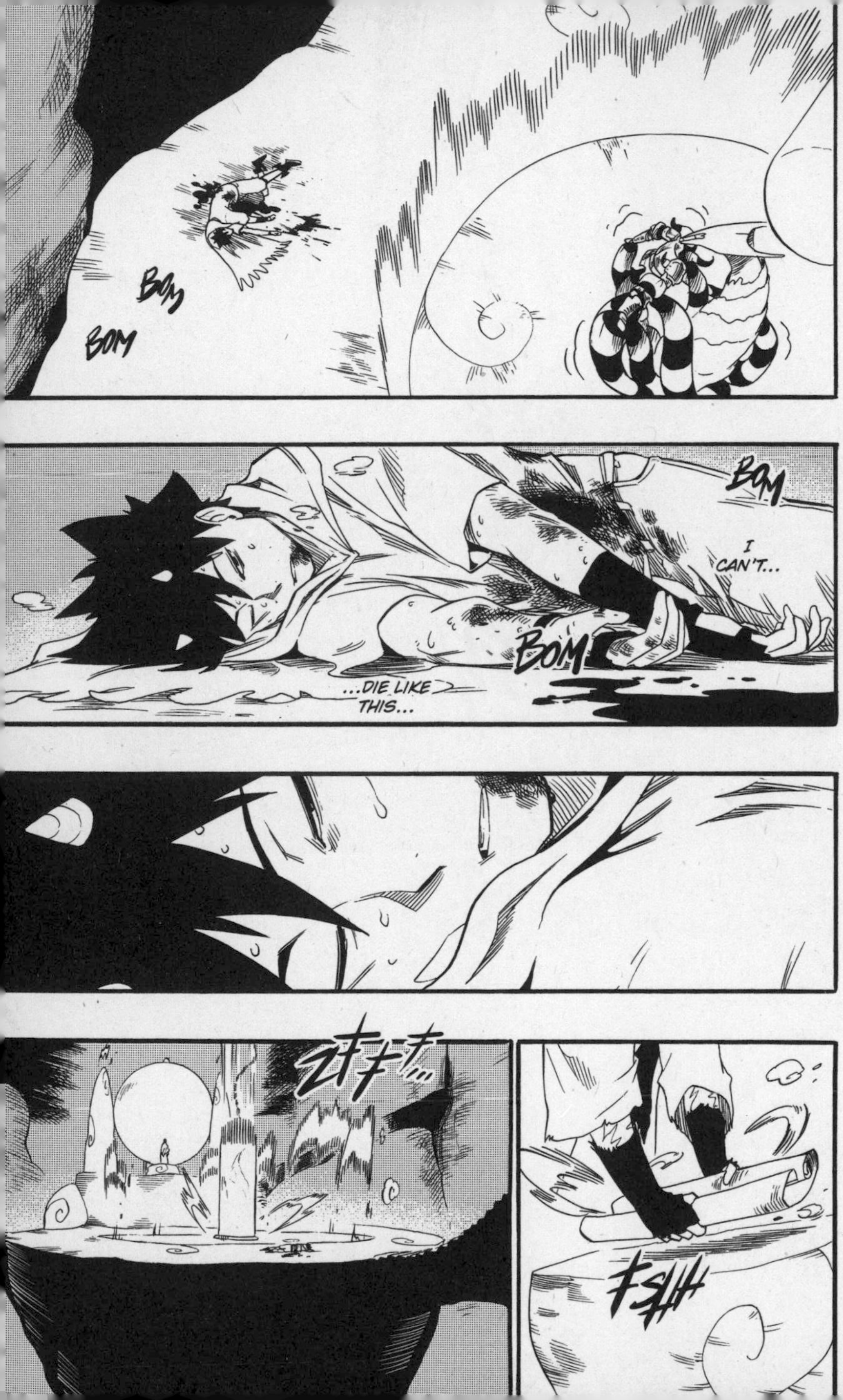
BOM
BOM
BOM
I CAN'T...
BOM
...DIE LIKE THIS...
FSHH

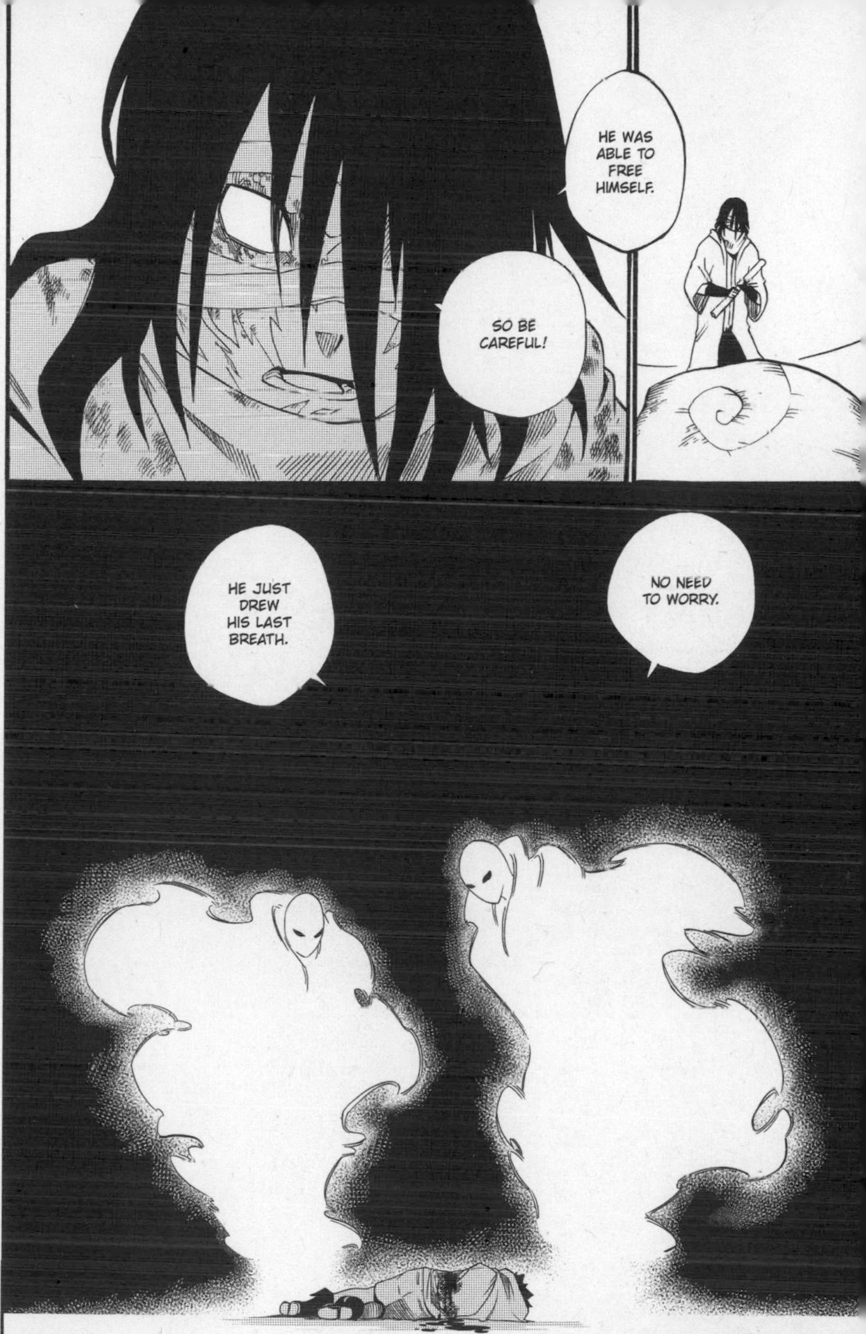
HE WAS ABLE TO FREE HIMSELF.
SO BE CAREFUL!
NO NEED TO WORRY.
HE JUST DREW HIS LAST BREATH.

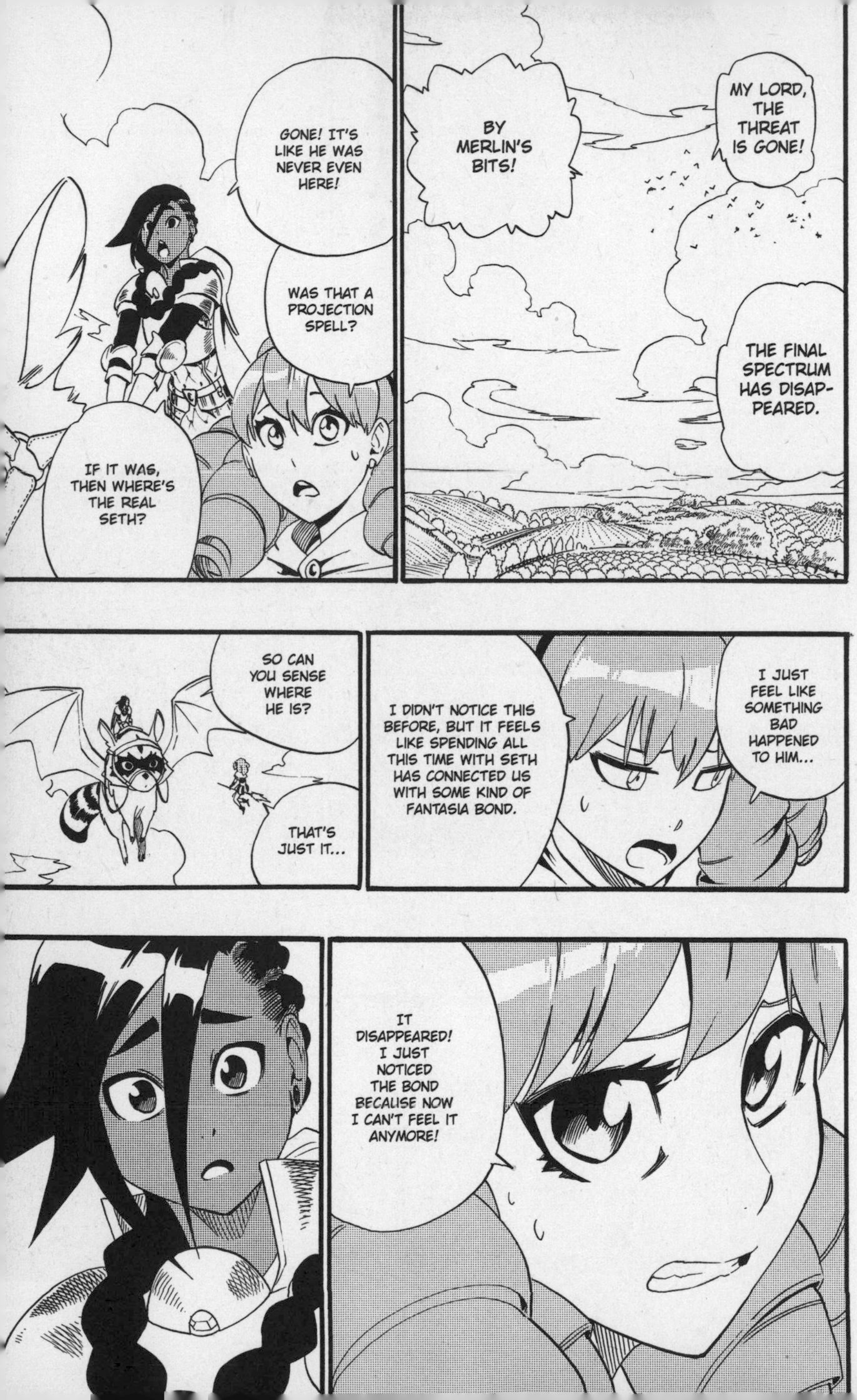
GONE! IT'S LIKE HE WAS NEVER EVEN HERE!
WAS THAT A PROJECTION SPELL?
IF IT WAS, THEN WHERE'S THE REAL SETH?
BY MERLIN'S BITS!
MY LORD, THE THREAT IS GONE!
THE FINAL SPECTRUM HAS DISAPPEARED.
SO CAN YOU SENSE WHERE HE IS?
THAT'S JUST IT...
I DIDN'T NOTICE THIS BEFORE, BUT IT FEELS LIKE SPENDING ALL THIS TIME WITH SETH HAS CONNECTED US WITH SOME KIND OF FANTASIA BOND.
I JUST FEEL LIKE SOMETHING BAD HAPPENED TO HIM...
IT DISAPPEARED! I JUST NOTICED THE BOND BECAUSE NOW I CAN'T FEEL IT ANYMORE!

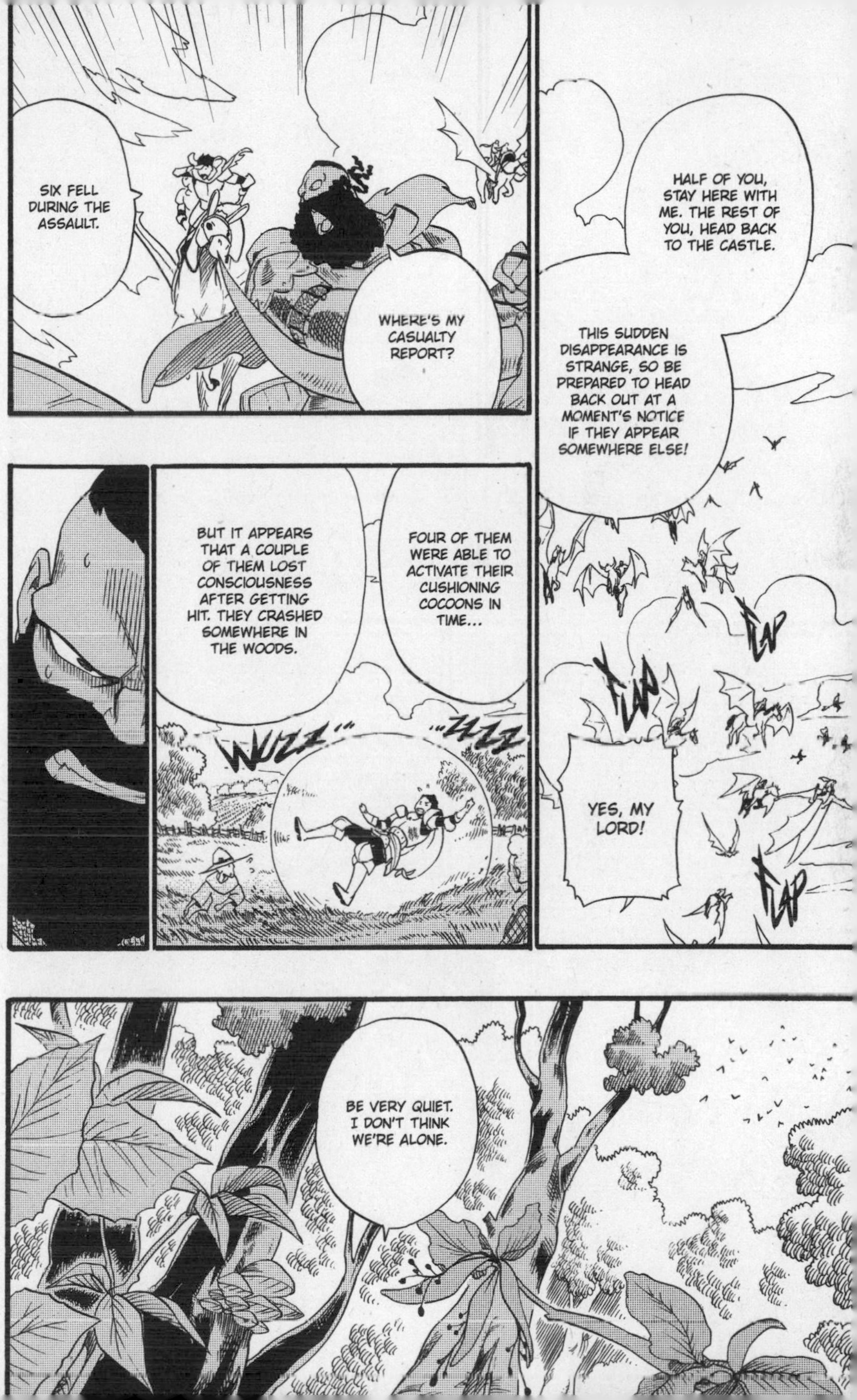
WHERE'S MY CASUALTY REPORT?
SIX FELL DURING THE ASSAULT.
FOUR OF THEM WERE ABLE TO ACTIVATE THEIR CUSHIONING COCOONS IN TIME...
BUT IT APPEARS THAT A COUPLE OF THEM LOST CONSCIOUSNESS AFTER GETTING HIT. THEY CRASHED SOMEWHERE IN THE WOODS.
WUZZ...
...ZZZZ
HALF OF YOU, STAY HERE WITH ME. THE REST OF YOU, HEAD BACK TO THE CASTLE.
THIS SUDDEN DISAPPEARANCE IS STRANGE, SO BE PREPARED TO HEAD BACK OUT AT A MOMENT'S NOTICE IF THEY APPEAR SOMEWHERE ELSE!
FLAP
FLAP
YES, MY LORD!
FLAP
BE VERY QUIET. I DON'T THINK WE'RE ALONE.

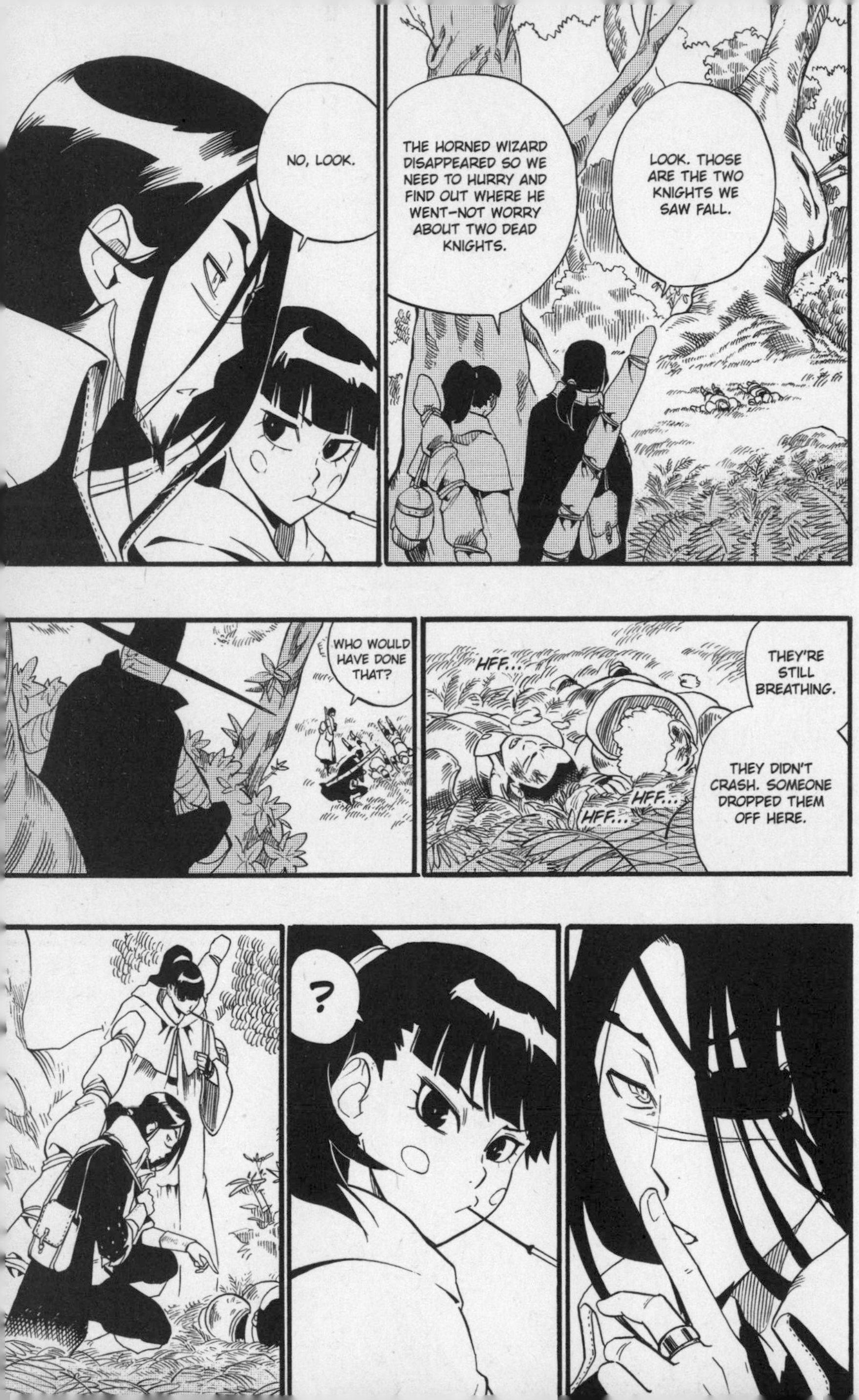
LOOK. THOSE ARE THE TWO KNIGHTS WE SAW FALL.
THE HORNED WIZARD DISAPPEARED SO WE NEED TO HURRY AND FIND OUT WHERE HE WENT–NOT WORRY ABOUT TWO DEAD KNIGHTS.
NO, LOOK.
THEY'RE STILL BREATHING.
HFF...
THEY DIDN'T CRASH. SOMEONE DROPPED THEM OFF HERE.
HFF...
HFF...
WHO WOULD HAVE DONE THAT?
?

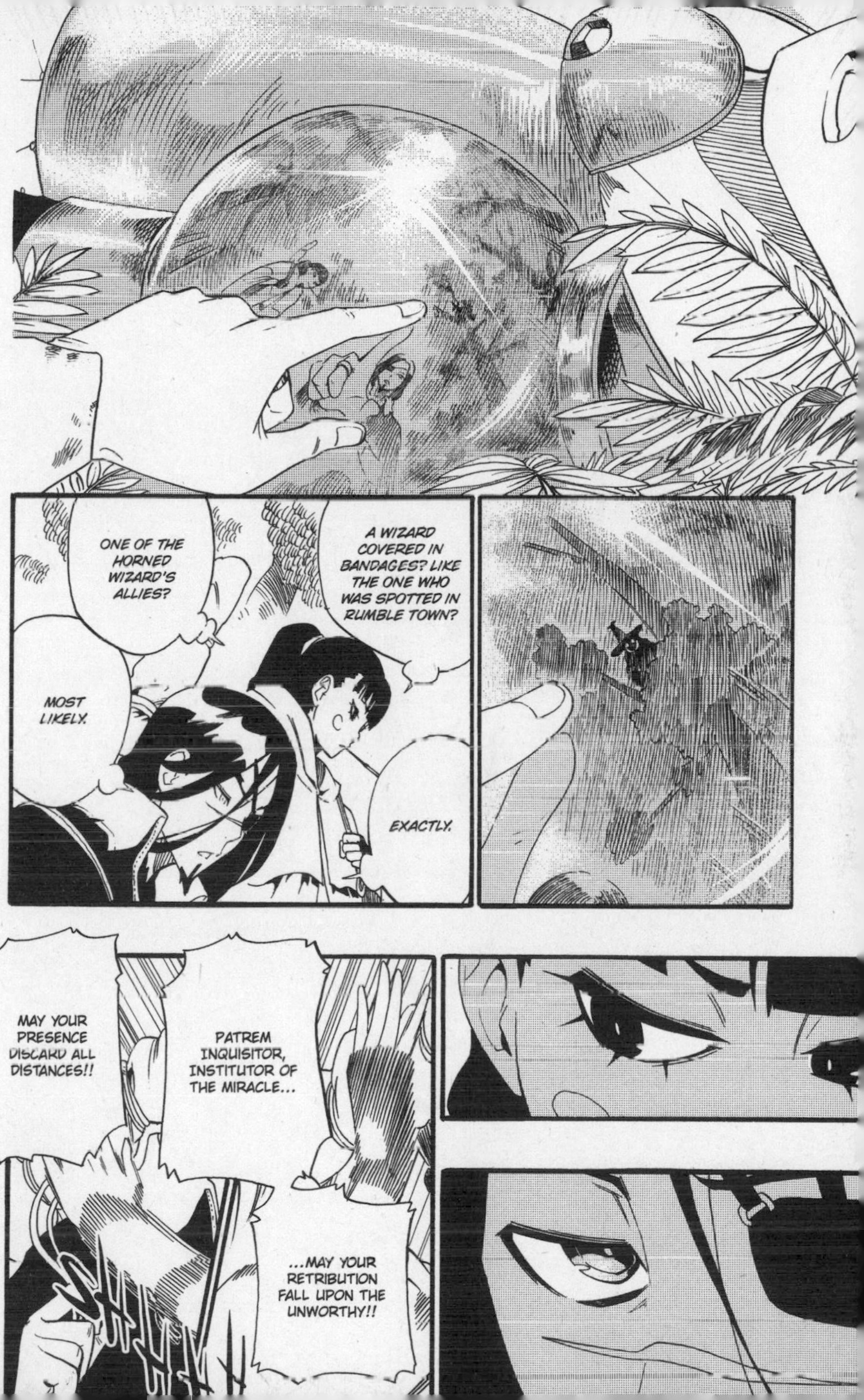
A WIZARD COVERED IN BANDAGES? LIKE THE ONE WHO WAS SPOTTED IN RUMBLE TOWN?
EXACTLY.
ONE OF THE HORNED WIZARD'S ALLIES?
MOST LIKELY.
PATREM INQUISITOR, INSTITUTOR OF THE MIRACLE...
MAY YOUR PRESENCE DISCARD ALL DISTANCES!!
...MAY YOUR RETRIBUTION FALL UPON THE UNWORTHY!!

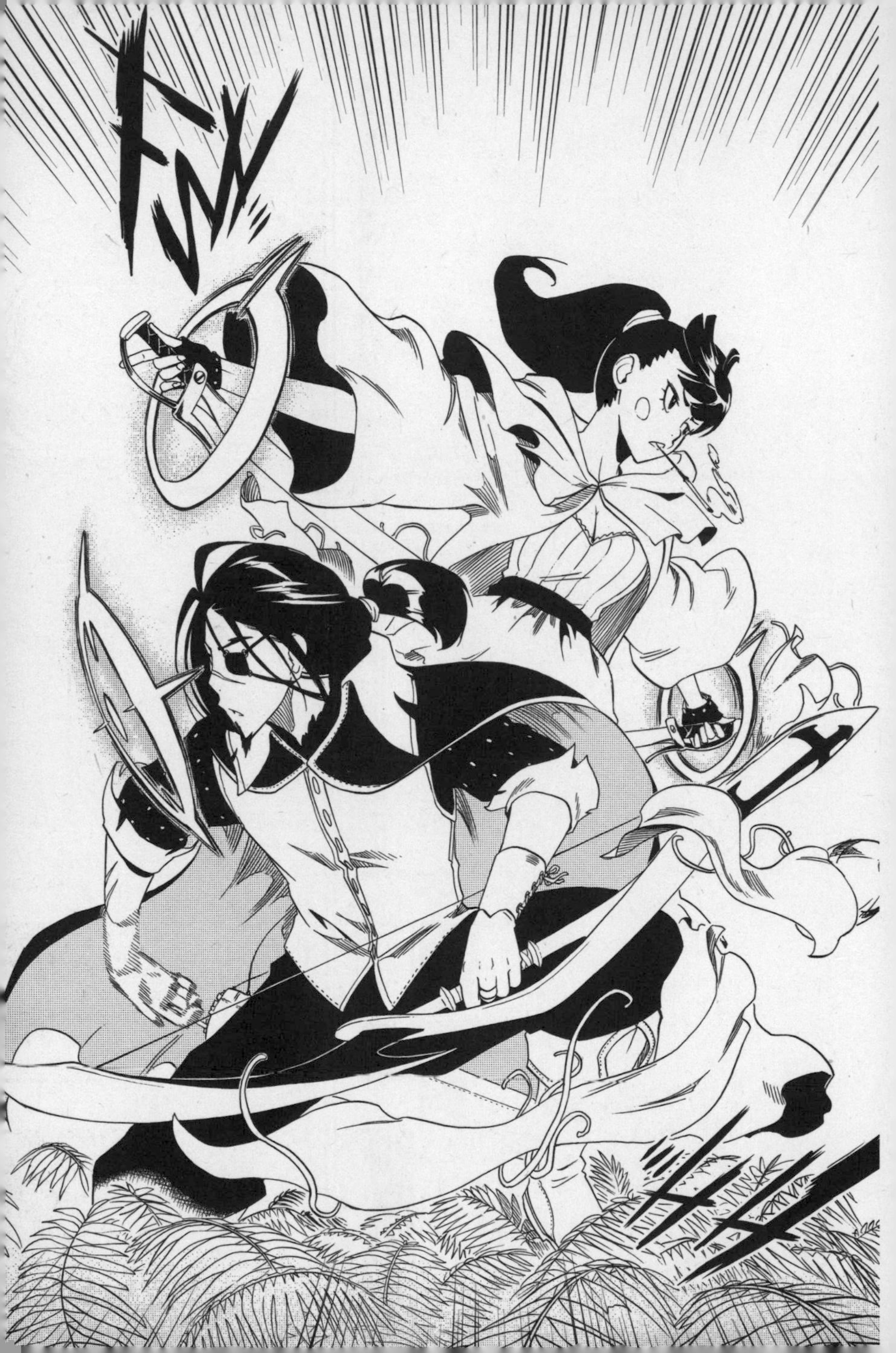

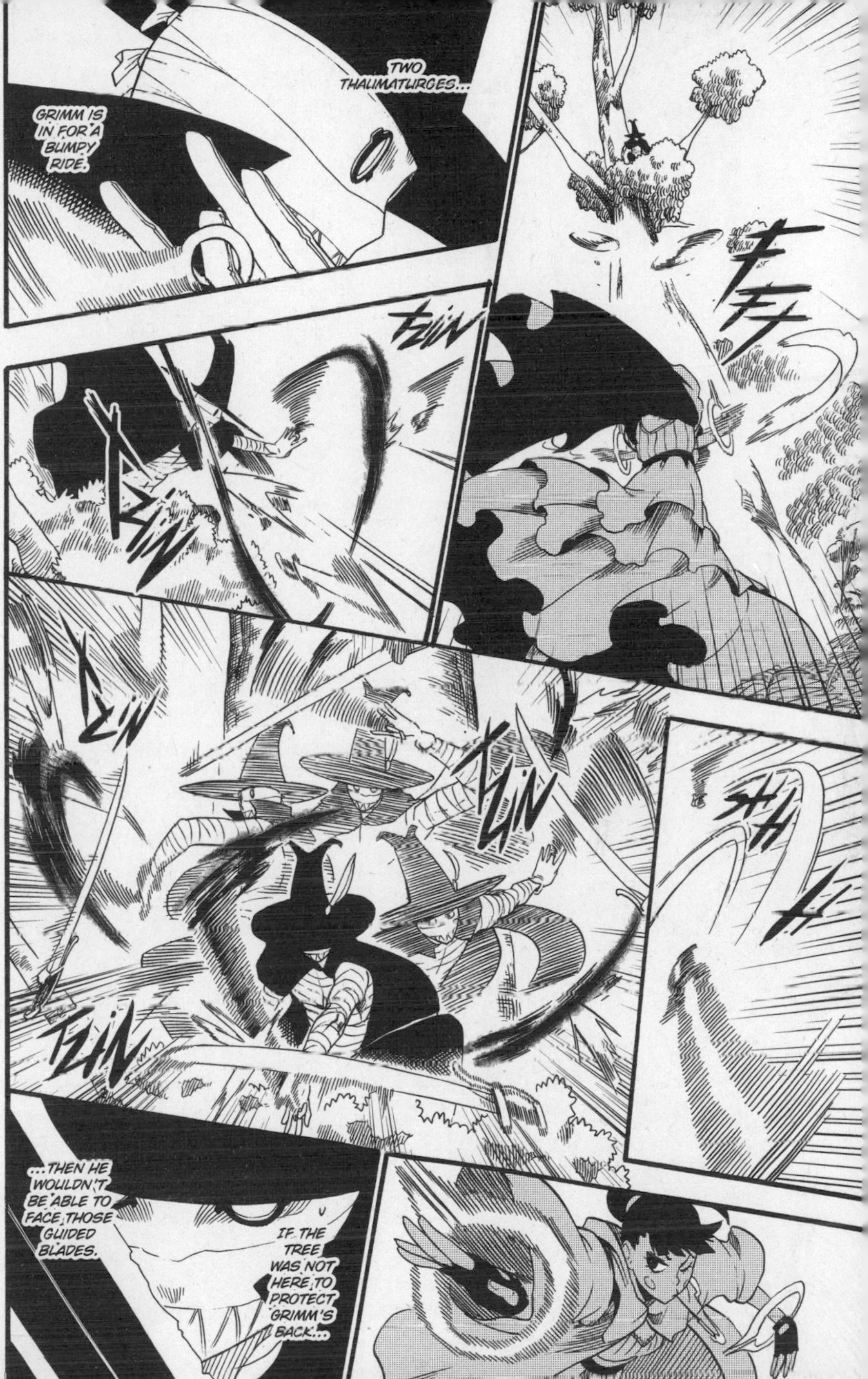
TWO THAUMATURGES...
GRIMM IS IN FOR A BUMPY RIDE.
TZIN
TZIN
IF THE TREE WAS NOT HERE TO PROTECT GRIMM'S BACK...
...THEN HE WOULDN'T BE ABLE TO FACE THOSE GUIDED BLADES.

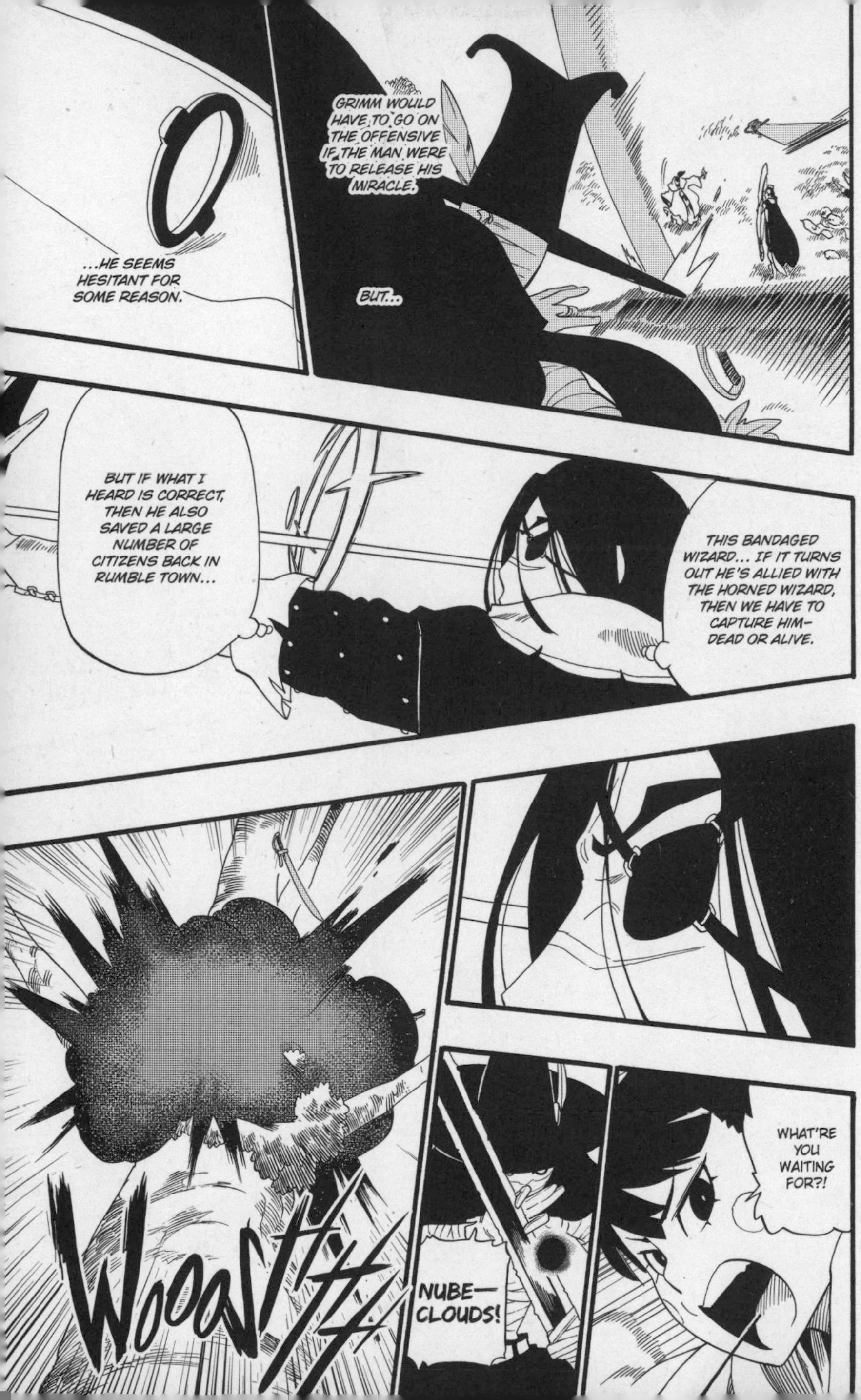
GRIMM WOULD HAVE TO GO ON THE OFFENSIVE IF THE MAN WERE TO RELEASE HIS MIRACLE.
BUT...
...HE SEEMS HESITANT FOR SOME REASON.
THIS BANDAGED WIZARD... IF IT TURNS OUT HE'S ALLIED WITH THE HORNED WIZARD, THEN WE HAVE TO CAPTURE HIM—DEAD OR ALIVE.
BUT IF WHAT I HEARD IS CORRECT, THEN HE ALSO SAVED A LARGE NUMBER OF CITIZENS BACK IN RUMBLE TOWN...
WHAT'RE YOU WAITING FOR?!
NUBE—CLOUDS!

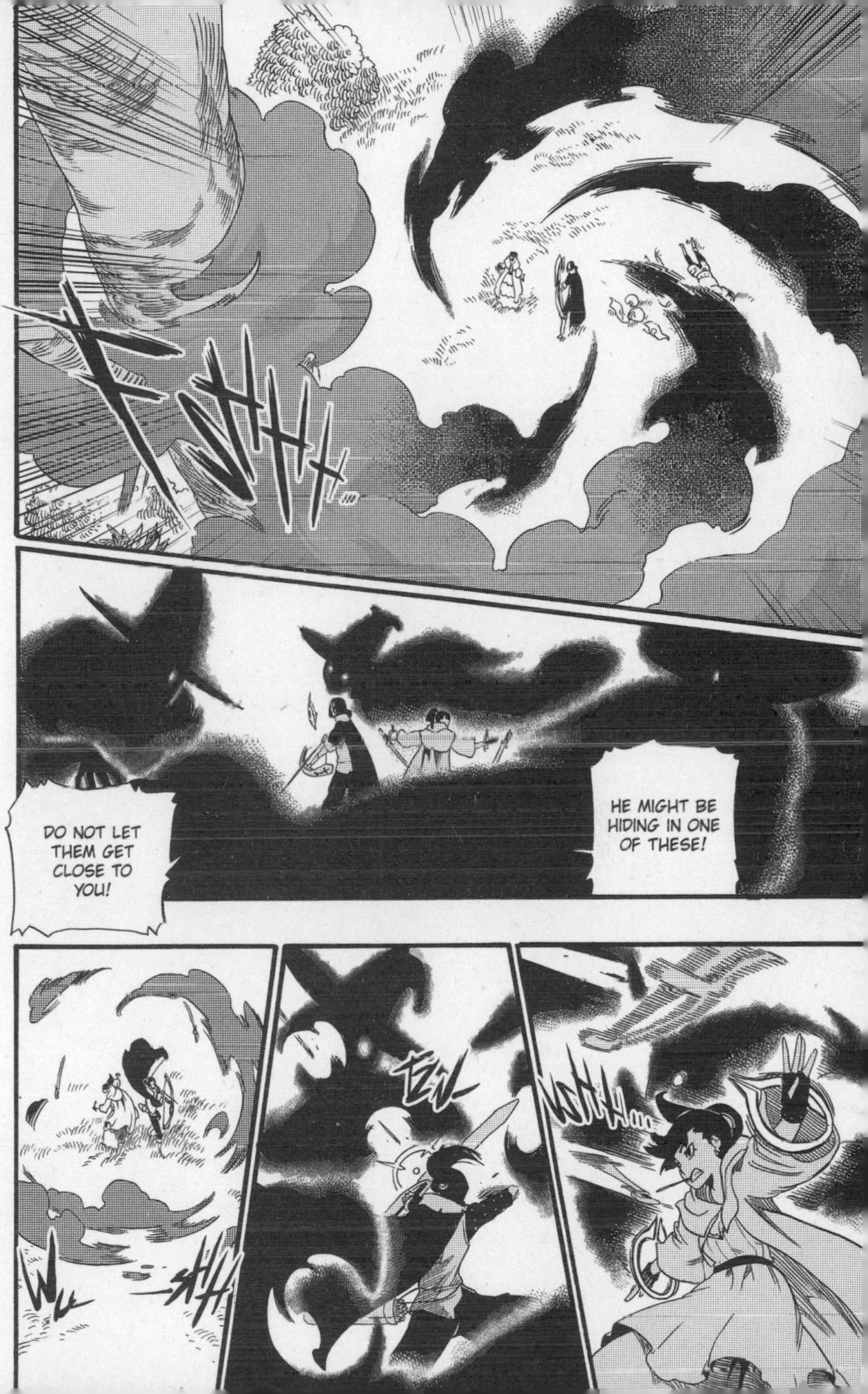
HE MIGHT BE HIDING IN ONE OF THESE!
DO NOT LET THEM GET CLOSE TO YOU!

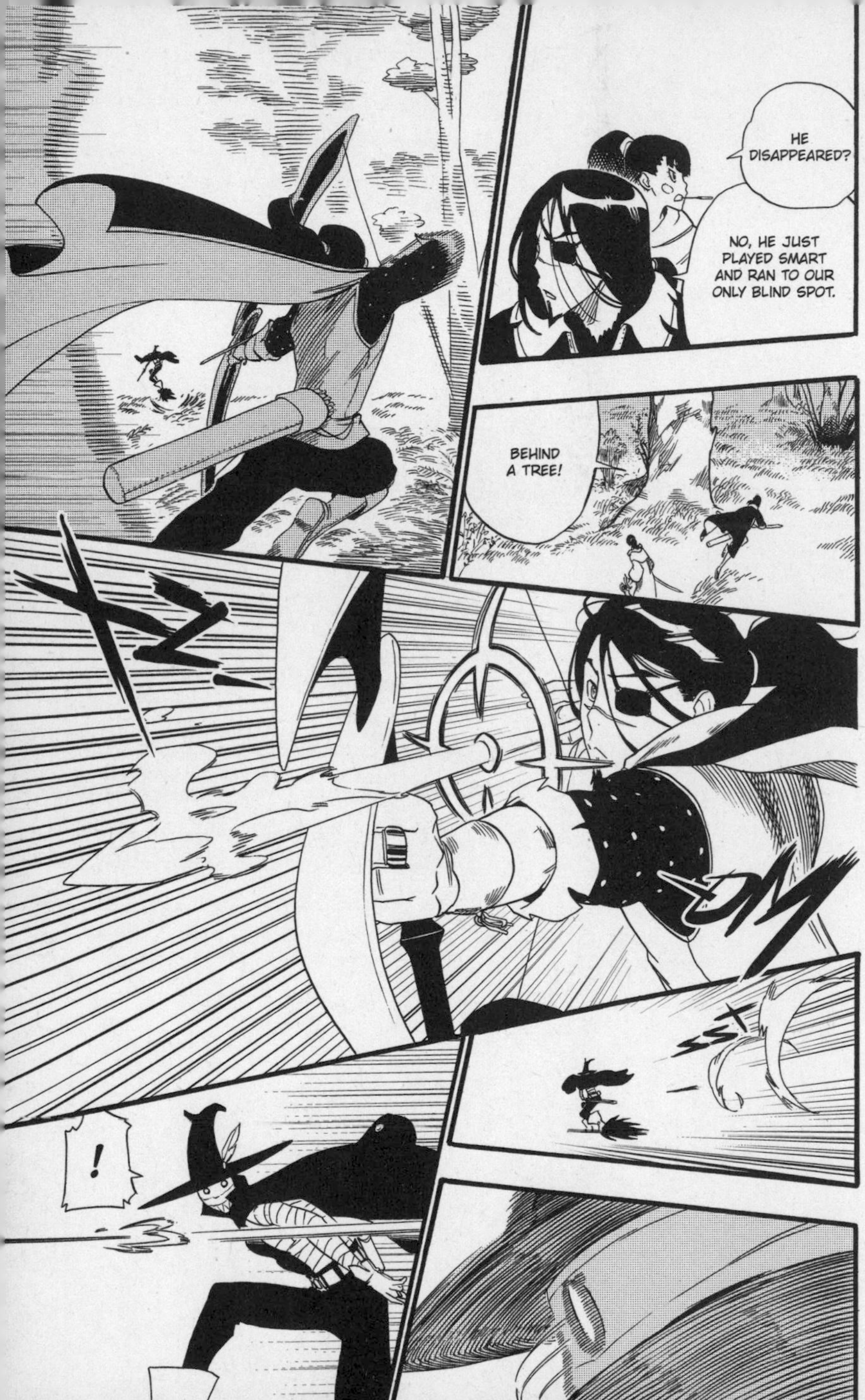
HE DISAPPEARED?
NO, HE JUST PLAYED SMART AND RAN TO OUR ONLY BLIND SPOT.
BEHIND A TREE!
!

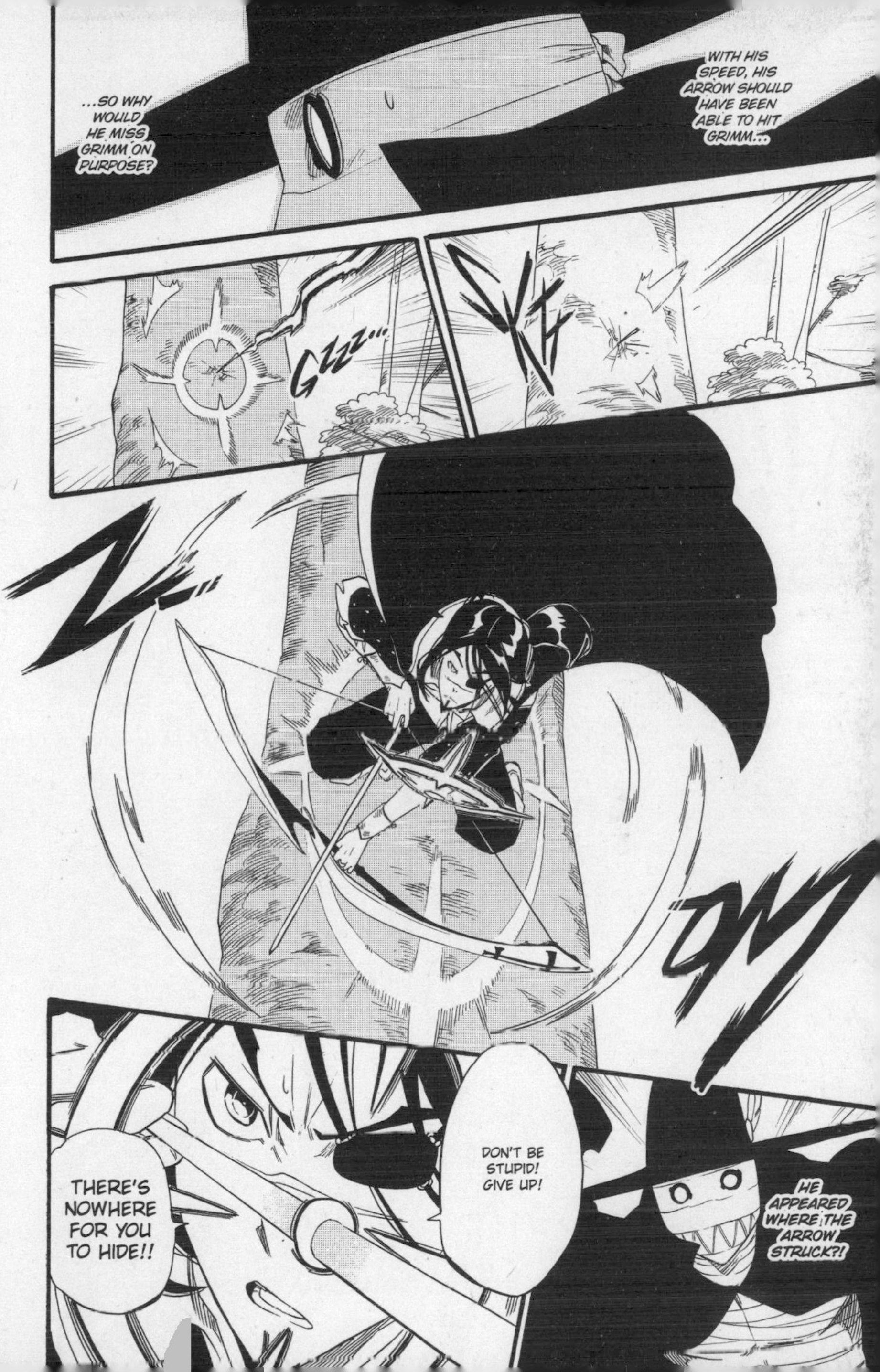
WITH HIS SPEED, HIS ARROW SHOULD HAVE BEEN ABLE TO HIT GRIMM...
...SO WHY WOULD HE MISS GRIMM ON PURPOSE?
GZZZ...
HE APPEARED WHERE THE ARROW STRUCK?!
DON'T BE STUPID! GIVE UP!
THERE'S NOWHERE FOR YOU TO HIDE!!

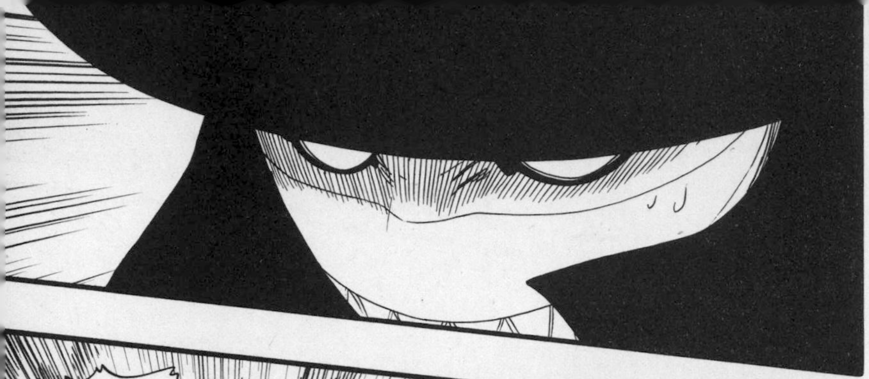

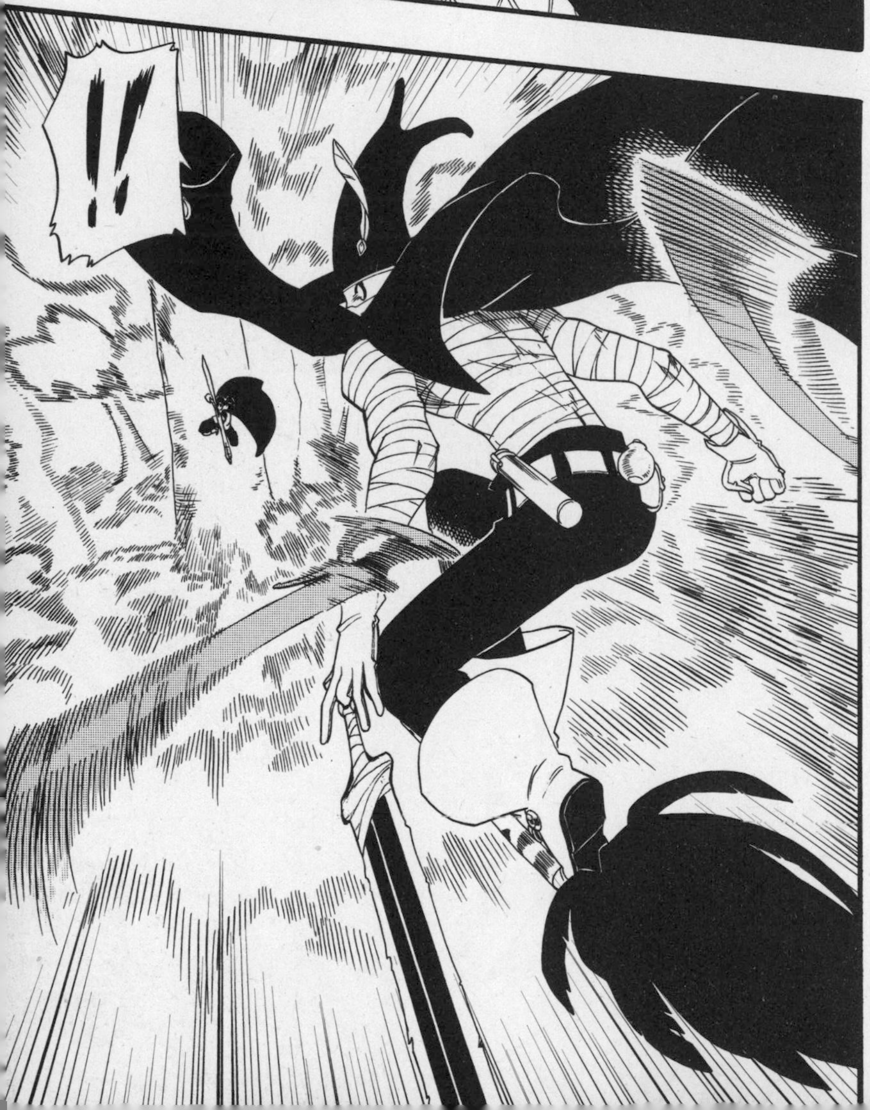
!!

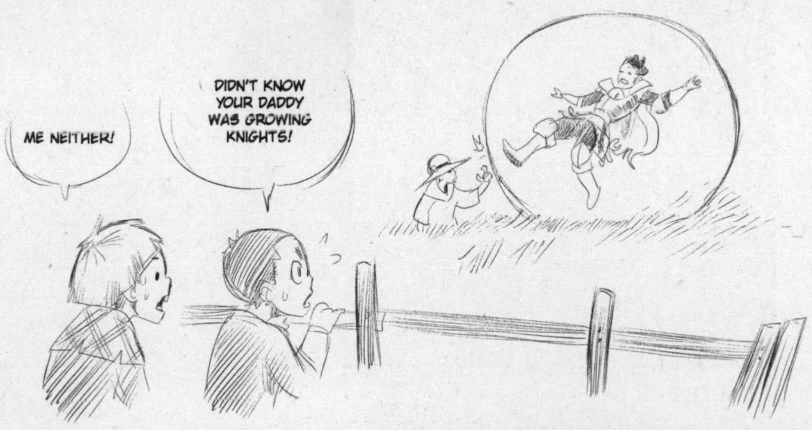
DIDN'T KNOW YOUR DADDY WAS GROWING KNIGHTS!
ME NEITHER!

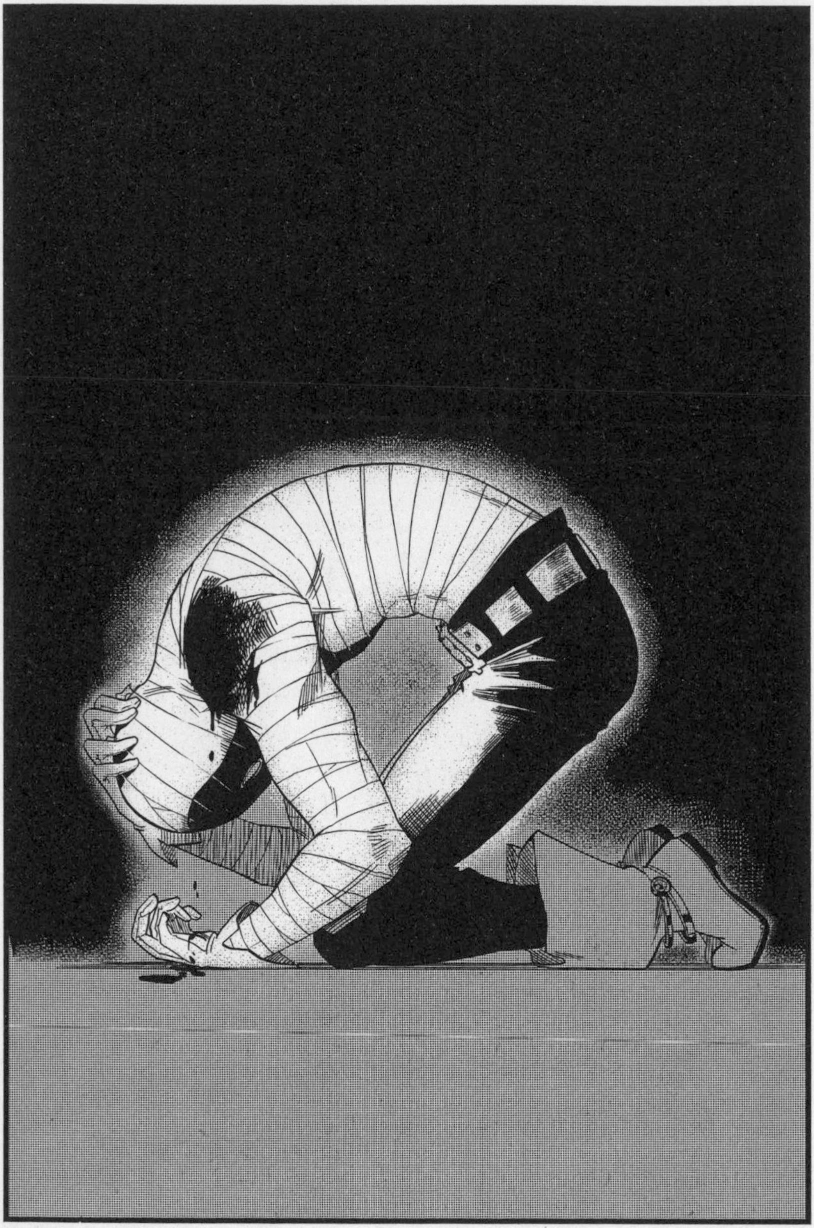

Chapter 39

Blood

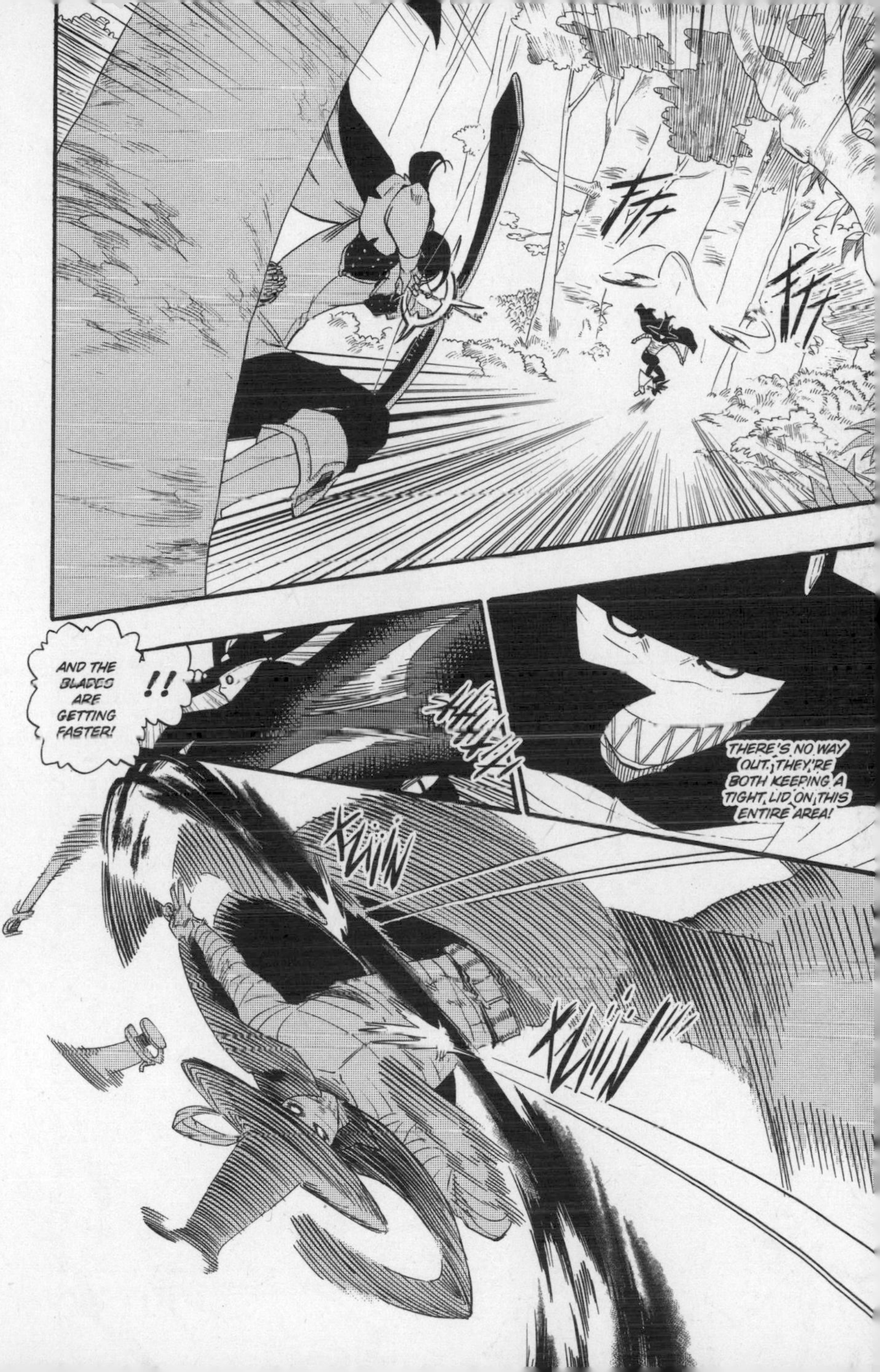
THERE'S NO WAY OUT, THEY'RE BOTH KEEPING A TIGHT LID ON THIS ENTIRE AREA!
!!
AND THE BLADES ARE GETTING FASTER!

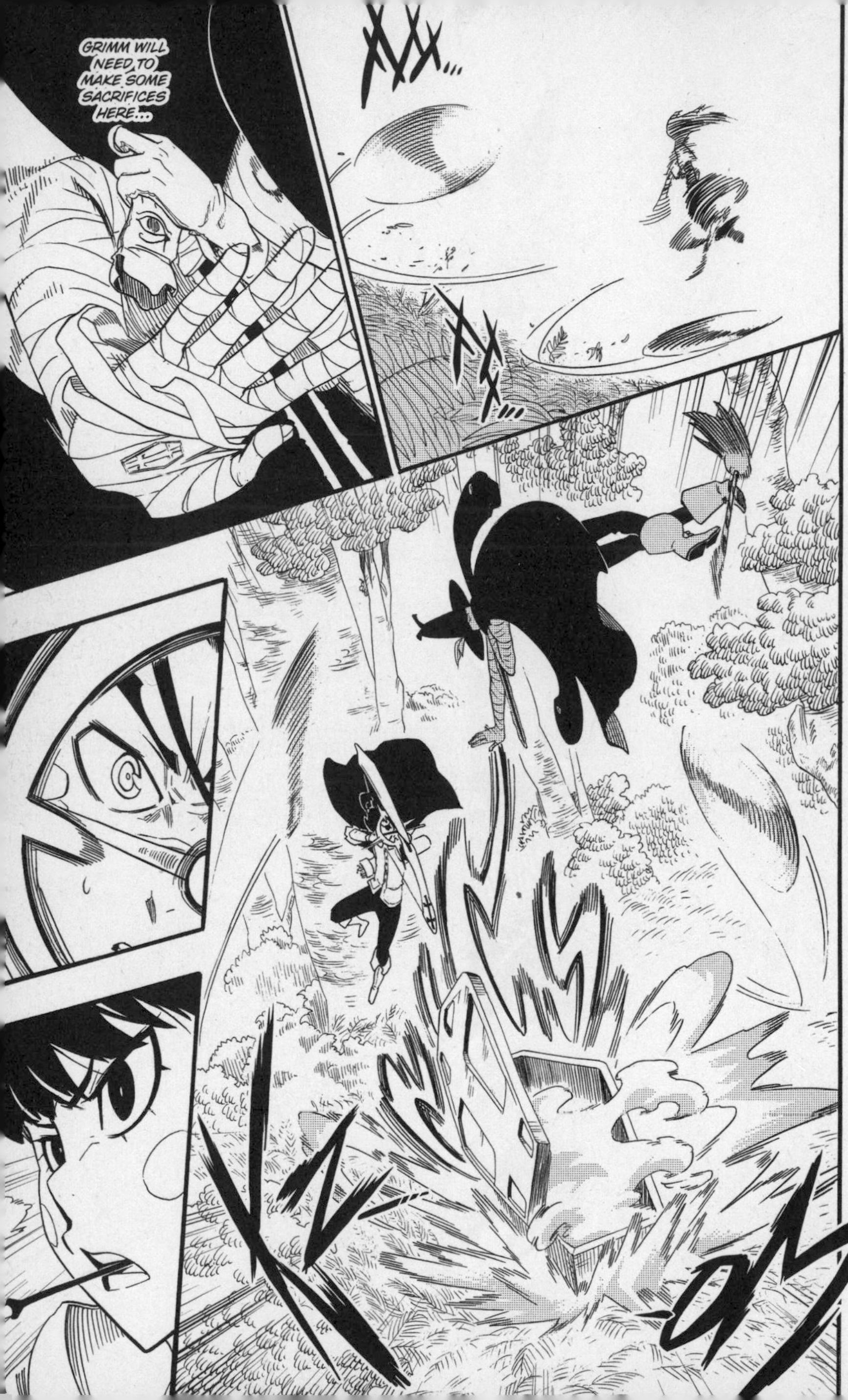
GRIMM WILL NEED TO MAKE SOME SACRIFICES HERE...

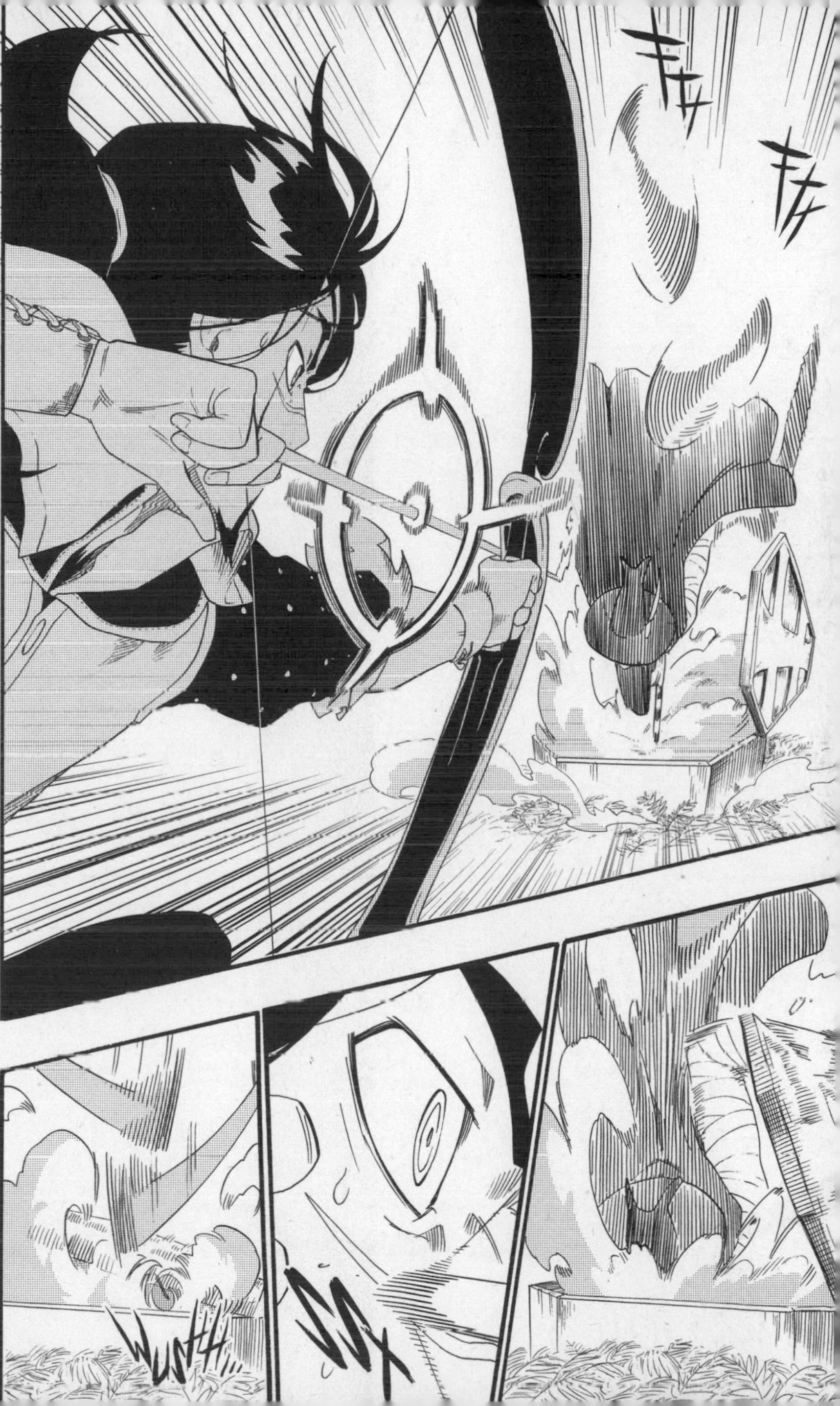
WUSH

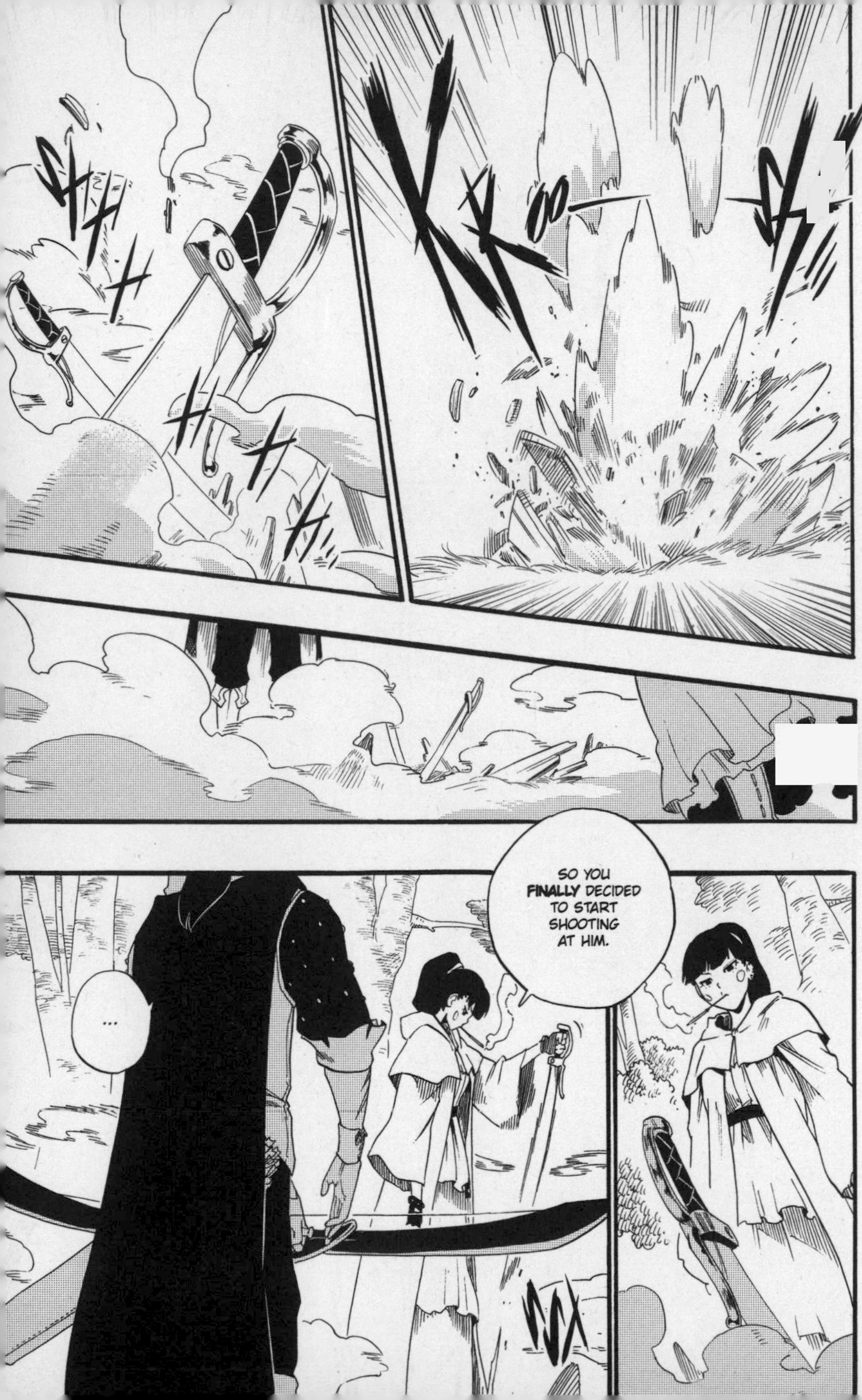

KKOO
SHH
SO YOU FINALLY DECIDED TO START SHOOTING AT HIM.
...

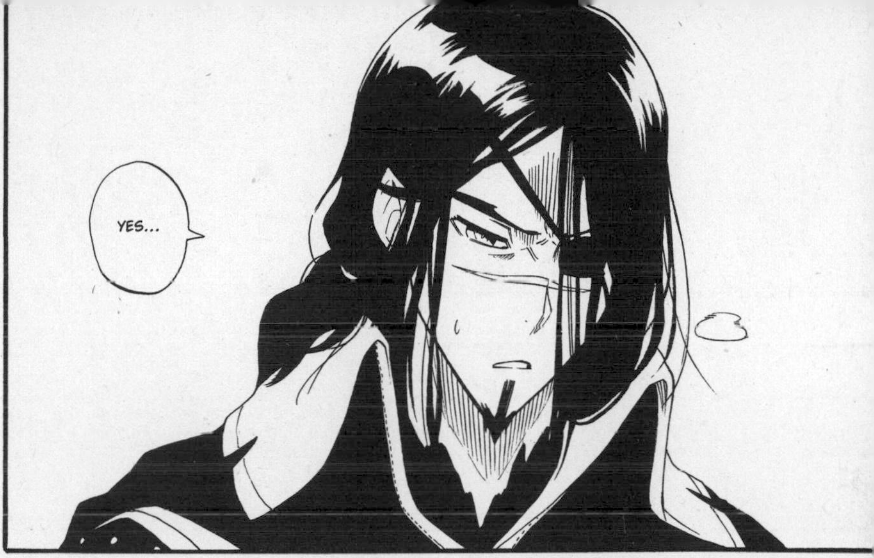
YES...
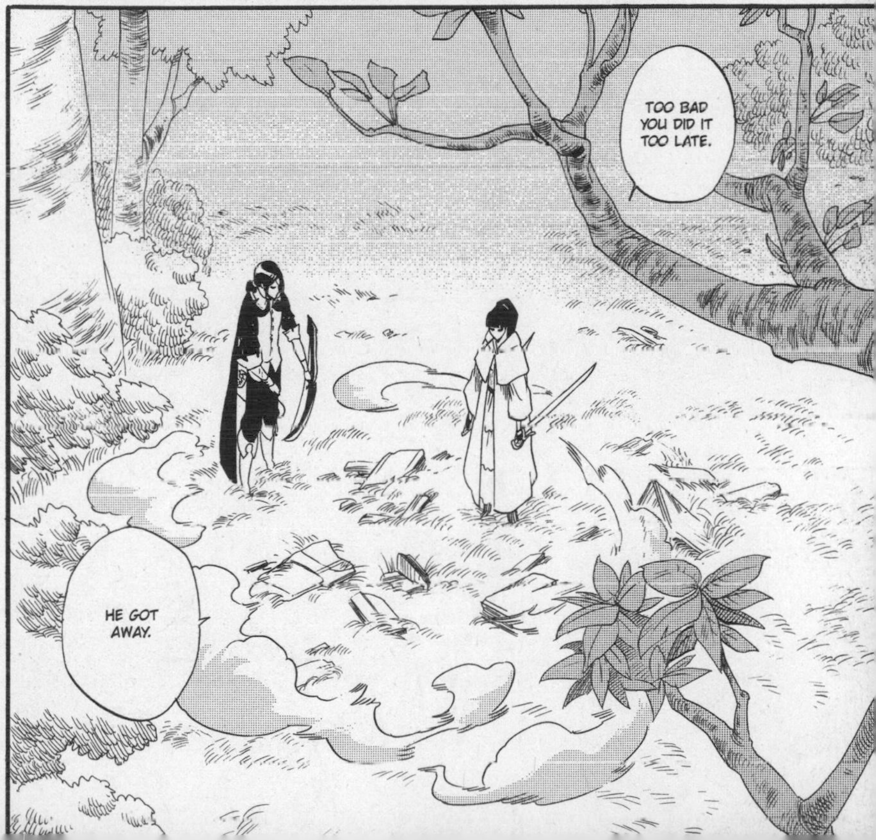
TOO BAD YOU DID IT TOO LATE.
HE GOT AWAY.

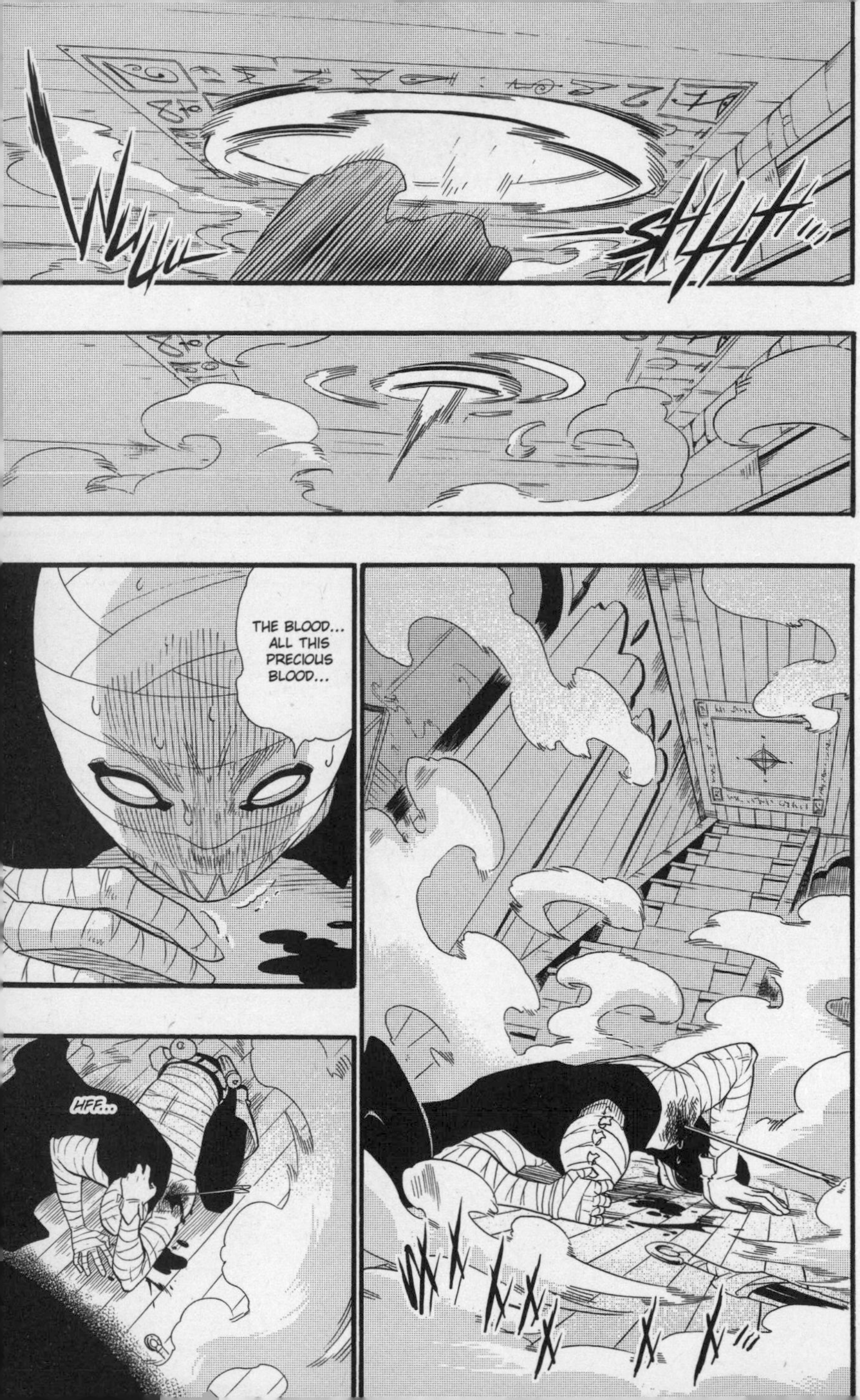
WHUUU
SHHH!!
THE BLOOD... ALL THIS PRECIOUS BLOOD...
HFF...

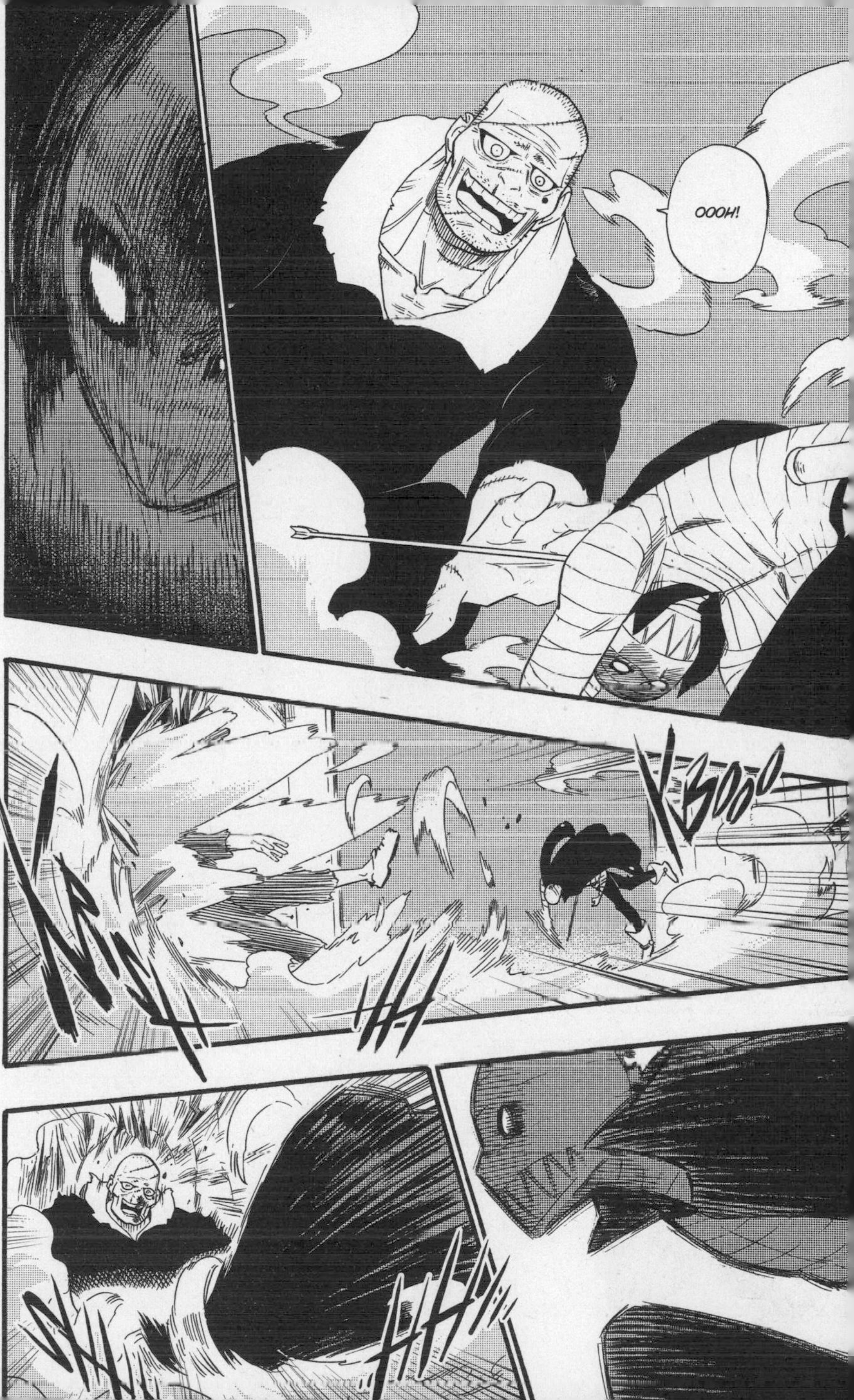
OOOH!
KBOOO

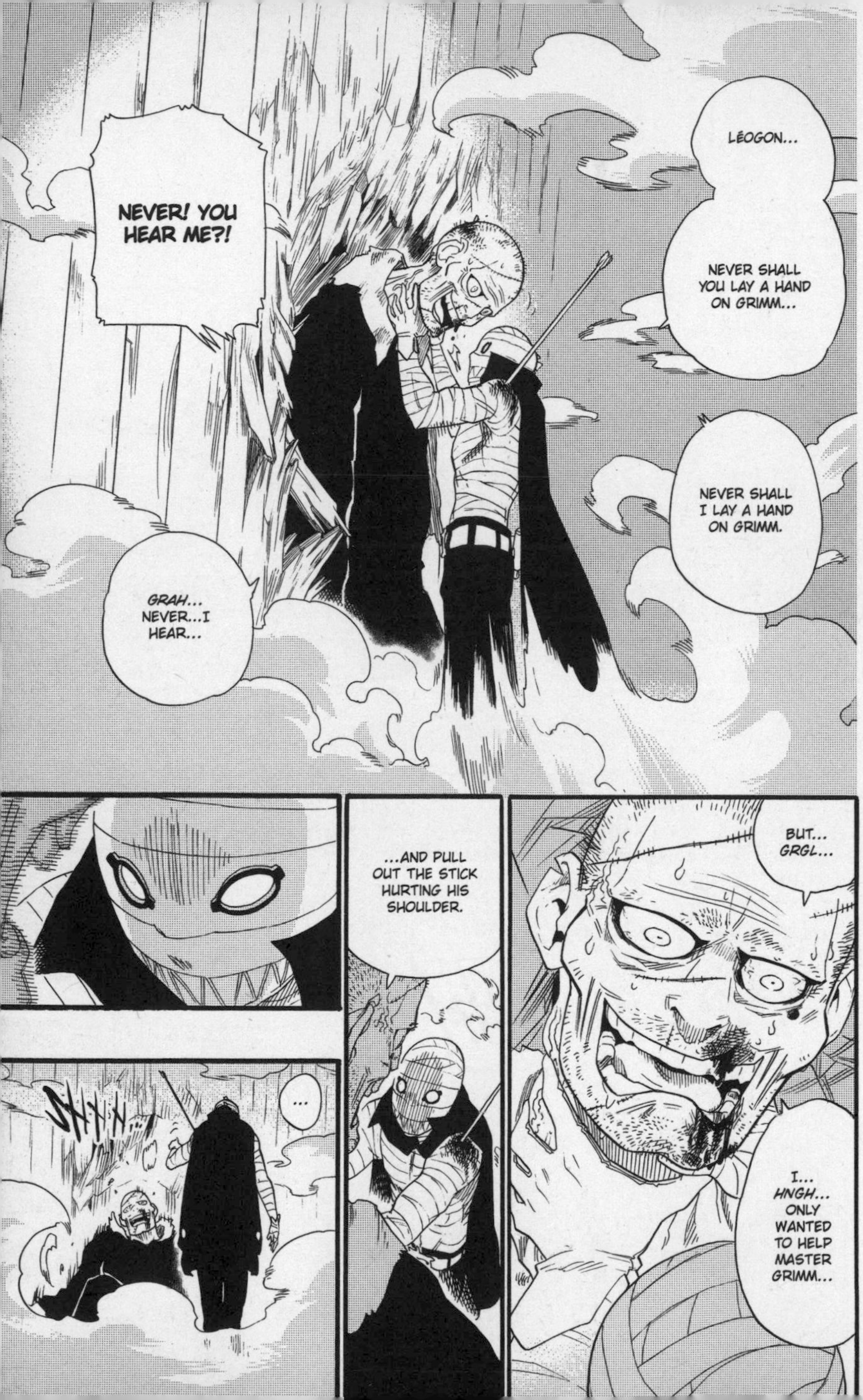
LÉOGON...
NEVER SHALL YOU LAY A HAND ON GRIMM...
NEVER! YOU HEAR ME?!
NEVER SHALL I LAY A HAND ON GRIMM.
GRAH... NEVER...I HEAR...
BUT... GRGL...
I... HNGH... ONLY WANTED TO HELP MASTER GRIMM...
...AND PULL OUT THE STICK HURTING HIS SHOULDER.
...

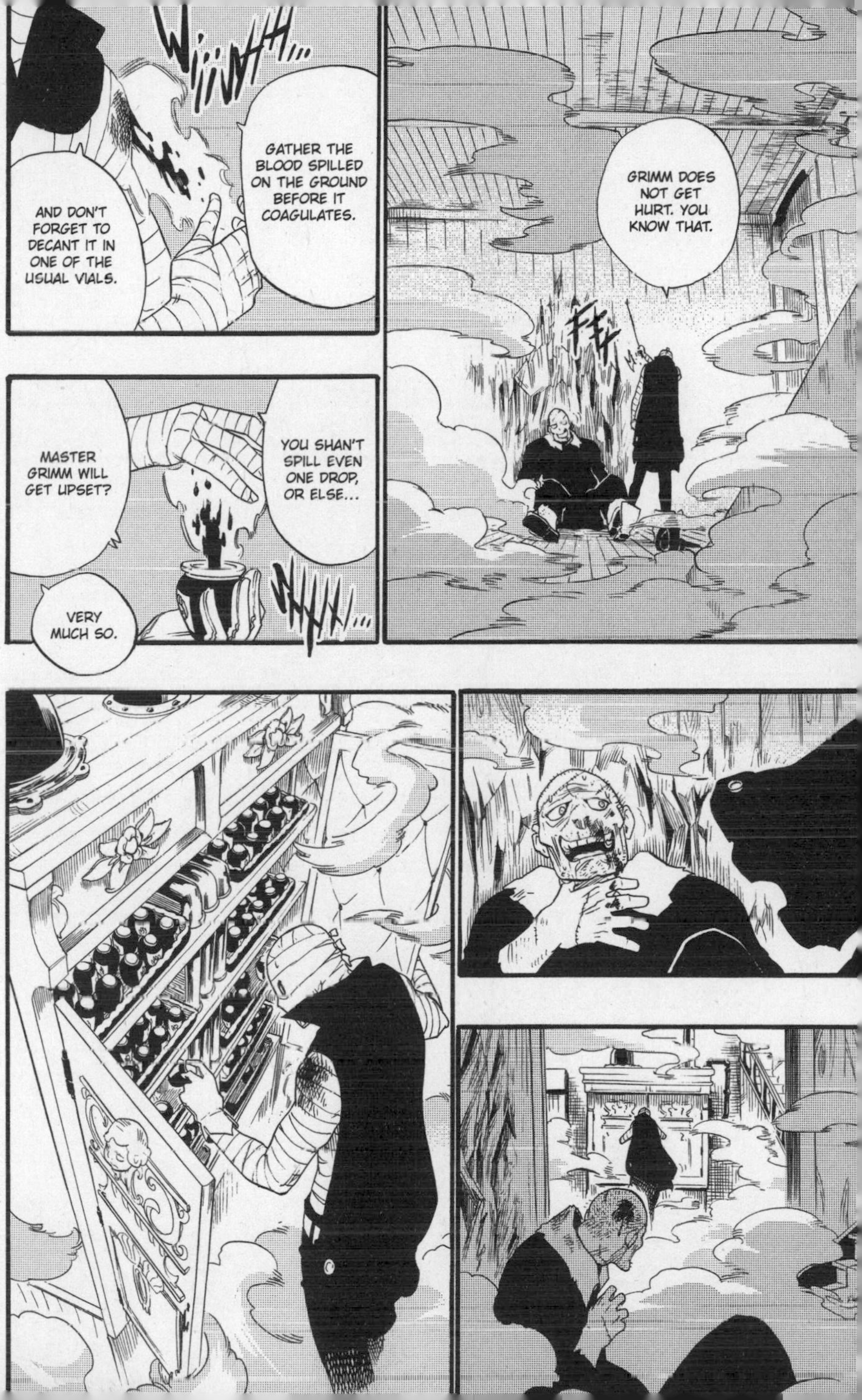
GRIMM DOES NOT GET HURT. YOU KNOW THAT.
GATHER THE BLOOD SPILLED ON THE GROUND BEFORE IT COAGULATES.
AND DON'T FORGET TO DECANT IT IN ONE OF THE USUAL VIALS.
YOU SHAN'T SPILL EVEN ONE DROP, OR ELSE...
MASTER GRIMM WILL GET UPSET?
VERY MUCH SO.

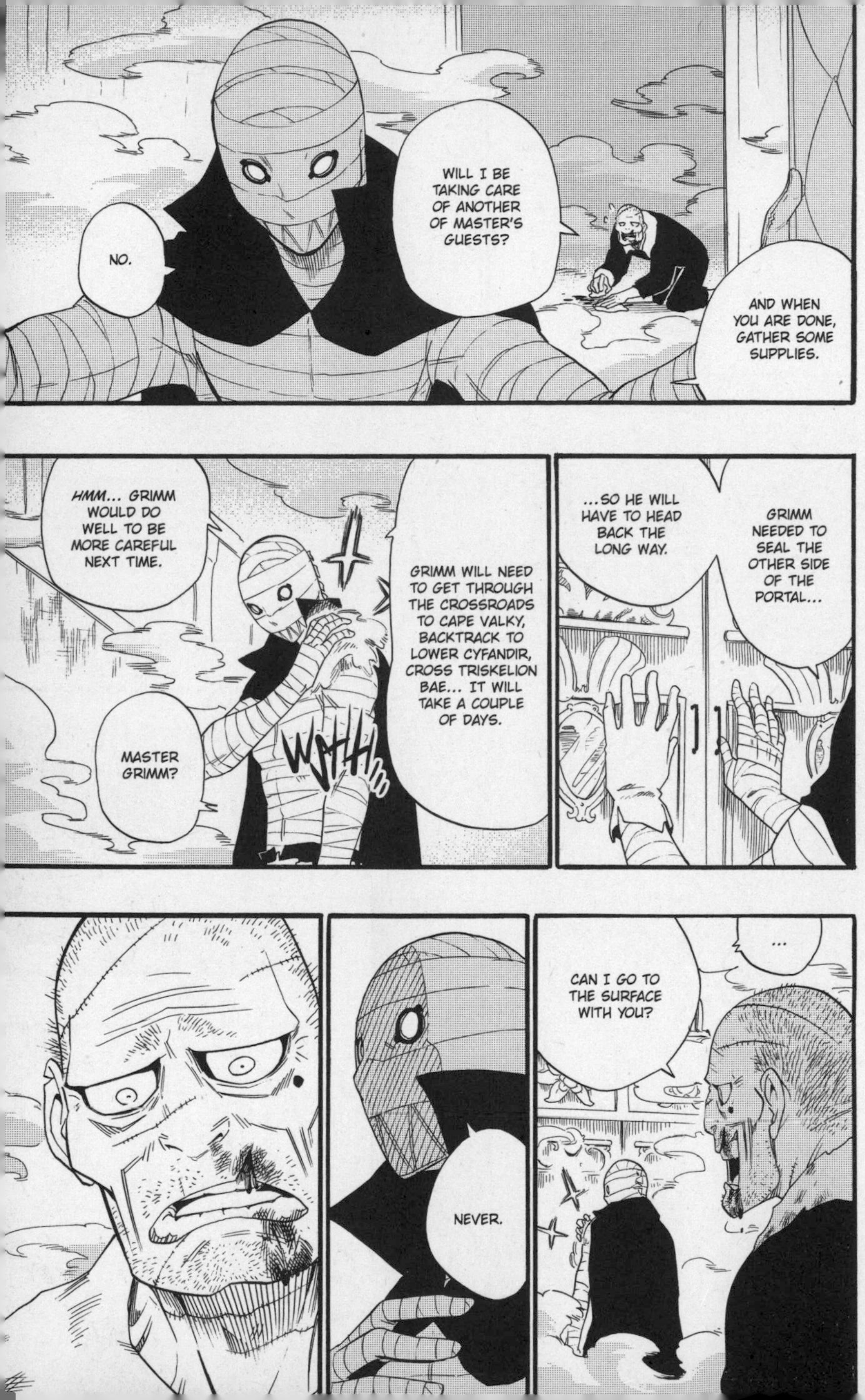
AND WHEN YOU ARE DONE, GATHER SOME SUPPLIES.
WILL I BE TAKING CARE OF ANOTHER OF MASTER'S GUESTS?
NO.
GRIMM NEEDED TO SEAL THE OTHER SIDE OF THE PORTAL...
...SO HE WILL HAVE TO HEAD BACK THE LONG WAY.
GRIMM WILL NEED TO GET THROUGH THE CROSSROADS TO CAPE VALKY, BACKTRACK TO LOWER CYFANDIR, CROSS TRISKELION BAE... IT WILL TAKE A COUPLE OF DAYS.
HMM... GRIMM WOULD DO WELL TO BE MORE CAREFUL NEXT TIME.
MASTER GRIMM?
...
CAN I GO TO THE SURFACE WITH YOU?
NEVER.

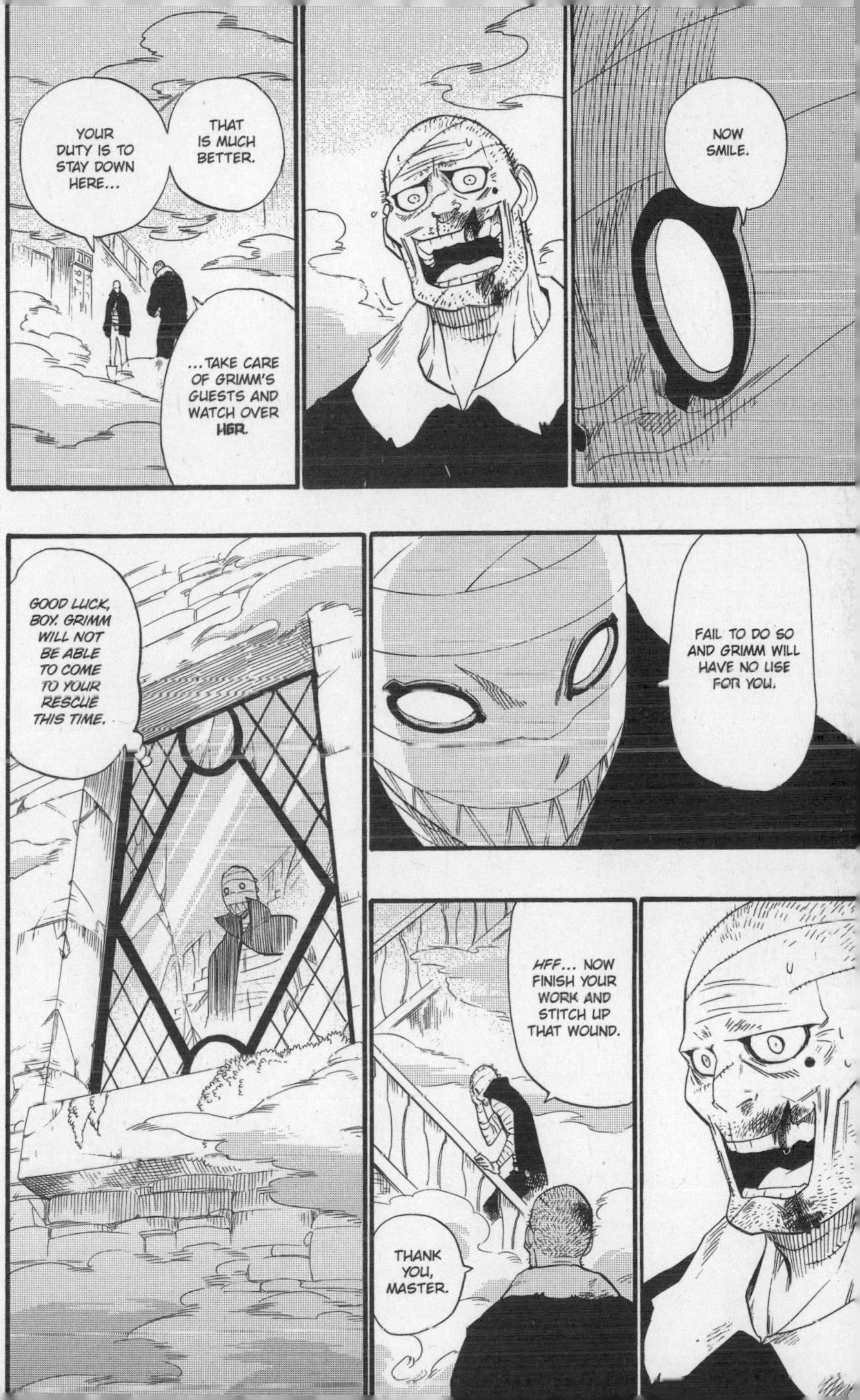
NOW SMILE.
THAT IS MUCH BETTER.
YOUR DUTY IS TO STAY DOWN HERE...
...TAKE CARE OF GRIMM'S GUESTS AND WATCH OVER HER.
FAIL TO DO SO AND GRIMM WILL HAVE NO USE FOR YOU.
HFF... NOW FINISH YOUR WORK AND STITCH UP THAT WOUND.
THANK YOU, MASTER.
GOOD LUCK, BOY. GRIMM WILL NOT BE ABLE TO COME TO YOUR RESCUE THIS TIME.

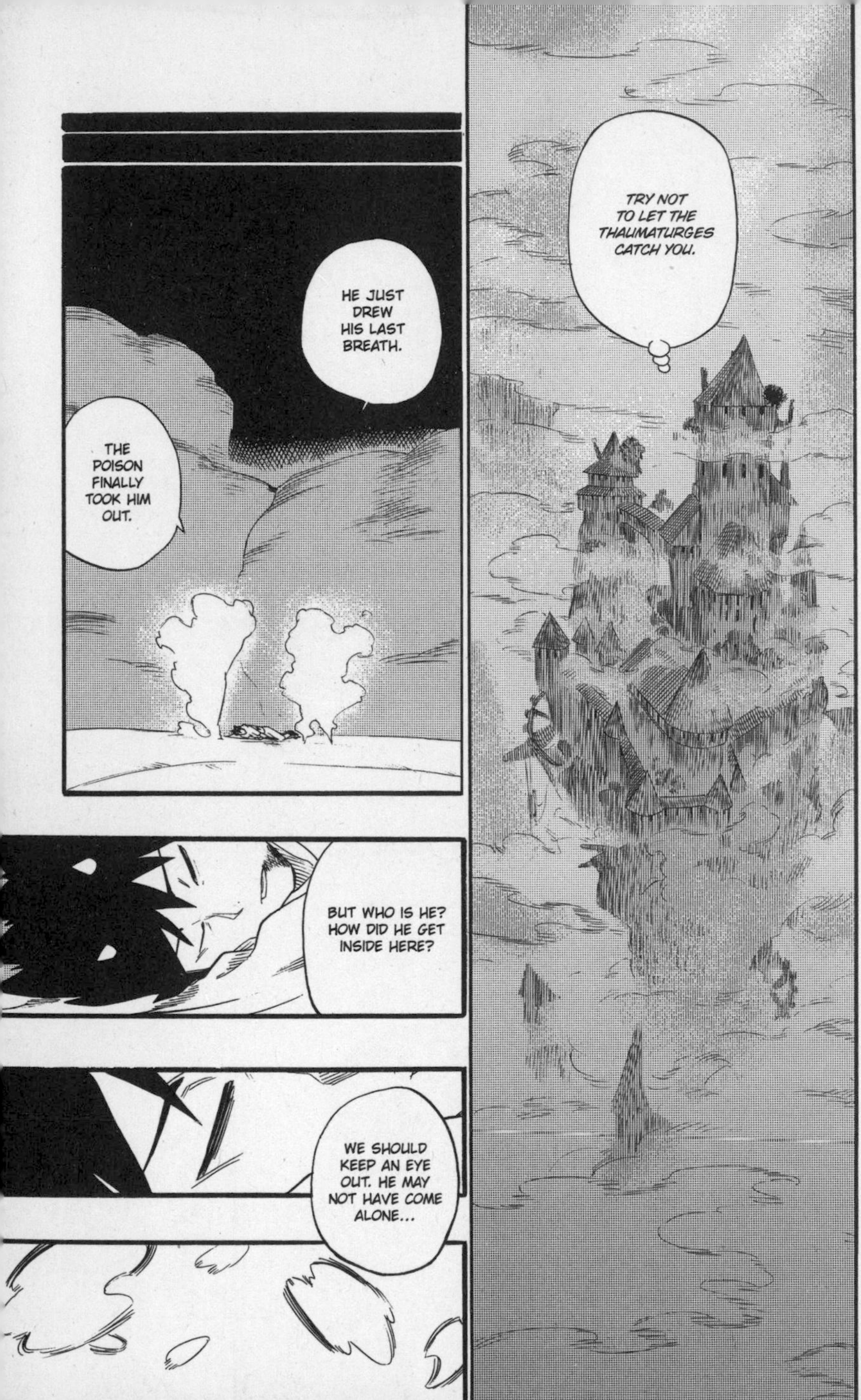
TRY NOT TO LET THE THAUMATURGES CATCH YOU.
HE JUST DREW HIS LAST BREATH.
THE POISON FINALLY TOOK HIM OUT.
BUT WHO IS HE? HOW DID HE GET INSIDE HERE?
WE SHOULD KEEP AN EYE OUT. HE MAY NOT HAVE COME ALONE...

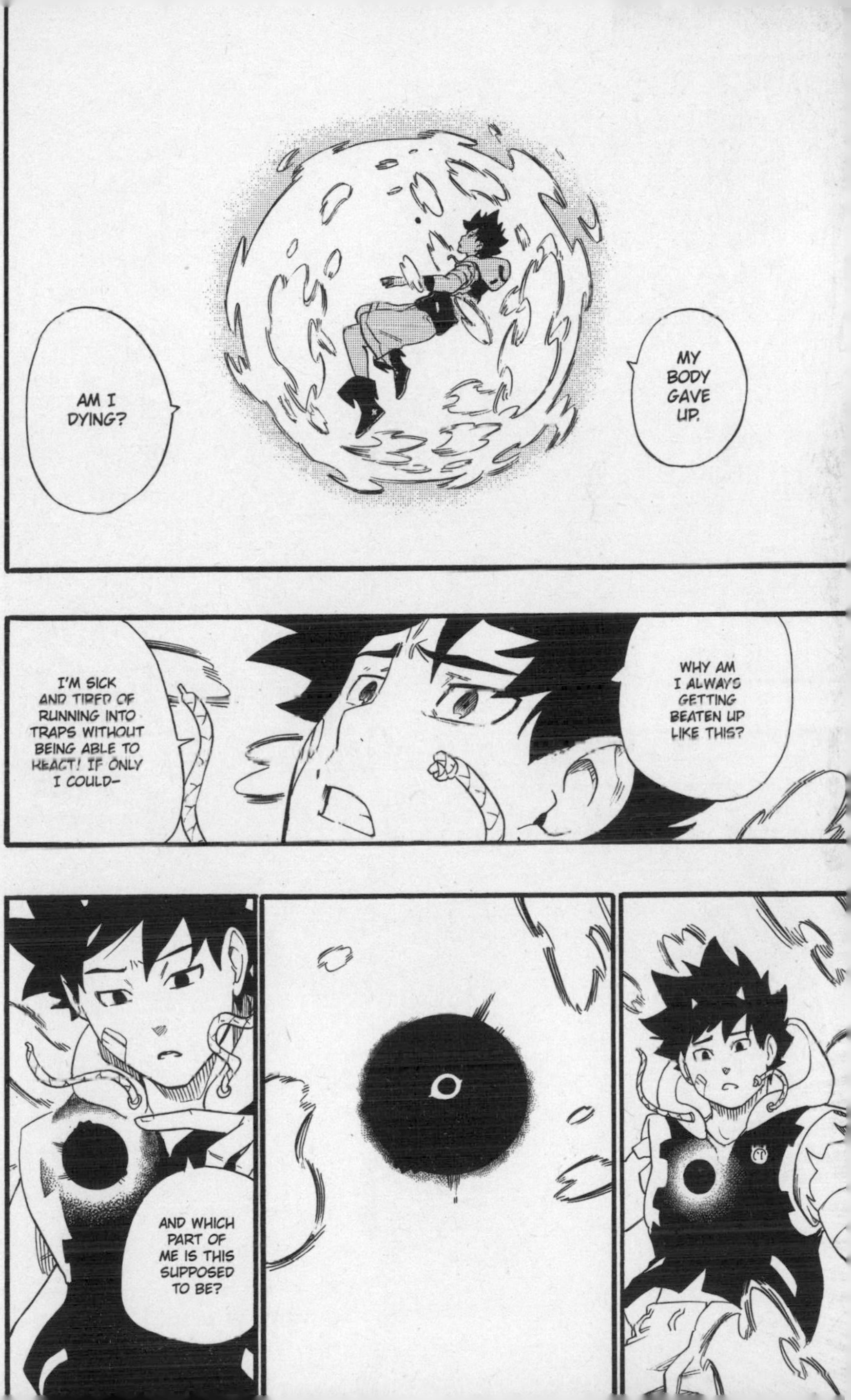
MY BODY GAVE UP.
AM I DYING?
WHY AM I ALWAYS GETTING BEATEN UP LIKE THIS?
I'M SICK AND TIRED OF RUNNING INTO TRAPS WITHOUT BEING ABLE TO REACT! IF ONLY I COULD–
AND WHICH PART OF ME IS THIS SUPPOSED TO BE?

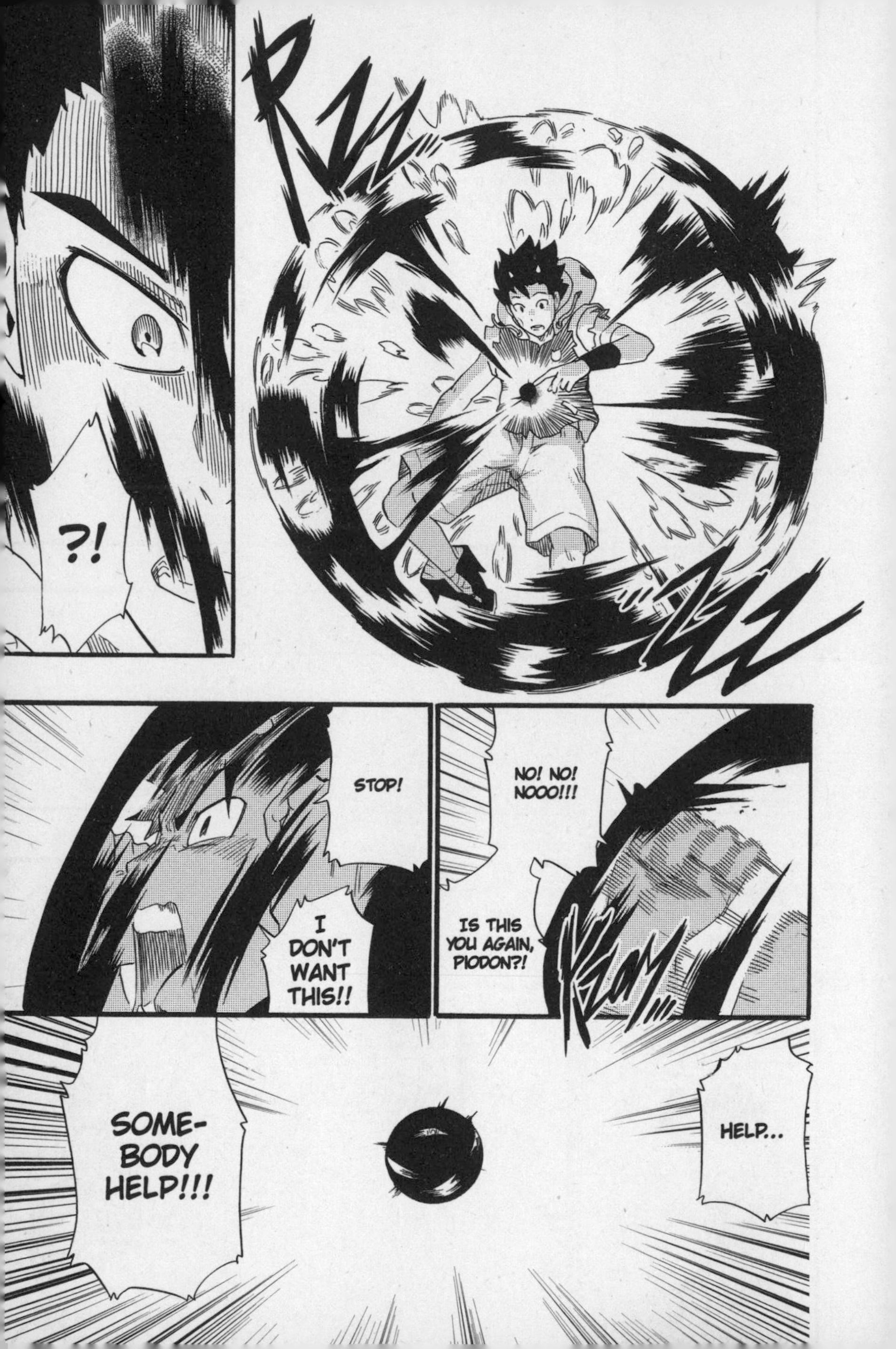
?!
NO! NO! NOOO!!!
IS THIS YOU AGAIN, PIODON?!
STOP!
I DON'T WANT THIS!!
HELP...
SOME-BODY HELP!!!

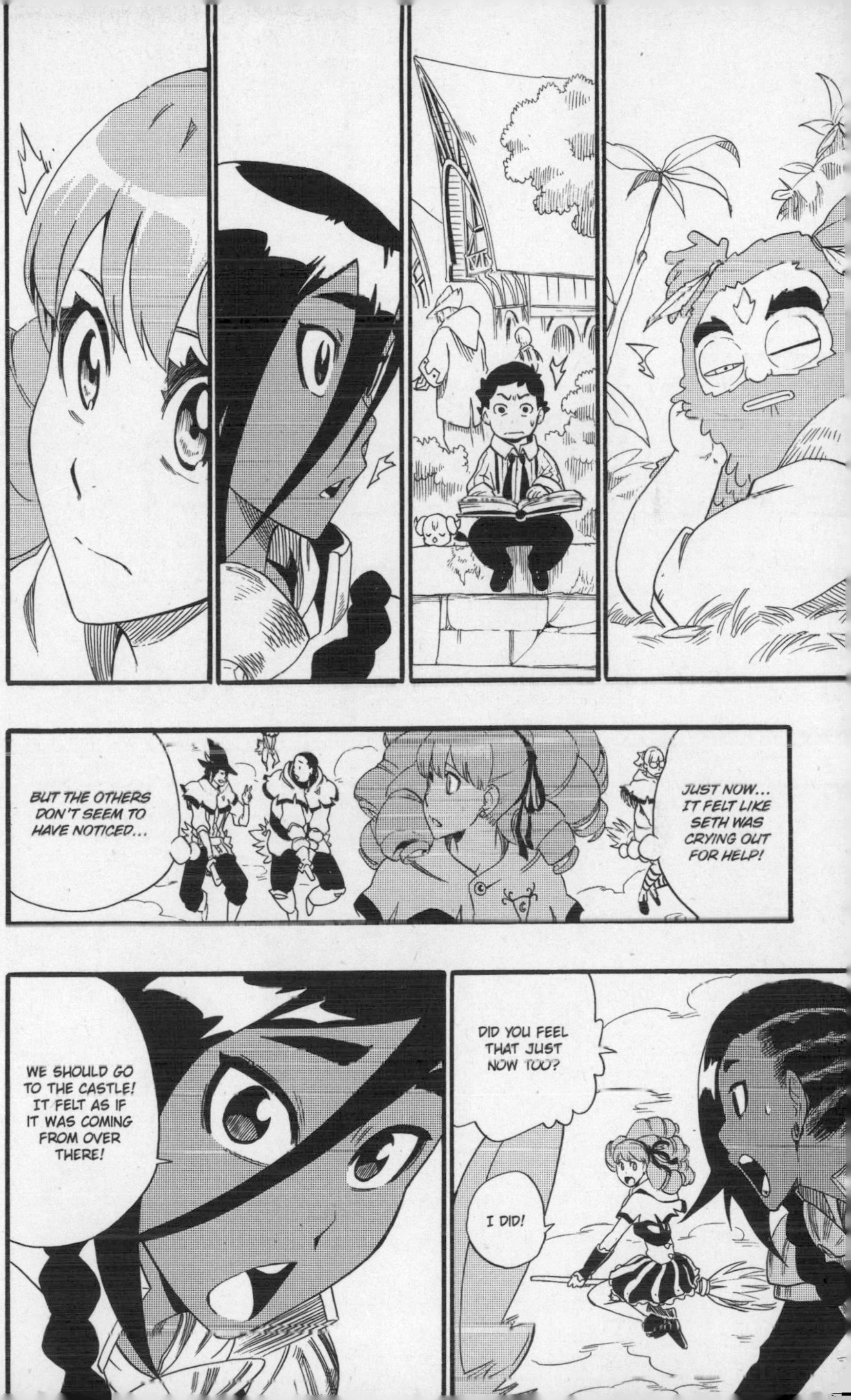
JUST NOW... IT FELT LIKE SETH WAS CRYING OUT FOR HELP!
BUT THE OTHERS DON'T SEEM TO HAVE NOTICED...
DID YOU FEEL THAT JUST NOW TOO?
I DID!
WE SHOULD GO TO THE CASTLE! IT FELT AS IF IT WAS COMING FROM OVER THERE!

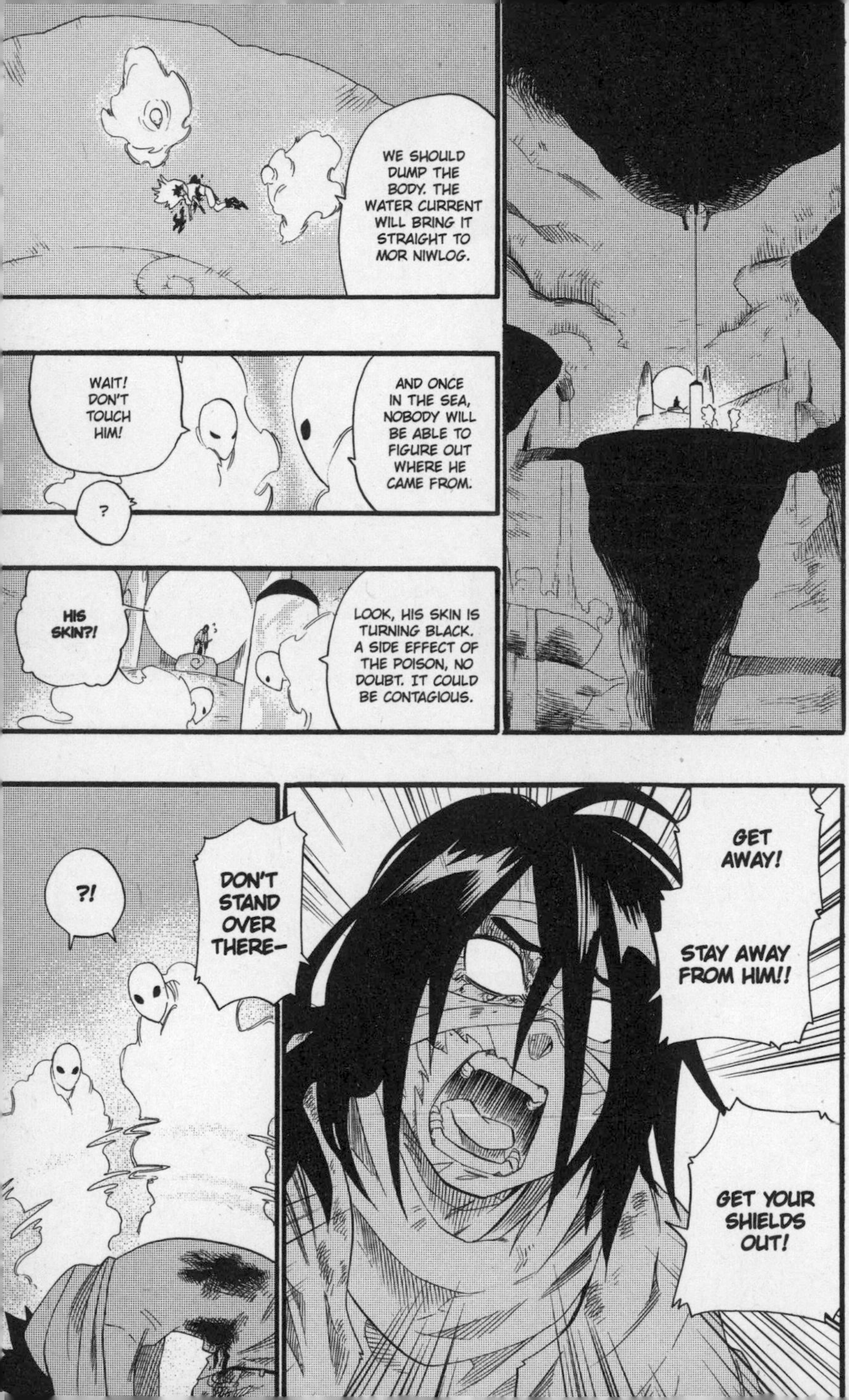
WE SHOULD DUMP THE BODY. THE WATER CURRENT WILL BRING IT STRAIGHT TO MOR NIWLOG.
AND ONCE IN THE SEA, NOBODY WILL BE ABLE TO FIGURE OUT WHERE HE CAME FROM.
WAIT! DON'T TOUCH HIM!
?
LOOK, HIS SKIN IS TURNING BLACK. A SIDE EFFECT OF THE POISON, NO DOUBT. IT COULD BE CONTAGIOUS.
HIS SKIN?!
DON'T STAND OVER THERE-
?!
GET AWAY!
STAY AWAY FROM HIM!!
GET YOUR SHIELDS OUT!

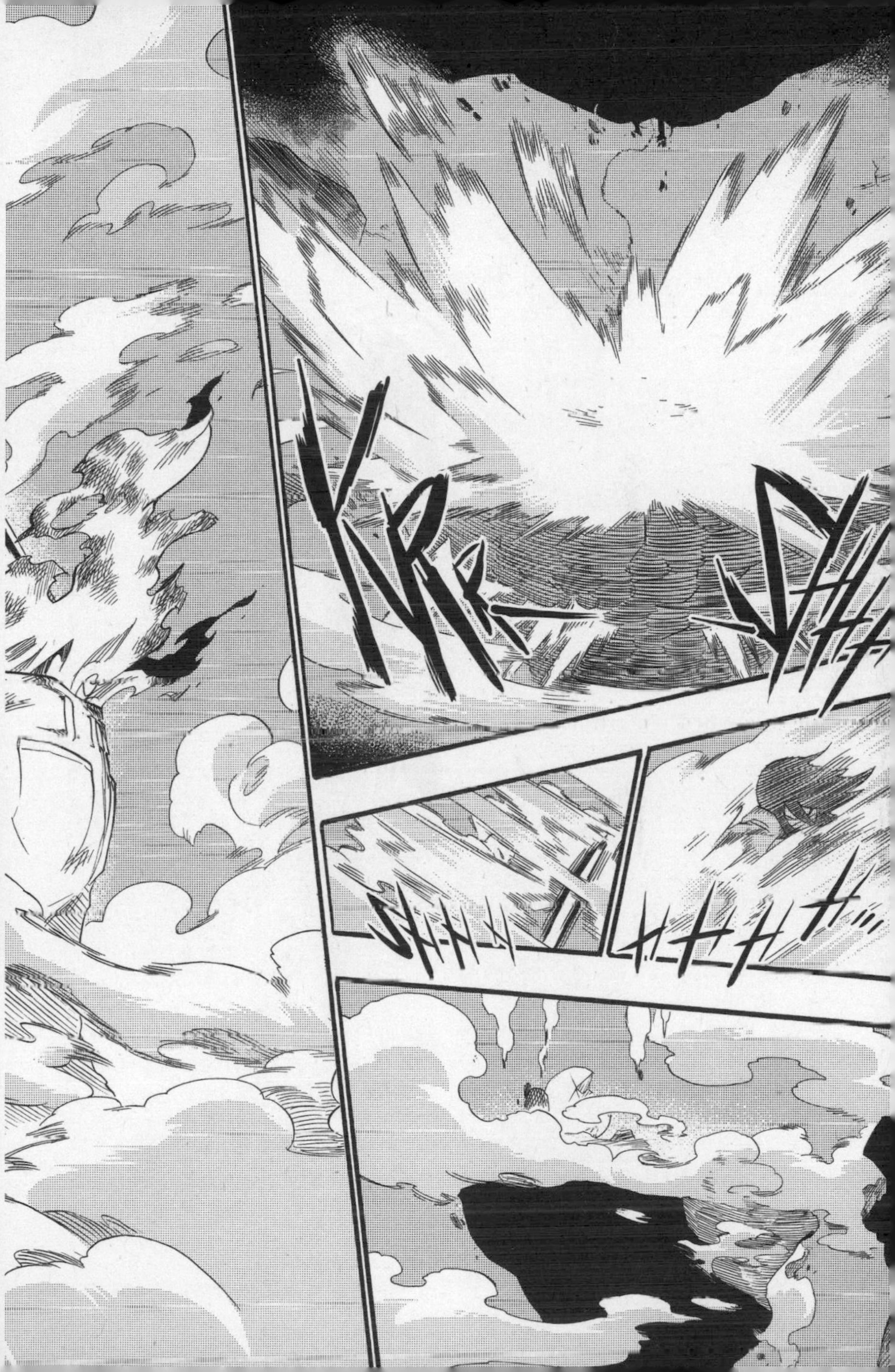
KRR—
HHHH...
SHHH

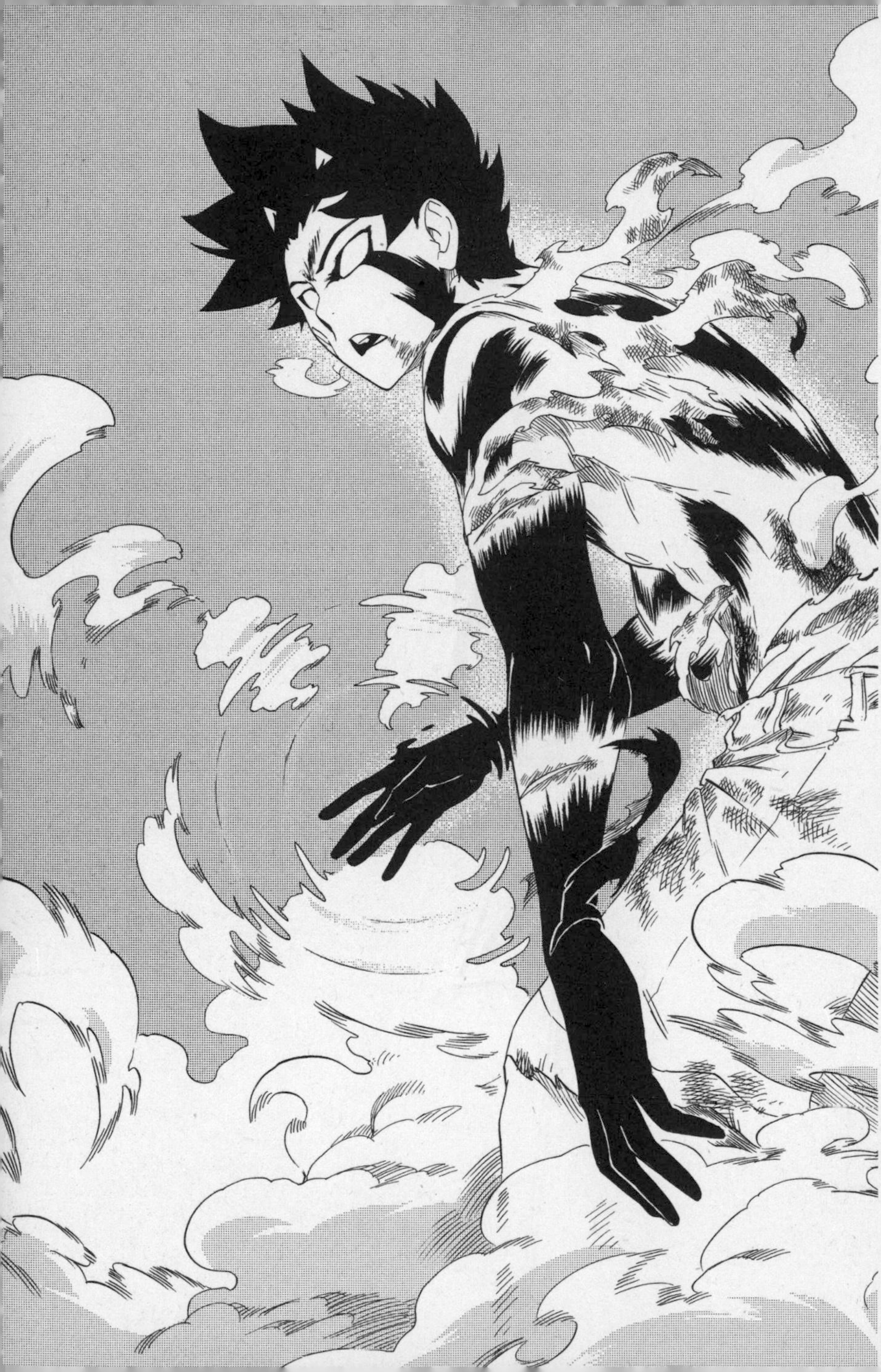

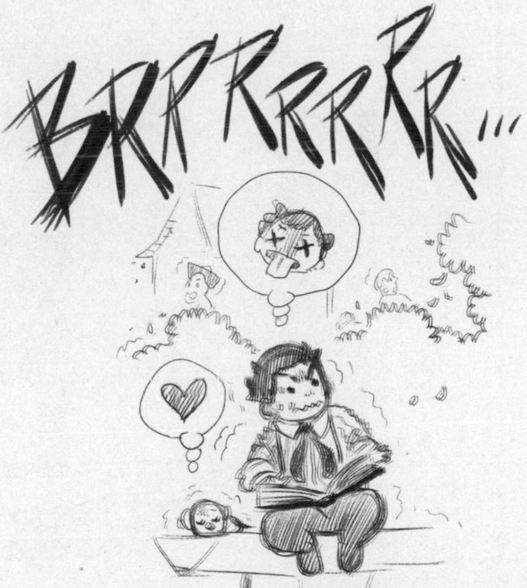
BRRRRRRR...

MEANWHILE, BACK ON THE GROUND...

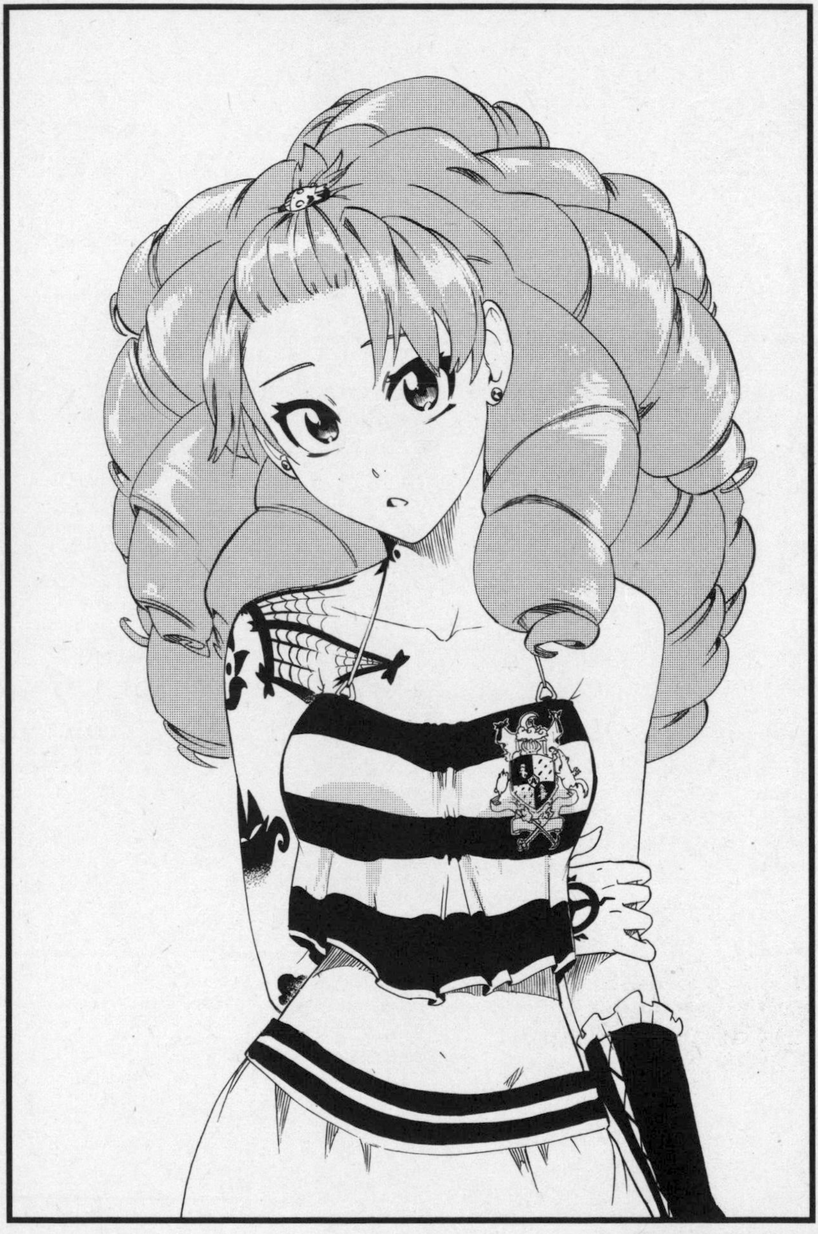

Chapter 40

Trapper

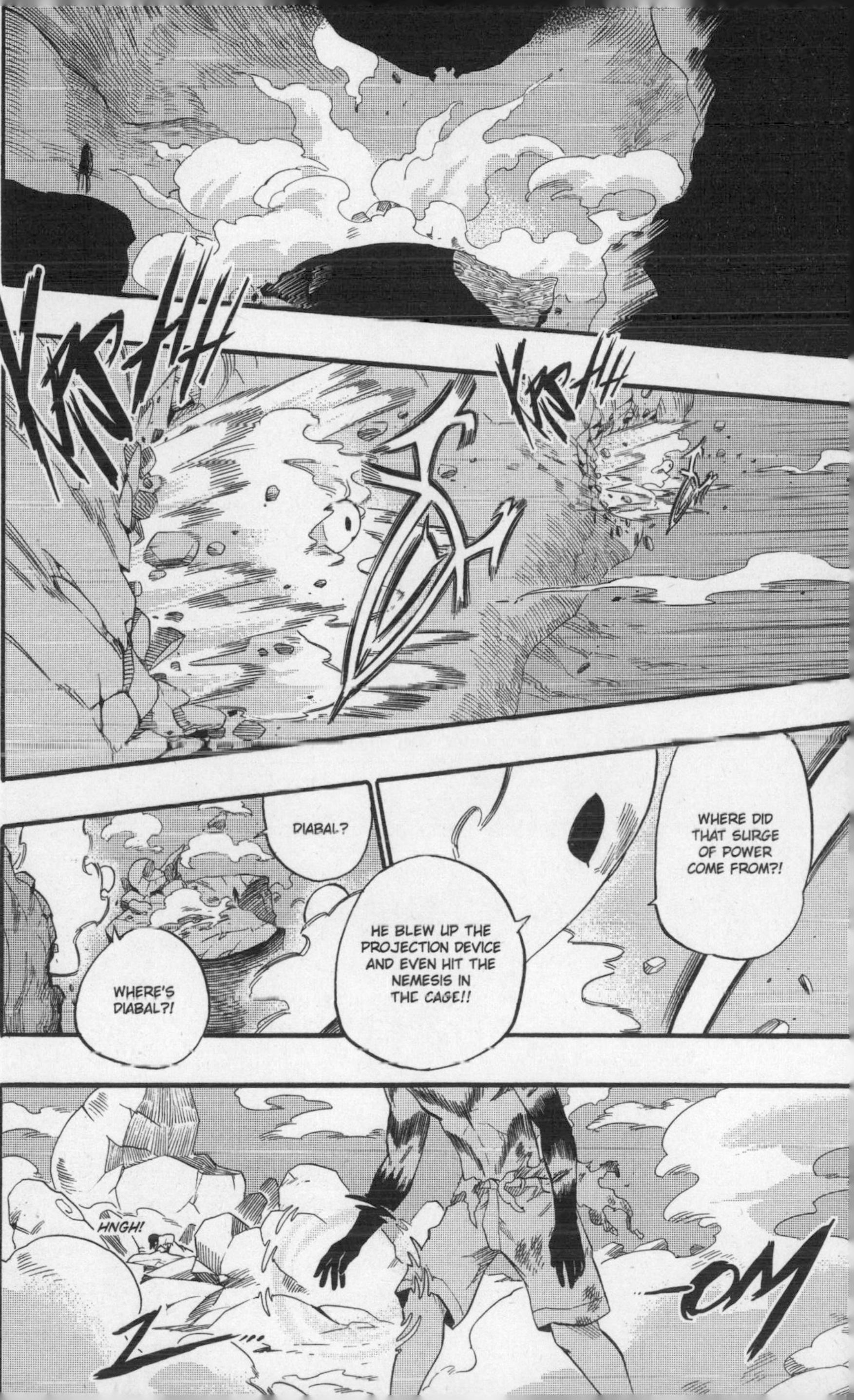
WHERE DID THAT SURGE OF POWER COME FROM?!
HE BLEW UP THE PROJECTION DEVICE AND EVEN HIT THE NEMESIS IN THE CAGE!!
DIABAL?
WHERE'S DIABAL?!
HNGH!

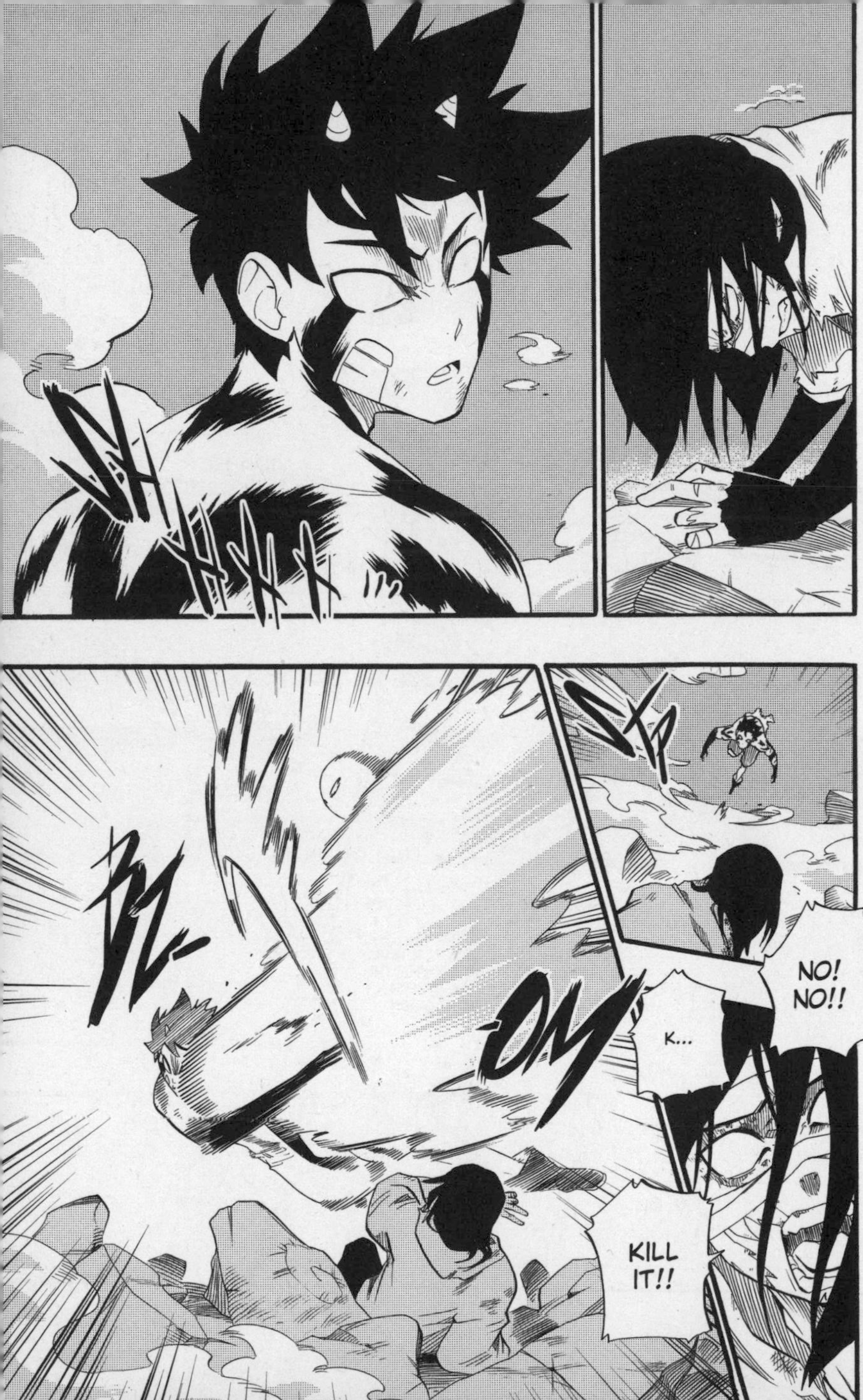
NO! NO!!
K...
KILL IT!!

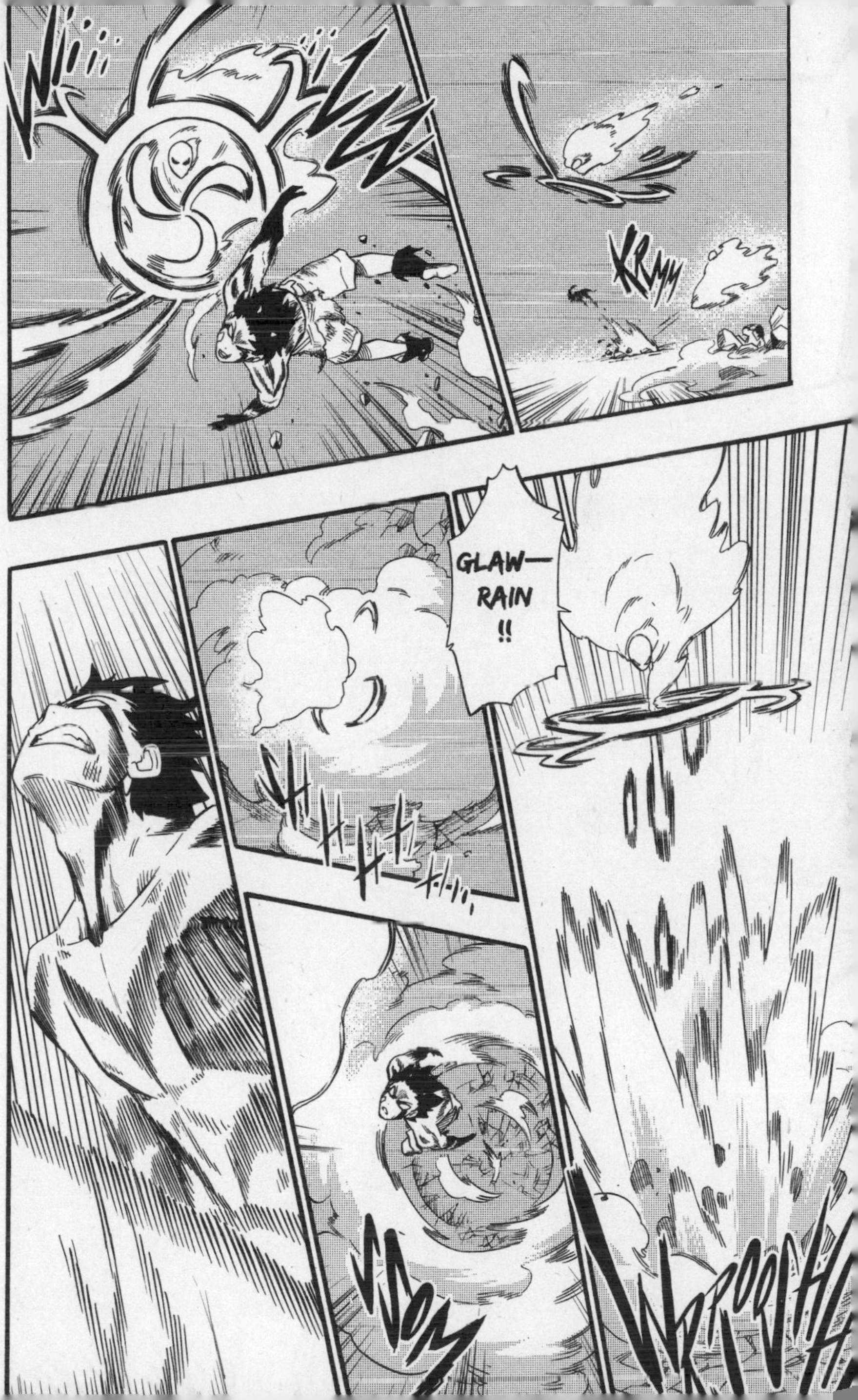
WIIII
ZWWW
KRMM
GLAW—
RAIN
!!
VSOOM
WHROOOSH

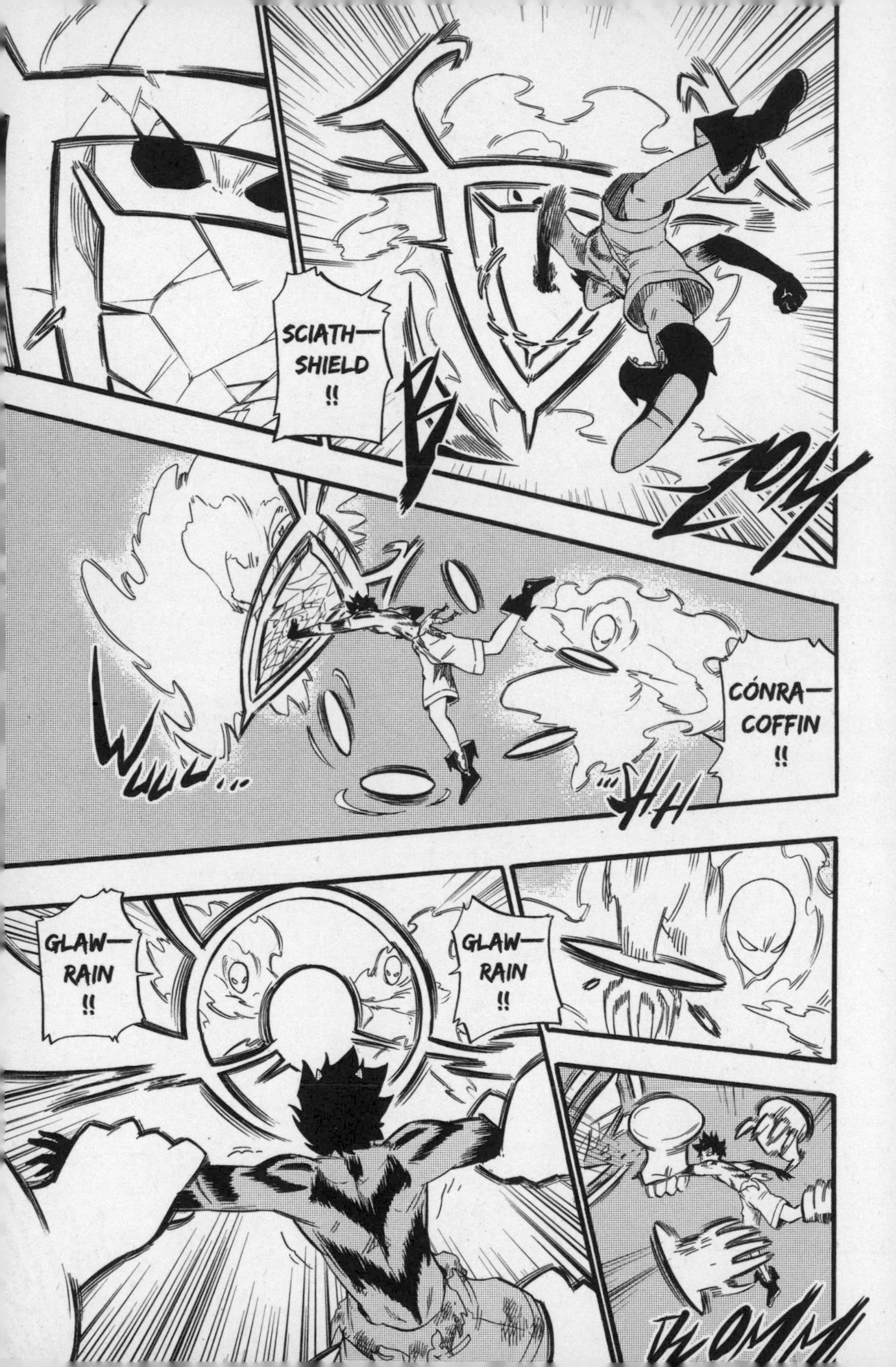
SCIATH— SHIELD !!
CÓNRA— COFFIN !!
GLAW— RAIN !!
GLAW— RAIN !!

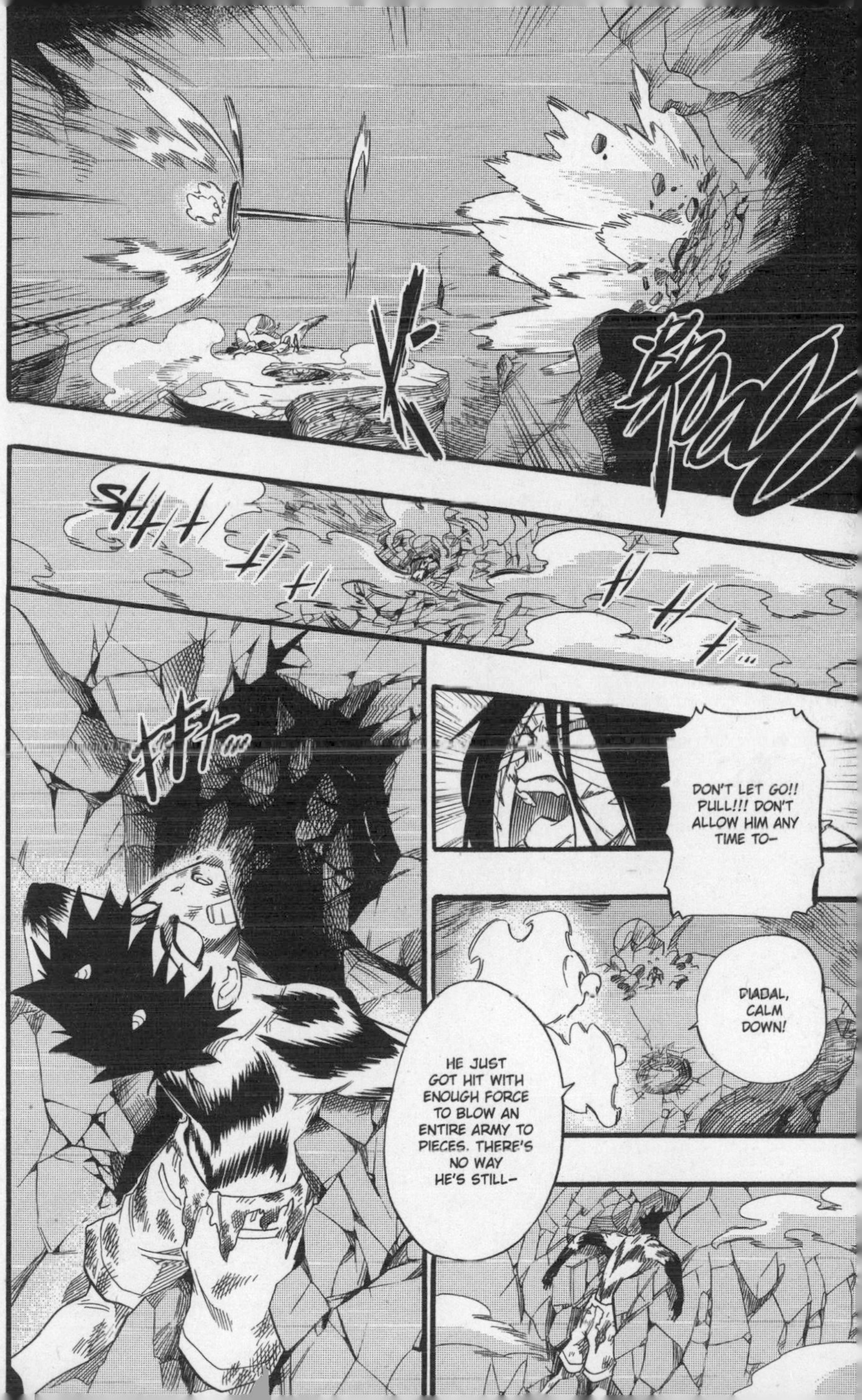
DON'T LET GO!! PULL!!! DON'T ALLOW HIM ANY TIME TO—
DIADAL, CALM DOWN!
HE JUST GOT HIT WITH ENOUGH FORCE TO BLOW AN ENTIRE ARMY TO PIECES. THERE'S NO WAY HE'S STILL—

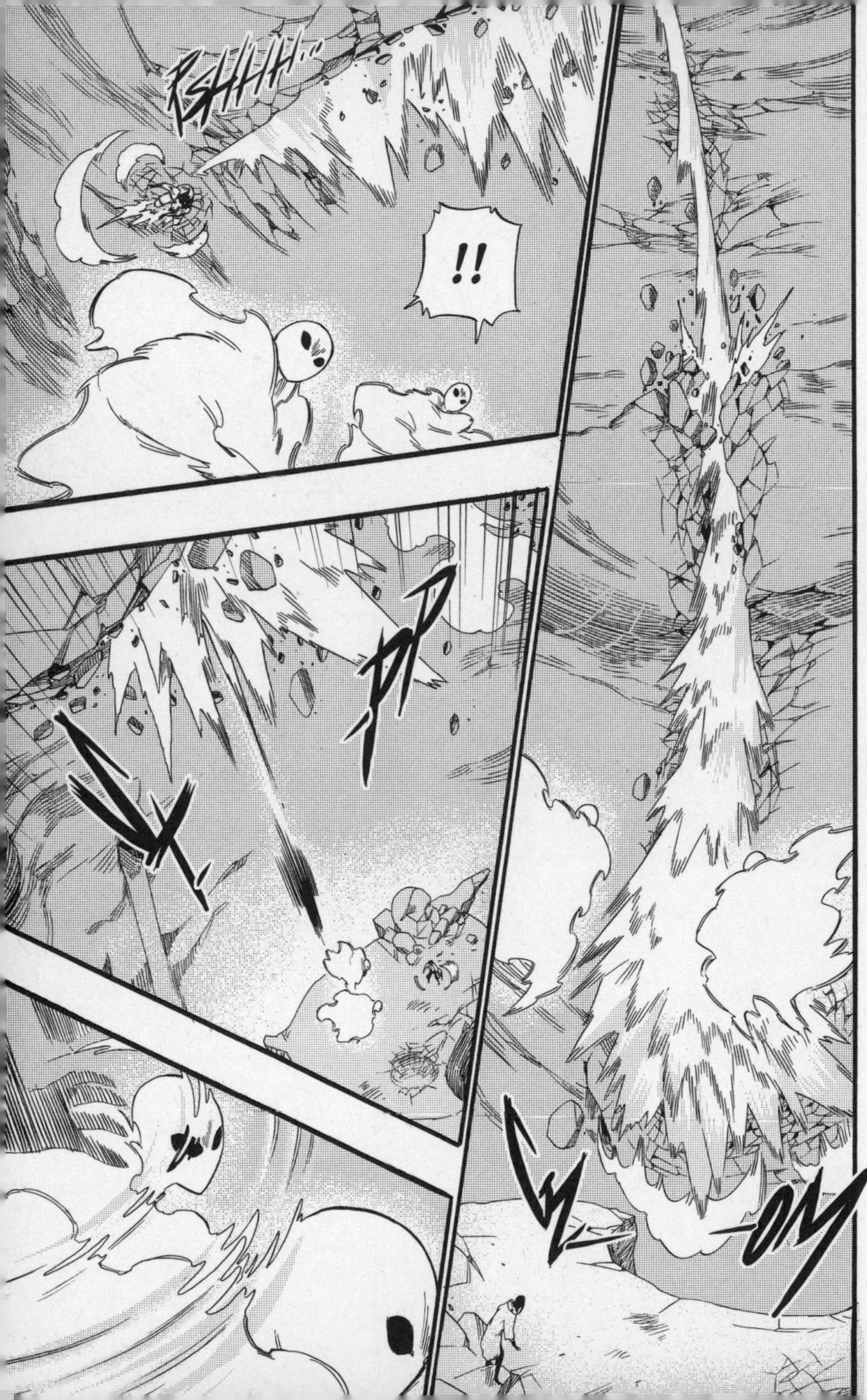

RSHHH...
!!
SK
DP
GA-OOM

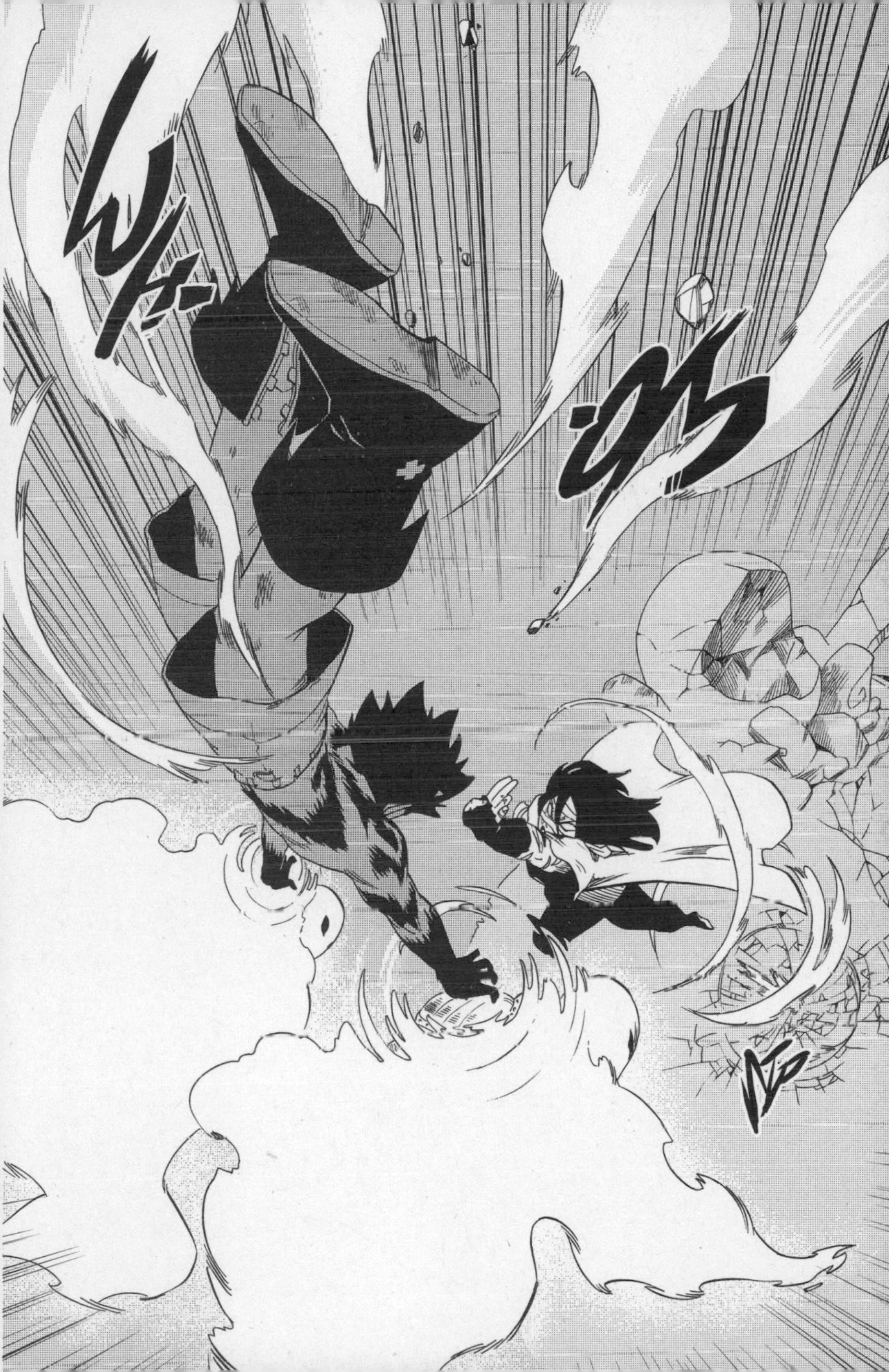

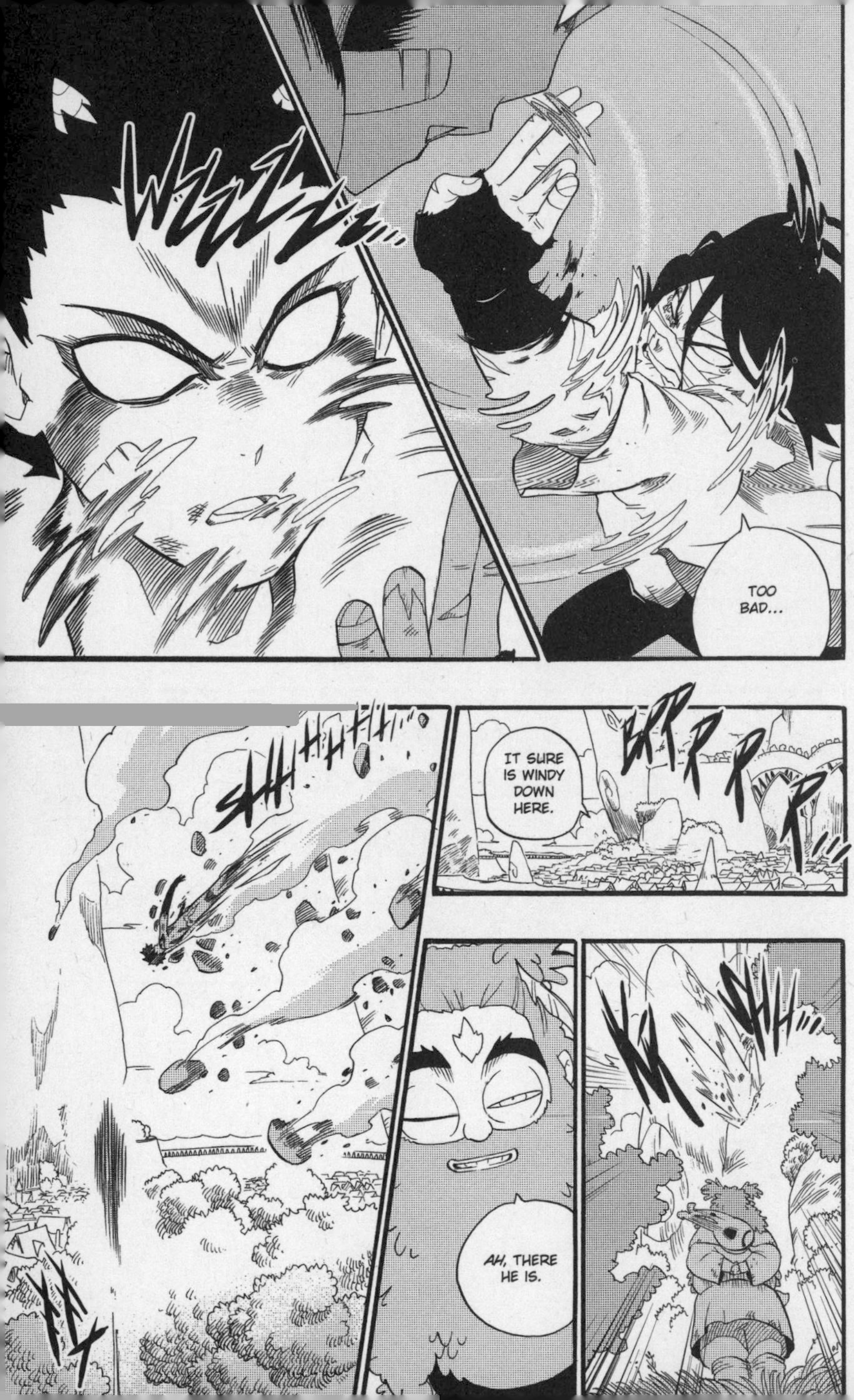
TOO BAD...
IT SURE IS WINDY DOWN HERE.
BRRRRR...
AH, THERE HE IS.
SHHHHHH!!

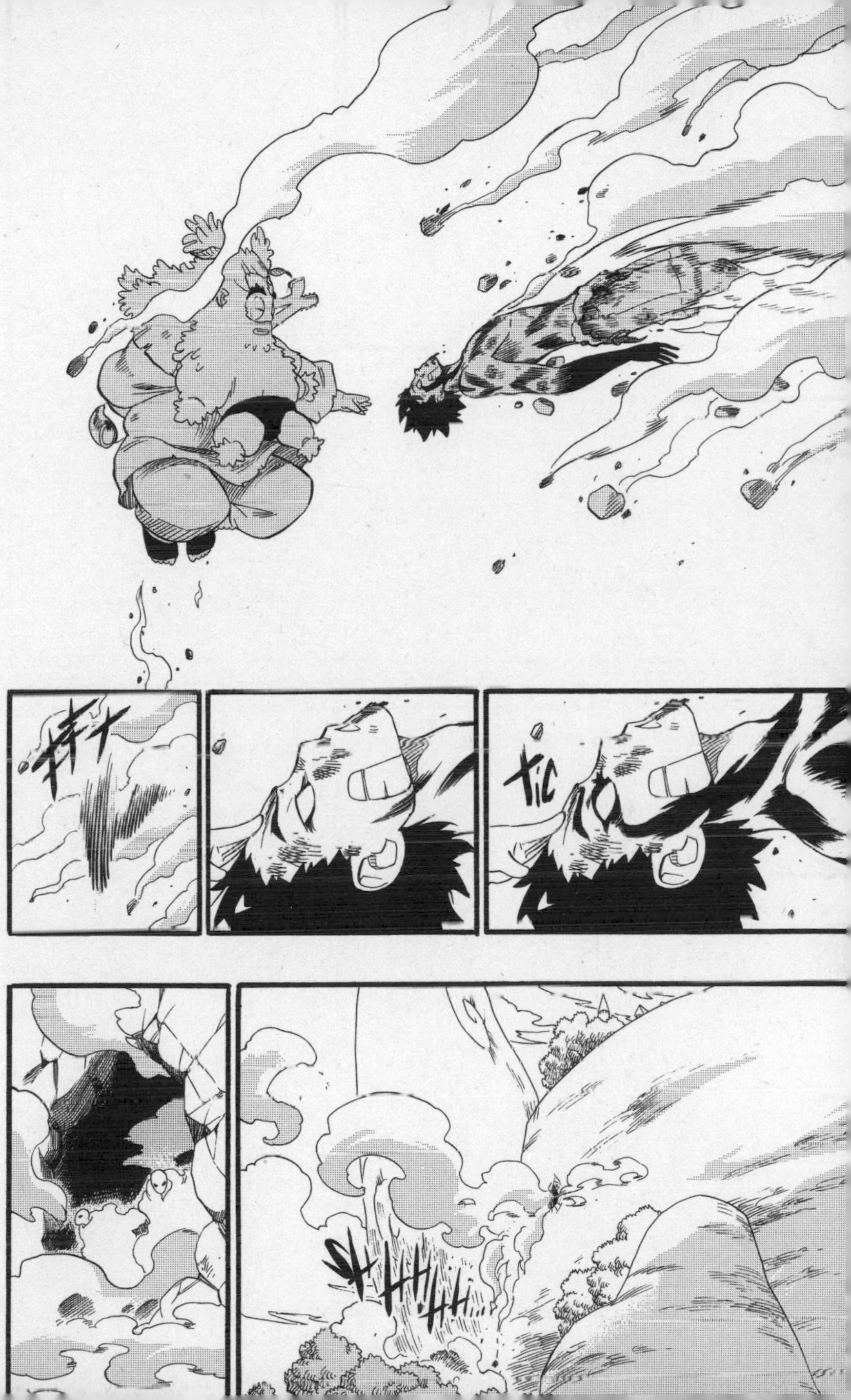
TIC
FFT
SHHHHH...

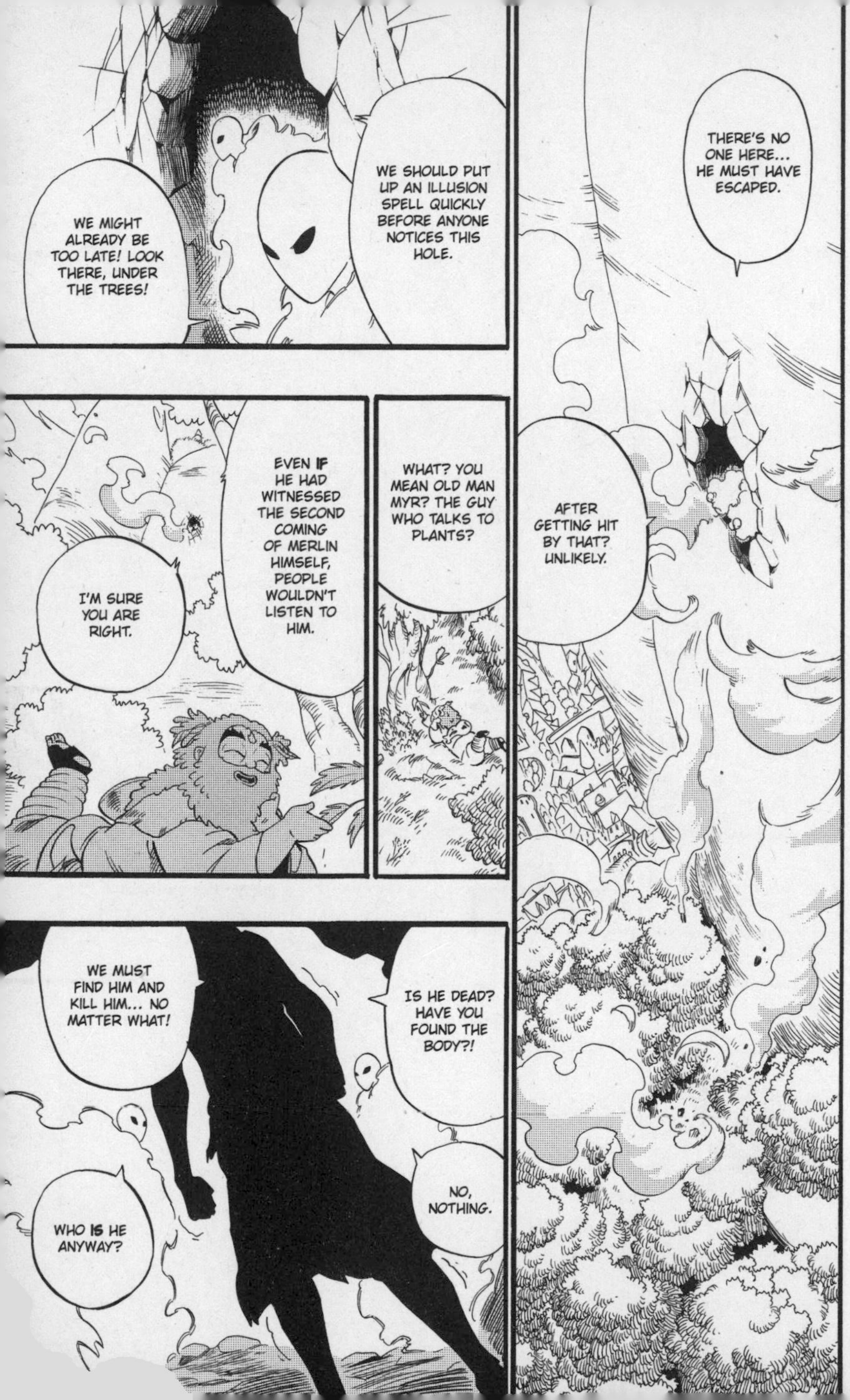
THERE'S NO ONE HERE... HE MUST HAVE ESCAPED.
AFTER GETTING HIT BY THAT? UNLIKELY.
WE SHOULD PUT UP AN ILLUSION SPELL QUICKLY BEFORE ANYONE NOTICES THIS HOLE.
WE MIGHT ALREADY BE TOO LATE! LOOK THERE, UNDER THE TREES!
WHAT? YOU MEAN OLD MAN MYR? THE GUY WHO TALKS TO PLANTS?
EVEN IF HE HAD WITNESSED THE SECOND COMING OF MERLIN HIMSELF, PEOPLE WOULDN'T LISTEN TO HIM.
I'M SURE YOU ARE RIGHT.
IS HE DEAD? HAVE YOU FOUND THE BODY?!
NO, NOTHING.
WE MUST FIND HIM AND KILL HIM... NO MATTER WHAT!
WHO IS HE ANYWAY?

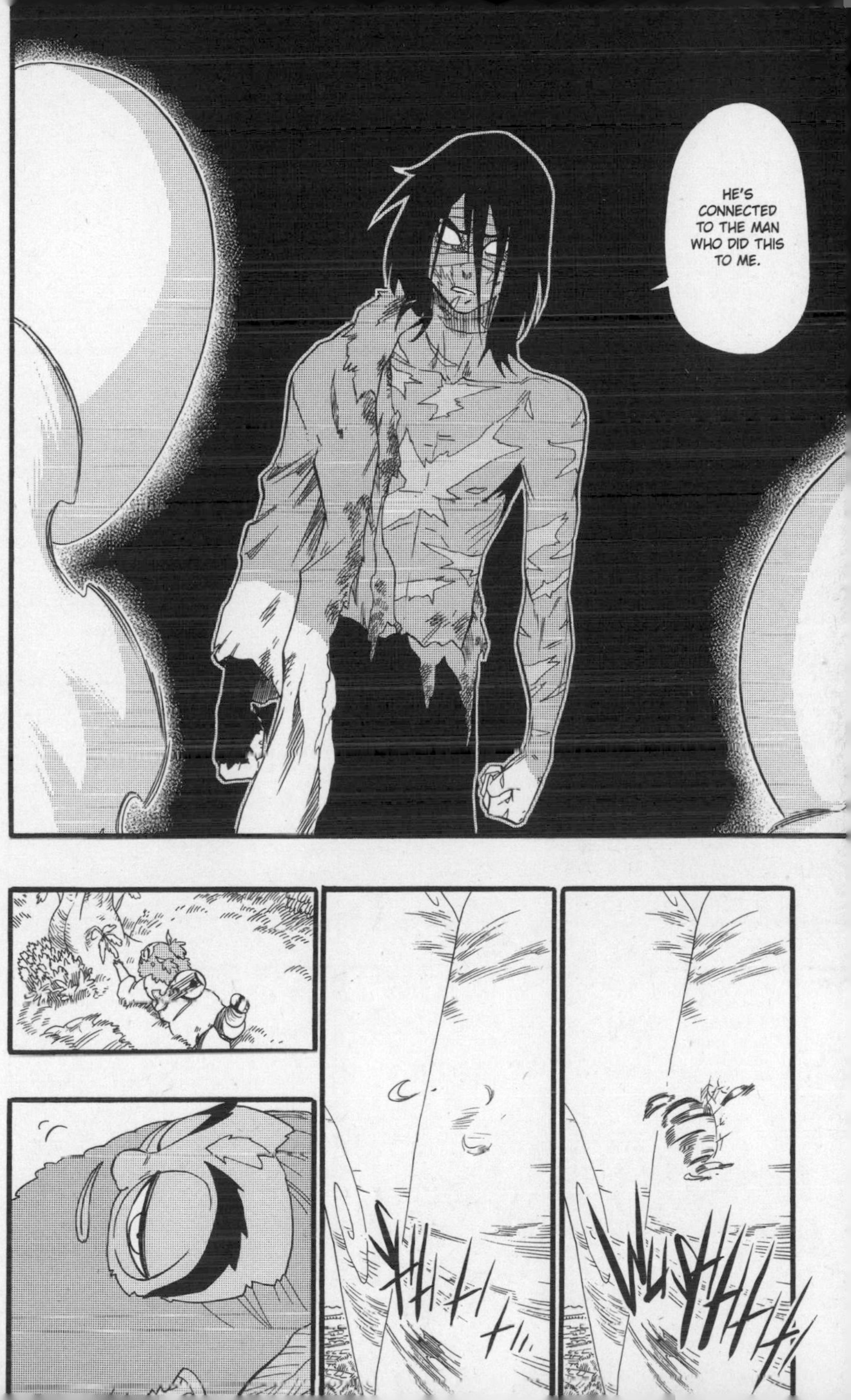
HE'S CONNECTED TO THE MAN WHO DID THIS TO ME.
WHSHHHHH
WHSHHHHH

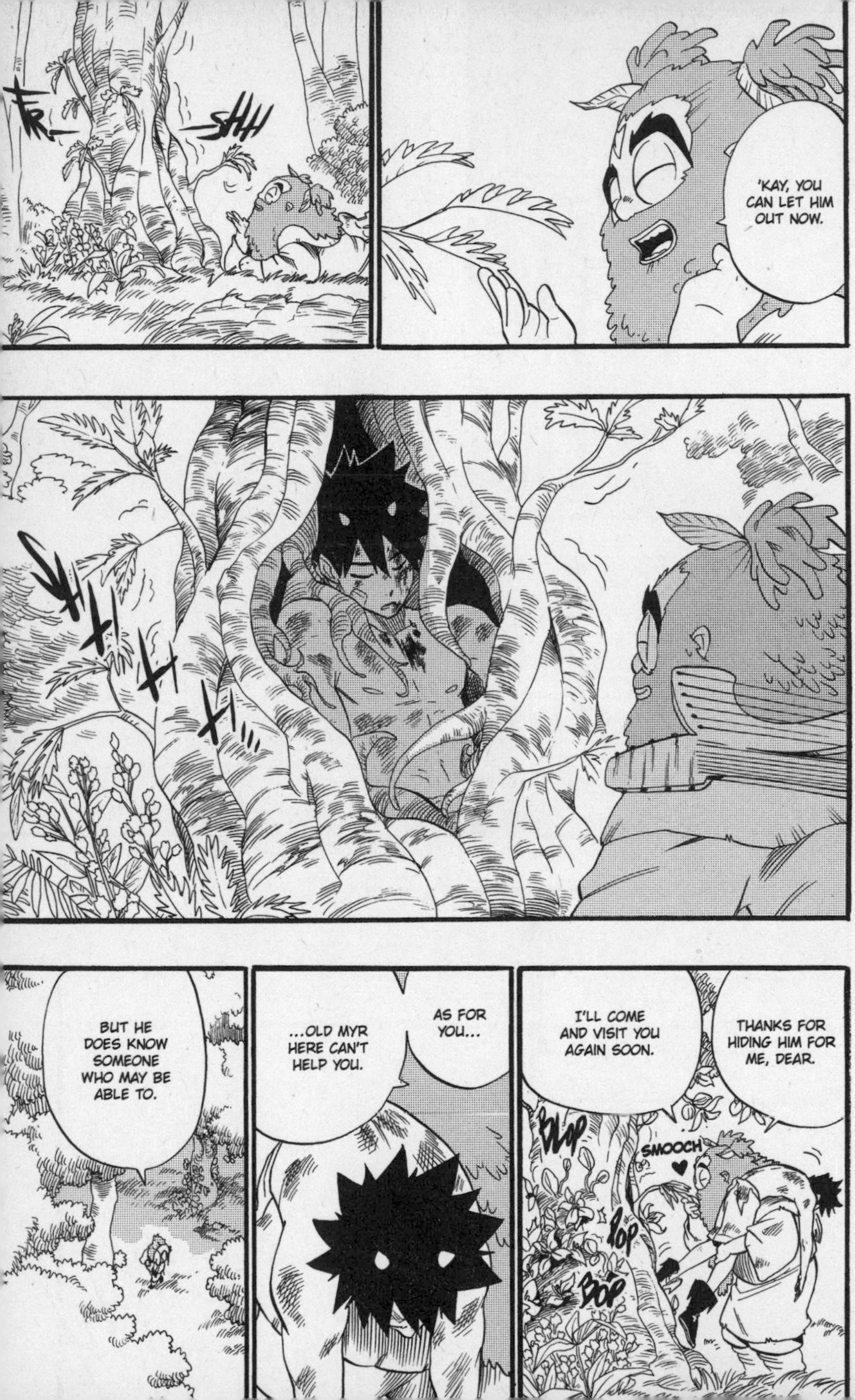
'KAY, YOU CAN LET HIM OUT NOW.
SHH
THANKS FOR HIDING HIM FOR ME, DEAR.
I'LL COME AND VISIT YOU AGAIN SOON.
SMOOCH
BLOP
POP
BOP
AS FOR YOU...
...OLD MYR HERE CAN'T HELP YOU.
BUT HE DOES KNOW SOMEONE WHO MAY BE ABLE TO.

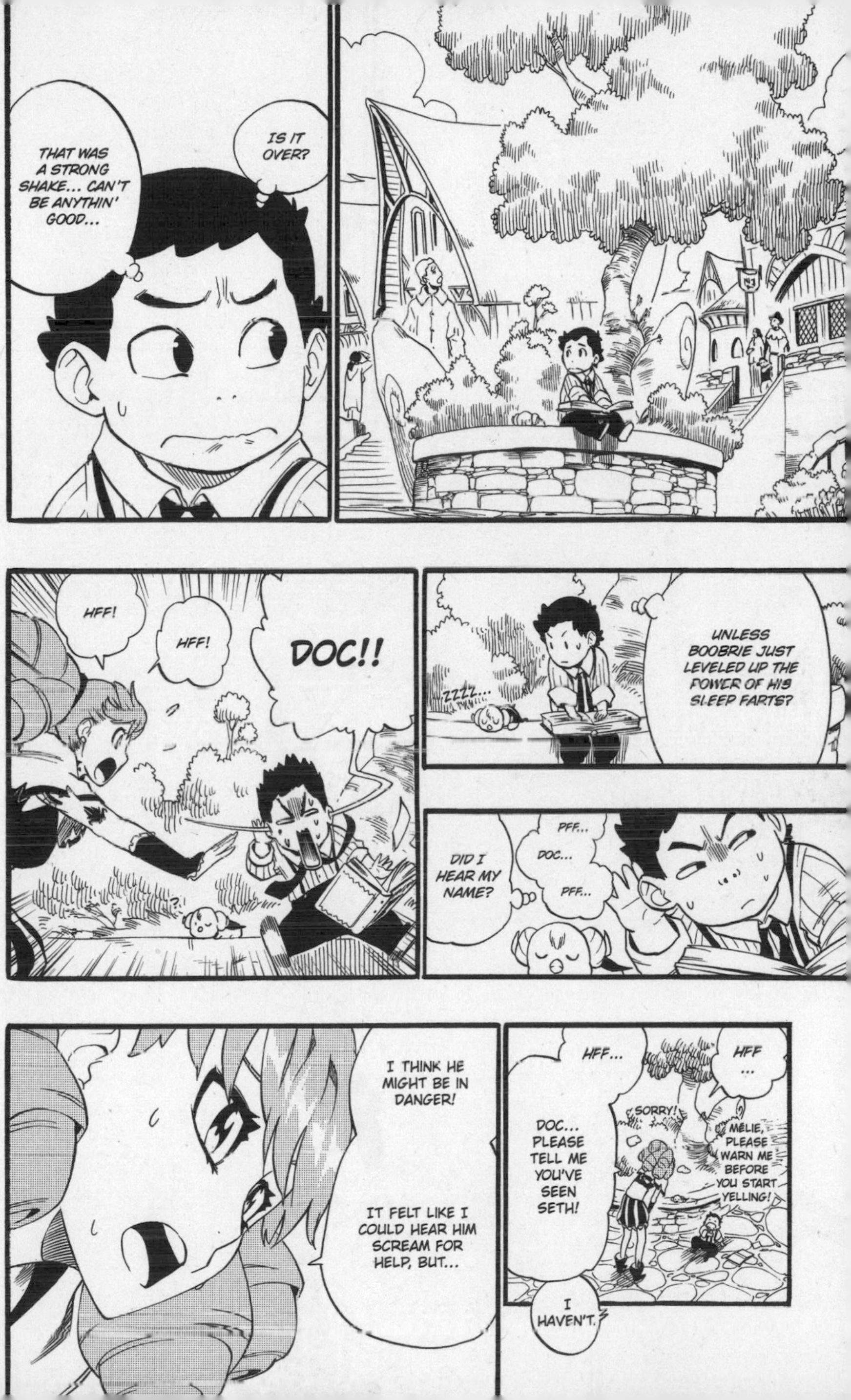
IS IT OVER?
THAT WAS A STRONG SHAKE... CAN'T BE ANYTHIN' GOOD...
UNLESS BOOBRIE JUST LEVELED UP THE POWER OF HIS SLEEP FARTS?
ZZZZ...
PFF...
DOC...
PFF...
DID I HEAR MY NAME?
DOC!!
HFF!
HFF!
HFF ...
HFF...
MÉLIE, PLEASE WARN ME BEFORE YOU START YELLING!
SORRY!
DOC... PLEASE TELL ME YOU'VE SEEN SETH!
I HAVEN'T.
I THINK HE MIGHT BE IN DANGER!
IT FELT LIKE I COULD HEAR HIM SCREAM FOR HELP, BUT...

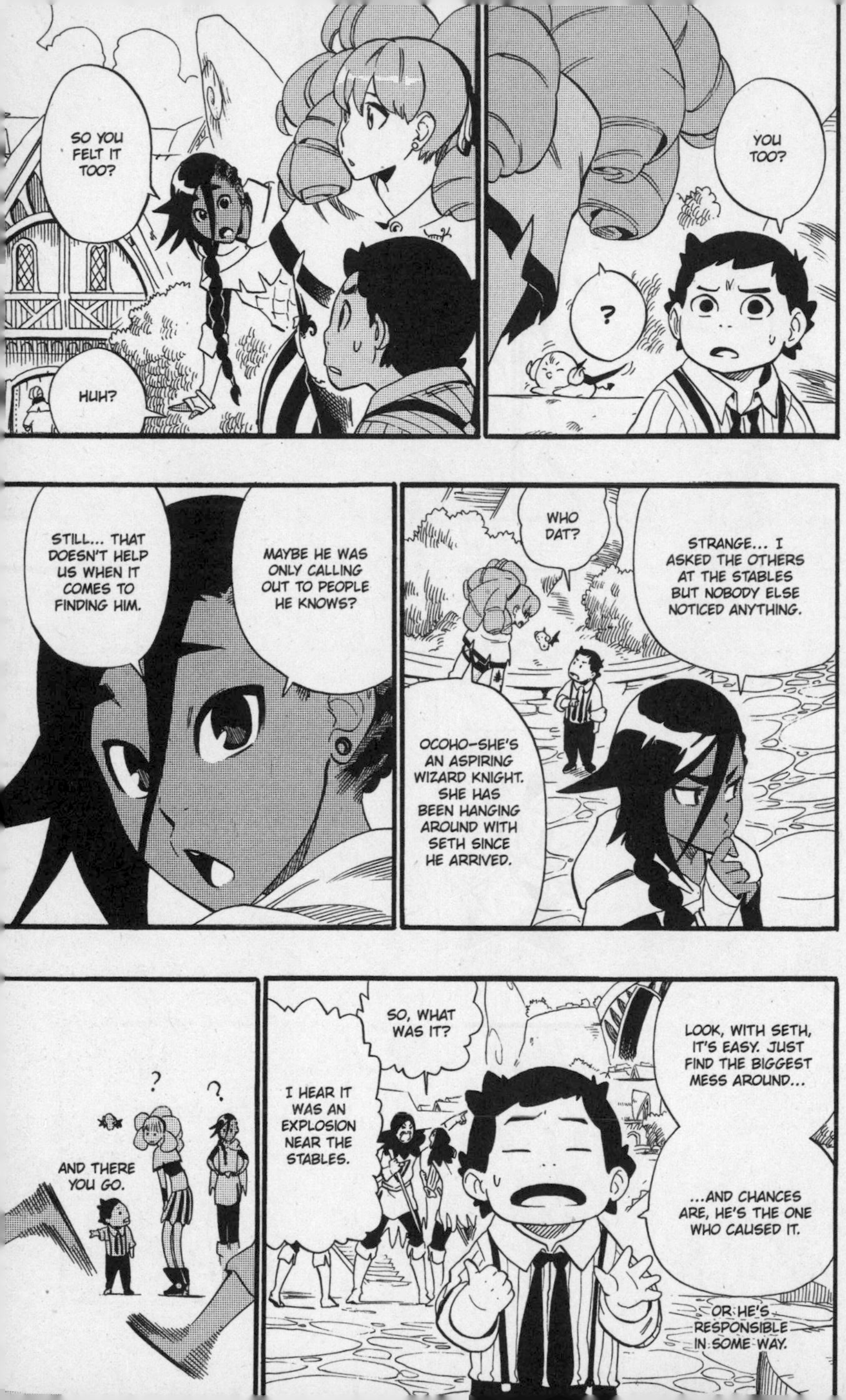
YOU TOO?
?
SO YOU FELT IT TOO?
HUH?
STRANGE... I ASKED THE OTHERS AT THE STABLES BUT NOBODY ELSE NOTICED ANYTHING.
WHO DAT?
OCOHO-SHE'S AN ASPIRING WIZARD KNIGHT. SHE HAS BEEN HANGING AROUND WITH SETH SINCE HE ARRIVED.
MAYBE HE WAS ONLY CALLING OUT TO PEOPLE HE KNOWS?
STILL... THAT DOESN'T HELP US WHEN IT COMES TO FINDING HIM.
LOOK, WITH SETH, IT'S EASY. JUST FIND THE BIGGEST MESS AROUND...
SO, WHAT WAS IT?
I HEAR IT WAS AN EXPLOSION NEAR THE STABLES.
...AND CHANCES ARE, HE'S THE ONE WHO CAUSED IT.
OR HE'S RESPONSIBLE IN SOME WAY.
?
?
AND THERE YOU GO.

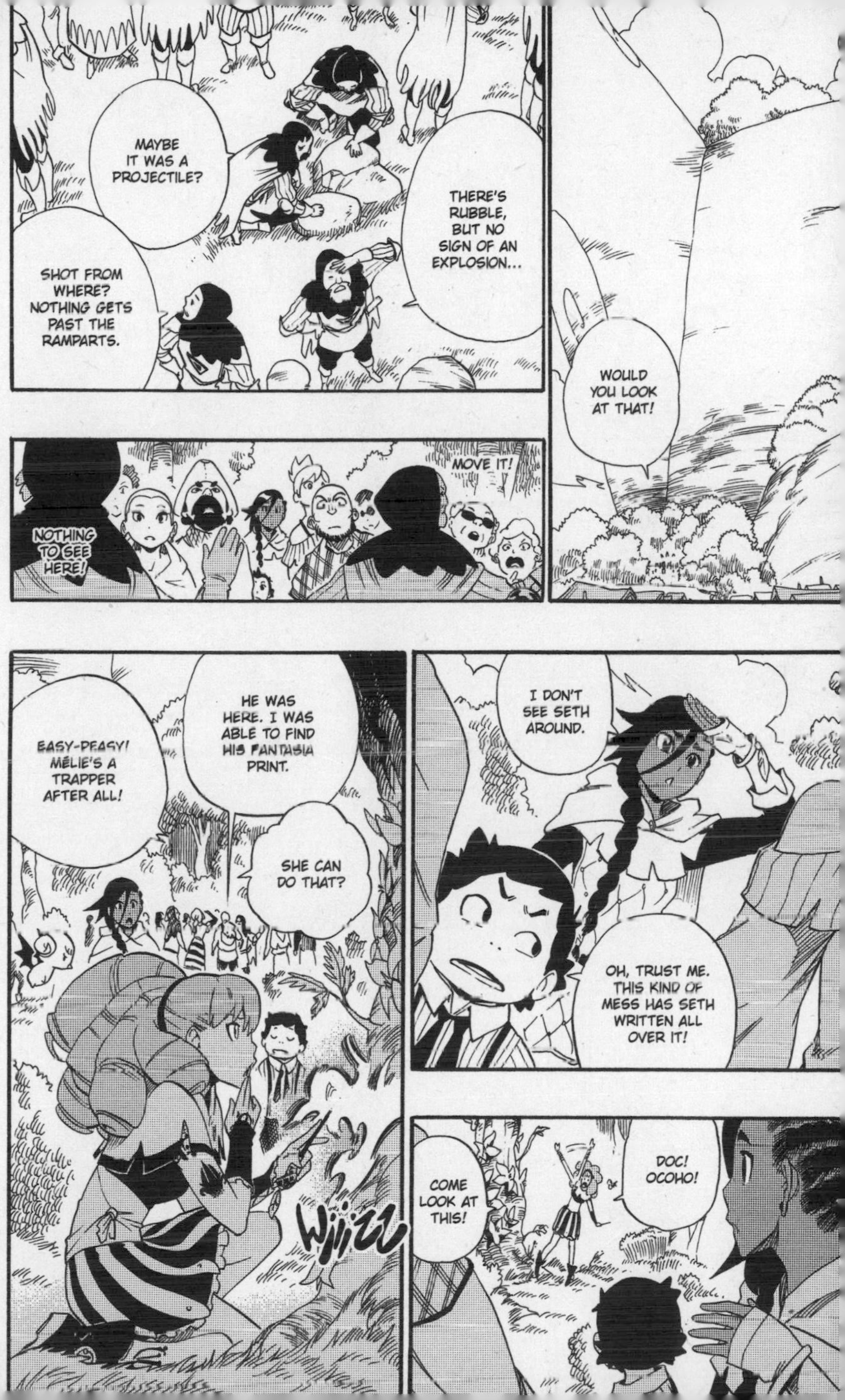
WOULD YOU LOOK AT THAT!
THERE'S RUBBLE, BUT NO SIGN OF AN EXPLOSION...
MAYBE IT WAS A PROJECTILE?
SHOT FROM WHERE? NOTHING GETS PAST THE RAMPARTS.
MOVE IT!
NOTHING TO SEE HERE!
I DON'T SEE SETH AROUND.
OH, TRUST ME. THIS KIND OF MESS HAS SETH WRITTEN ALL OVER IT!
DOC! OCOHO!
COME LOOK AT THIS!
HE WAS HERE. I WAS ABLE TO FIND HIS FANTASIA PRINT.
EASY-PEASY! MÉLIE'S A TRAPPER AFTER ALL!
SHE CAN DO THAT?
WJIIZZ

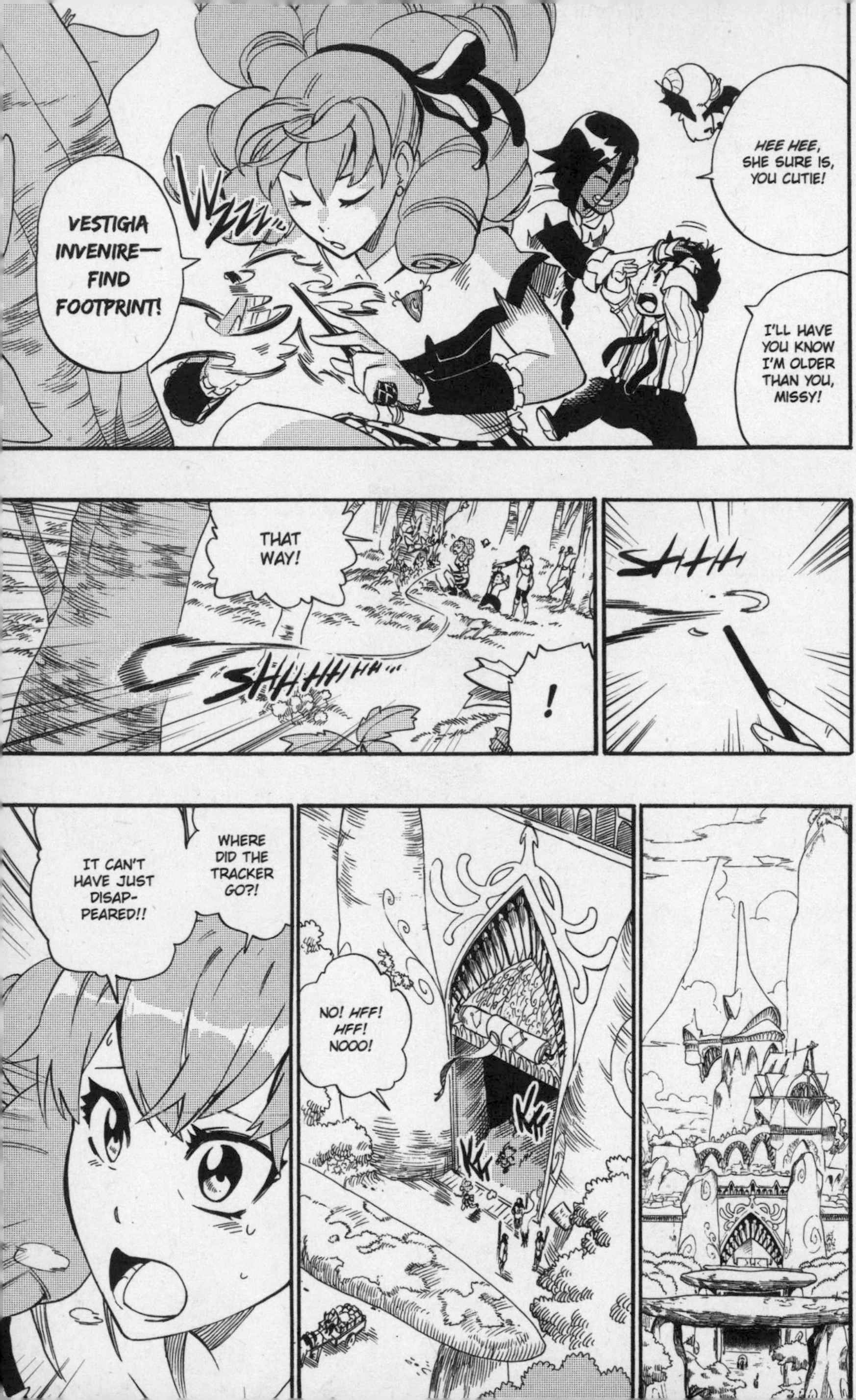
HEE HEE, SHE SURE IS, YOU CUTIE!
I'LL HAVE YOU KNOW I'M OLDER THAN YOU, MISSY!
VESTIGIA INVENIRE— FIND FOOTPRINT!
WZZZZ
SHHHH
THAT WAY!
SHHHHHHH...
!
NO! HFF! HFF! NOOO!
KH
KH
WHERE DID THE TRACKER GO?!
IT CAN'T HAVE JUST DISAP-PEARED!!

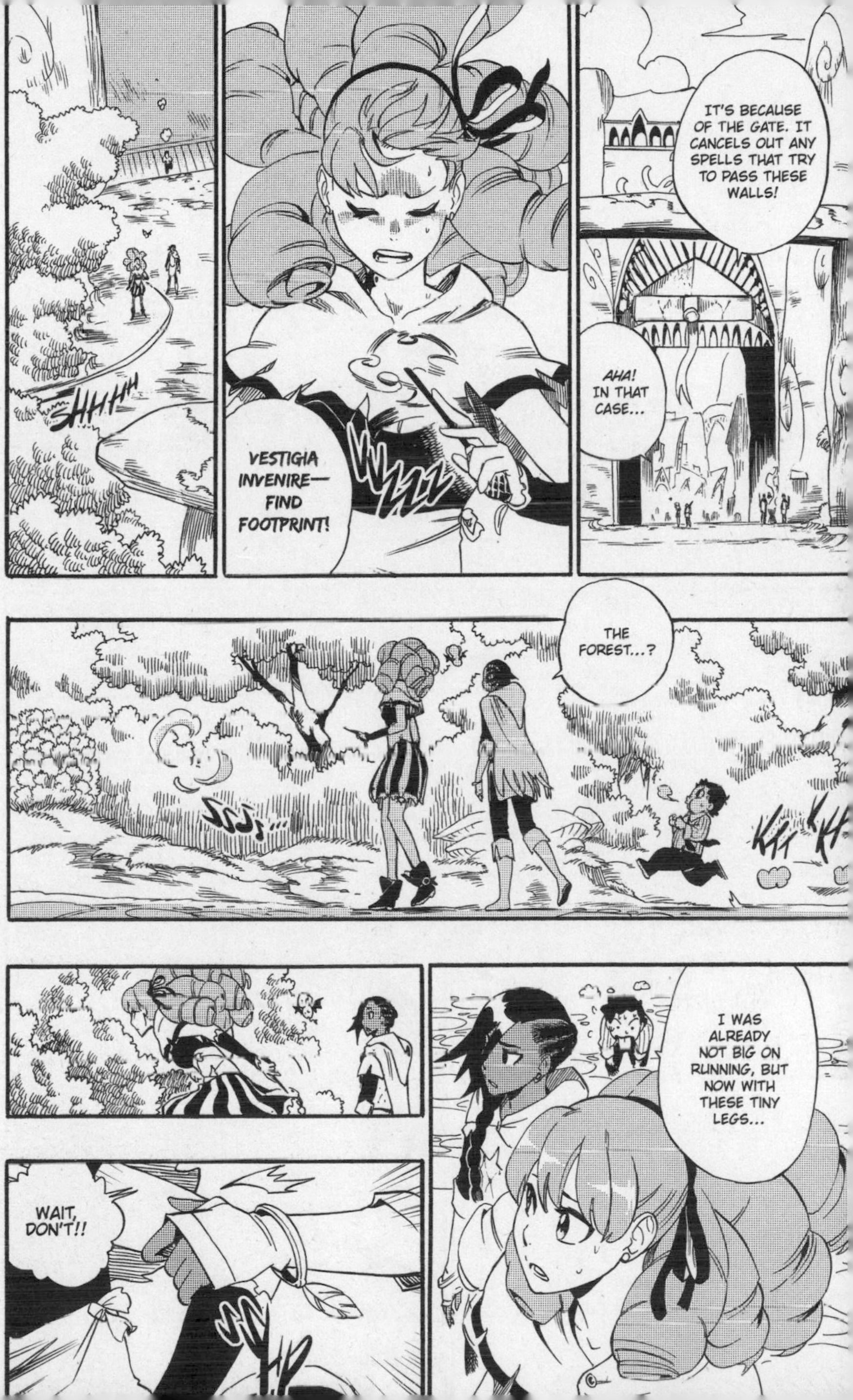
IT'S BECAUSE OF THE GATE. IT CANCELS OUT ANY SPELLS THAT TRY TO PASS THESE WALLS!
AHA! IN THAT CASE...
VESTIGIA INVENIRE—FIND FOOTPRINT!
THE FOREST...?
I WAS ALREADY NOT BIG ON RUNNING, BUT NOW WITH THESE TINY LEGS...
WAIT, DON'T!!

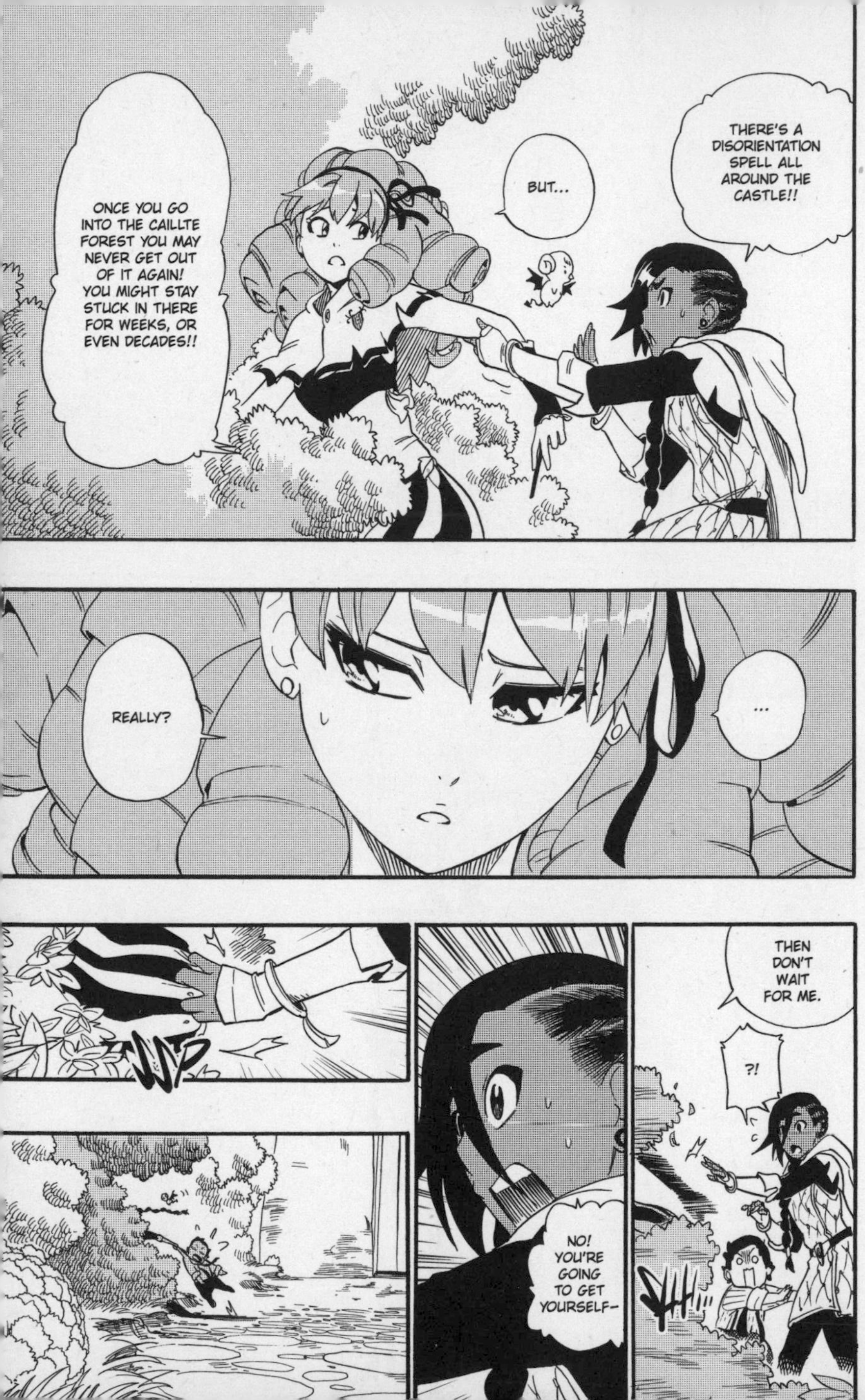
THERE'S A DISORIENTATION SPELL ALL AROUND THE CASTLE!!
BUT...
ONCE YOU GO INTO THE CAILLTE FOREST YOU MAY NEVER GET OUT OF IT AGAIN! YOU MIGHT STAY STUCK IN THERE FOR WEEKS, OR EVEN DECADES!!
...
REALLY?
THEN DON'T WAIT FOR ME.
?!
NO! YOU'RE GOING TO GET YOURSELF–

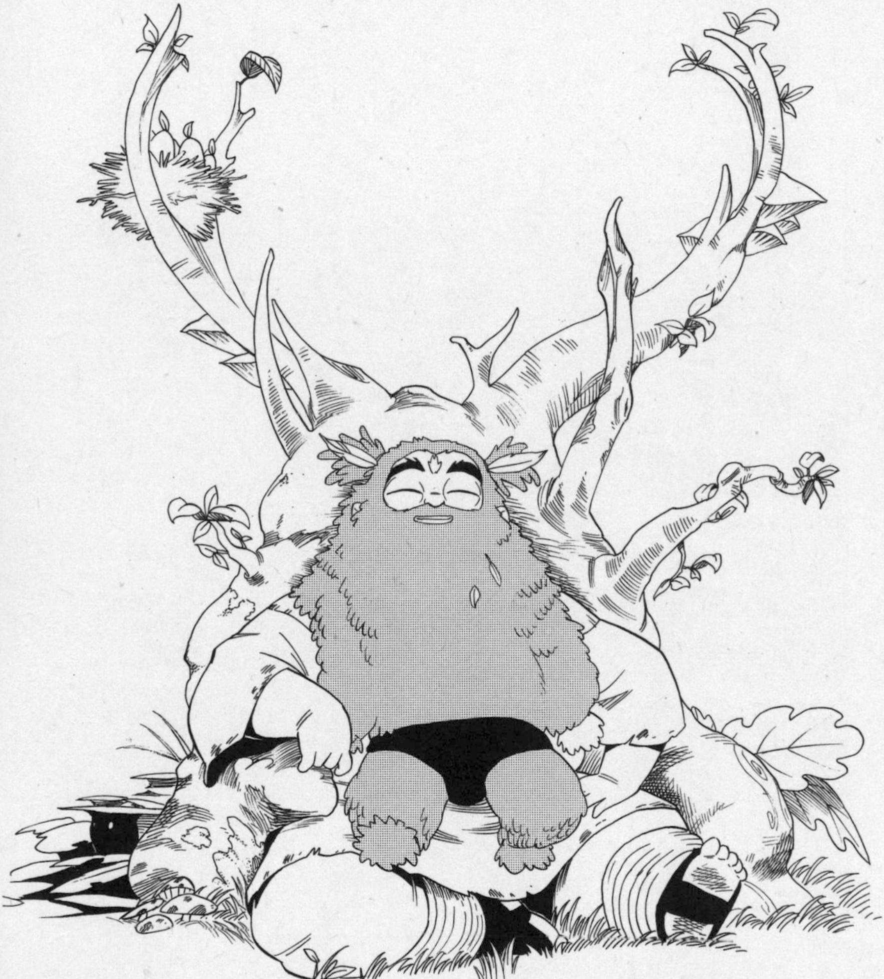

Chapter 41

The Imp of the Forest

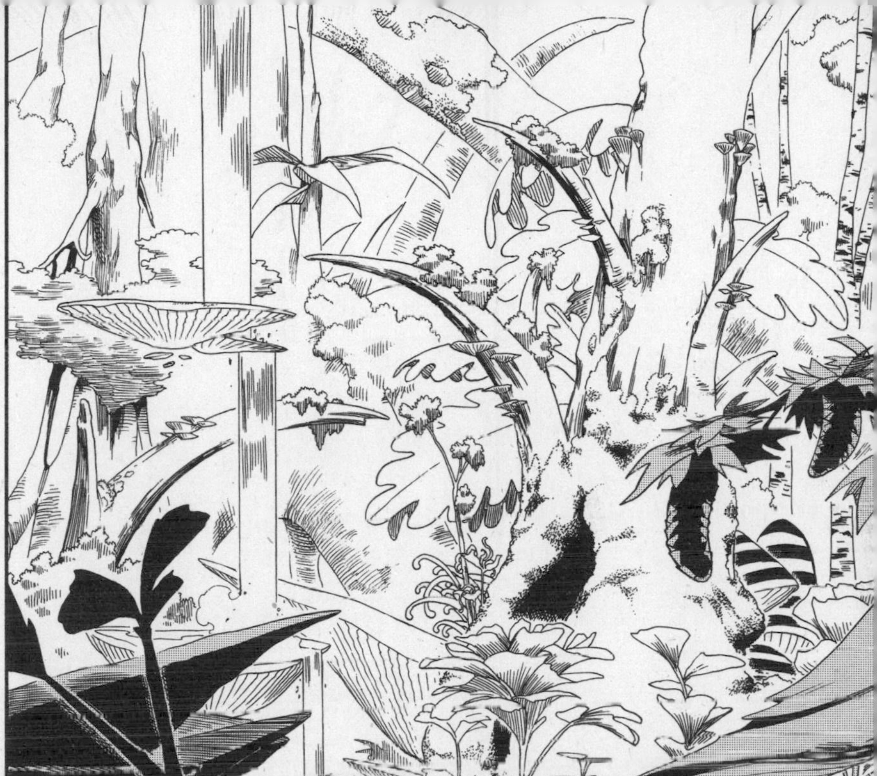

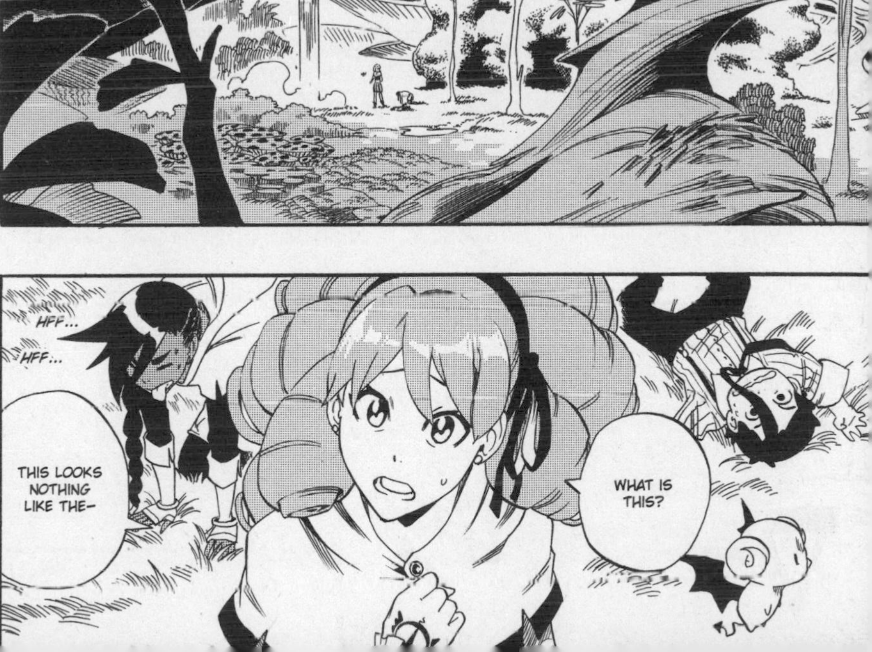
WHAT IS THIS?
HFF...
HFF...
THIS LOOKS NOTHING LIKE THE-

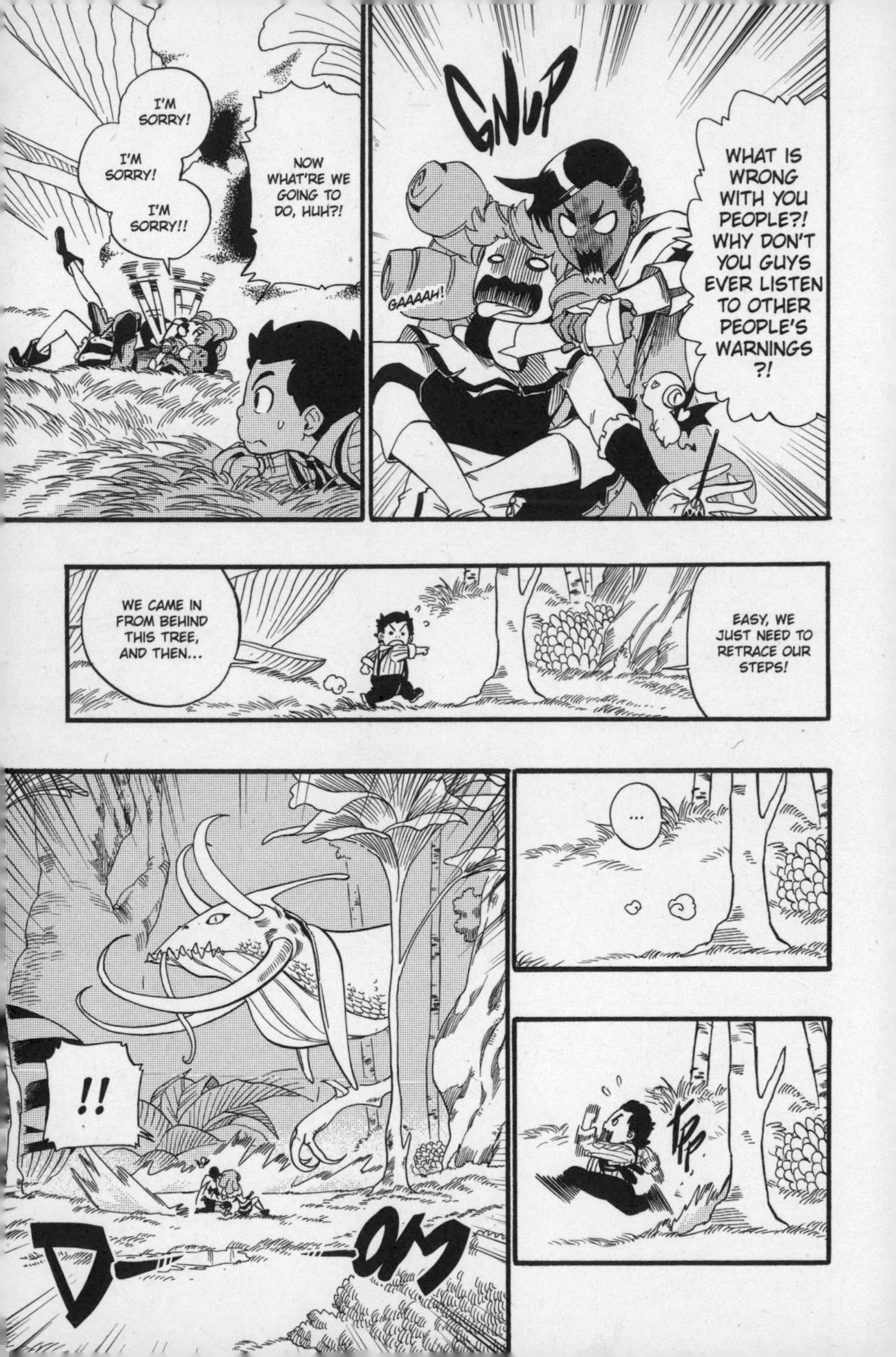
GNUP
WHAT IS WRONG WITH YOU PEOPLE?! WHY DON'T YOU GUYS EVER LISTEN TO OTHER PEOPLE'S WARNINGS?!
GAAAAH!
NOW WHAT'RE WE GOING TO DO, HUH?!
I'M SORRY! I'M SORRY! I'M SORRY!!
EASY, WE JUST NEED TO RETRACE OUR STEPS!
WE CAME IN FROM BEHIND THIS TREE, AND THEN...
...
TPP
!!
D—OM

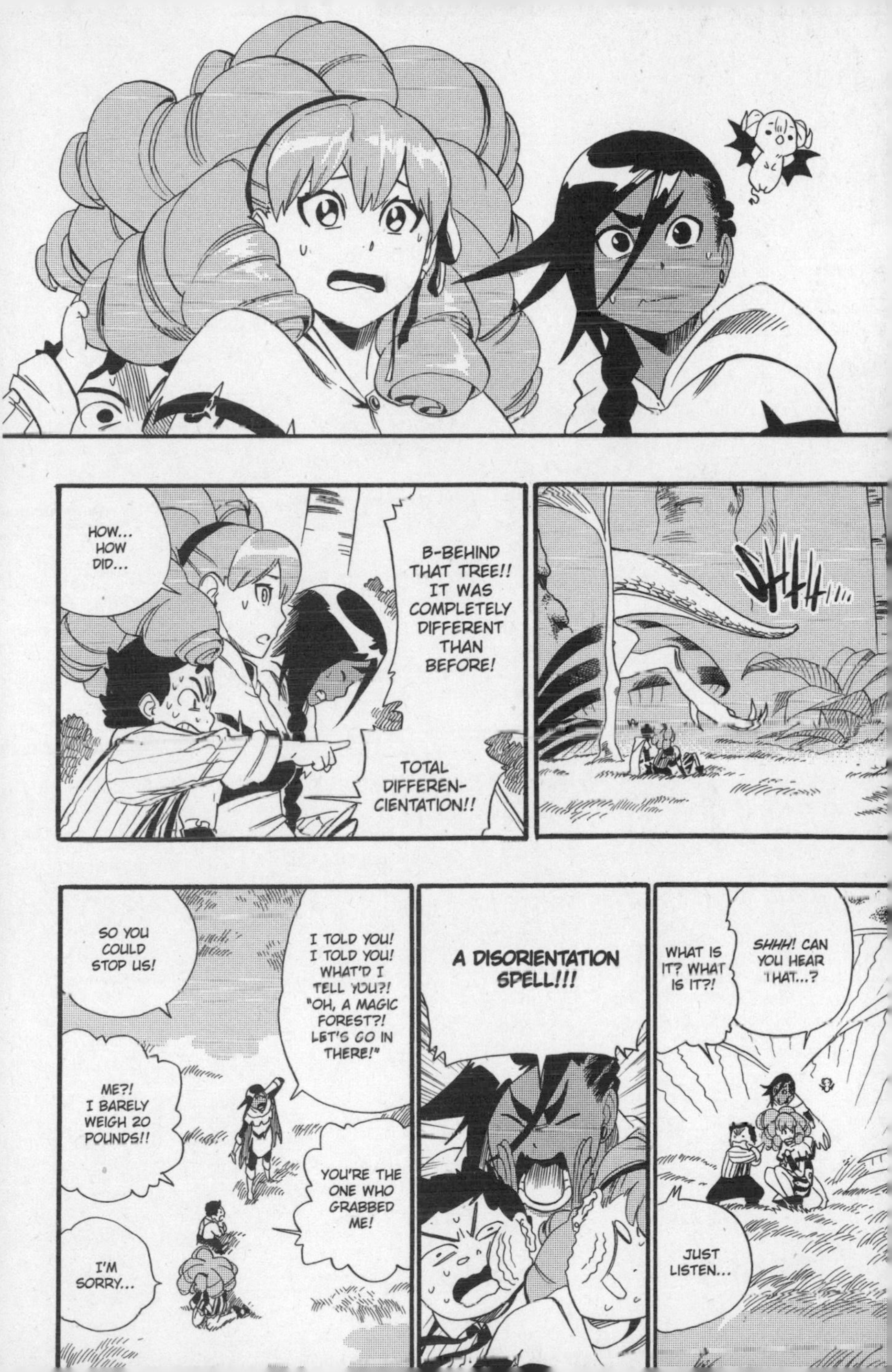
HOW... HOW DID...
B-BEHIND THAT TREE!! IT WAS COMPLETELY DIFFERENT THAN BEFORE!
TOTAL DIFFEREN-CIENTATION!!
SHHH
I TOLD YOU! I TOLD YOU! WHAT'D I TELL YOU?! "OH, A MAGIC FOREST?! LET'S GO IN THERE!"
SO YOU COULD STOP US!
ME?! I BARELY WEIGH 20 POUNDS!!
YOU'RE THE ONE WHO GRABBED ME!
I'M SORRY...
A DISORIENTATION SPELL!!!
WHAT IS IT? WHAT IS IT?!
SHHH! CAN YOU HEAR THAT...?
JUST LISTEN...

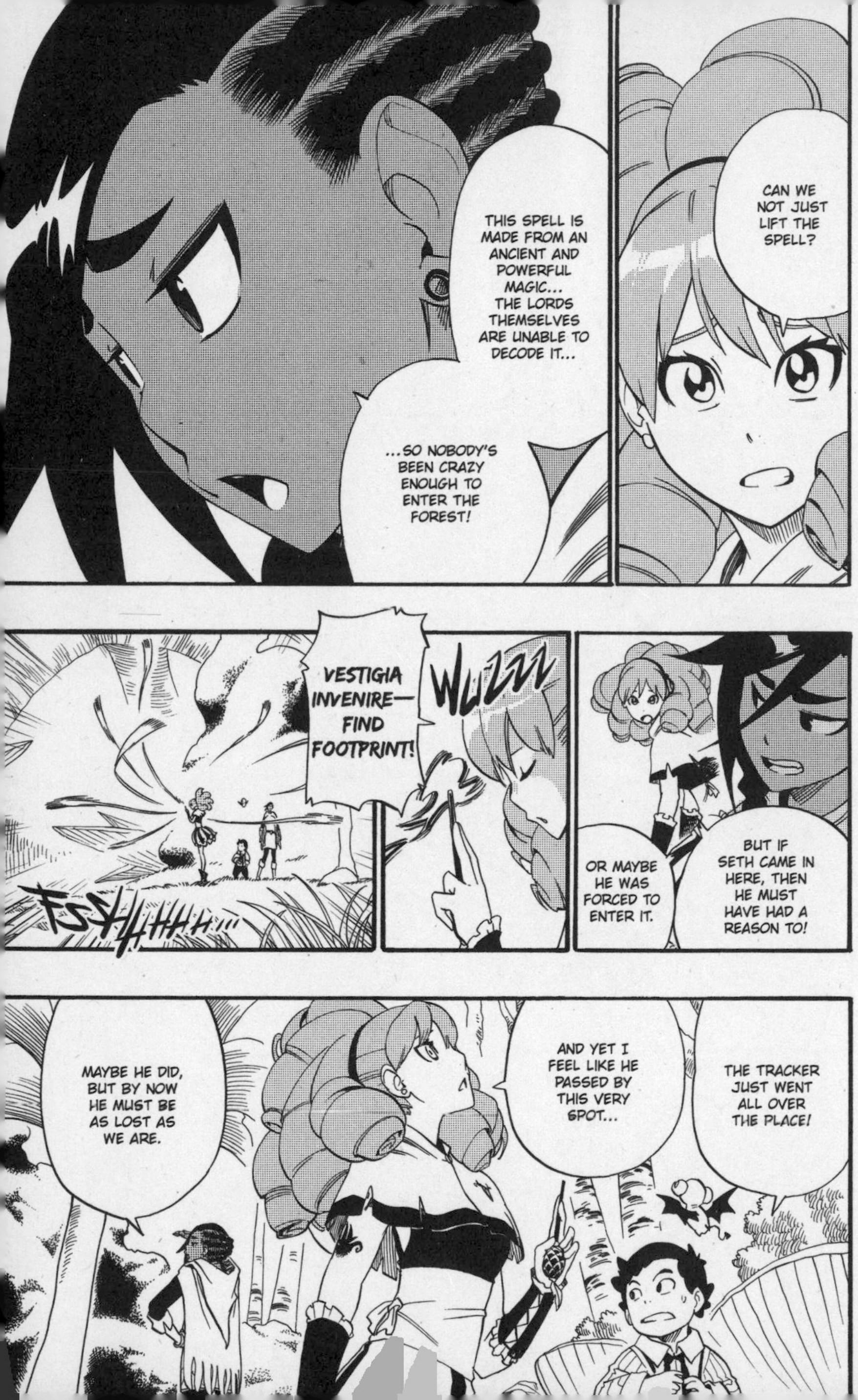
CAN WE NOT JUST LIFT THE SPELL?
THIS SPELL IS MADE FROM AN ANCIENT AND POWERFUL MAGIC... THE LORDS THEMSELVES ARE UNABLE TO DECODE IT...
...SO NOBODY'S BEEN CRAZY ENOUGH TO ENTER THE FOREST!
BUT IF SETH CAME IN HERE, THEN HE MUST HAVE HAD A REASON TO!
OR MAYBE HE WAS FORCED TO ENTER IT.
VESTIGIA INVENIRE— FIND FOOTPRINT!
WUZZZ
FSSHHHH...
THE TRACKER JUST WENT ALL OVER THE PLACE!
AND YET I FEEL LIKE HE PASSED BY THIS VERY SPOT...
MAYBE HE DID, BUT BY NOW HE MUST BE AS LOST AS WE ARE.

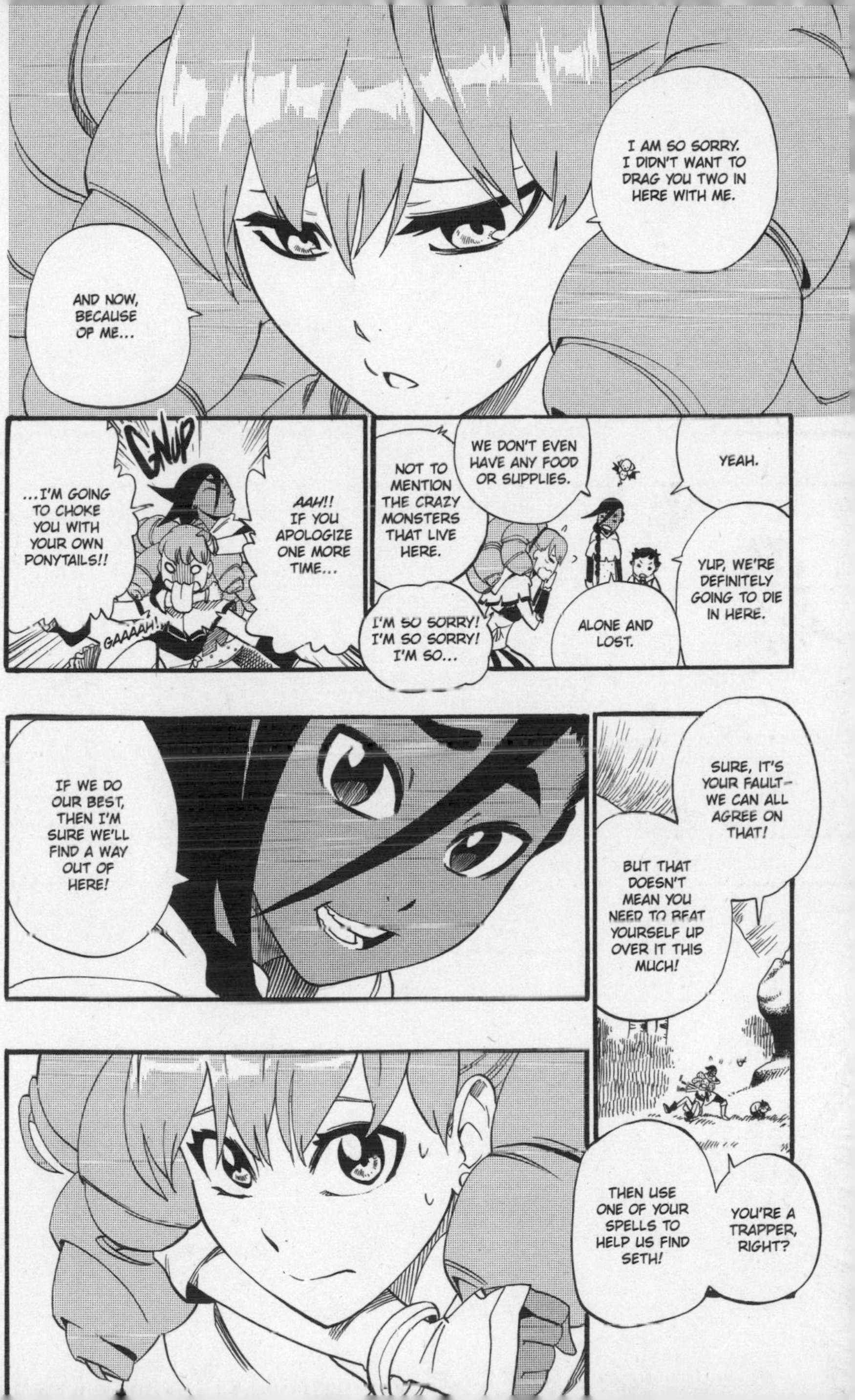
I AM SO SORRY. I DIDN'T WANT TO DRAG YOU TWO IN HERE WITH ME.
AND NOW, BECAUSE OF ME...
YEAH.
YUP, WE'RE DEFINITELY GOING TO DIE IN HERE.
ALONE AND LOST.
WE DON'T EVEN HAVE ANY FOOD OR SUPPLIES.
NOT TO MENTION THE CRAZY MONSTERS THAT LIVE HERE.
I'M SO SORRY! I'M SO SORRY! I'M SO...
GNUP
AAH!! IF YOU APOLOGIZE ONE MORE TIME...
...I'M GOING TO CHOKE YOU WITH YOUR OWN PONYTAILS!!
GAAAAH!
SURE, IT'S YOUR FAULT— WE CAN ALL AGREE ON THAT!
BUT THAT DOESN'T MEAN YOU NEED TO BEAT YOURSELF UP OVER IT THIS MUCH!
IF WE DO OUR BEST, THEN I'M SURE WE'LL FIND A WAY OUT OF HERE!
YOU'RE A TRAPPER, RIGHT?
THEN USE ONE OF YOUR SPELLS TO HELP US FIND SETH!

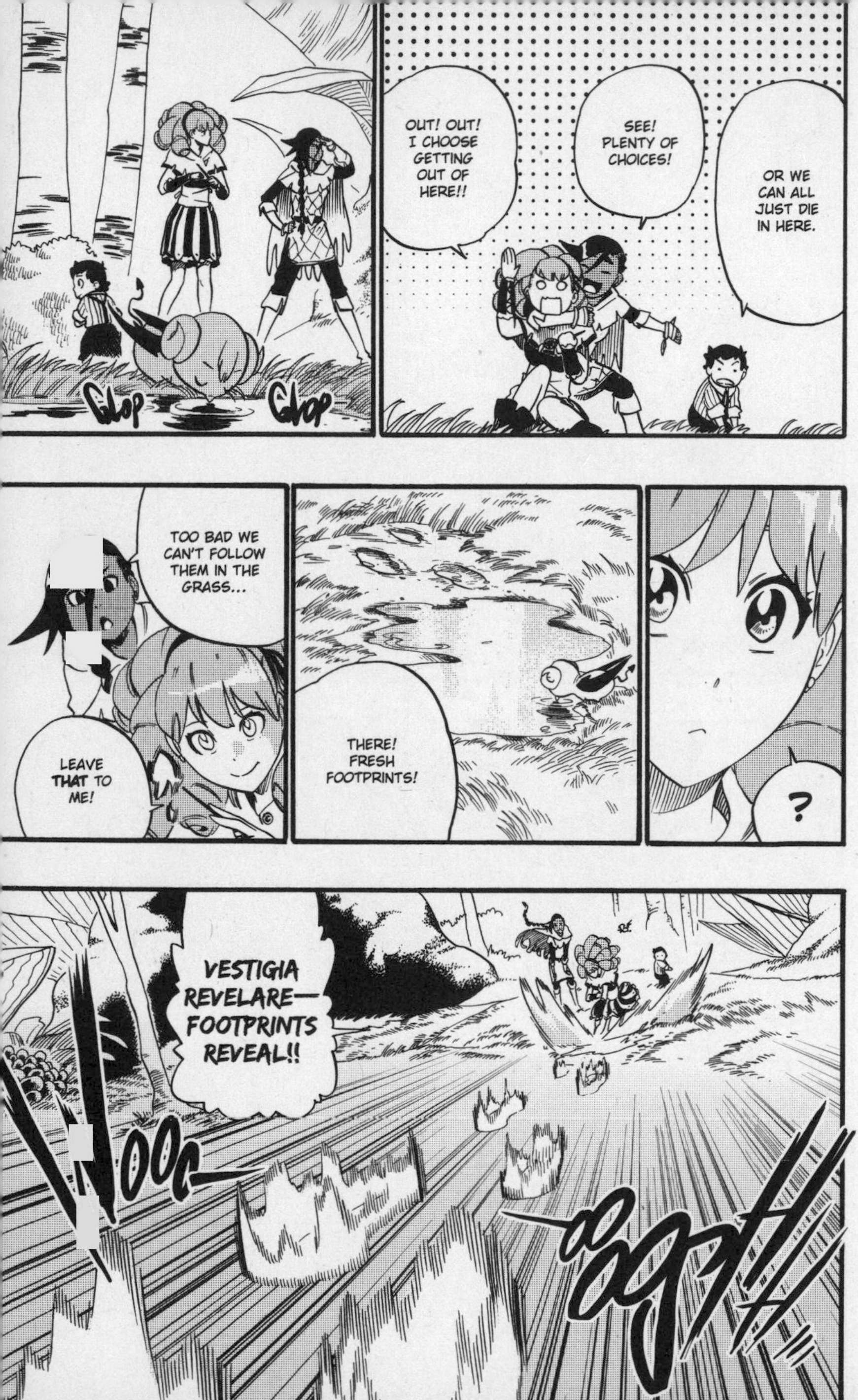
GLOP
GLOP
OUT! OUT! I CHOOSE GETTING OUT OF HERE!!
SEE! PLENTY OF CHOICES!
OR WE CAN ALL JUST DIE IN HERE.
TOO BAD WE CAN'T FOLLOW THEM IN THE GRASS...
LEAVE THAT TO ME!
THERE! FRESH FOOTPRINTS!
?
VESTIGIA REVELARE— FOOTPRINTS REVEAL!!

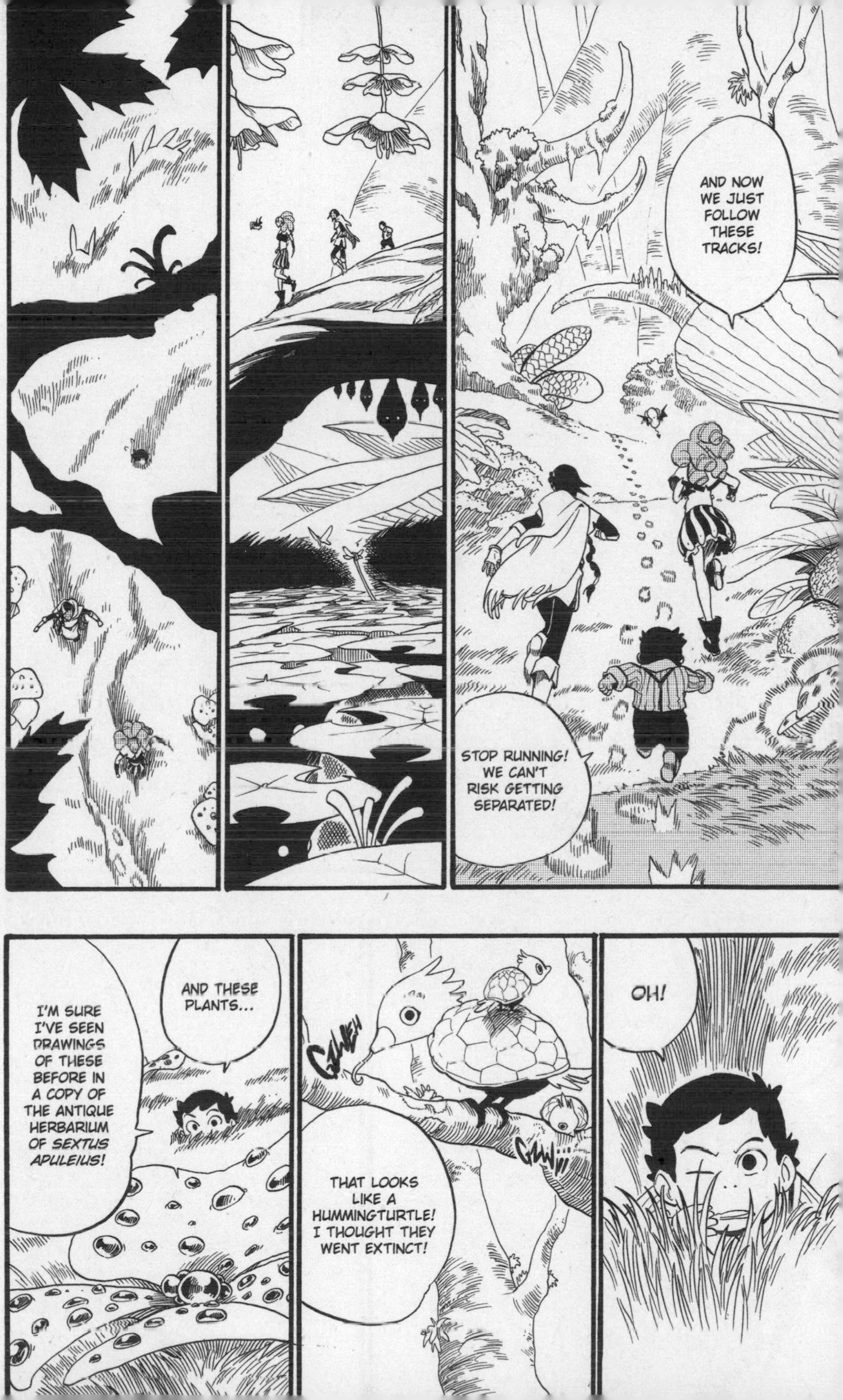
AND NOW WE JUST FOLLOW THESE TRACKS!
STOP RUNNING! WE CAN'T RISK GETTING SEPARATED!
OH!
THAT LOOKS LIKE A HUMMINGTURTLE! I THOUGHT THEY WENT EXTINCT!
AND THESE PLANTS...
I'M SURE I'VE SEEN DRAWINGS OF THESE BEFORE IN A COPY OF THE ANTIQUE HERBARIUM OF *SEXTUS APULEIUS*!

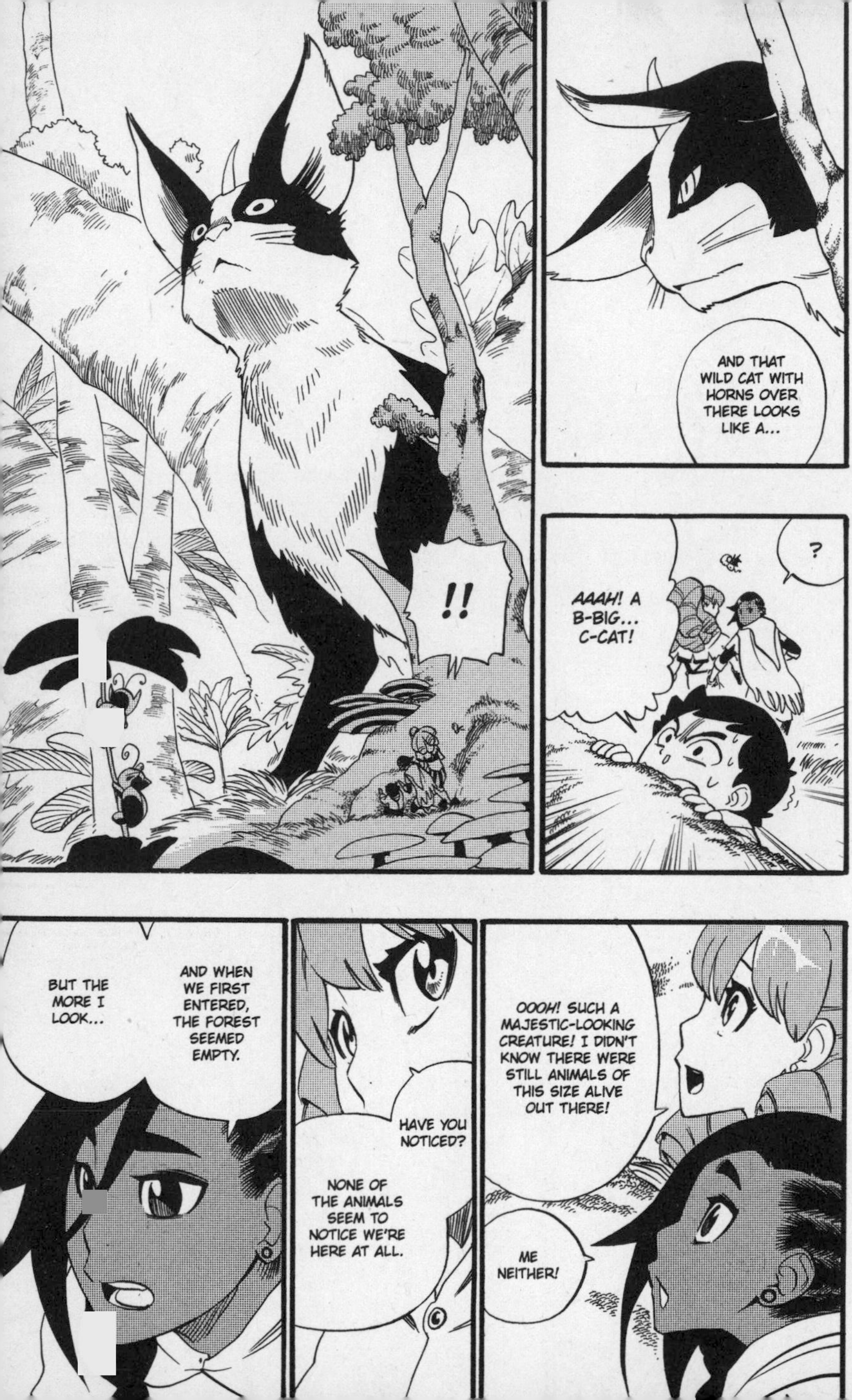
AND THAT WILD CAT WITH HORNS OVER THERE LOOKS LIKE A...
?
AAAH! A B-BIG... C-CAT!
!!
OOOH! SUCH A MAJESTIC-LOOKING CREATURE! I DIDN'T KNOW THERE WERE STILL ANIMALS OF THIS SIZE ALIVE OUT THERE!
ME NEITHER!
HAVE YOU NOTICED?
NONE OF THE ANIMALS SEEM TO NOTICE WE'RE HERE AT ALL.
AND WHEN WE FIRST ENTERED, THE FOREST SEEMED EMPTY.
BUT THE MORE I LOOK...

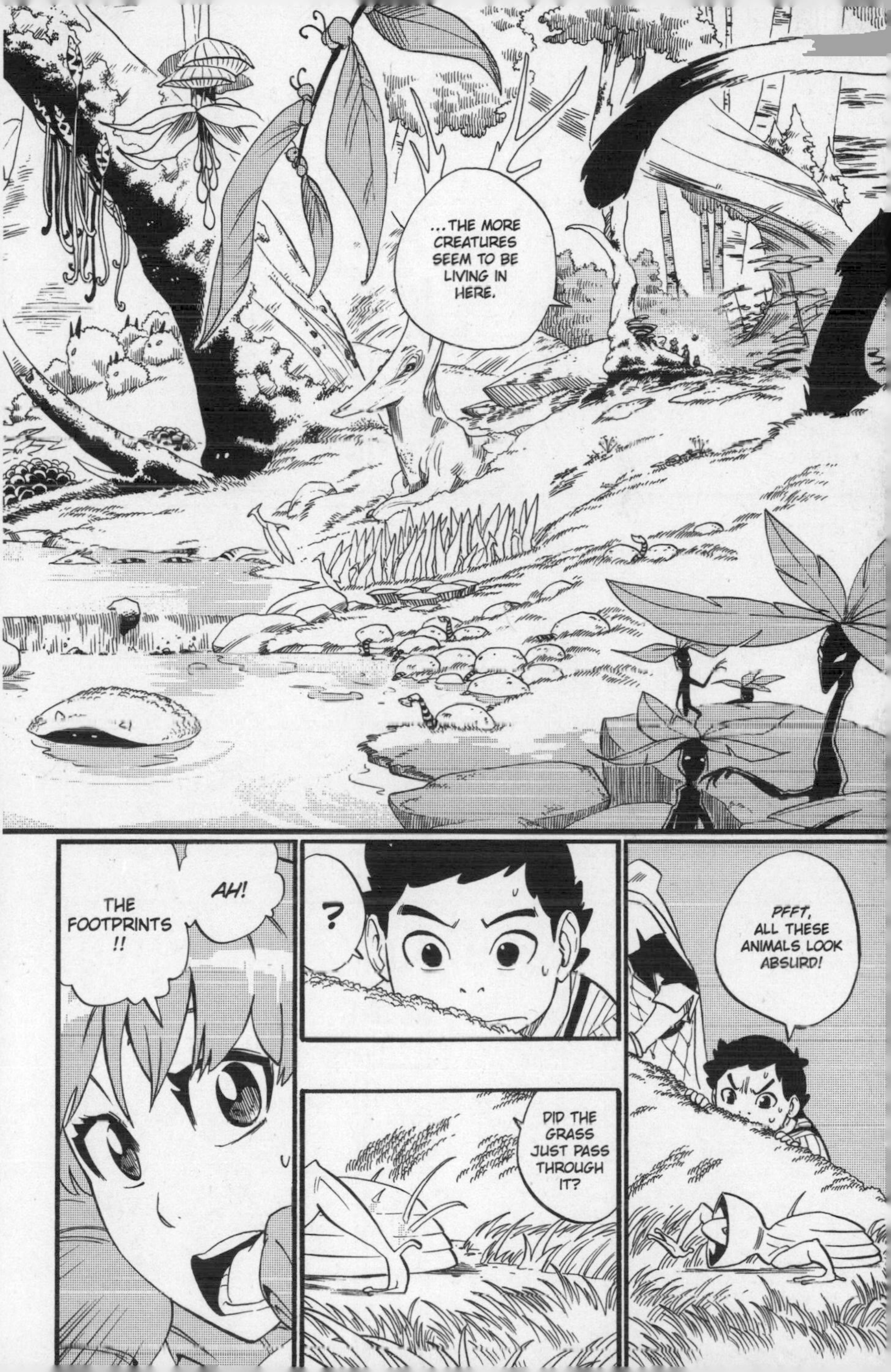
...THE MORE CREATURES SEEM TO BE LIVING IN HERE.
PFFT, ALL THESE ANIMALS LOOK ABSURD!
?
DID THE GRASS JUST PASS THROUGH IT?
AH!
THE FOOTPRINTS !!

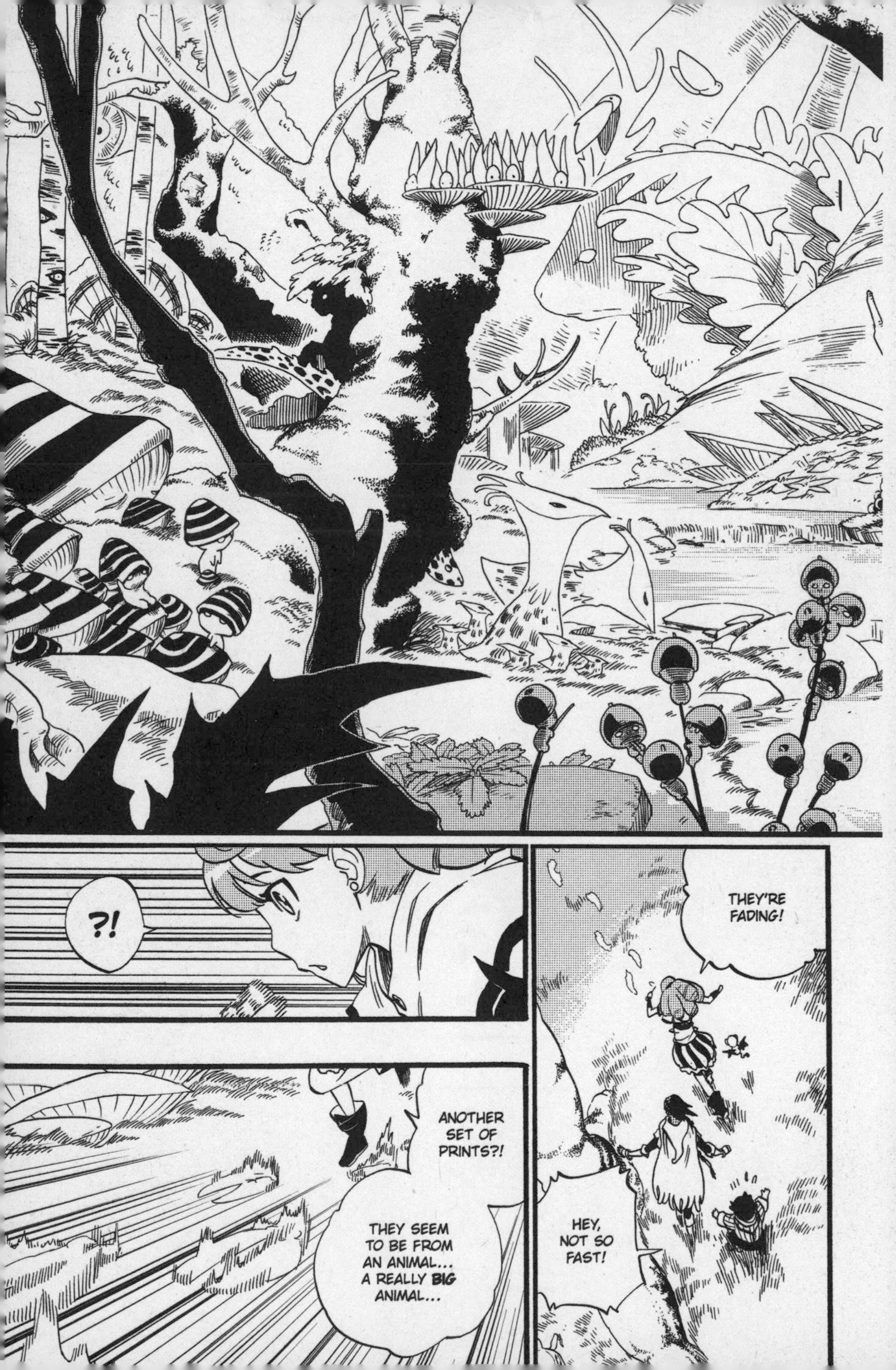
THEY'RE FADING!
HEY, NOT SO FAST!
?!
ANOTHER SET OF PRINTS?!
THEY SEEM TO BE FROM AN ANIMAL... A REALLY BIG ANIMAL...

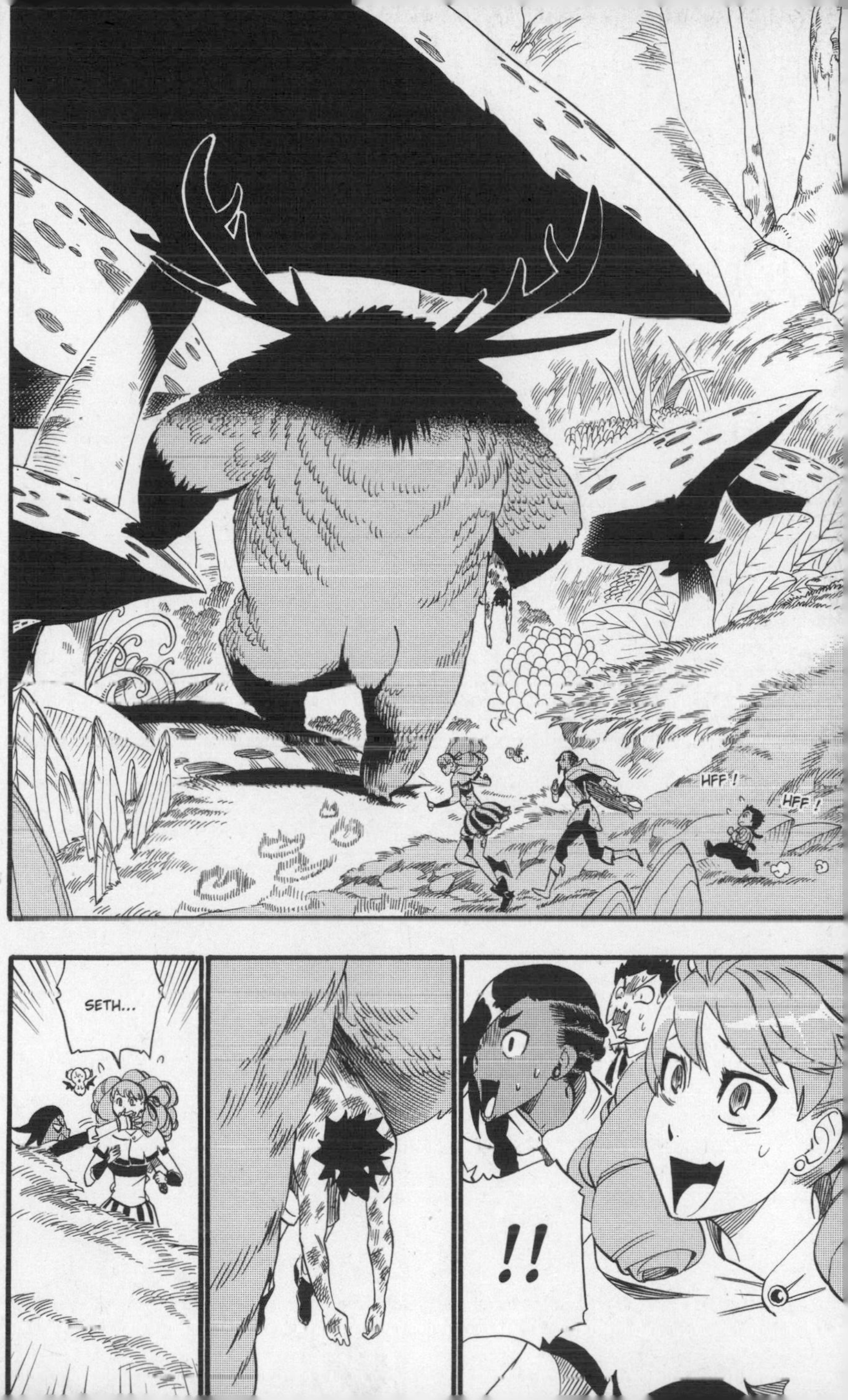
HFF!
HFF!
!!
SETH...

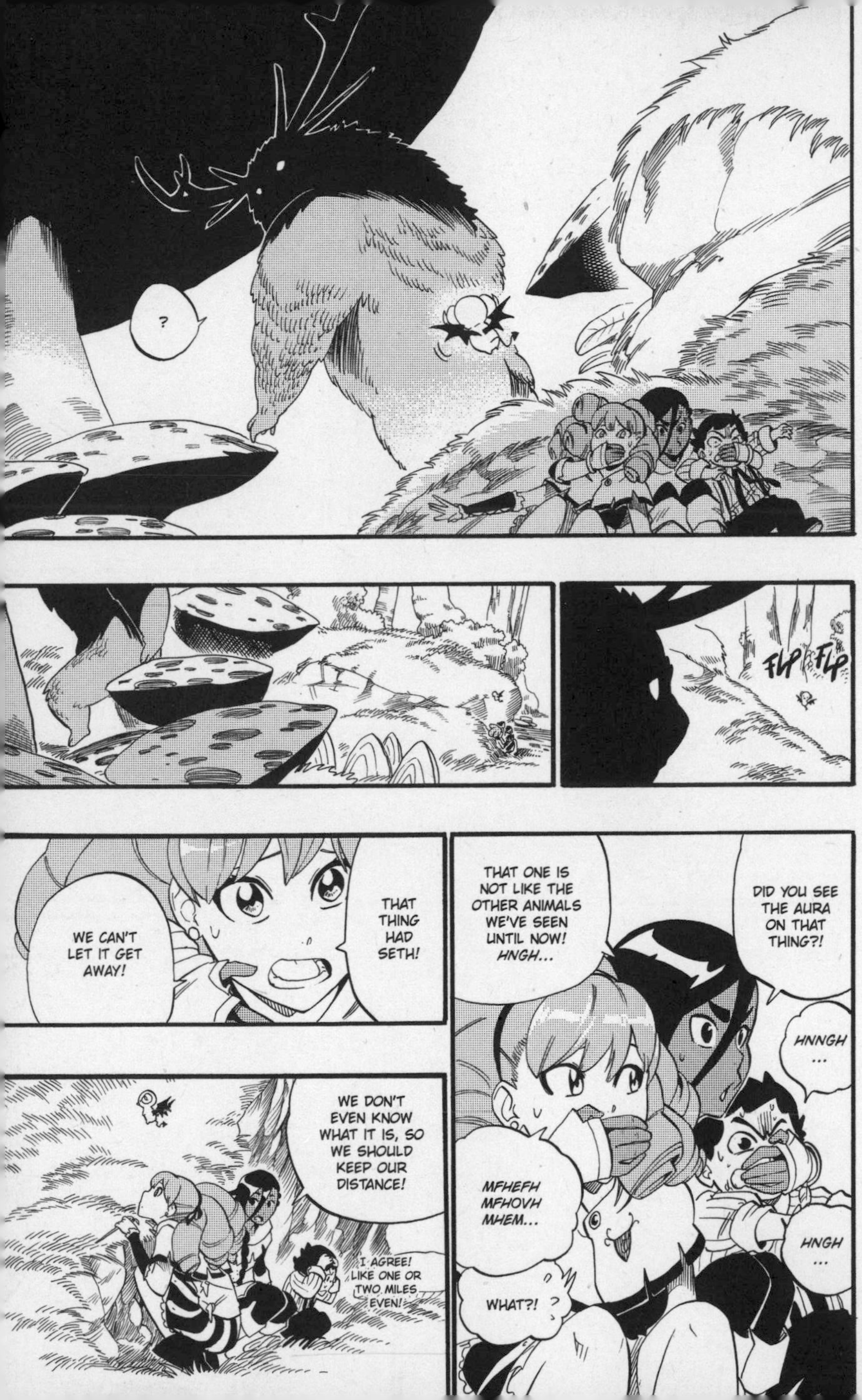
?
FLP FLP
DID YOU SEE THE AURA ON THAT THING?!
THAT ONE IS NOT LIKE THE OTHER ANIMALS WE'VE SEEN UNTIL NOW! HNGH...
HNNGH ...
HNGH ...
MFHEFH MFHOVH MHEM...
WHAT?!
THAT THING HAD SETH!
WE CAN'T LET IT GET AWAY!
WE DON'T EVEN KNOW WHAT IT IS, SO WE SHOULD KEEP OUR DISTANCE!
I AGREE! LIKE ONE OR TWO MILES, EVEN!

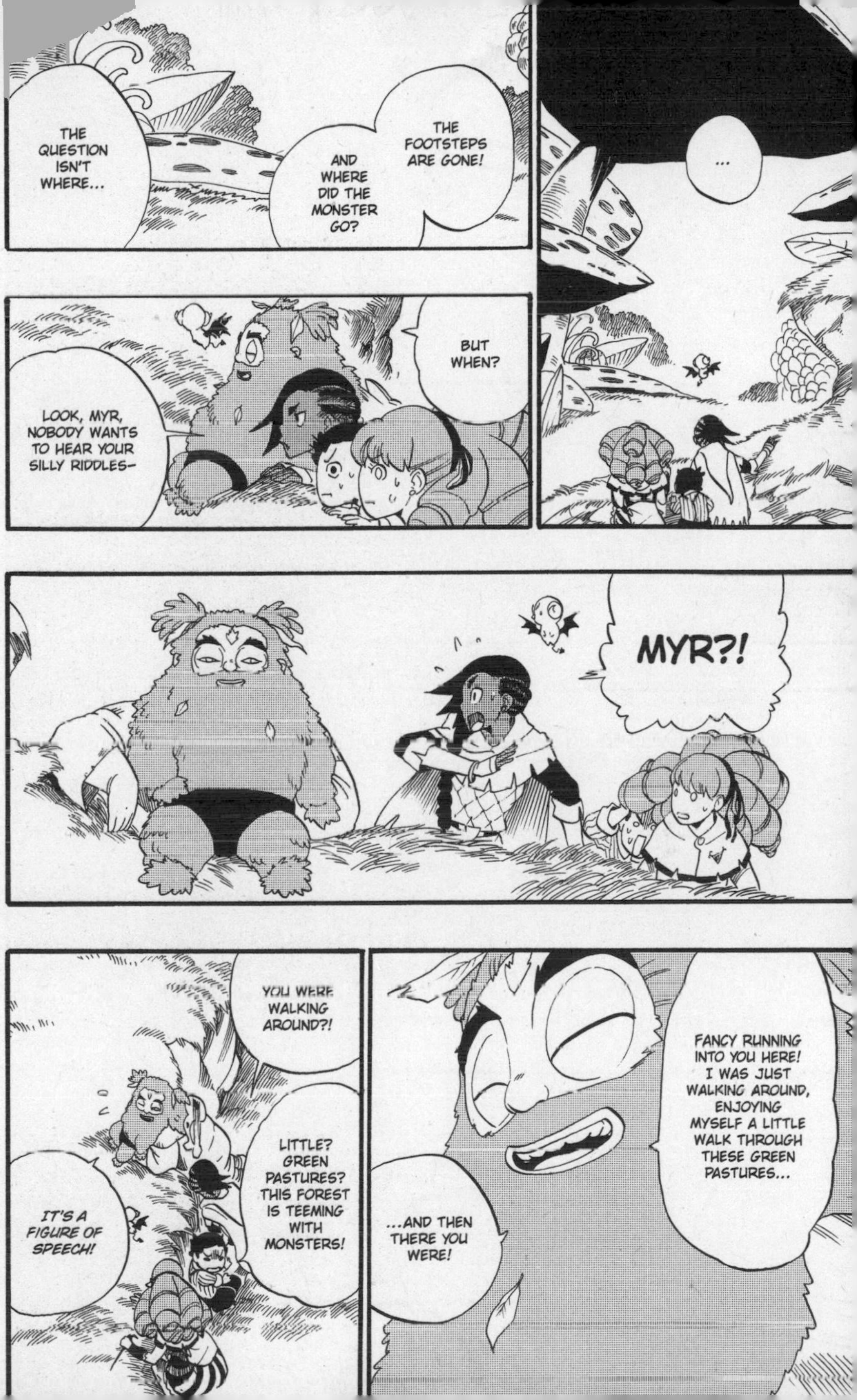
...
THE FOOTSTEPS ARE GONE!
AND WHERE DID THE MONSTER GO?
THE QUESTION ISN'T WHERE...
BUT WHEN?
LOOK, MYR, NOBODY WANTS TO HEAR YOUR SILLY RIDDLES—
MYR?!
FANCY RUNNING INTO YOU HERE! I WAS JUST WALKING AROUND, ENJOYING MYSELF A LITTLE WALK THROUGH THESE GREEN PASTURES...
...AND THEN THERE YOU WERE!
YOU WERE WALKING AROUND?!
LITTLE? GREEN PASTURES? THIS FOREST IS TEEMING WITH MONSTERS!
IT'S A FIGURE OF SPEECH!

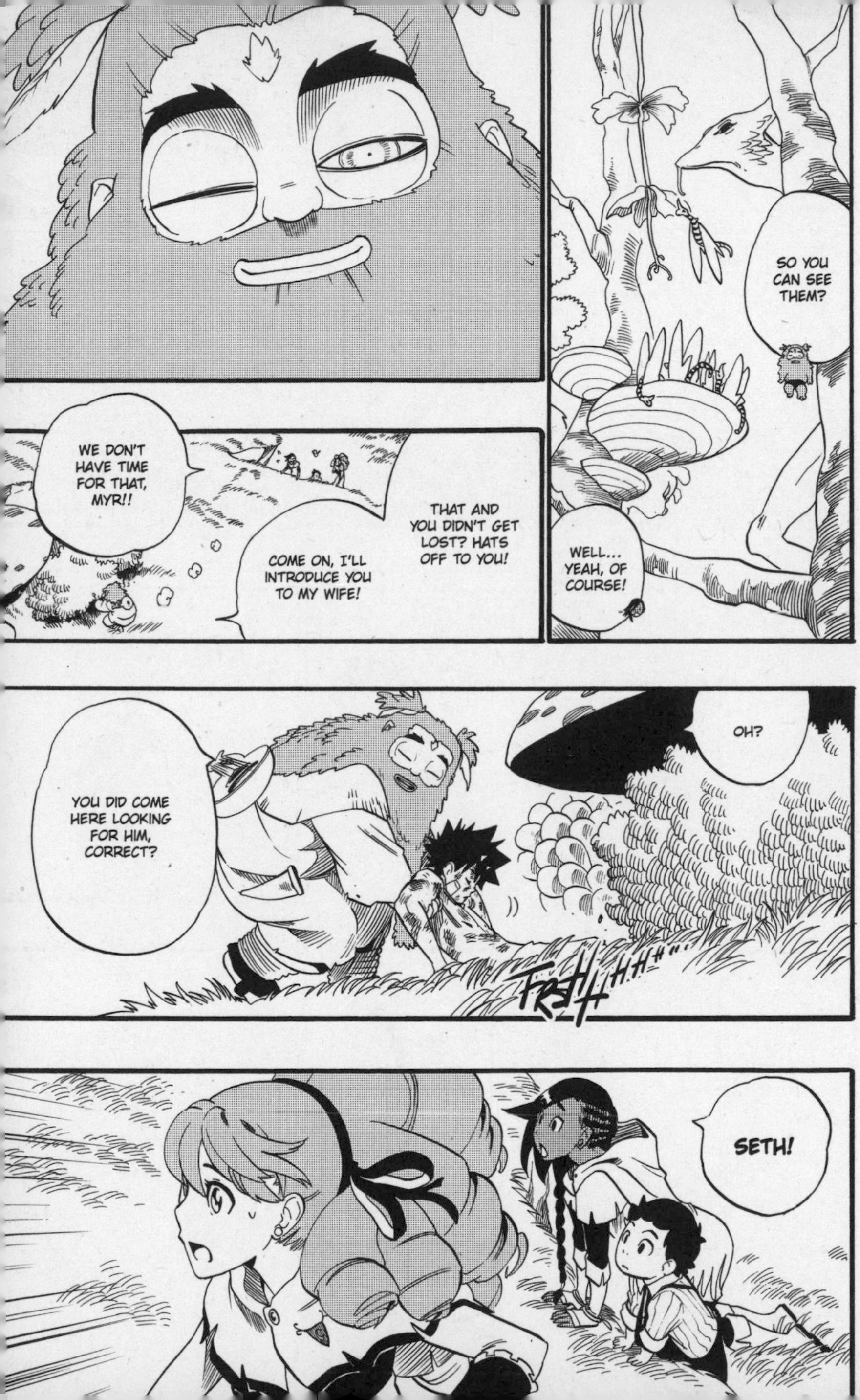
SO YOU CAN SEE THEM?
WELL... YEAH, OF COURSE!
THAT AND YOU DIDN'T GET LOST? HATS OFF TO YOU!
COME ON, I'LL INTRODUCE YOU TO MY WIFE!
WE DON'T HAVE TIME FOR THAT, MYR!!
OH?
YOU DID COME HERE LOOKING FOR HIM, CORRECT?
SETH!

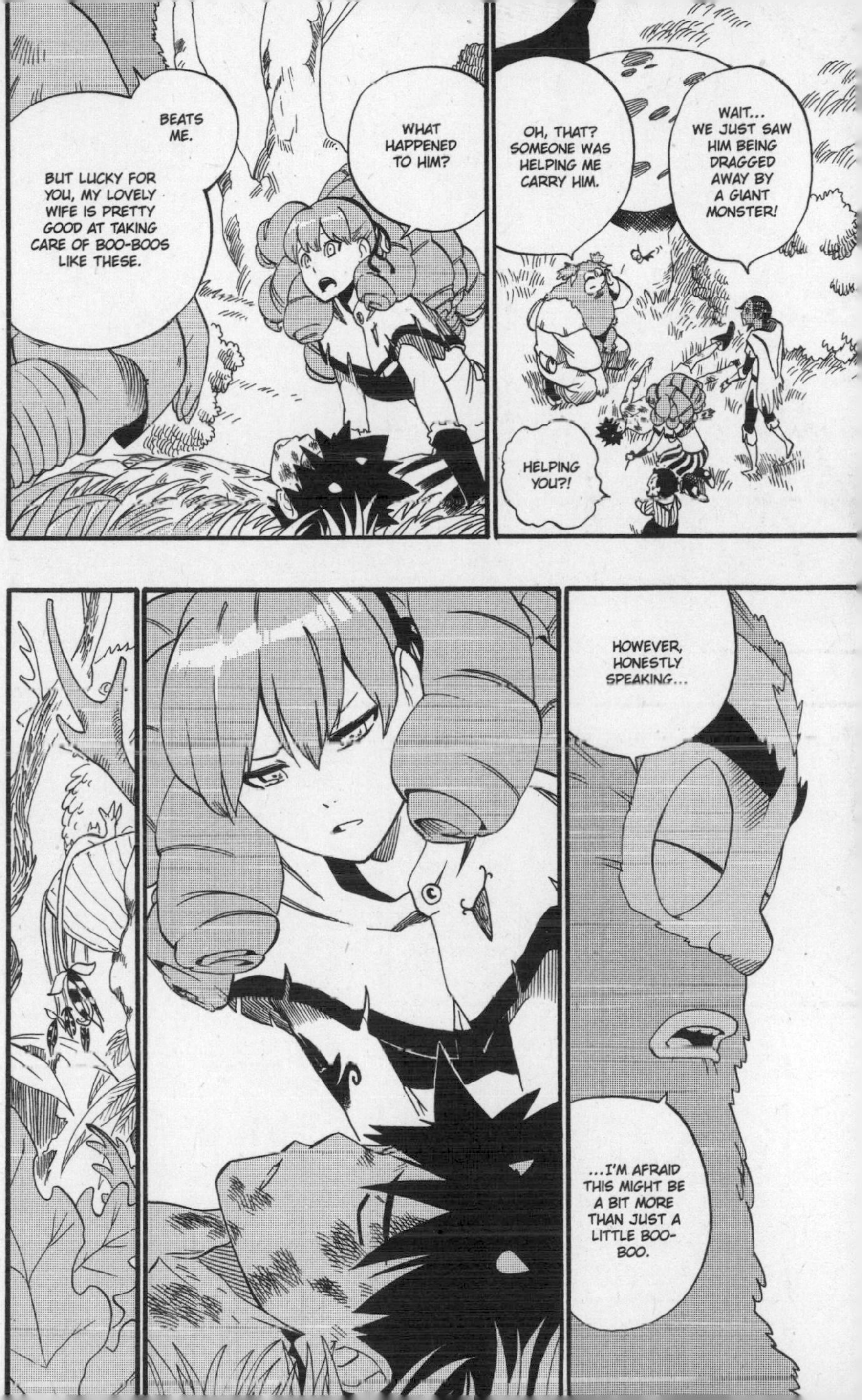
WHAT HAPPENED TO HIM?
BEATS ME.
BUT LUCKY FOR YOU, MY LOVELY WIFE IS PRETTY GOOD AT TAKING CARE OF BOO-BOOS LIKE THESE.
WAIT... WE JUST SAW HIM BEING DRAGGED AWAY BY A GIANT MONSTER!
OH, THAT? SOMEONE WAS HELPING ME CARRY HIM.
HELPING YOU?!
HOWEVER, HONESTLY SPEAKING...
...I'M AFRAID THIS MIGHT BE A BIT MORE THAN JUST A LITTLE BOO-BOO.

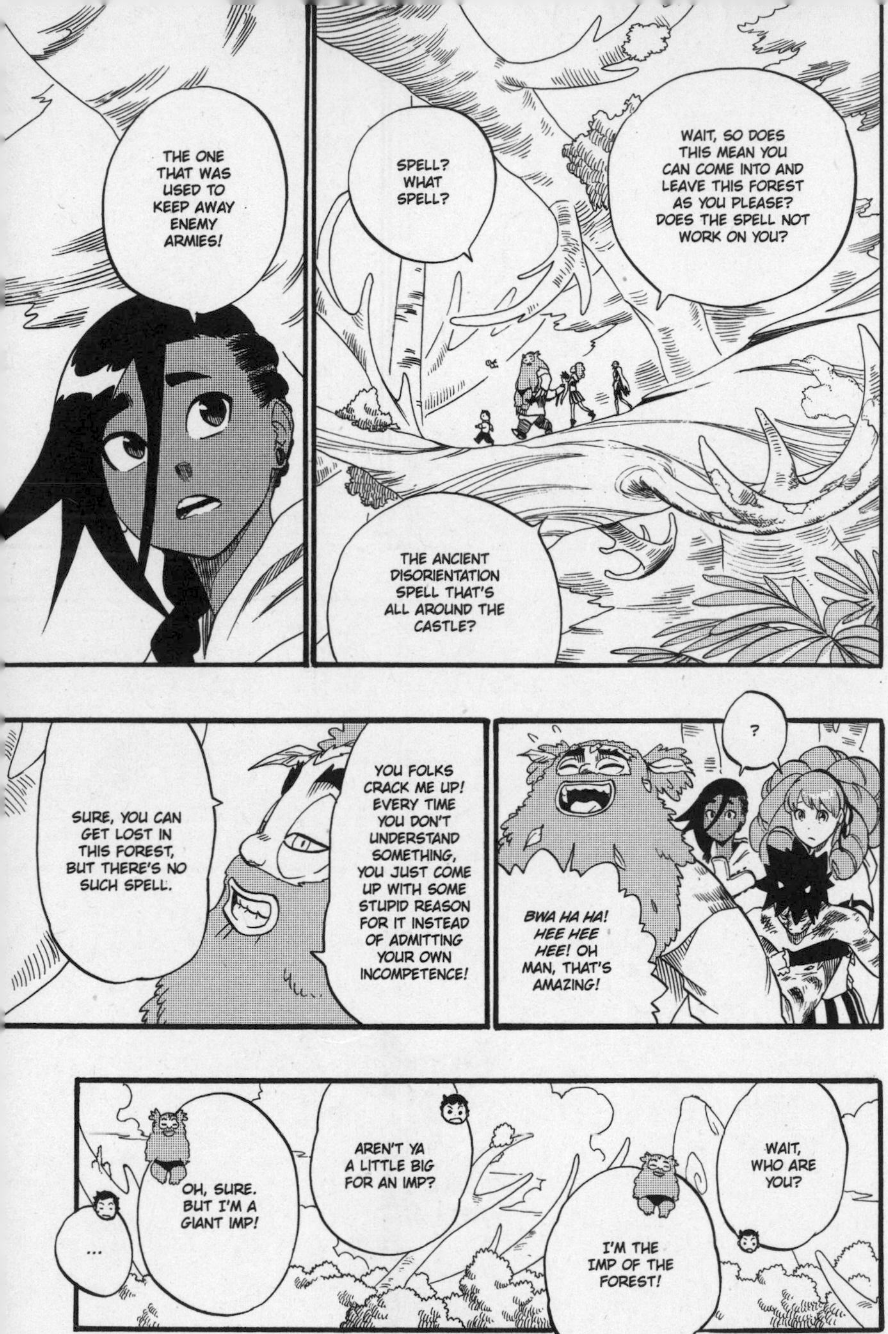
WAIT, SO DOES THIS MEAN YOU CAN COME INTO AND LEAVE THIS FOREST AS YOU PLEASE? DOES THE SPELL NOT WORK ON YOU?
SPELL? WHAT SPELL?
THE ANCIENT DISORIENTATION SPELL THAT'S ALL AROUND THE CASTLE?
THE ONE THAT WAS USED TO KEEP AWAY ENEMY ARMIES!
?
BWA HA HA! HEE HEE HEE! OH MAN, THAT'S AMAZING!
YOU FOLKS CRACK ME UP! EVERY TIME YOU DON'T UNDERSTAND SOMETHING, YOU JUST COME UP WITH SOME STUPID REASON FOR IT INSTEAD OF ADMITTING YOUR OWN INCOMPETENCE!
SURE, YOU CAN GET LOST IN THIS FOREST, BUT THERE'S NO SUCH SPELL.
WAIT, WHO ARE YOU?
I'M THE IMP OF THE FOREST!
AREN'T YA A LITTLE BIG FOR AN IMP?
OH, SURE. BUT I'M A GIANT IMP!
...

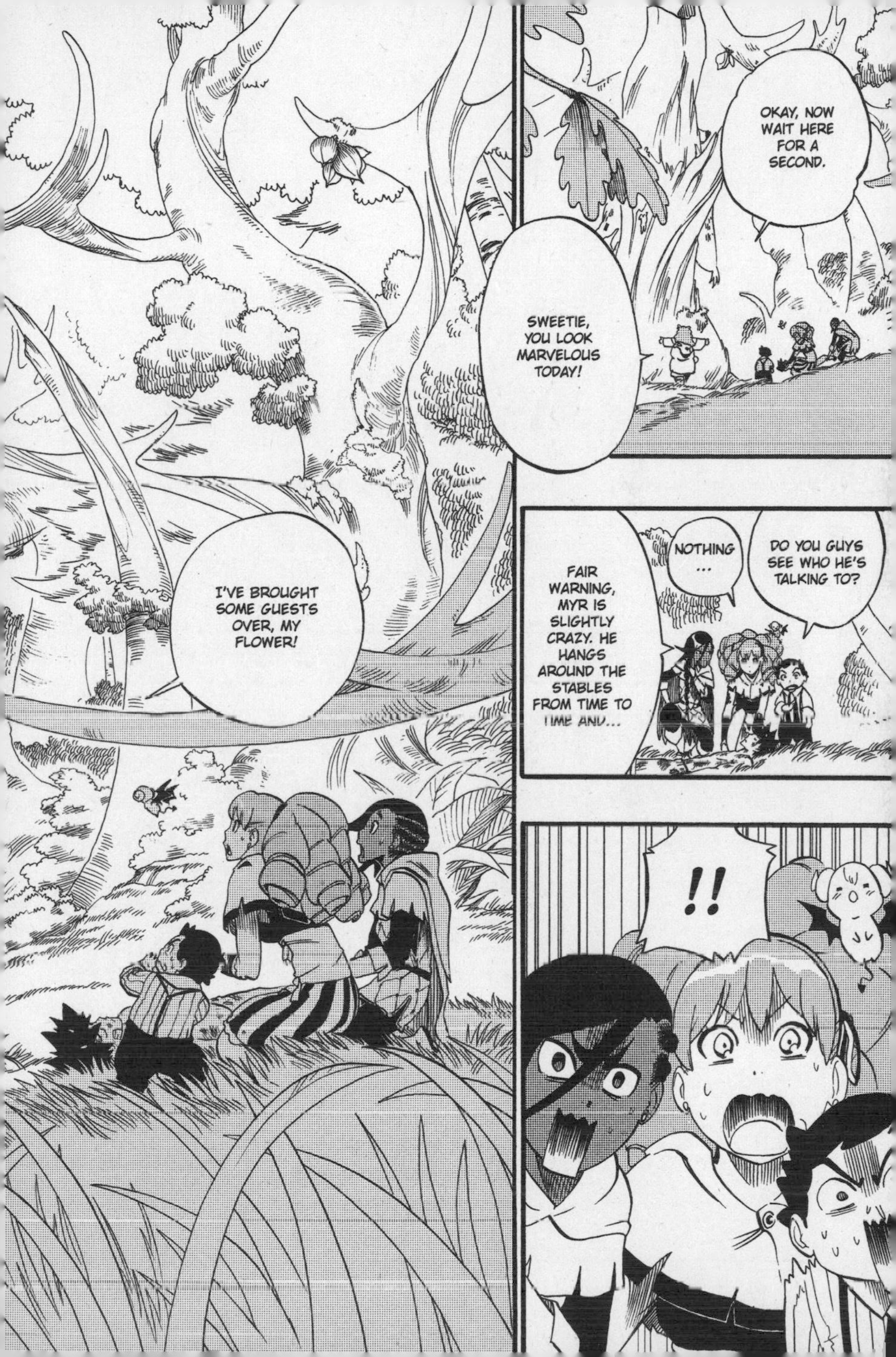
OKAY, NOW WAIT HERE FOR A SECOND.
SWEETIE, YOU LOOK MARVELOUS TODAY!
DO YOU GUYS SEE WHO HE'S TALKING TO?
NOTHING ...
FAIR WARNING, MYR IS SLIGHTLY CRAZY. HE HANGS AROUND THE STABLES FROM TIME TO TIME AND...
!!
I'VE BROUGHT SOME GUESTS OVER, MY FLOWER!

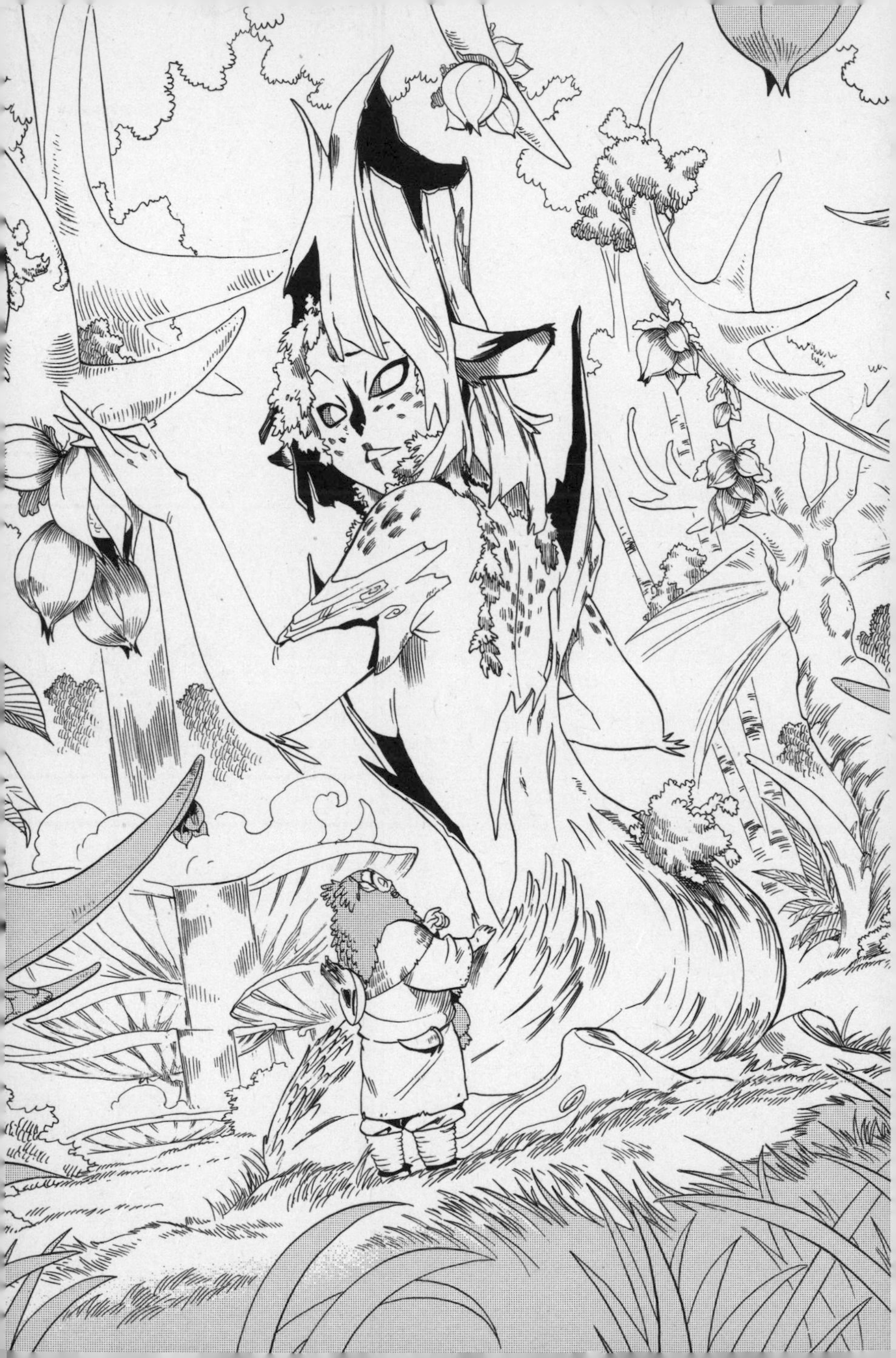

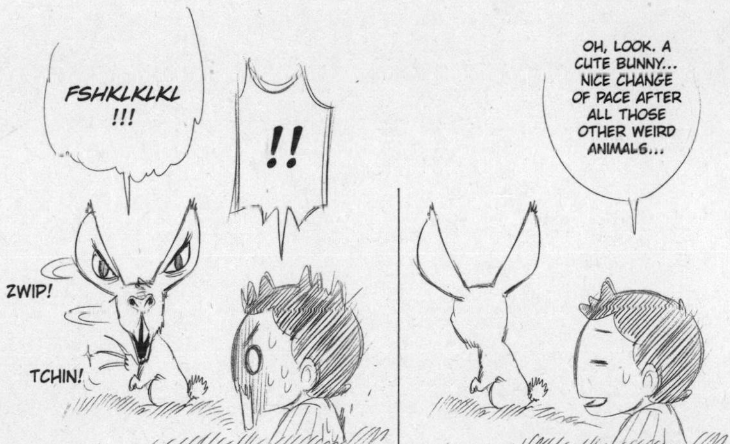
OH, LOOK. A CUTE BUNNY... NICE CHANGE OF PACE AFTER ALL THOSE OTHER WEIRD ANIMALS...
FSHKLKLKL !!!
!!
ZWIP!
TCHIN!

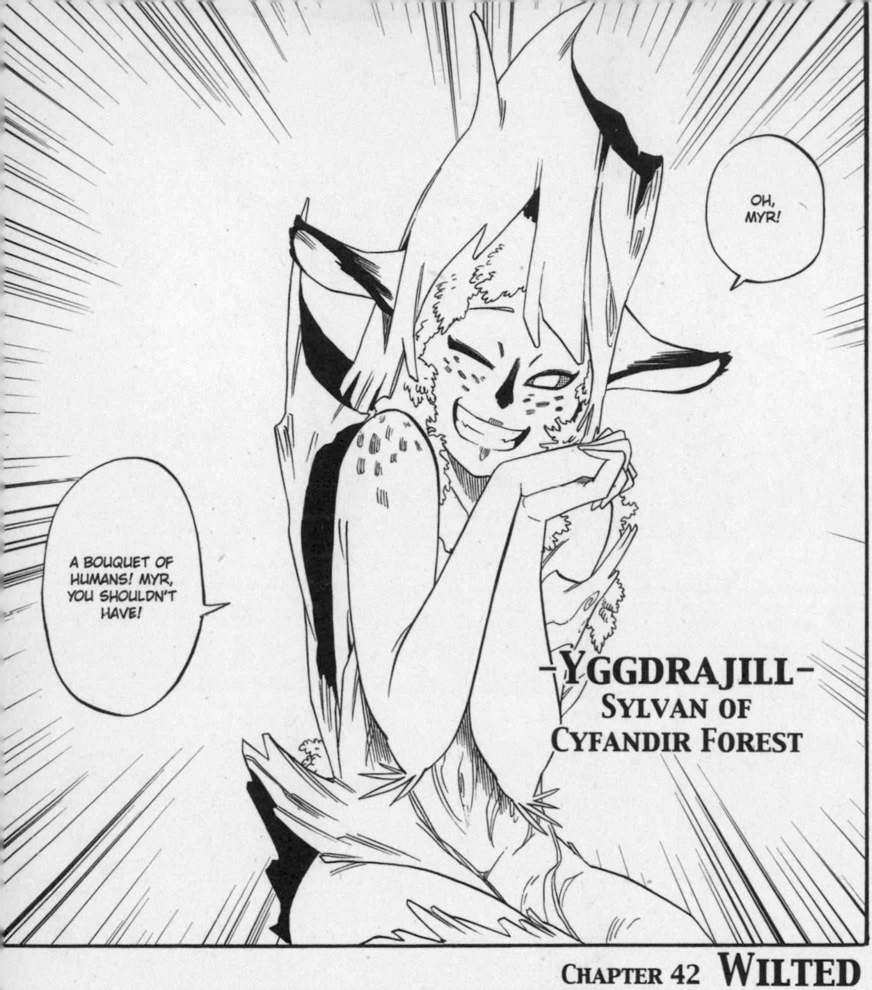
OH, MYR!
A BOUQUET OF HUMANS! MYR, YOU SHOULDN'T HAVE!
-YGGDRAJILL-
SYLVAN OF CYFANDIR FOREST

CHAPTER 42 WILTED

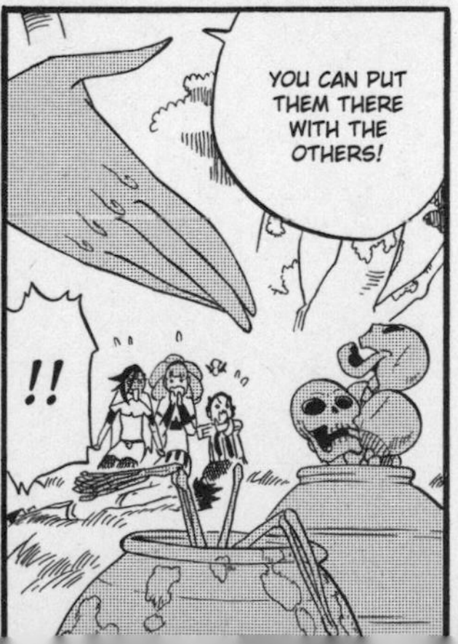
YOU CAN PUT THEM THERE WITH THE OTHERS!
!!

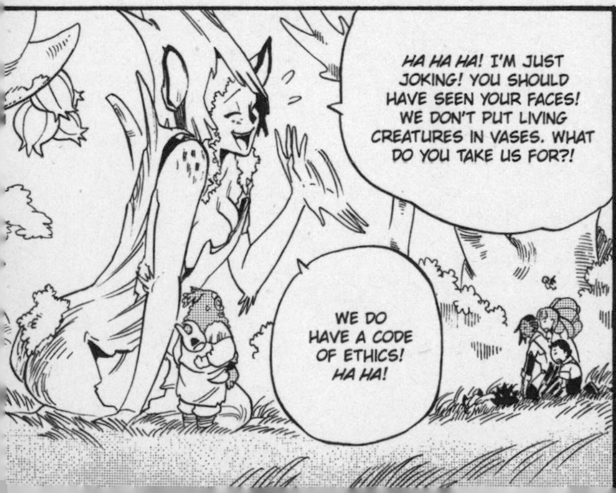
HA HA HA! I'M JUST JOKING! YOU SHOULD HAVE SEEN YOUR FACES! WE DON'T PUT LIVING CREATURES IN VASES. WHAT DO YOU TAKE US FOR?!
WE DO HAVE A CODE OF ETHICS! HA HA!

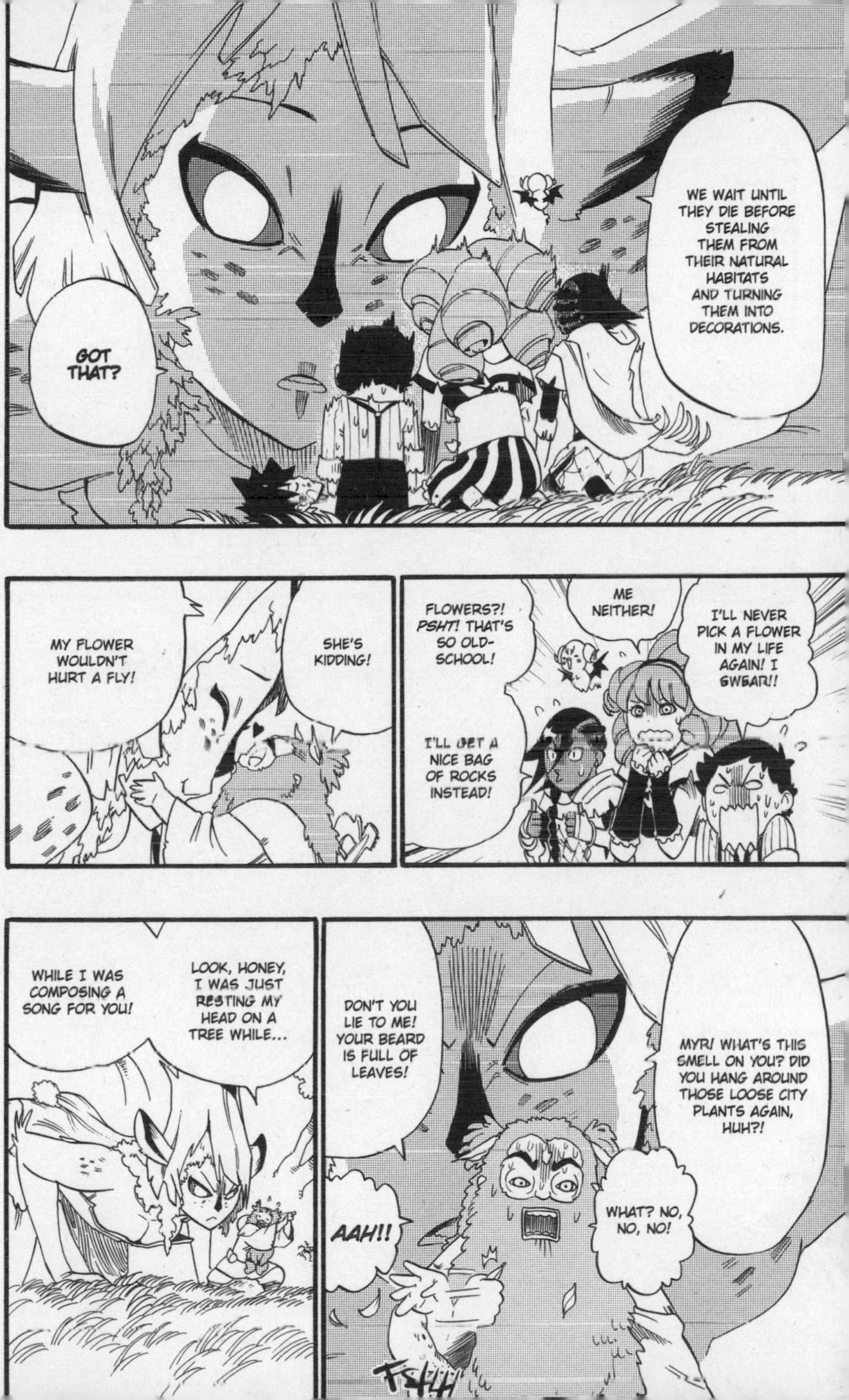

WE WAIT UNTIL THEY DIE BEFORE STEALING THEM FROM THEIR NATURAL HABITATS AND TURNING THEM INTO DECORATIONS.
GOT THAT?
I'LL NEVER PICK A FLOWER IN MY LIFE AGAIN! I SWEAR!!
ME NEITHER!
FLOWERS?! PSHT! THAT'S SO OLD-SCHOOL!
I'LL GET A NICE BAG OF ROCKS INSTEAD!
SHE'S KIDDING!
MY FLOWER WOULDN'T HURT A FLY!
MYR! WHAT'S THIS SMELL ON YOU? DID YOU HANG AROUND THOSE LOOSE CITY PLANTS AGAIN, HUH?!
WHAT? NO, NO, NO!
DON'T YOU LIE TO ME! YOUR BEARD IS FULL OF LEAVES!
AAH!!
LOOK, HONEY, I WAS JUST RESTING MY HEAD ON A TREE WHILE...
WHILE I WAS COMPOSING A SONG FOR YOU!

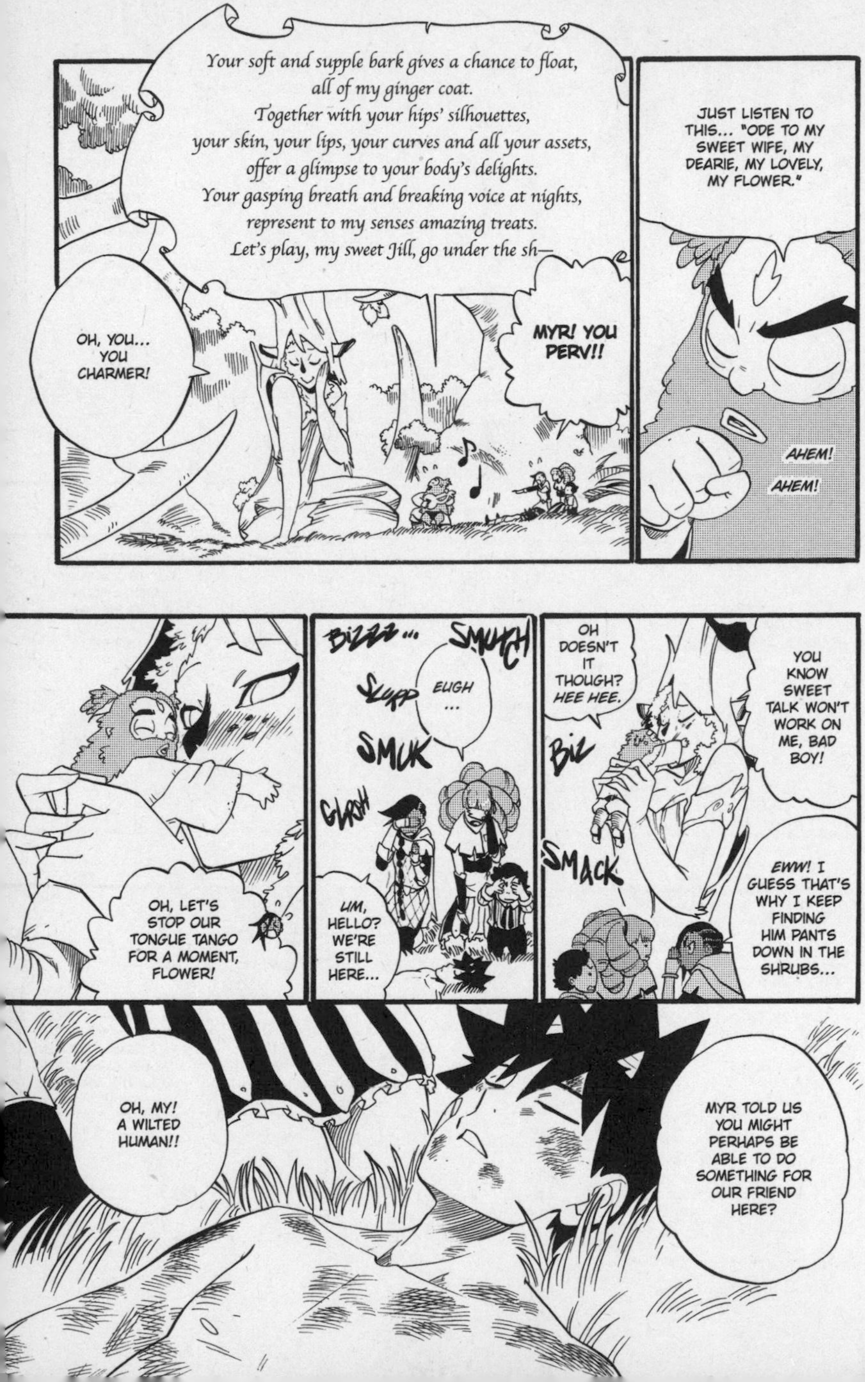
JUST LISTEN TO THIS... "ODE TO MY SWEET WIFE, MY DEARIE, MY LOVELY, MY FLOWER."
AHEM!
AHEM!
Your soft and supple bark gives a chance to float, all of my ginger coat. Together with your hips' silhouettes, your skin, your lips, your curves and all your assets, offer a glimpse to your body's delights. Your gasping breath and breaking voice at nights, represent to my senses amazing treats. Let's play, my sweet Jill, go under the sh—
MYR! YOU PERV!!
OH, YOU... YOU CHARMER!
YOU KNOW SWEET TALK WON'T WORK ON ME, BAD BOY!
OH DOESN'T IT THOUGH? HEE HEE.
BIZ
SMACK
EWW! I GUESS THAT'S WHY I KEEP FINDING HIM PANTS DOWN IN THE SHRUBS...
BIZZZ...
SMUCH
EUGH ...
SLURP
SMUK
GLRSH
UM, HELLO? WE'RE STILL HERE...
OH, LET'S STOP OUR TONGUE TANGO FOR A MOMENT, FLOWER!
MYR TOLD US YOU MIGHT PERHAPS BE ABLE TO DO SOMETHING FOR OUR FRIEND HERE?
OH, MY! A WILTED HUMAN!!

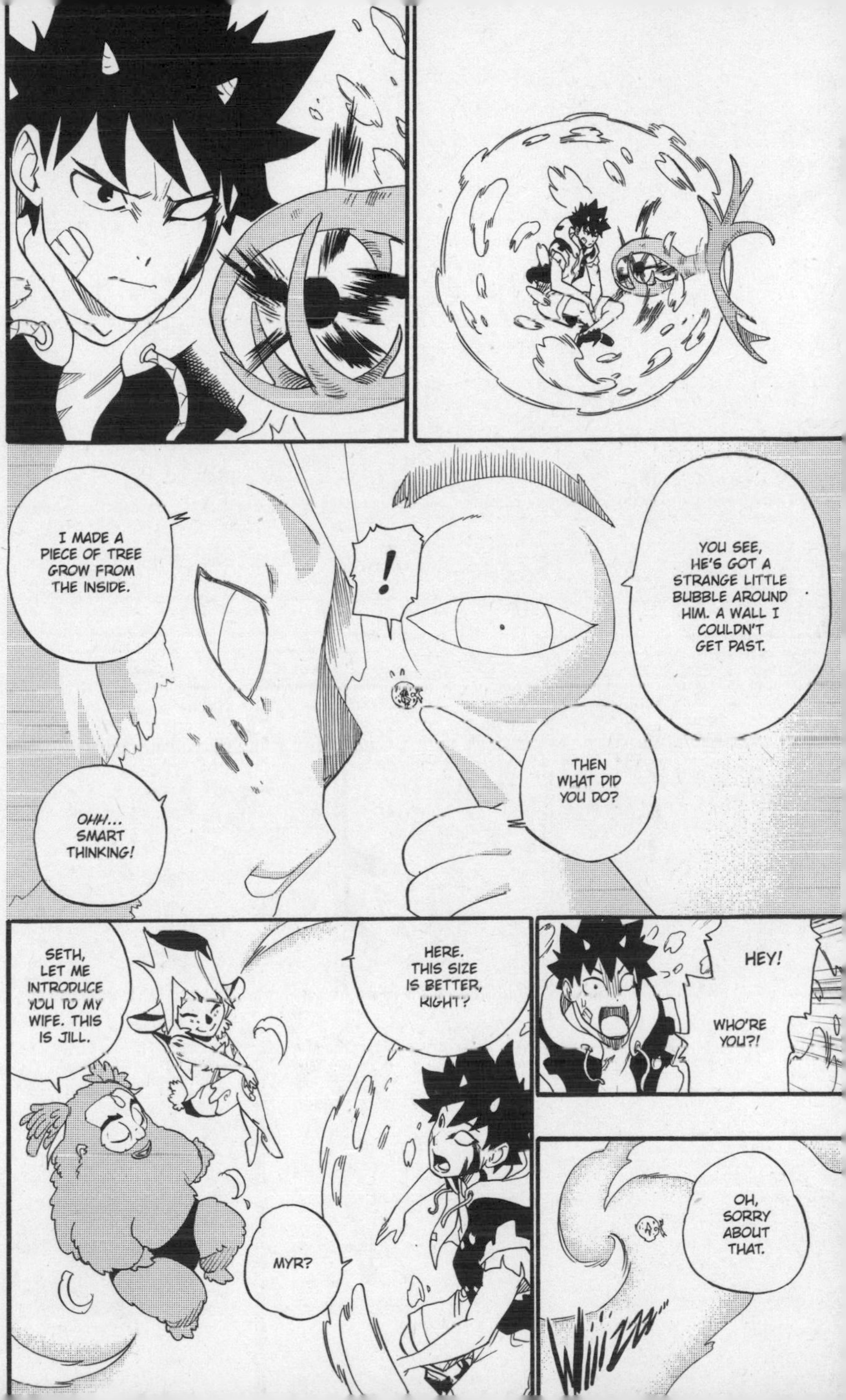
YOU SEE, HE'S GOT A STRANGE LITTLE BUBBLE AROUND HIM. A WALL I COULDN'T GET PAST.
!
THEN WHAT DID YOU DO?
I MADE A PIECE OF TREE GROW FROM THE INSIDE.
OHH... SMART THINKING!
HEY!
WHO'RE YOU?!
OH, SORRY ABOUT THAT.
WIIIZZZ
HERE. THIS SIZE IS BETTER, RIGHT?
SETH, LET ME INTRODUCE YOU TO MY WIFE. THIS IS JILL.
MYR?

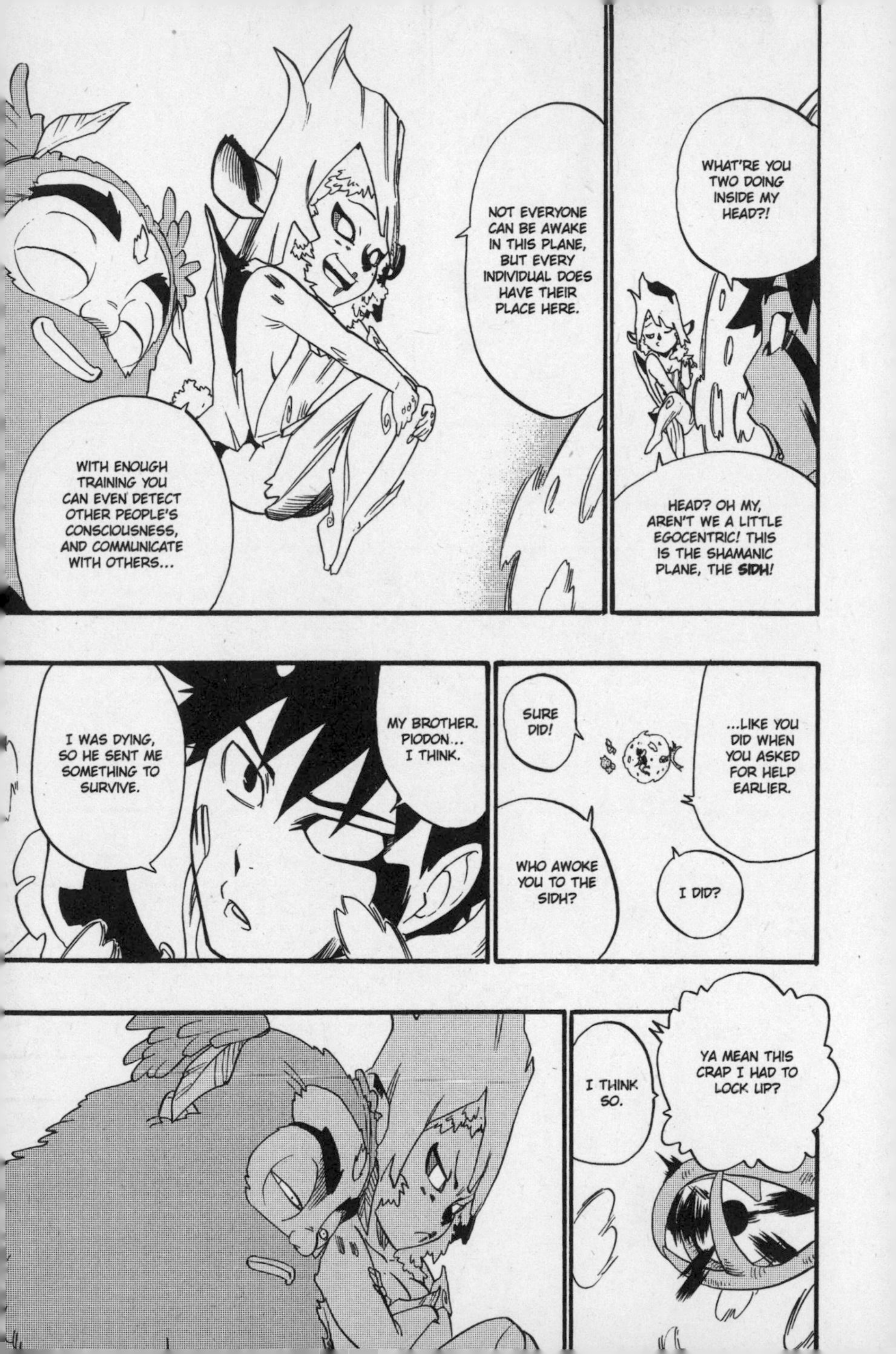
WHAT'RE YOU TWO DOING INSIDE MY HEAD?!
HEAD? OH MY, AREN'T WE A LITTLE EGOCENTRIC! THIS IS THE SHAMANIC PLANE, THE **SIDH**!
NOT EVERYONE CAN BE AWAKE IN THIS PLANE, BUT EVERY INDIVIDUAL DOES HAVE THEIR PLACE HERE.
WITH ENOUGH TRAINING YOU CAN EVEN DETECT OTHER PEOPLE'S CONSCIOUSNESS, AND COMMUNICATE WITH OTHERS...
...LIKE YOU DID WHEN YOU ASKED FOR HELP EARLIER.
I DID?
SURE DID!
WHO AWOKE YOU TO THE SIDH?
MY BROTHER. PIODON... I THINK.
I WAS DYING, SO HE SENT ME SOMETHING TO SURVIVE.
YA MEAN THIS CRAP I HAD TO LOCK UP?
I THINK SO.

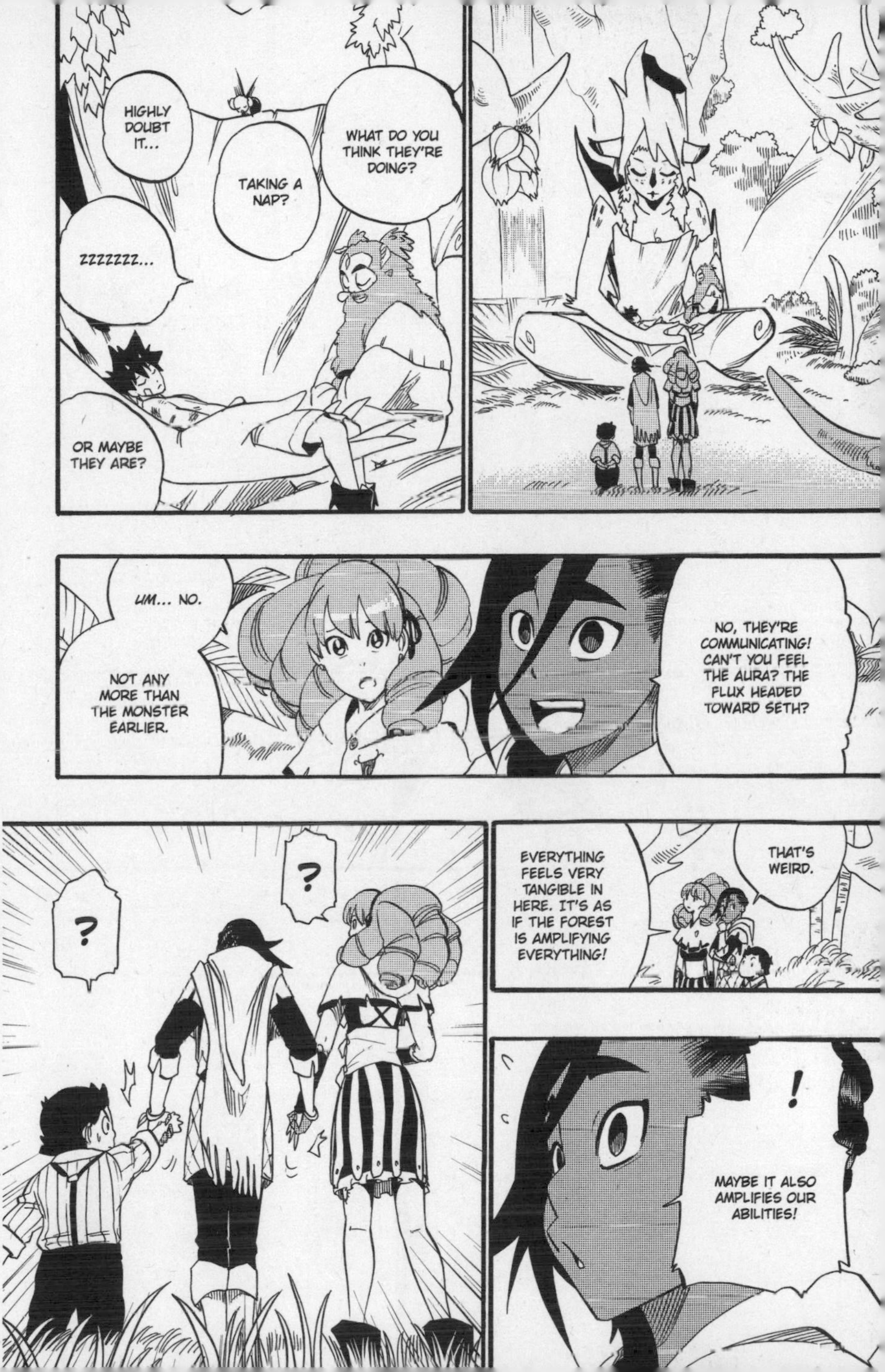
WHAT DO YOU THINK THEY'RE DOING?
TAKING A NAP?
HIGHLY DOUBT IT...
ZZZZZZZ...
OR MAYBE THEY ARE?
NO, THEY'RE COMMUNICATING! CAN'T YOU FEEL THE AURA? THE FLUX HEADED TOWARD SETH?
UM... NO.
NOT ANY MORE THAN THE MONSTER EARLIER.
THAT'S WEIRD.
EVERYTHING FEELS VERY TANGIBLE IN HERE. IT'S AS IF THE FOREST IS AMPLIFYING EVERYTHING!
!
MAYBE IT ALSO AMPLIFIES OUR ABILITIES!
?
?

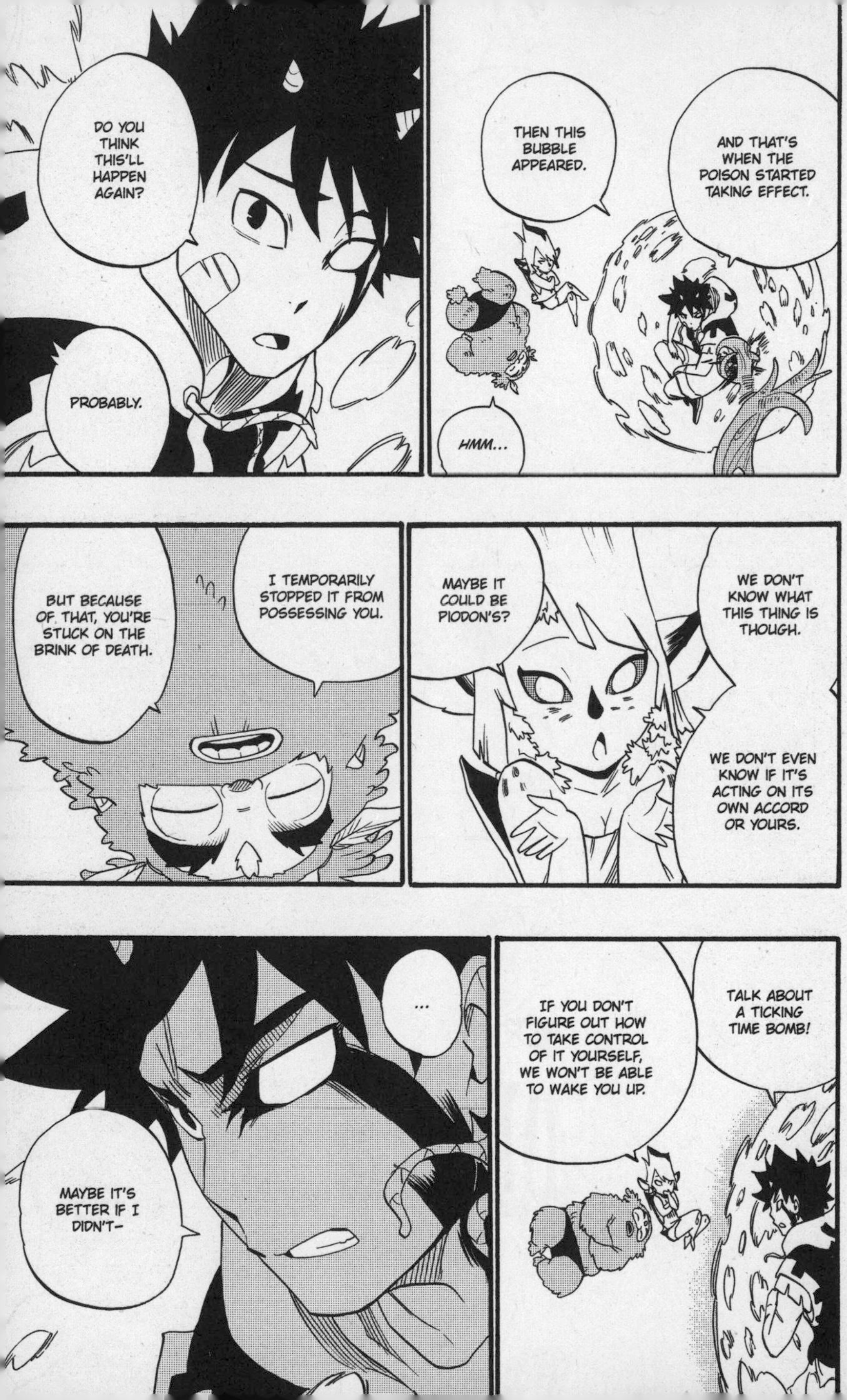
AND THAT'S WHEN THE POISON STARTED TAKING EFFECT.
THEN THIS BUBBLE APPEARED.
HMM...
DO YOU THINK THIS'LL HAPPEN AGAIN?
PROBABLY.
WE DON'T KNOW WHAT THIS THING IS THOUGH.
MAYBE IT COULD BE PIODON'S?
WE DON'T EVEN KNOW IF IT'S ACTING ON ITS OWN ACCORD OR YOURS.
I TEMPORARILY STOPPED IT FROM POSSESSING YOU.
BUT BECAUSE OF THAT, YOU'RE STUCK ON THE BRINK OF DEATH.
TALK ABOUT A TICKING TIME BOMB!
IF YOU DON'T FIGURE OUT HOW TO TAKE CONTROL OF IT YOURSELF, WE WON'T BE ABLE TO WAKE YOU UP.
...
MAYBE IT'S BETTER IF I DIDN'T-

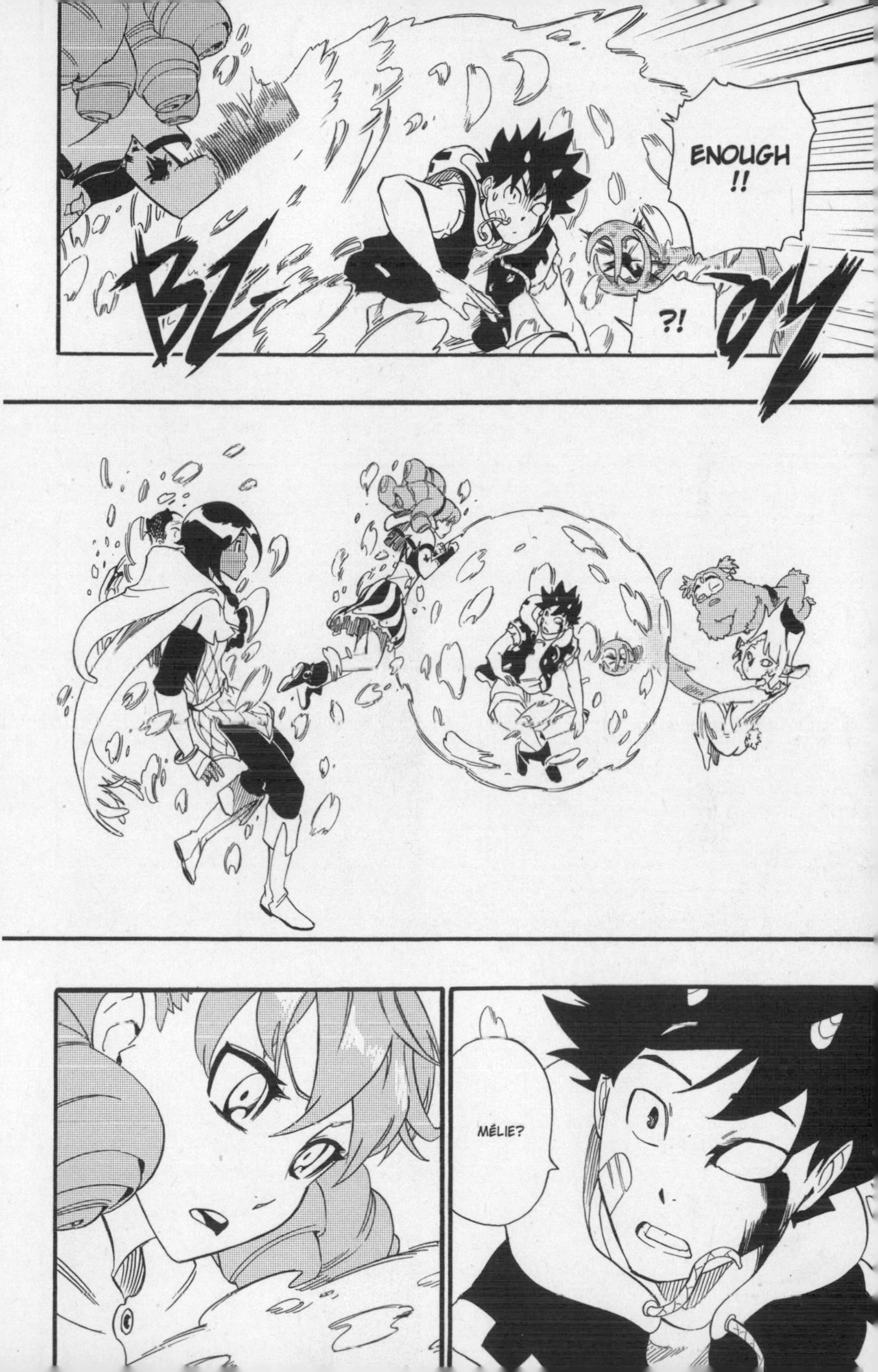
ENOUGH !!
?!
BZ-OOM
MÉLIE?

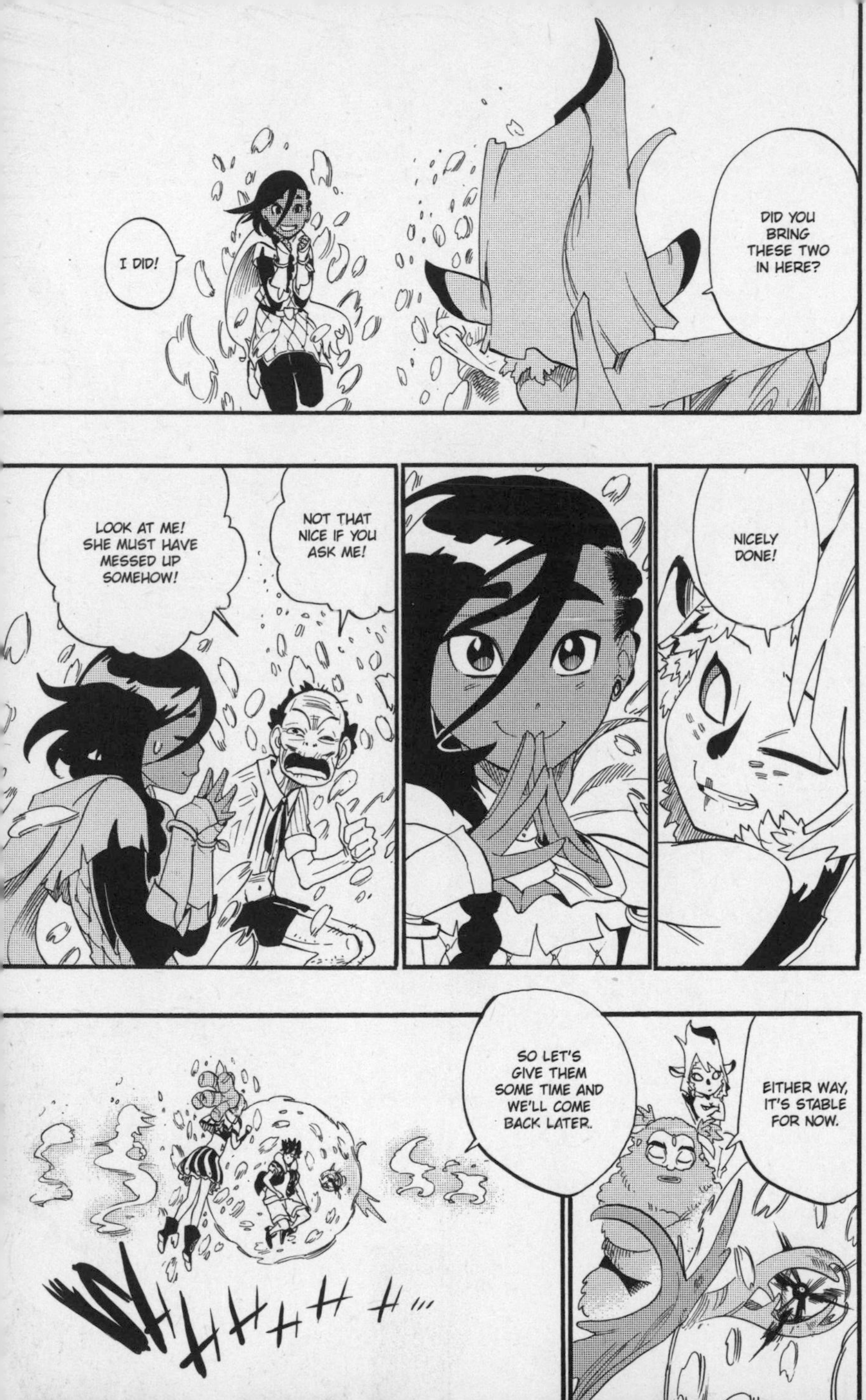
DID YOU BRING THESE TWO IN HERE?
I DID!
NICELY DONE!
NOT THAT NICE IF YOU ASK ME!
LOOK AT ME! SHE MUST HAVE MESSED UP SOMEHOW!
EITHER WAY, IT'S STABLE FOR NOW.
SO LET'S GIVE THEM SOME TIME AND WE'LL COME BACK LATER.

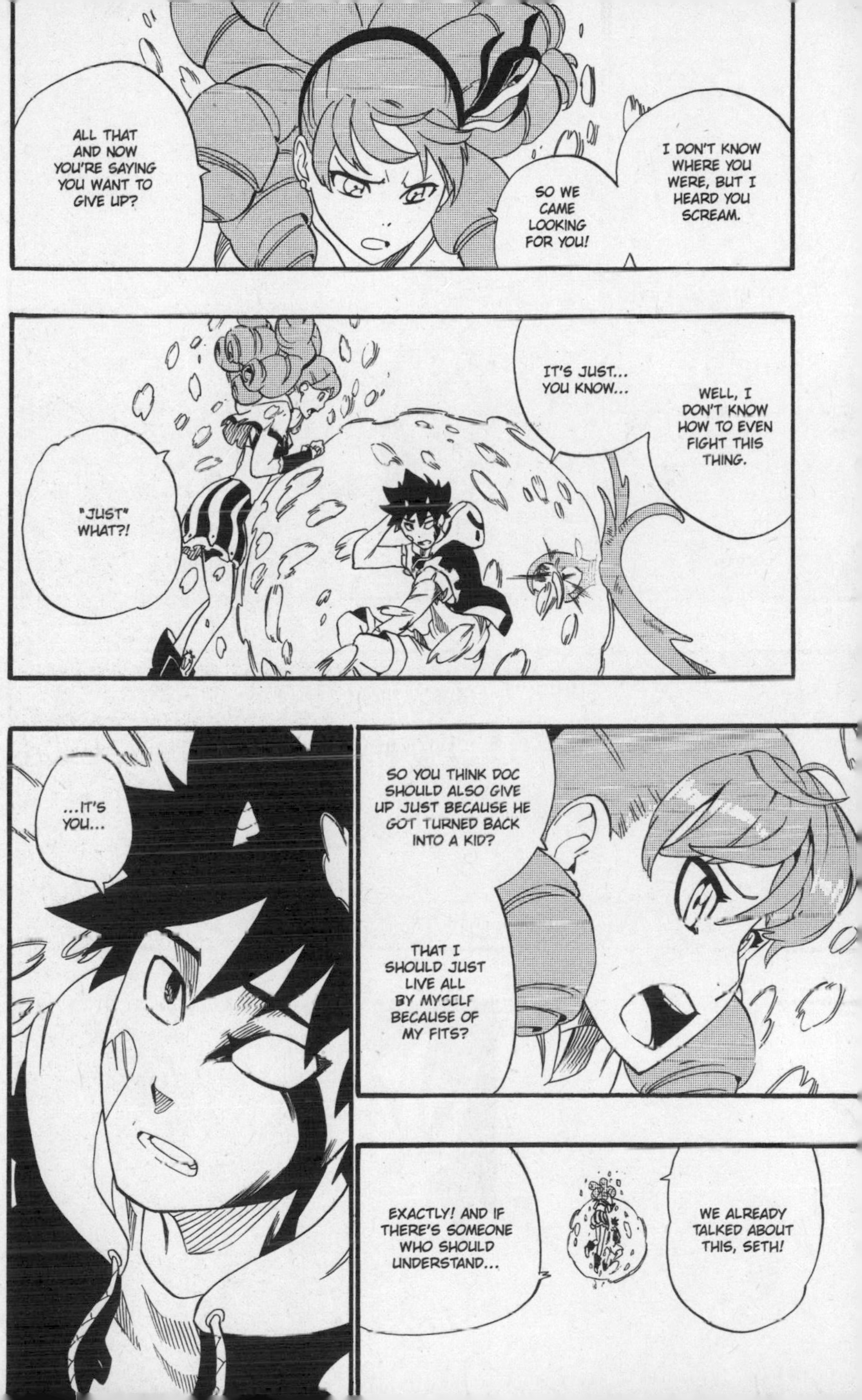
I DON'T KNOW WHERE YOU WERE, BUT I HEARD YOU SCREAM.
SO WE CAME LOOKING FOR YOU!
ALL THAT AND NOW YOU'RE SAYING YOU WANT TO GIVE UP?
WELL, I DON'T KNOW HOW TO EVEN FIGHT THIS THING.
IT'S JUST... YOU KNOW...
"JUST" WHAT?!
SO YOU THINK DOC SHOULD ALSO GIVE UP JUST BECAUSE HE GOT TURNED BACK INTO A KID?
THAT I SHOULD JUST LIVE ALL BY MYSELF BECAUSE OF MY FITS?
WE ALREADY TALKED ABOUT THIS, SETH!
EXACTLY! AND IF THERE'S SOMEONE WHO SHOULD UNDERSTAND...
...IT'S YOU...

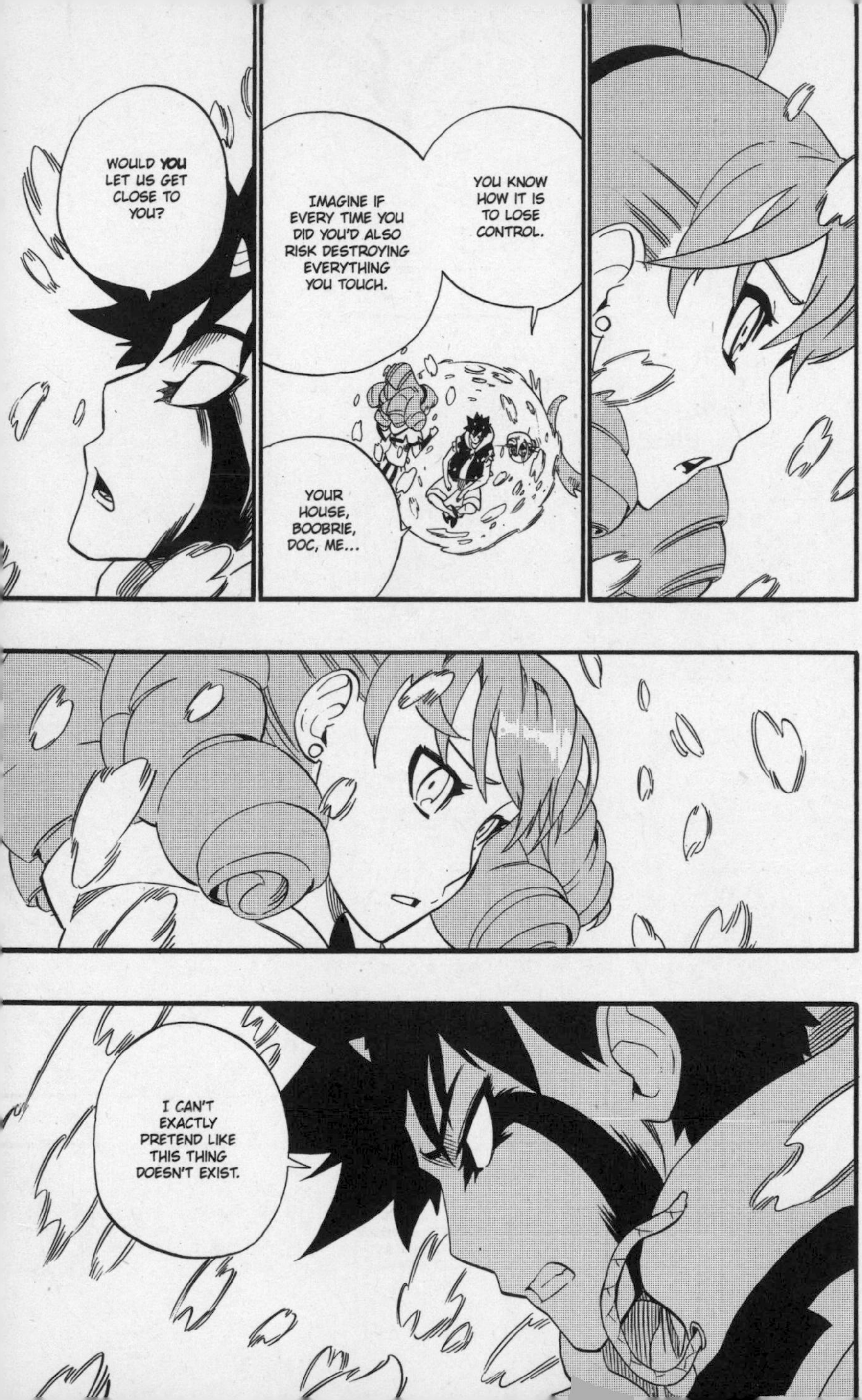
YOU KNOW HOW IT IS TO LOSE CONTROL.
IMAGINE IF EVERY TIME YOU DID YOU'D ALSO RISK DESTROYING EVERYTHING YOU TOUCH.
YOUR HOUSE, BOOBRIE, DOC, ME...
WOULD **YOU** LET US GET CLOSE TO YOU?
I CAN'T EXACTLY PRETEND LIKE THIS THING DOESN'T EXIST.

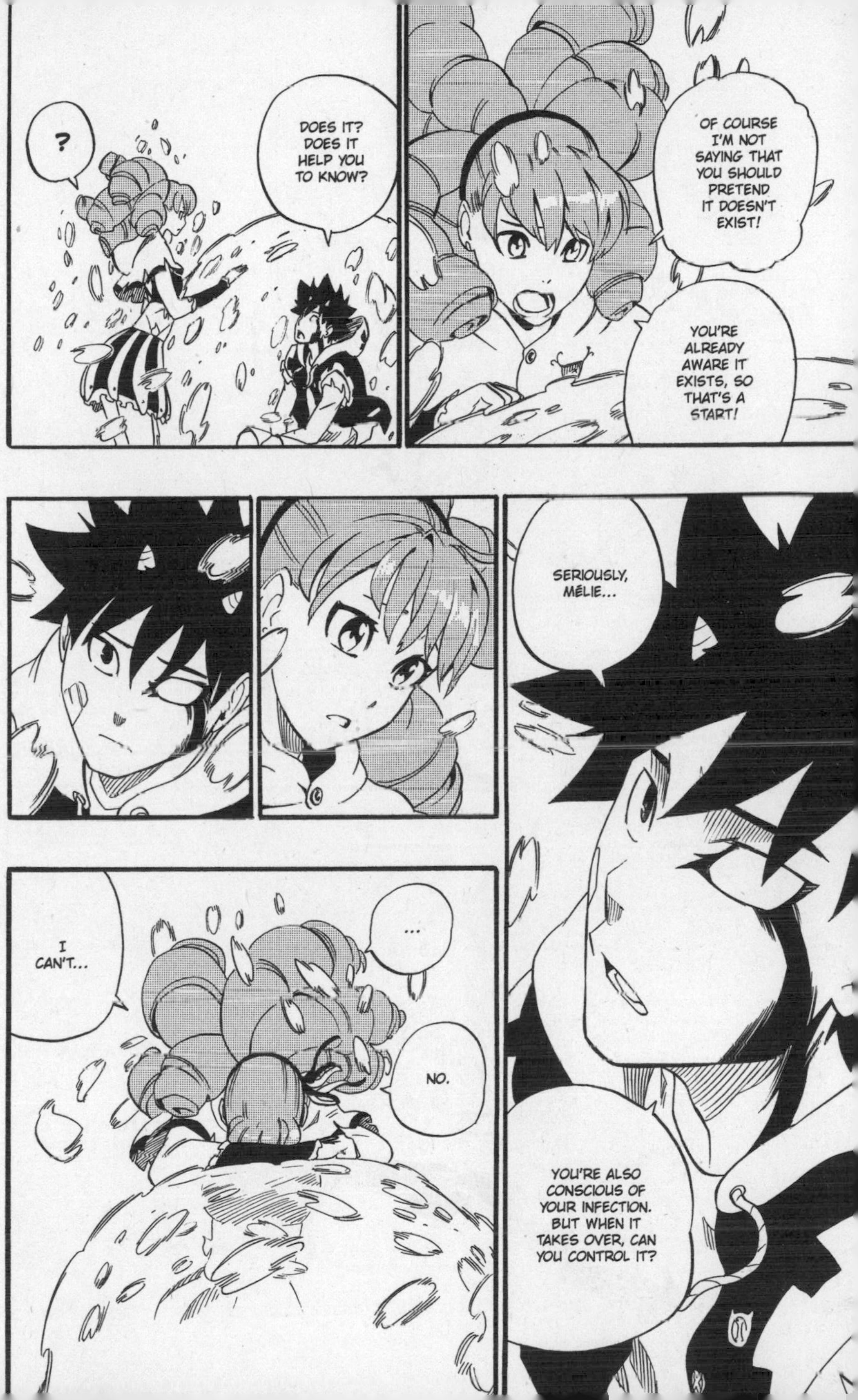
OF COURSE I'M NOT SAYING THAT YOU SHOULD PRETEND IT DOESN'T EXIST!
YOU'RE ALREADY AWARE IT EXISTS, SO THAT'S A START!
DOES IT? DOES IT HELP YOU TO KNOW?
?
SERIOUSLY, MÉLIE...
YOU'RE ALSO CONSCIOUS OF YOUR INFECTION. BUT WHEN IT TAKES OVER, CAN YOU CONTROL IT?
...
NO.
I CAN'T...

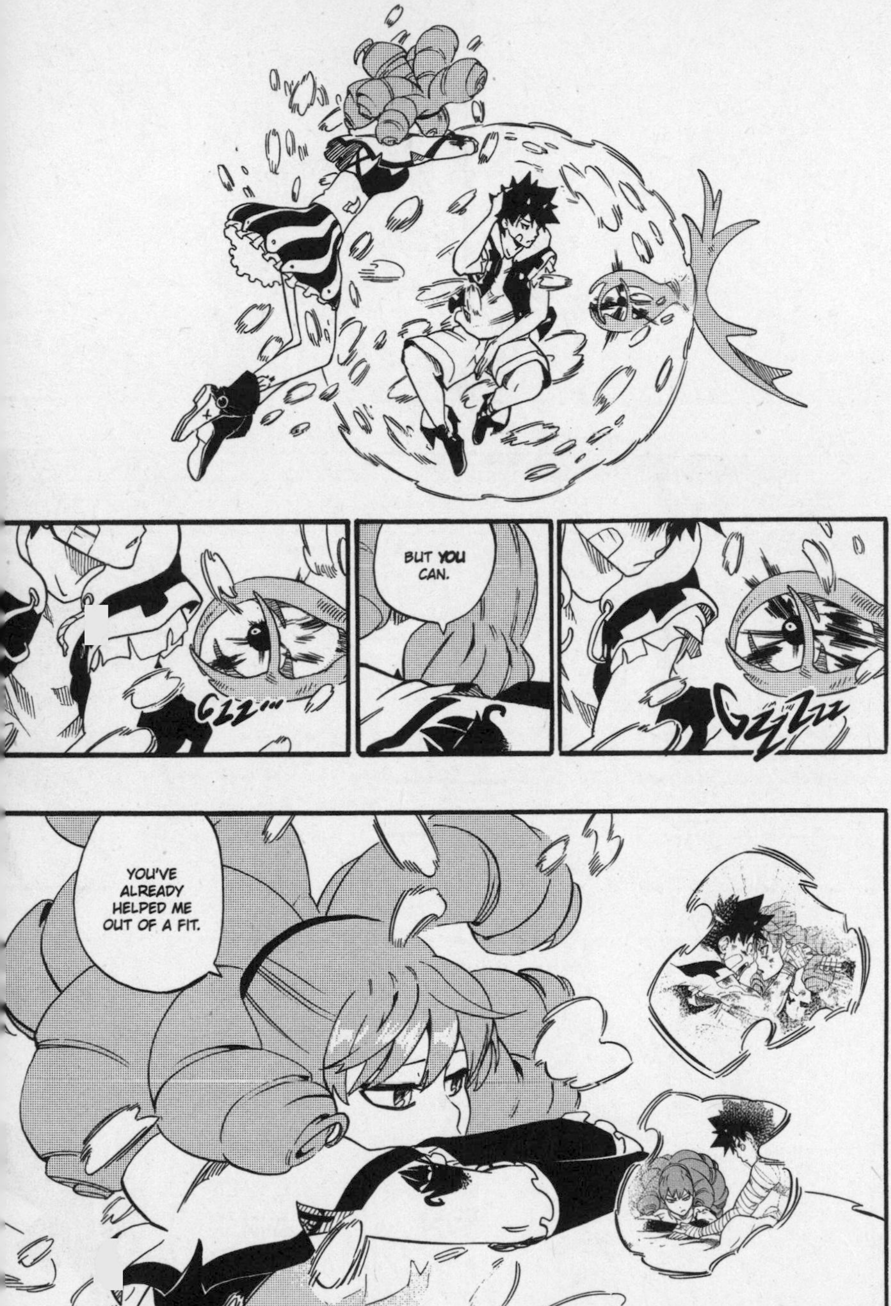
GZZZZ
BUT YOU CAN.
GZZ...
YOU'VE ALREADY HELPED ME OUT OF A FIT.

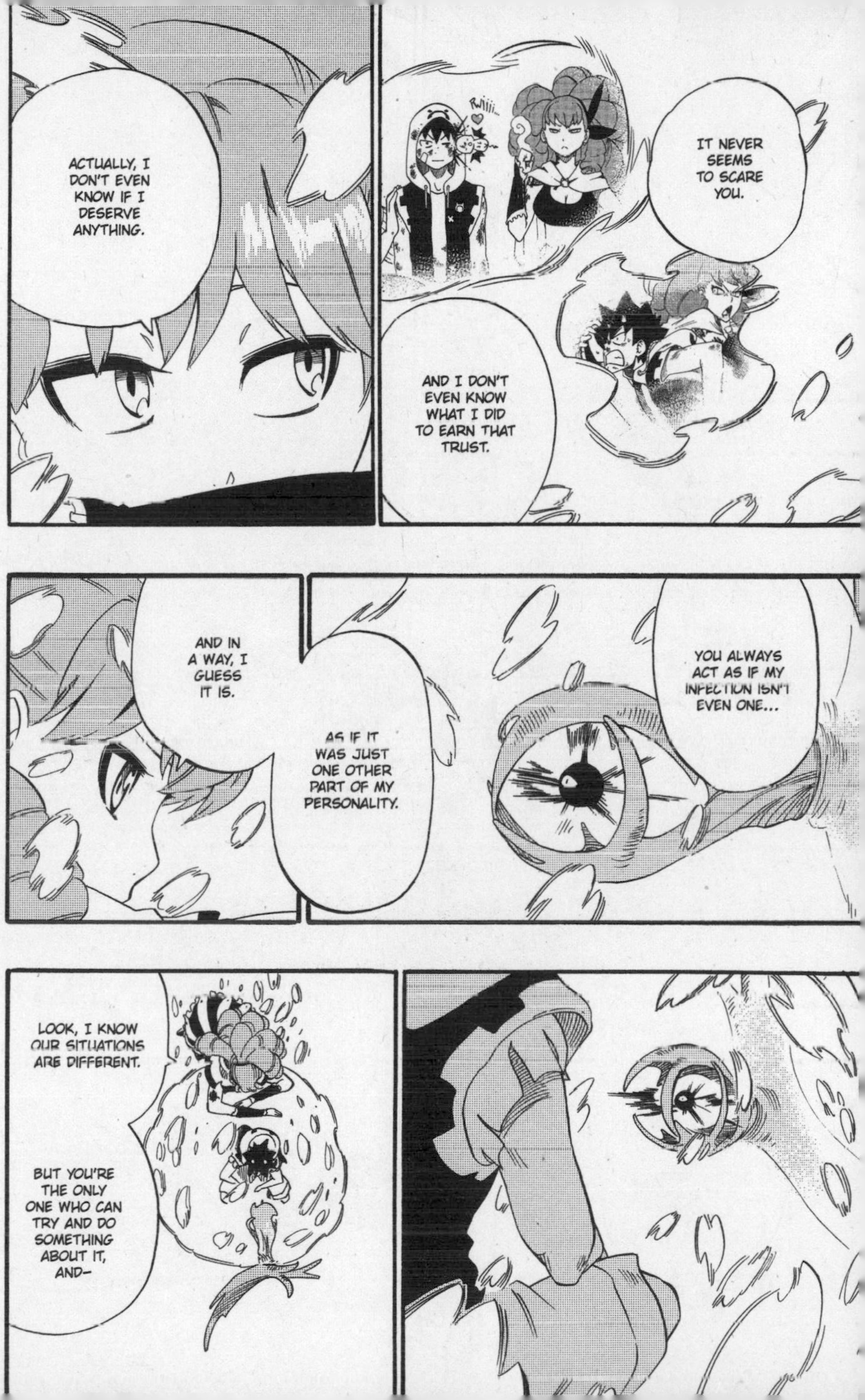
IT NEVER SEEMS TO SCARE YOU.
AND I DON'T EVEN KNOW WHAT I DID TO EARN THAT TRUST.
ACTUALLY, I DON'T EVEN KNOW IF I DESERVE ANYTHING.
YOU ALWAYS ACT AS IF MY INFECTION ISN'T EVEN ONE...
AS IF IT WAS JUST ONE OTHER PART OF MY PERSONALITY.
AND IN A WAY, I GUESS IT IS.
LOOK, I KNOW OUR SITUATIONS ARE DIFFERENT.
BUT YOU'RE THE ONLY ONE WHO CAN TRY AND DO SOMETHING ABOUT IT, AND–

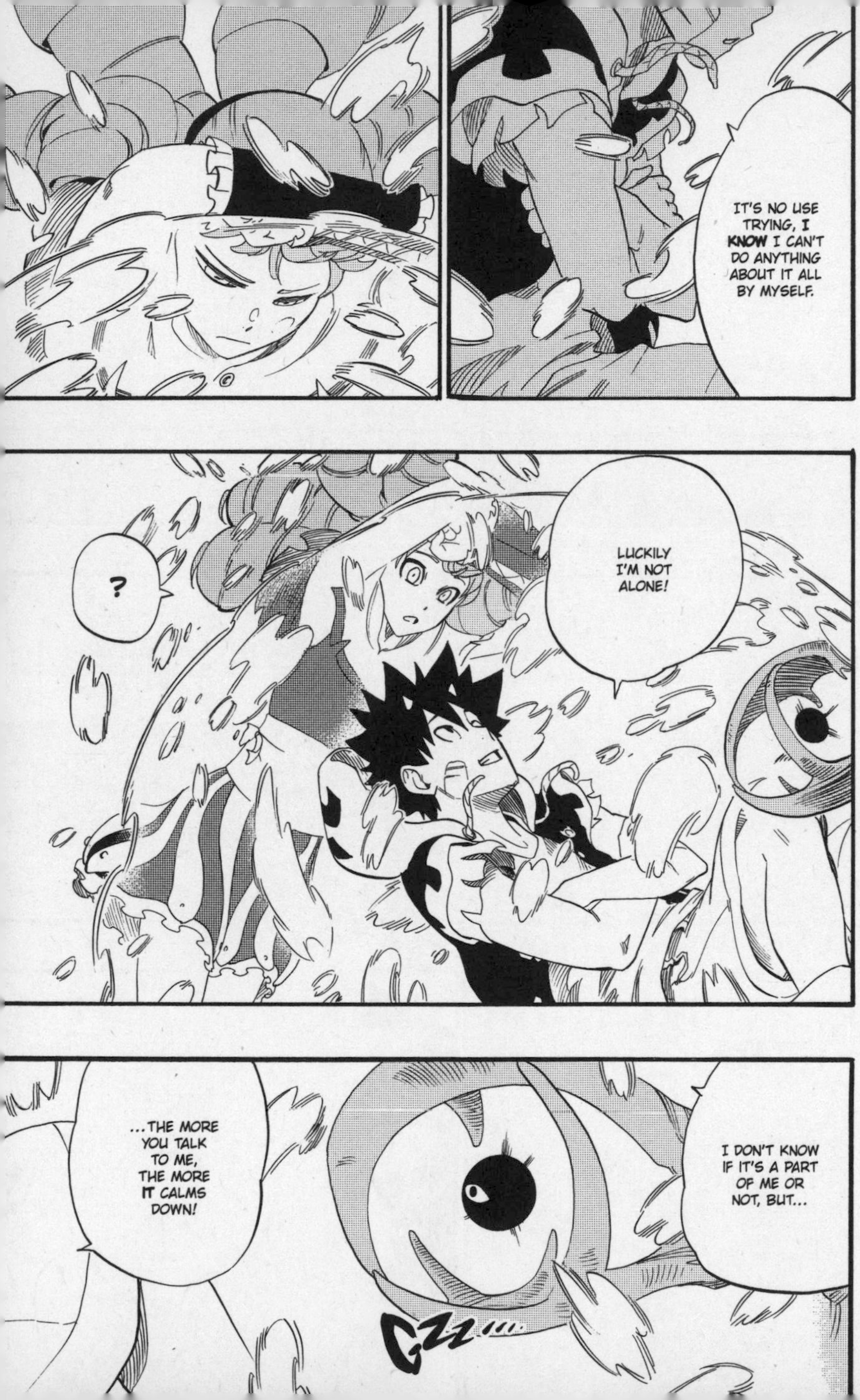
IT'S NO USE TRYING, I KNOW I CAN'T DO ANYTHING ABOUT IT ALL BY MYSELF.
LUCKILY I'M NOT ALONE!
?
I DON'T KNOW IF IT'S A PART OF ME OR NOT, BUT...
...THE MORE YOU TALK TO ME, THE MORE IT CALMS DOWN!
GZZ...

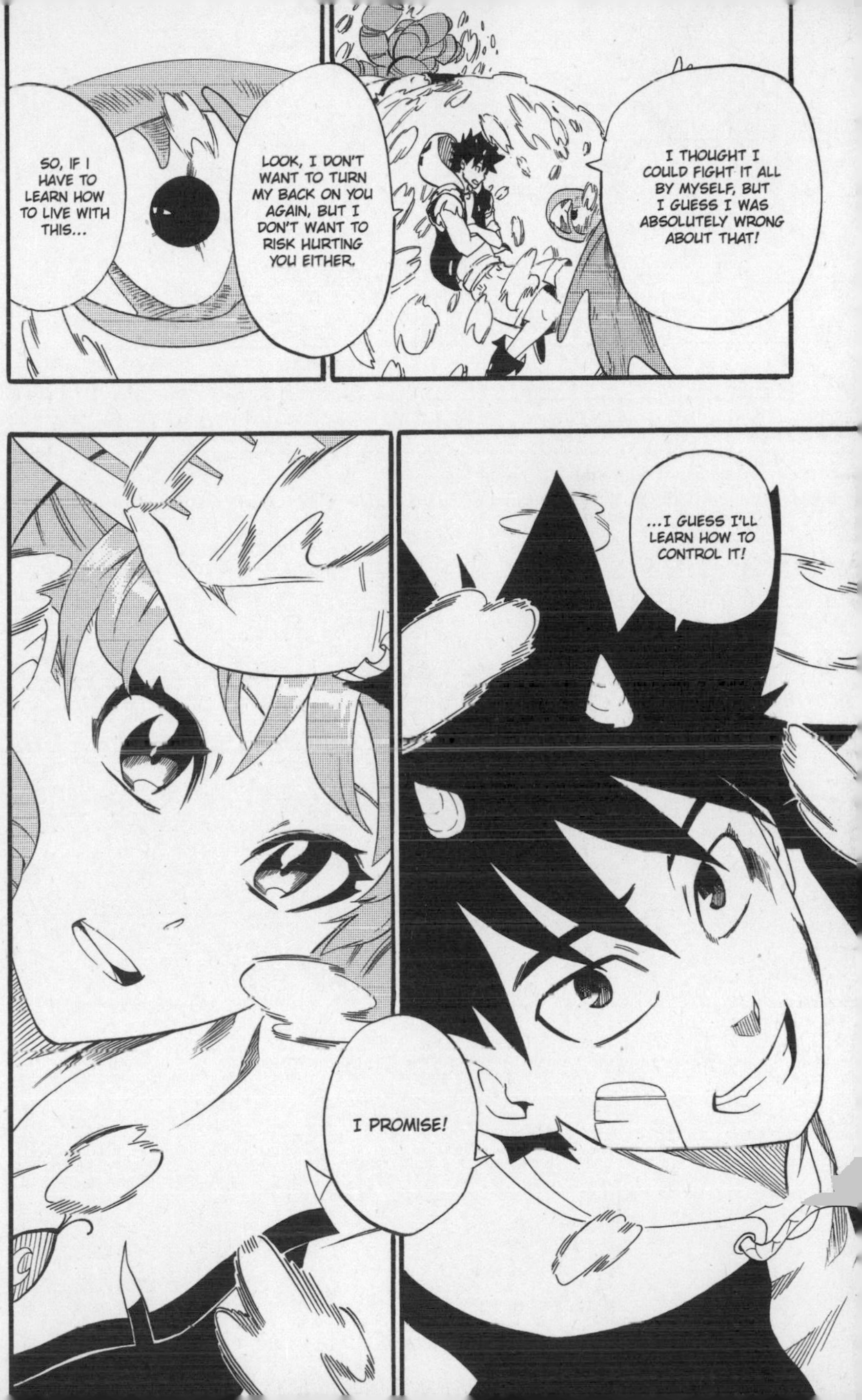
I THOUGHT I COULD FIGHT IT ALL BY MYSELF, BUT I GUESS I WAS ABSOLUTELY WRONG ABOUT THAT!
LOOK, I DON'T WANT TO TURN MY BACK ON YOU AGAIN, BUT I DON'T WANT TO RISK HURTING YOU EITHER.
SO, IF I HAVE TO LEARN HOW TO LIVE WITH THIS...
...I GUESS I'LL LEARN HOW TO CONTROL IT!
I PROMISE!

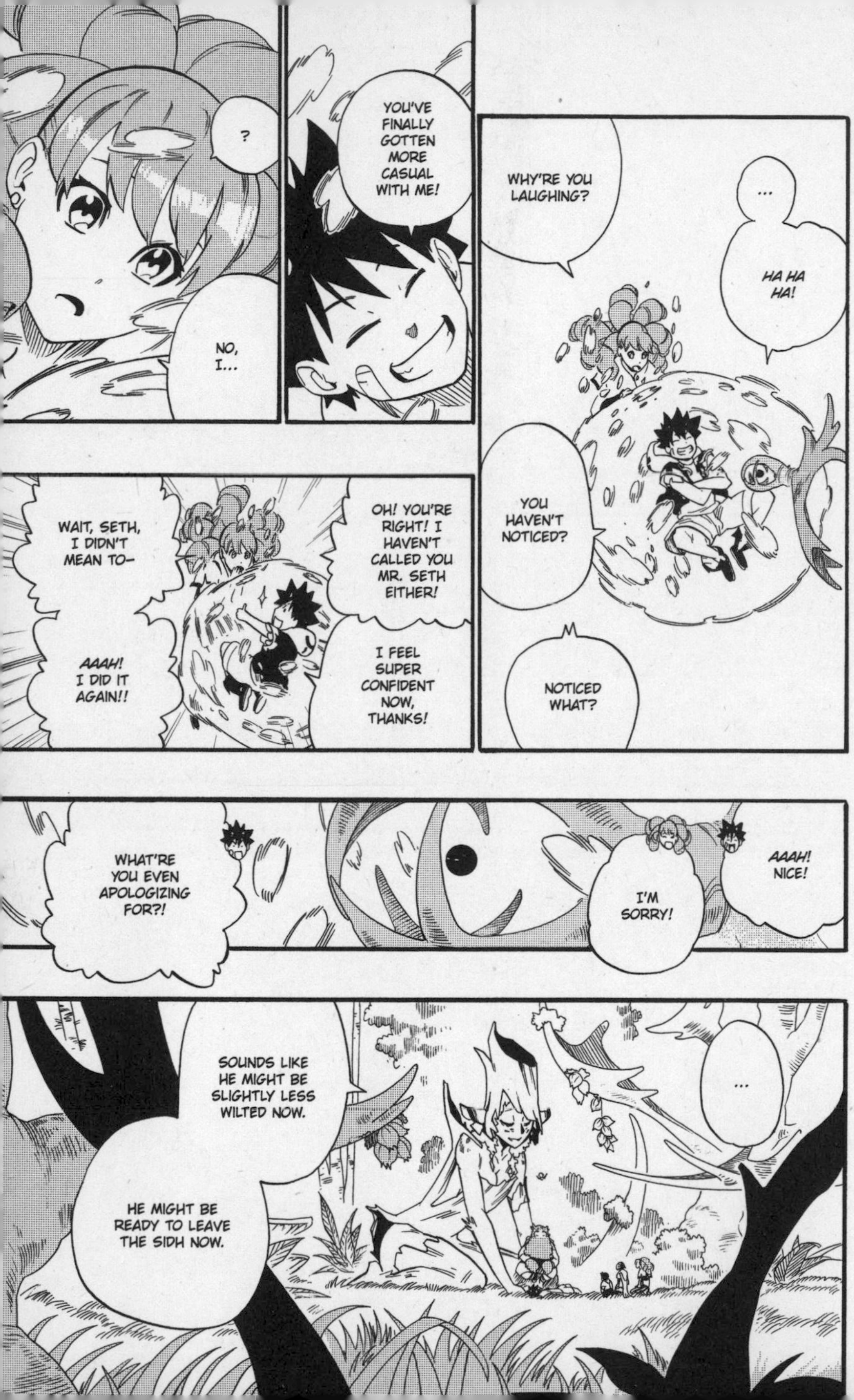
...
HA HA HA!
WHY'RE YOU LAUGHING?
YOU HAVEN'T NOTICED?
NOTICED WHAT?
YOU'VE FINALLY GOTTEN MORE CASUAL WITH ME!
?
NO, I...
OH! YOU'RE RIGHT! I HAVEN'T CALLED YOU MR. SETH EITHER!
I FEEL SUPER CONFIDENT NOW, THANKS!
WAIT, SETH, I DIDN'T MEAN TO-
AAAH! I DID IT AGAIN!!
AAAH! NICE!
I'M SORRY!
WHAT'RE YOU EVEN APOLOGIZING FOR?!
...
SOUNDS LIKE HE MIGHT BE SLIGHTLY LESS WILTED NOW.
HE MIGHT BE READY TO LEAVE THE SIDH NOW.

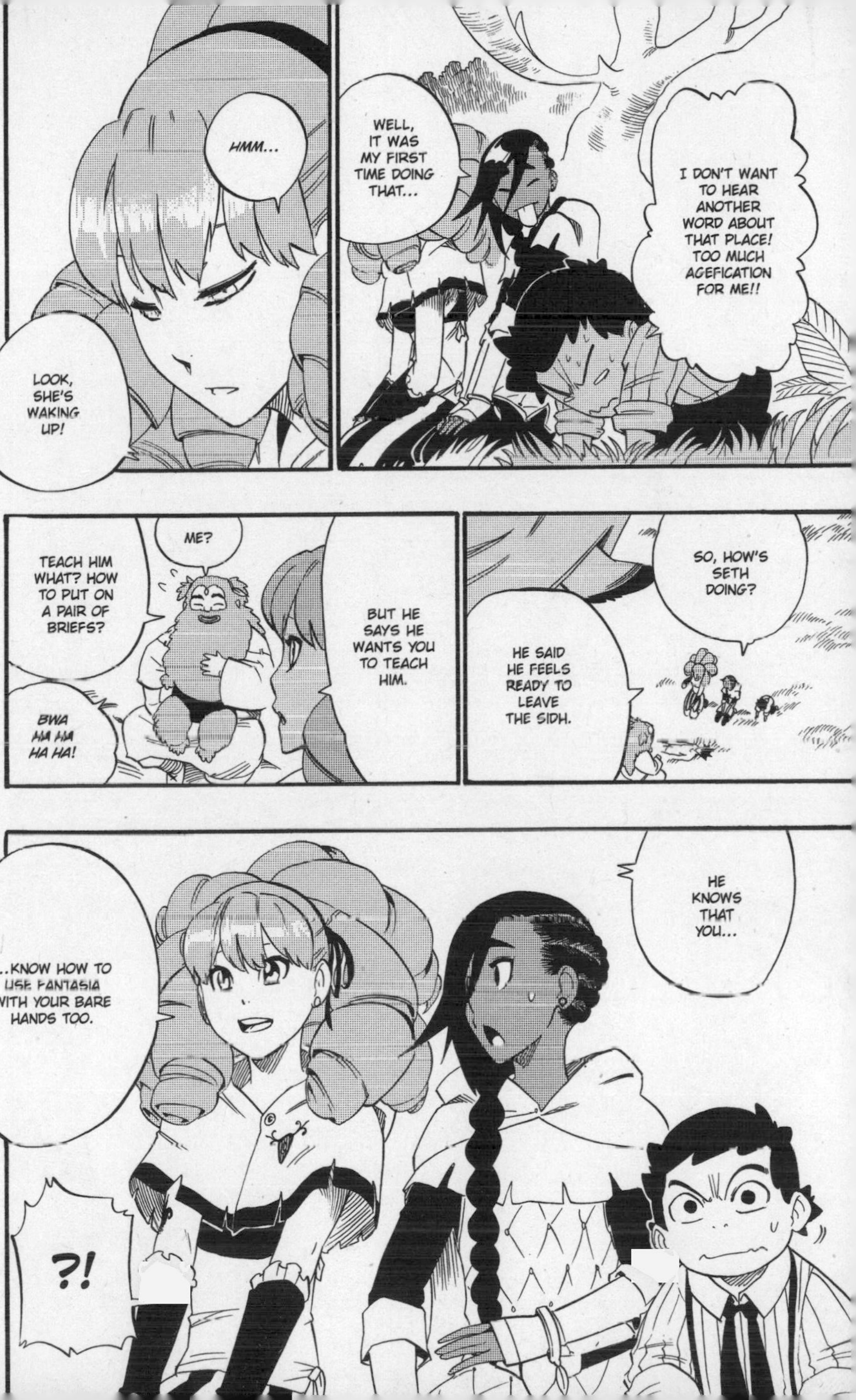
I DON'T WANT TO HEAR ANOTHER WORD ABOUT THAT PLACE! TOO MUCH AGEFICATION FOR ME!!
WELL, IT WAS MY FIRST TIME DOING THAT...
HMM...
LOOK, SHE'S WAKING UP!
SO, HOW'S SETH DOING?
HE SAID HE FEELS READY TO LEAVE THE SIDH.
BUT HE SAYS HE WANTS YOU TO TEACH HIM.
ME?
TEACH HIM WHAT? HOW TO PUT ON A PAIR OF BRIEFS?
BWA HA HA HA HA!
HE KNOWS THAT YOU...
...KNOW HOW TO USE FANTASIA WITH YOUR BARE HANDS TOO.
?!

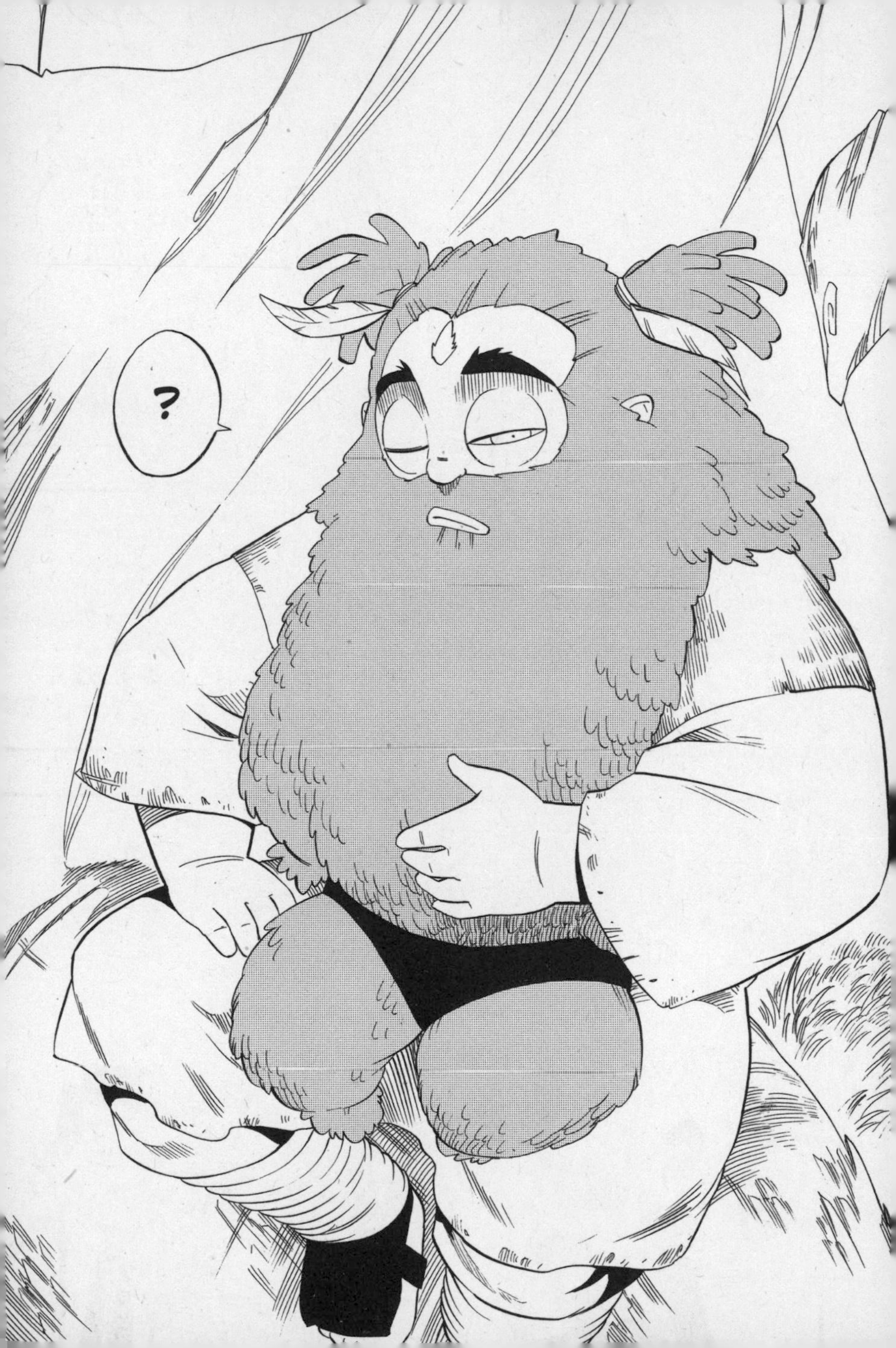
?

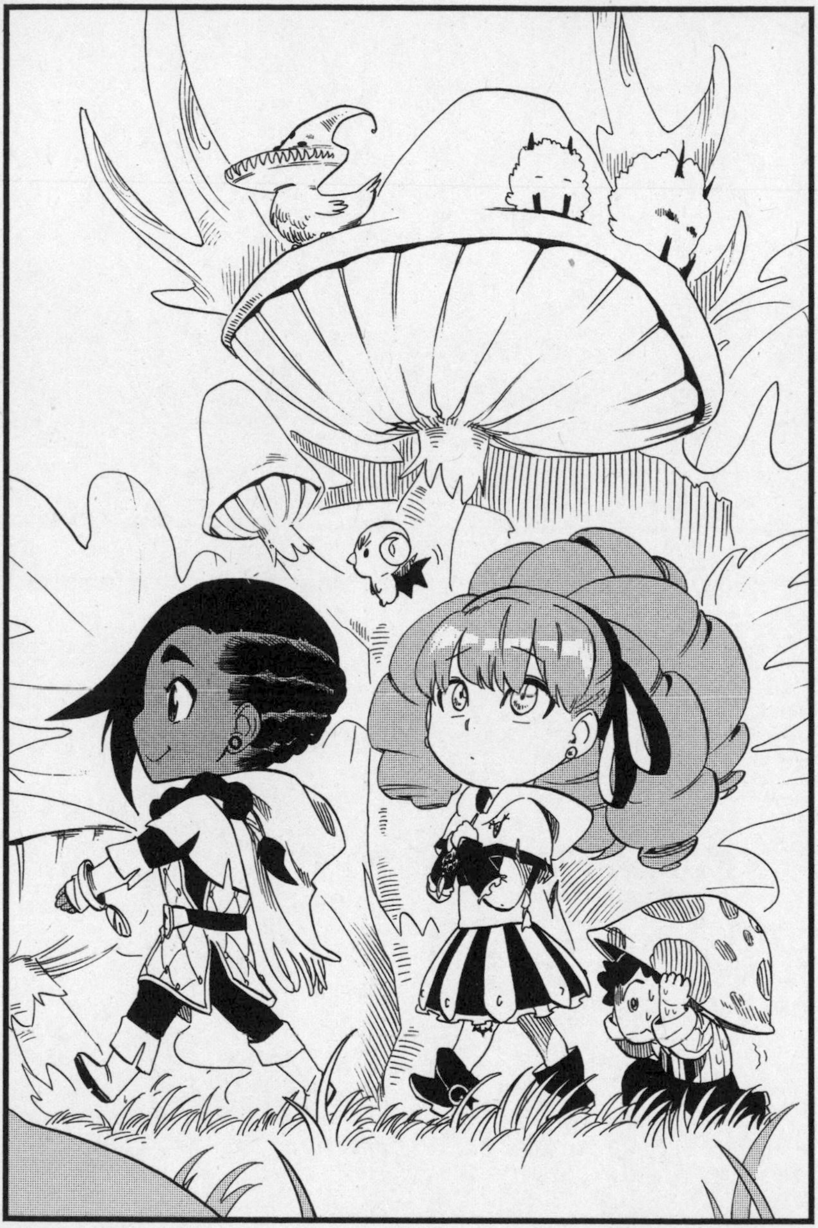

Chapter 43

The Rebel

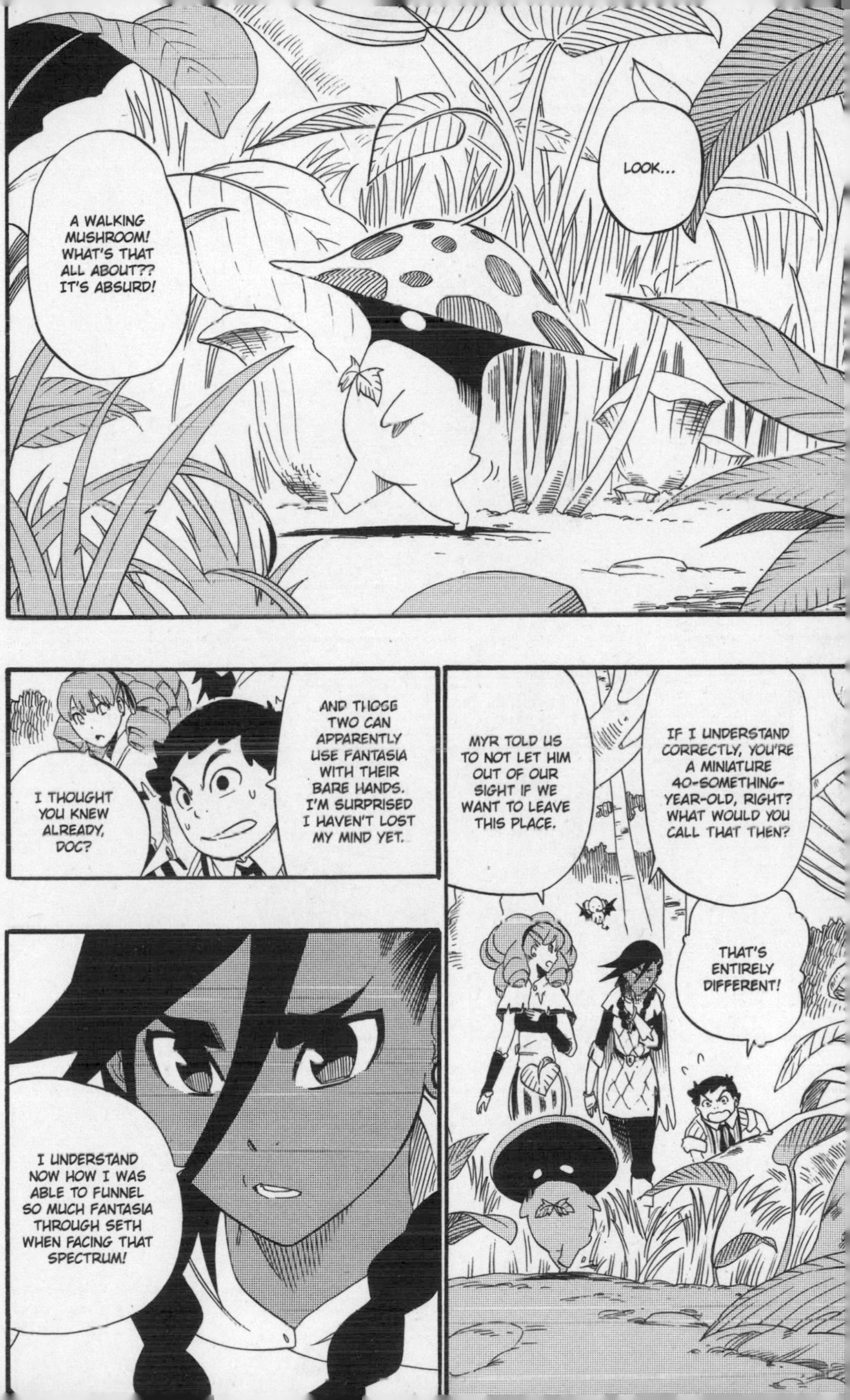
LOOK...
A WALKING MUSHROOM! WHAT'S THAT ALL ABOUT?? IT'S ABSURD!
MYR TOLD US TO NOT LET HIM OUT OF OUR SIGHT IF WE WANT TO LEAVE THIS PLACE.
IF I UNDERSTAND CORRECTLY, YOU'RE A MINIATURE 40-SOMETHING-YEAR-OLD, RIGHT? WHAT WOULD YOU CALL THAT THEN?
THAT'S ENTIRELY DIFFERENT!
AND THOSE TWO CAN APPARENTLY USE FANTASIA WITH THEIR BARE HANDS. I'M SURPRISED I HAVEN'T LOST MY MIND YET.
I THOUGHT YOU KNEW ALREADY, DOC?
I UNDERSTAND NOW HOW I WAS ABLE TO FUNNEL SO MUCH FANTASIA THROUGH SETH WHEN FACING THAT SPECTRUM!

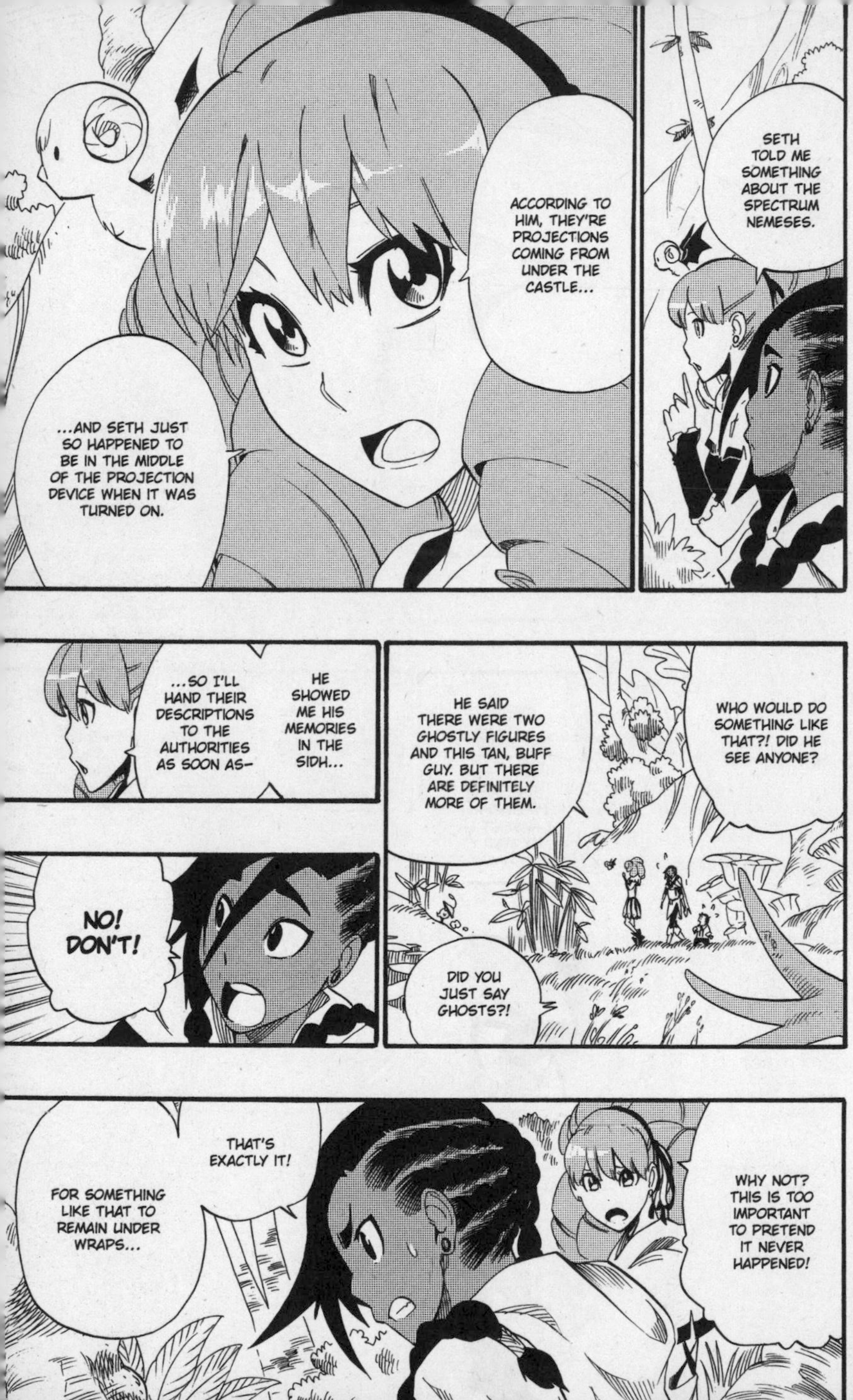
SETH TOLD ME SOMETHING ABOUT THE SPECTRUM NEMESES.
ACCORDING TO HIM, THEY'RE PROJECTIONS COMING FROM UNDER THE CASTLE...
...AND SETH JUST SO HAPPENED TO BE IN THE MIDDLE OF THE PROJECTION DEVICE WHEN IT WAS TURNED ON.
WHO WOULD DO SOMETHING LIKE THAT?! DID HE SEE ANYONE?
HE SAID THERE WERE TWO GHOSTLY FIGURES AND THIS TAN, BUFF GUY. BUT THERE ARE DEFINITELY MORE OF THEM.
DID YOU JUST SAY GHOSTS?!
HE SHOWED ME HIS MEMORIES IN THE SIDH...
...SO I'LL HAND THEIR DESCRIPTIONS TO THE AUTHORITIES AS SOON AS-
NO! DON'T!
WHY NOT? THIS IS TOO IMPORTANT TO PRETEND IT NEVER HAPPENED!
THAT'S EXACTLY IT!
FOR SOMETHING LIKE THAT TO REMAIN UNDER WRAPS...

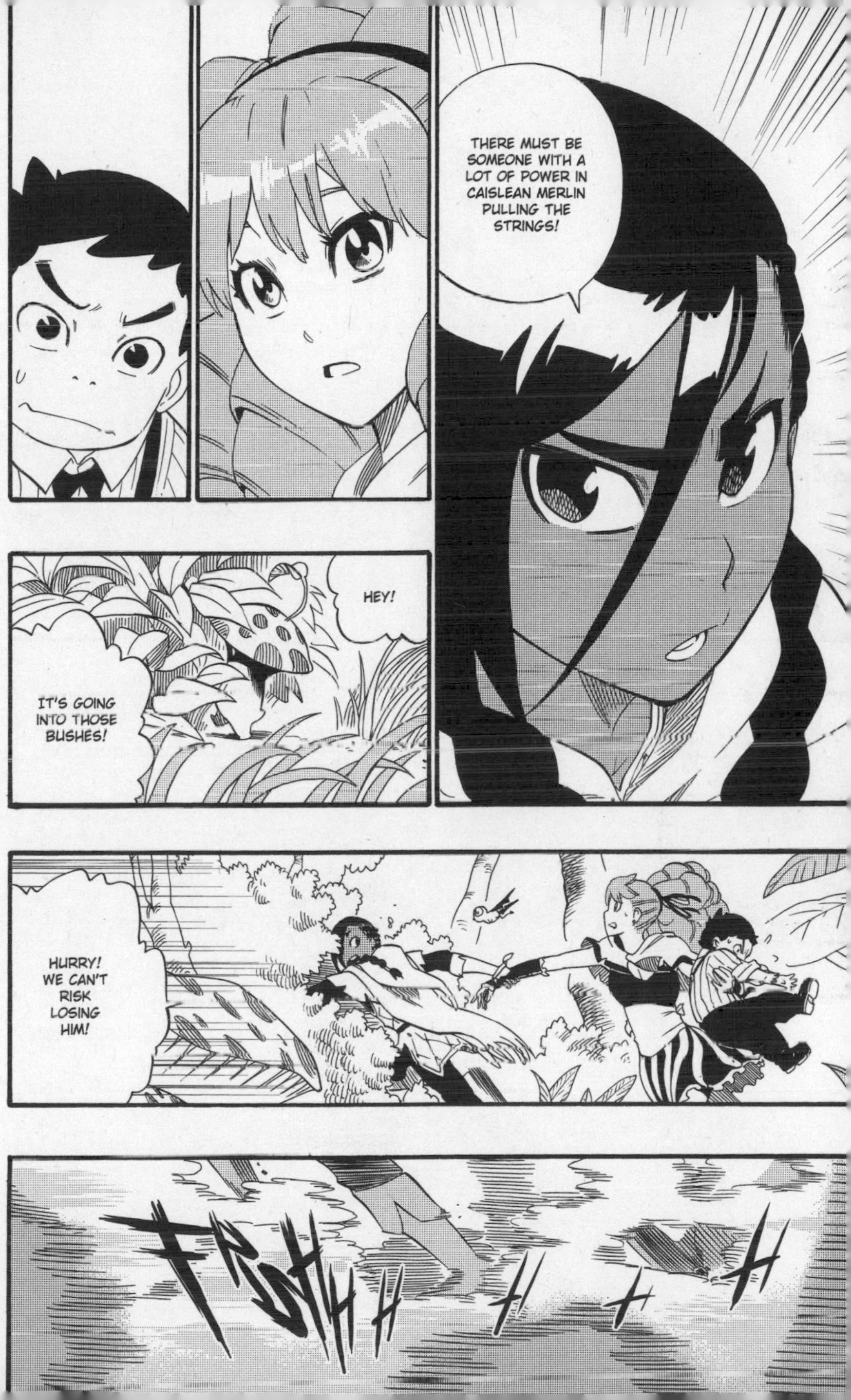
THERE MUST BE SOMEONE WITH A LOT OF POWER IN CAISLEAN MERLIN PULLING THE STRINGS!
HEY!
IT'S GOING INTO THOSE BUSHES!
HURRY! WE CAN'T RISK LOSING HIM!
FRSHHHHH

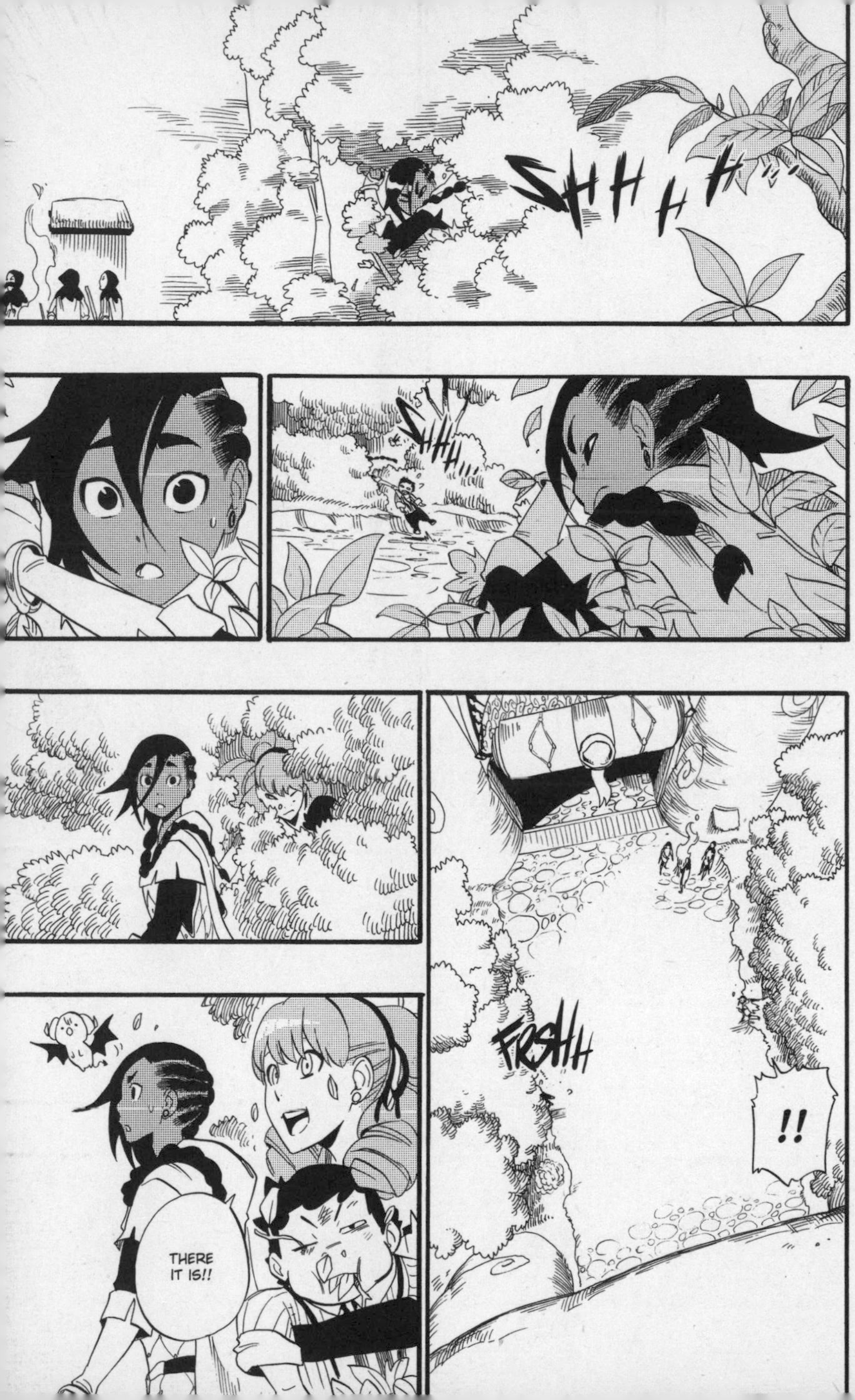
SHHHH
SHHH
!!
FRSHH
THERE IT IS!!

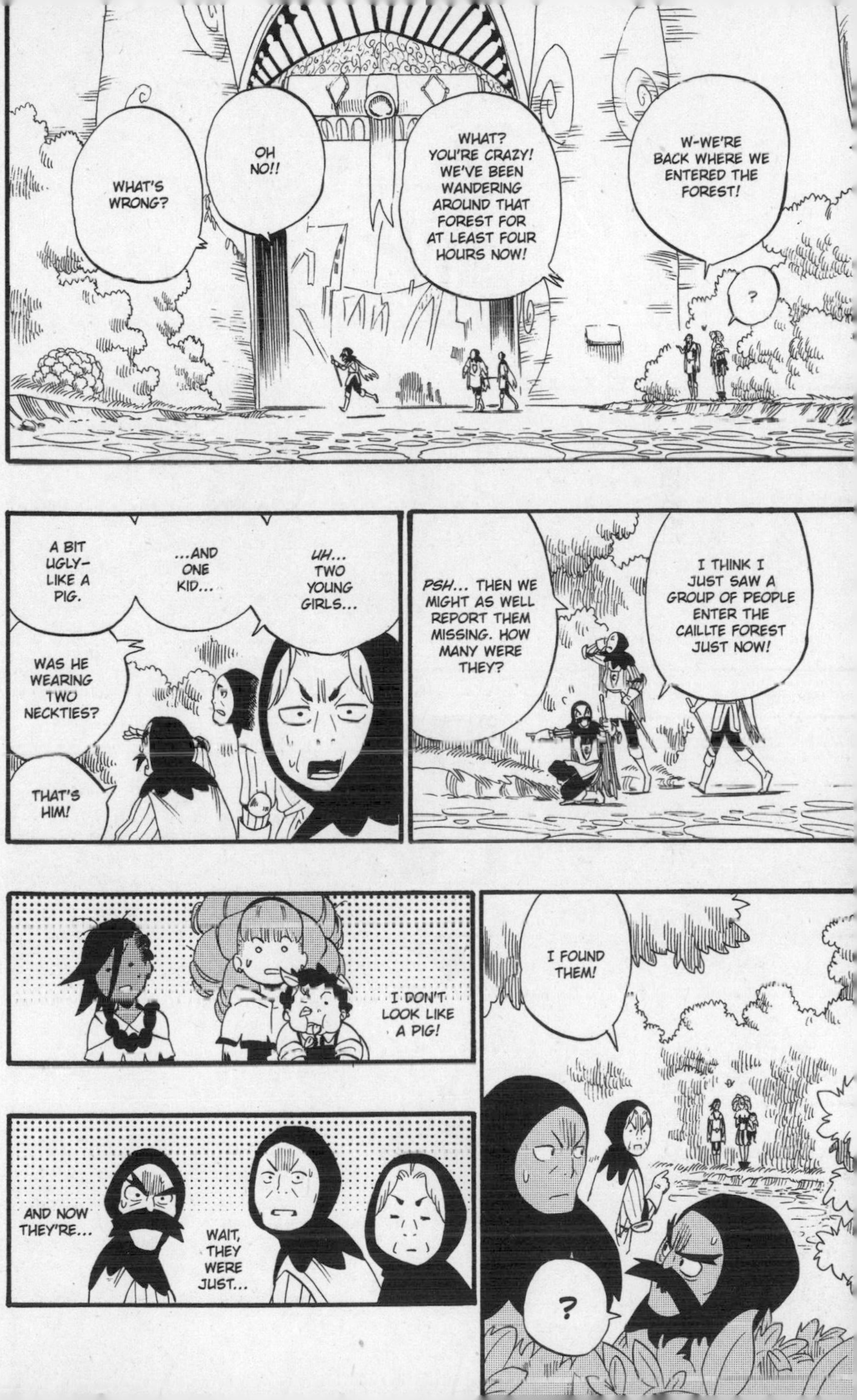
W-WE'RE BACK WHERE WE ENTERED THE FOREST!
?
WHAT? YOU'RE CRAZY! WE'VE BEEN WANDERING AROUND THAT FOREST FOR AT LEAST FOUR HOURS NOW!
OH NO!!
WHAT'S WRONG?
I THINK I JUST SAW A GROUP OF PEOPLE ENTER THE CAILLTE FOREST JUST NOW!
PSH... THEN WE MIGHT AS WELL REPORT THEM MISSING. HOW MANY WERE THEY?
UH... TWO YOUNG GIRLS...
...AND ONE KID...
A BIT UGLY- LIKE A PIG.
WAS HE WEARING TWO NECKTIES?
THAT'S HIM!
I DON'T LOOK LIKE A PIG!
WAIT, THEY WERE JUST...
AND NOW THEY'RE...
I FOUND THEM!
?

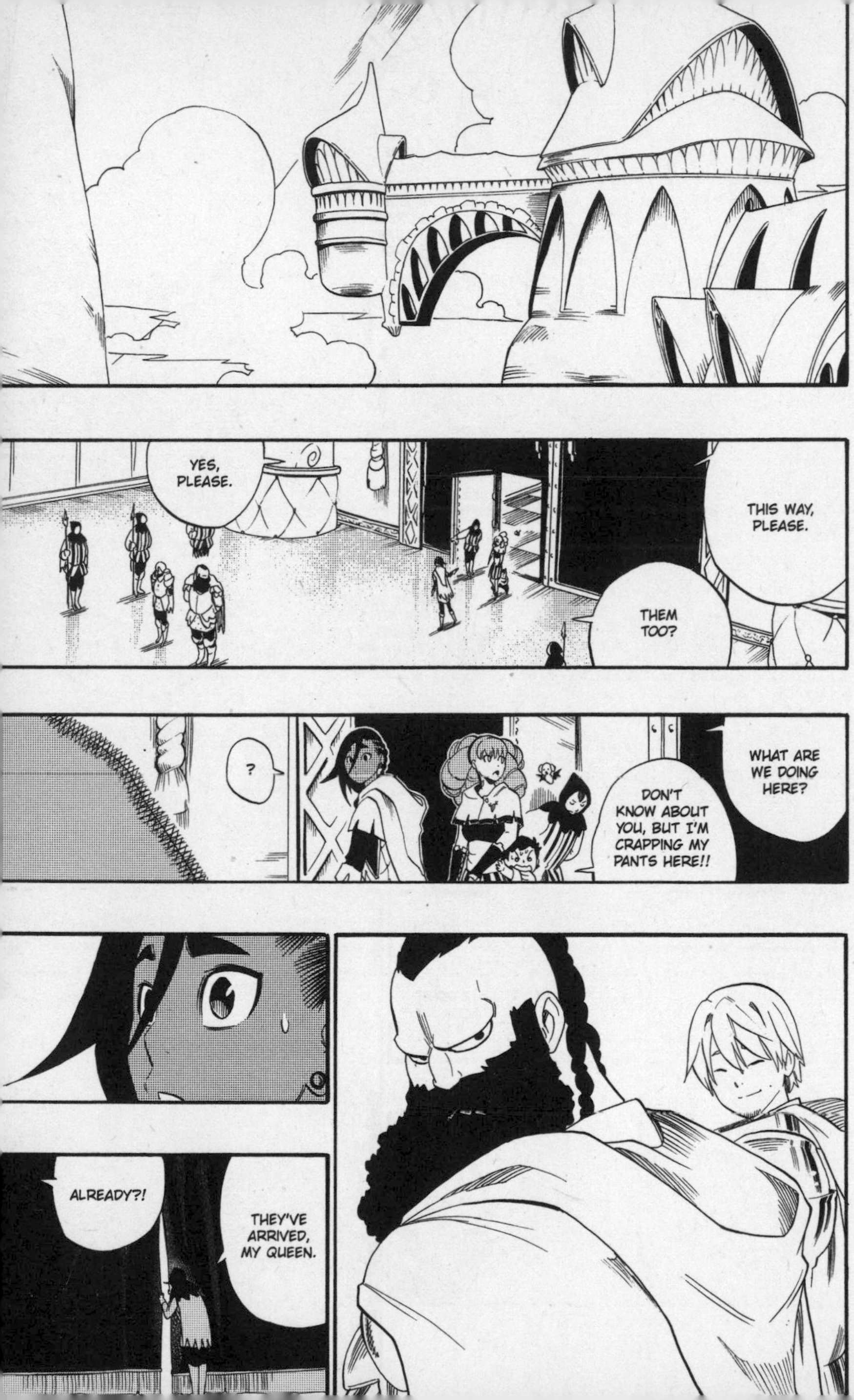
THIS WAY, PLEASE.
THEM TOO?
YES, PLEASE.
WHAT ARE WE DOING HERE?
DON'T KNOW ABOUT YOU, BUT I'M CRAPPING MY PANTS HERE!!
?
THEY'VE ARRIVED, MY QUEEN.
ALREADY?!

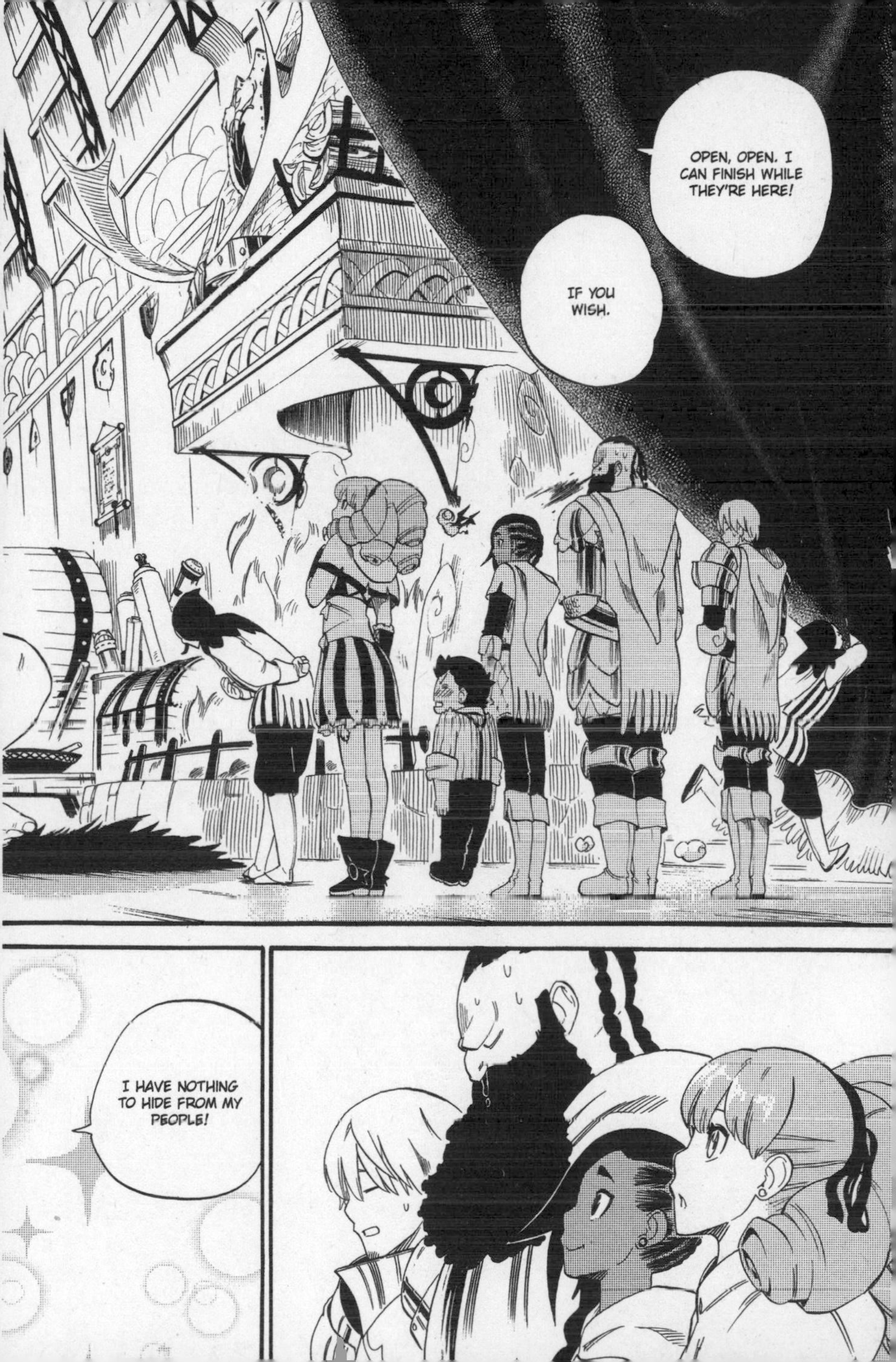
OPEN, OPEN. I CAN FINISH WHILE THEY'RE HERE!
IF YOU WISH.
I HAVE NOTHING TO HIDE FROM MY PEOPLE!

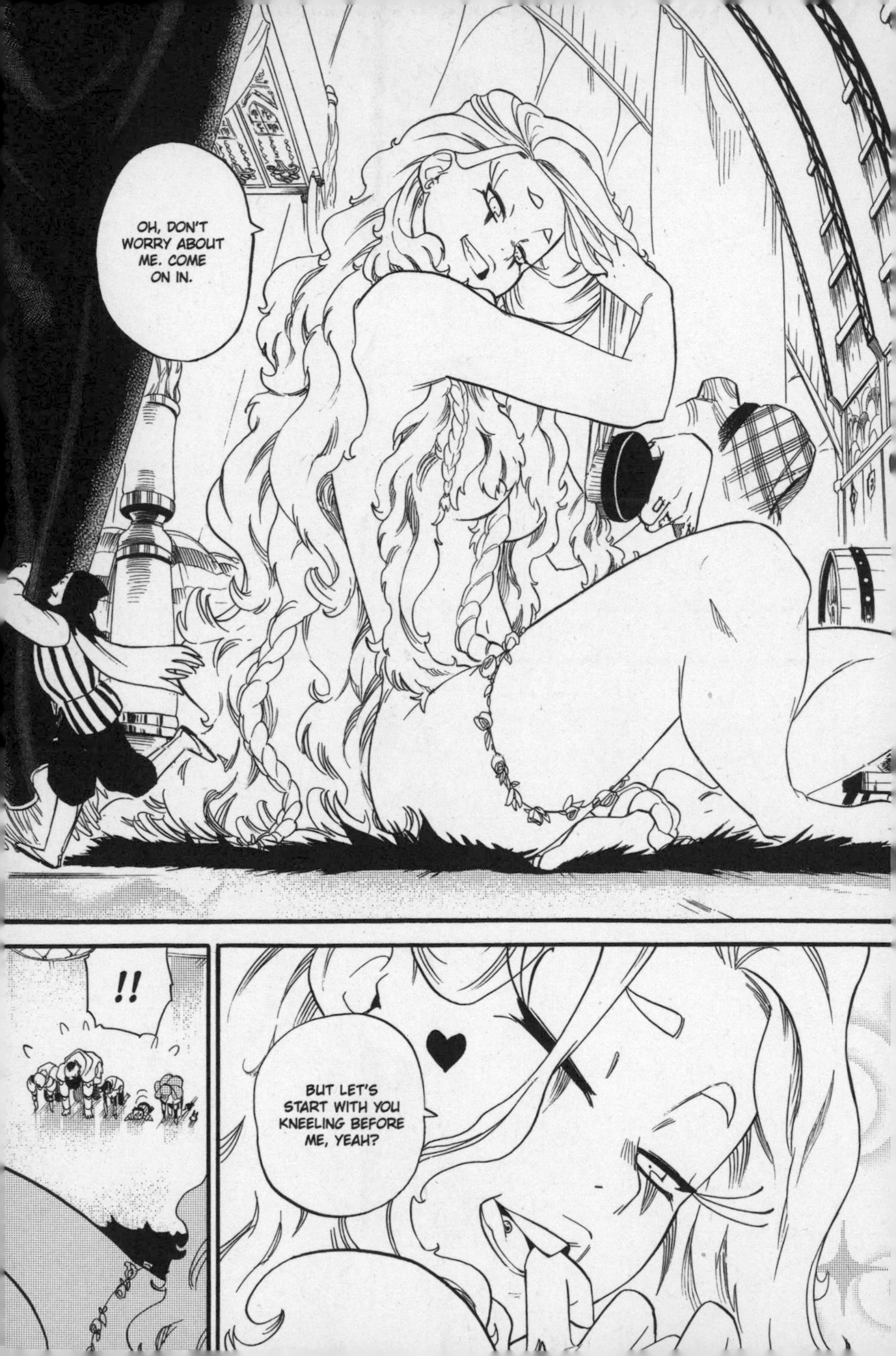
OH, DON'T WORRY ABOUT ME. COME ON IN.
BUT LET'S START WITH YOU KNEELING BEFORE ME, YEAH?
!!

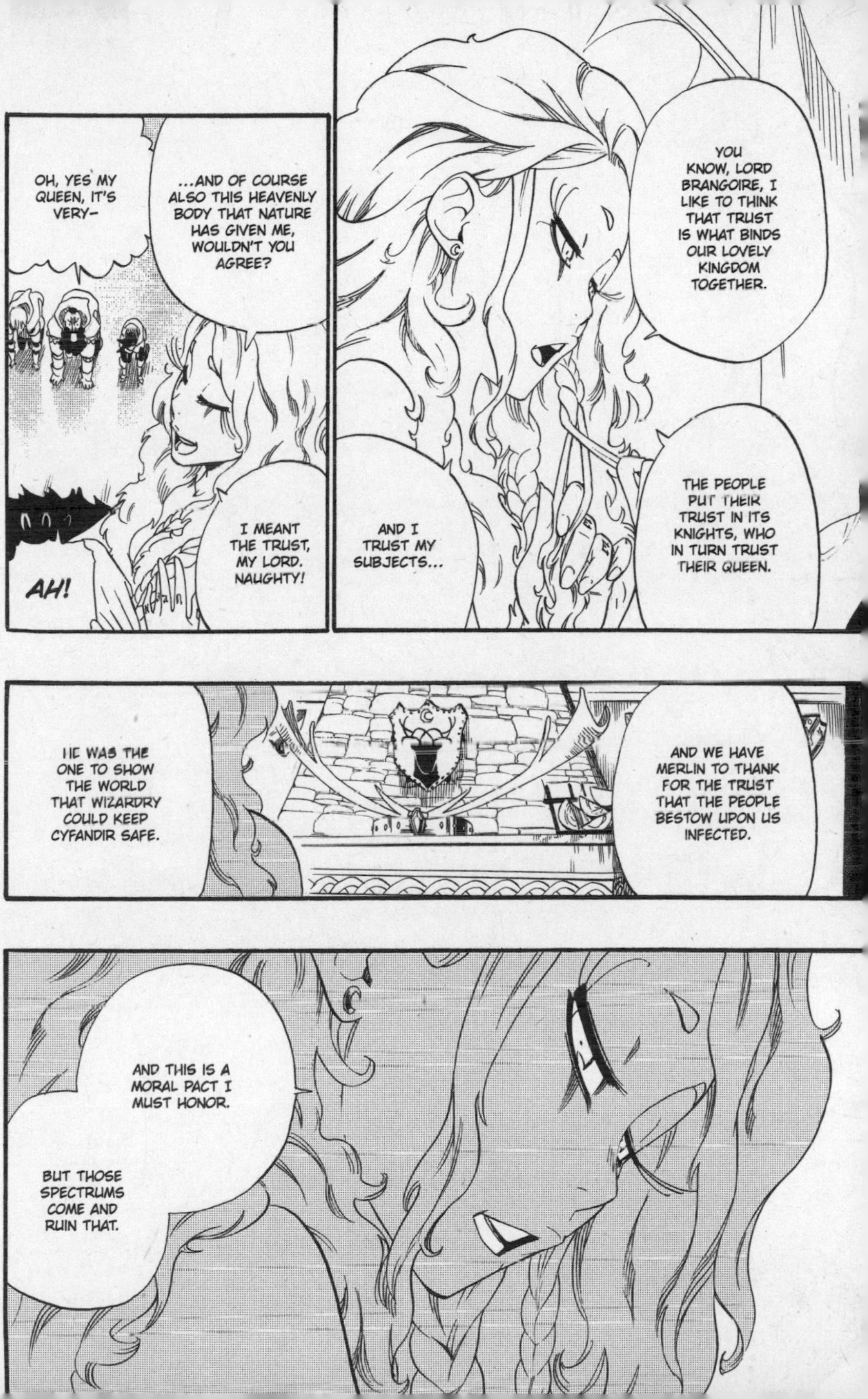
YOU KNOW, LORD BRANGOIRE, I LIKE TO THINK THAT TRUST IS WHAT BINDS OUR LOVELY KINGDOM TOGETHER.
THE PEOPLE PUT THEIR TRUST IN ITS KNIGHTS, WHO IN TURN TRUST THEIR QUEEN.
AND I TRUST MY SUBJECTS...
...AND OF COURSE ALSO THIS HEAVENLY BODY THAT NATURE HAS GIVEN ME, WOULDN'T YOU AGREE?
OH, YES MY QUEEN, IT'S VERY-
I MEANT THE TRUST, MY LORD. NAUGHTY!
AH!
AND WE HAVE MERLIN TO THANK FOR THE TRUST THAT THE PEOPLE BESTOW UPON US INFECTED.
HE WAS THE ONE TO SHOW THE WORLD THAT WIZARDRY COULD KEEP CYFANDIR SAFE.
AND THIS IS A MORAL PACT I MUST HONOR.
BUT THOSE SPECTRUMS COME AND RUIN THAT.

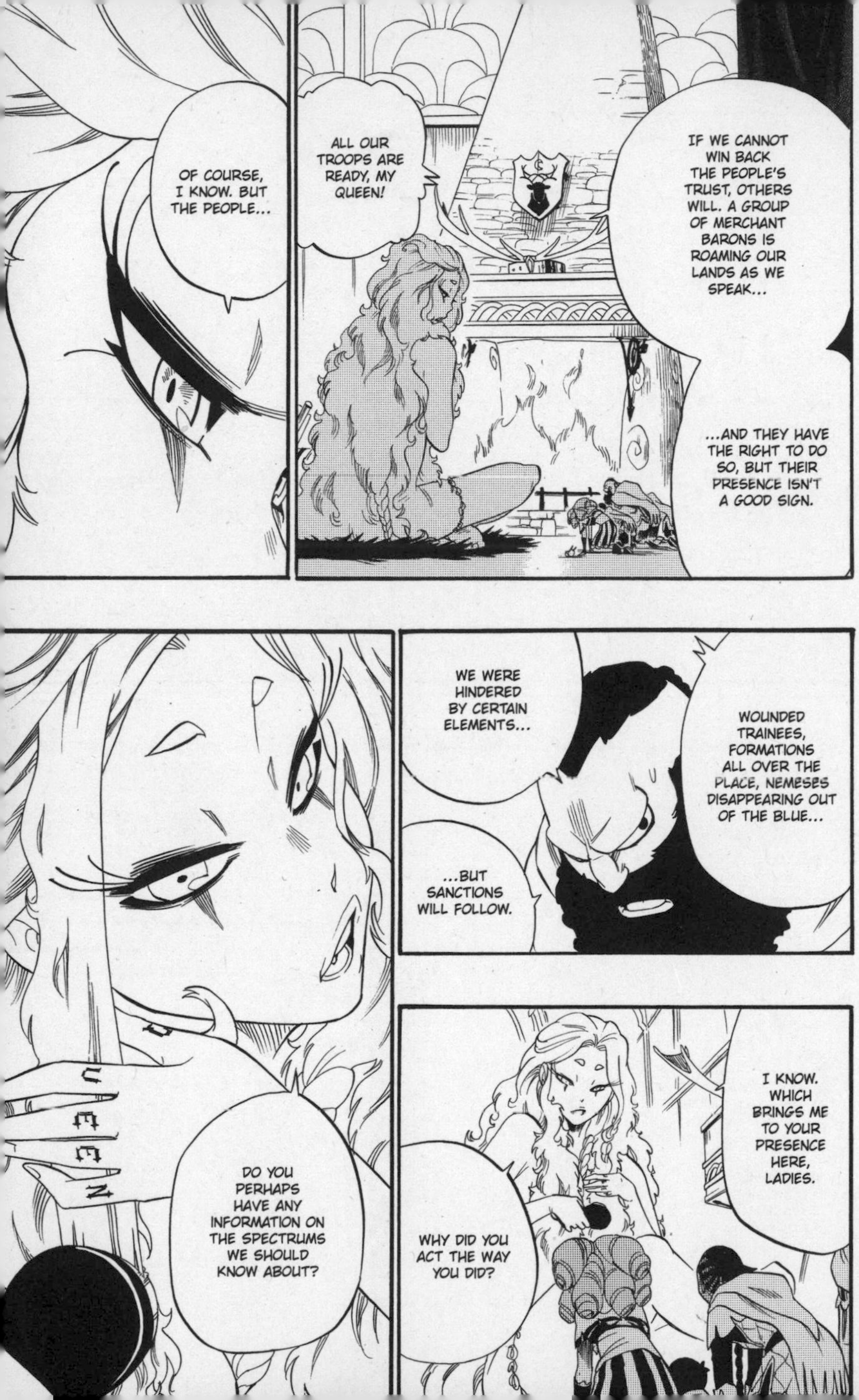
IF WE CANNOT WIN BACK THE PEOPLE'S TRUST, OTHERS WILL. A GROUP OF MERCHANT BARONS IS ROAMING OUR LANDS AS WE SPEAK...
...AND THEY HAVE THE RIGHT TO DO SO, BUT THEIR PRESENCE ISN'T A GOOD SIGN.
ALL OUR TROOPS ARE READY, MY QUEEN!
OF COURSE, I KNOW. BUT THE PEOPLE...
WE WERE HINDERED BY CERTAIN ELEMENTS...
WOUNDED TRAINEES, FORMATIONS ALL OVER THE PLACE, NEMESES DISAPPEARING OUT OF THE BLUE...
...BUT SANCTIONS WILL FOLLOW.
I KNOW. WHICH BRINGS ME TO YOUR PRESENCE HERE, LADIES.
WHY DID YOU ACT THE WAY YOU DID?
DO YOU PERHAPS HAVE ANY INFORMATION ON THE SPECTRUMS WE SHOULD KNOW ABOUT?
QUEEN

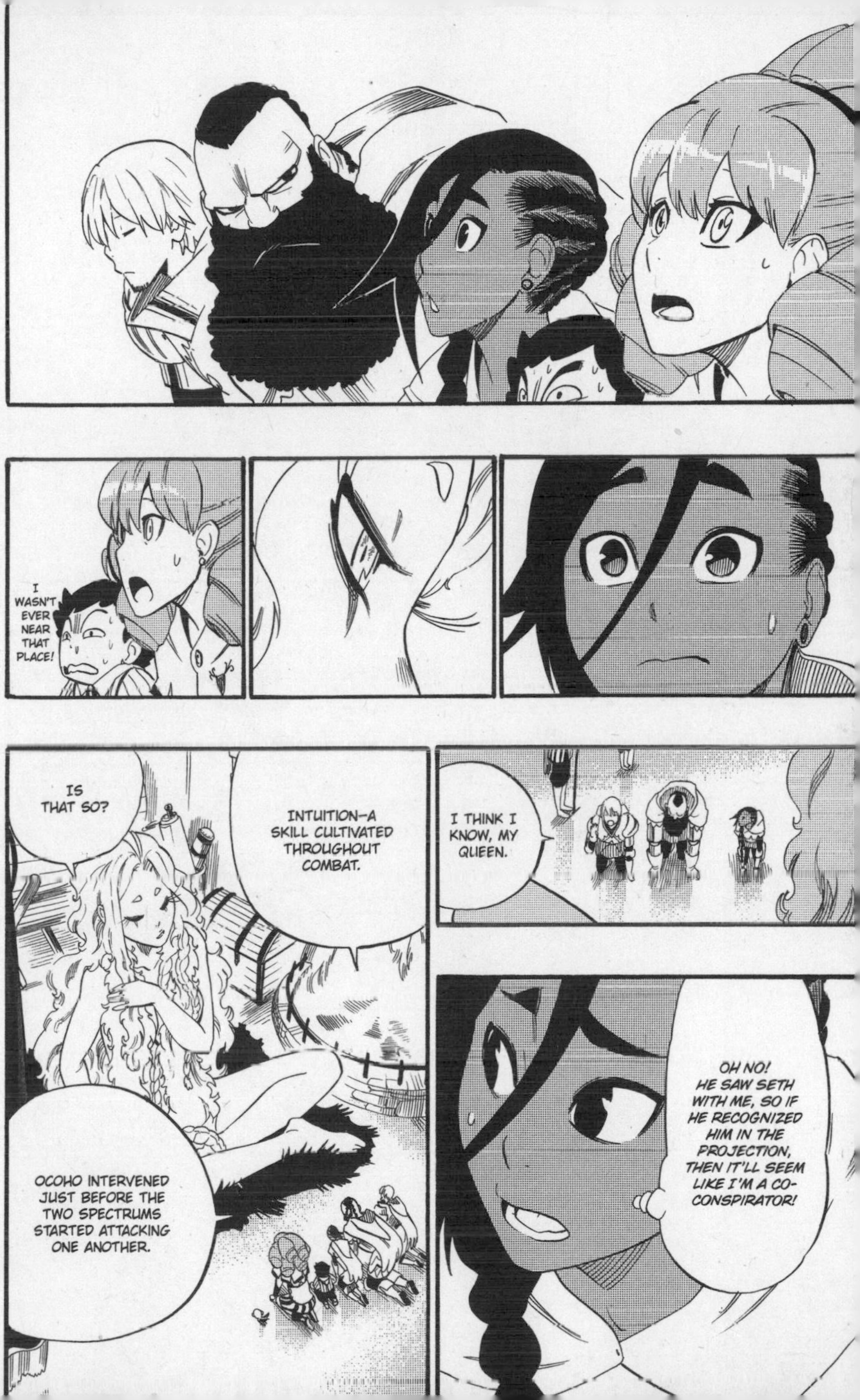
I WASN'T EVER NEAR THAT PLACE!
I THINK I KNOW, MY QUEEN.
OH NO! HE SAW SETH WITH ME, SO IF HE RECOGNIZED HIM IN THE PROJECTION, THEN IT'LL SEEM LIKE I'M A CO-CONSPIRATOR!
INTUITION—A SKILL CULTIVATED THROUGHOUT COMBAT.
IS THAT SO?
OCOHO INTERVENED JUST BEFORE THE TWO SPECTRUMS STARTED ATTACKING ONE ANOTHER.

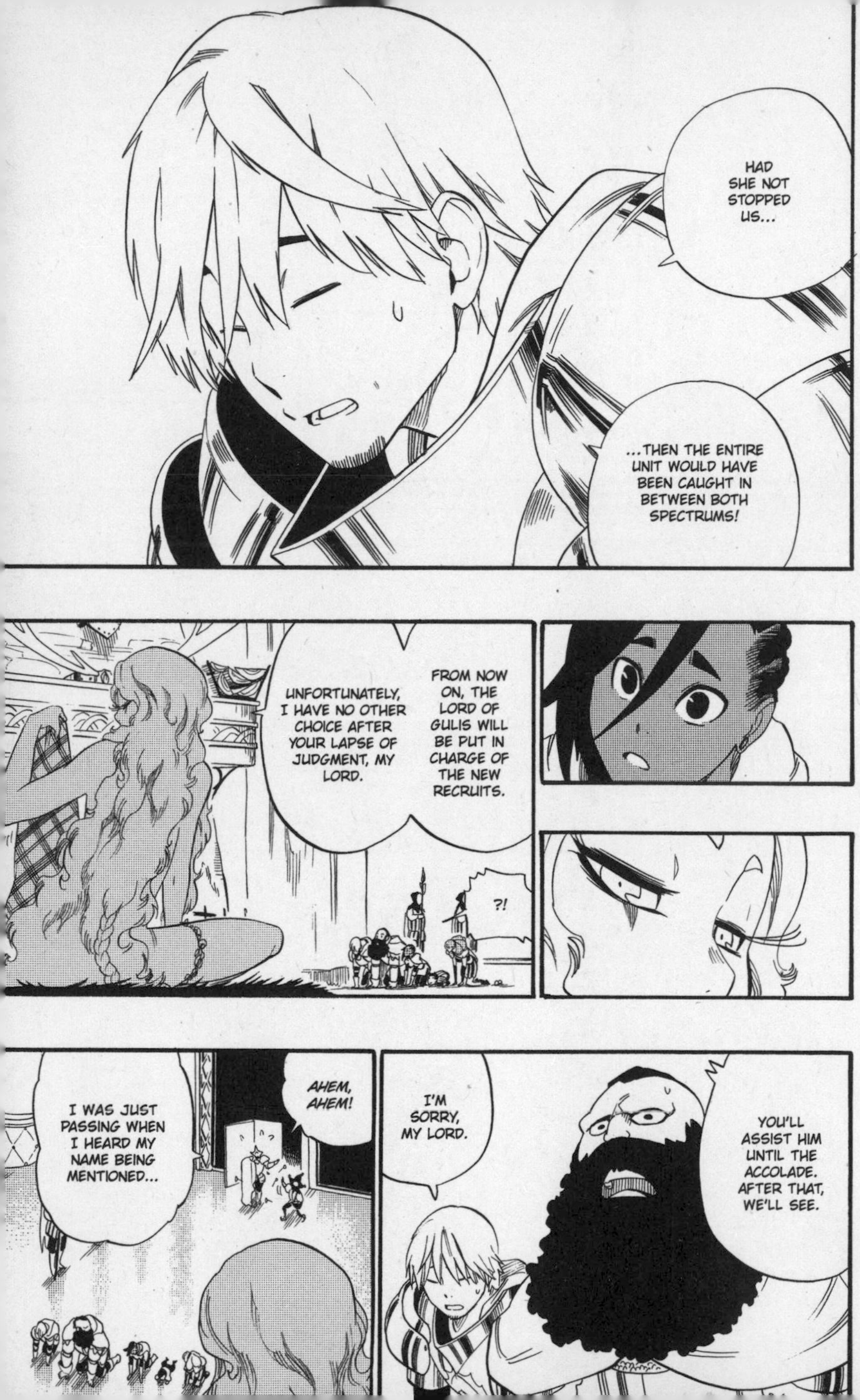
HAD SHE NOT STOPPED US...
...THEN THE ENTIRE UNIT WOULD HAVE BEEN CAUGHT IN BETWEEN BOTH SPECTRUMS!
FROM NOW ON, THE LORD OF GULIS WILL BE PUT IN CHARGE OF THE NEW RECRUITS.
UNFORTUNATELY, I HAVE NO OTHER CHOICE AFTER YOUR LAPSE OF JUDGMENT, MY LORD.
?!
YOU'LL ASSIST HIM UNTIL THE ACCOLADE. AFTER THAT, WE'LL SEE.
I'M SORRY, MY LORD.
AHEM, AHEM!
I WAS JUST PASSING WHEN I HEARD MY NAME BEING MENTIONED...

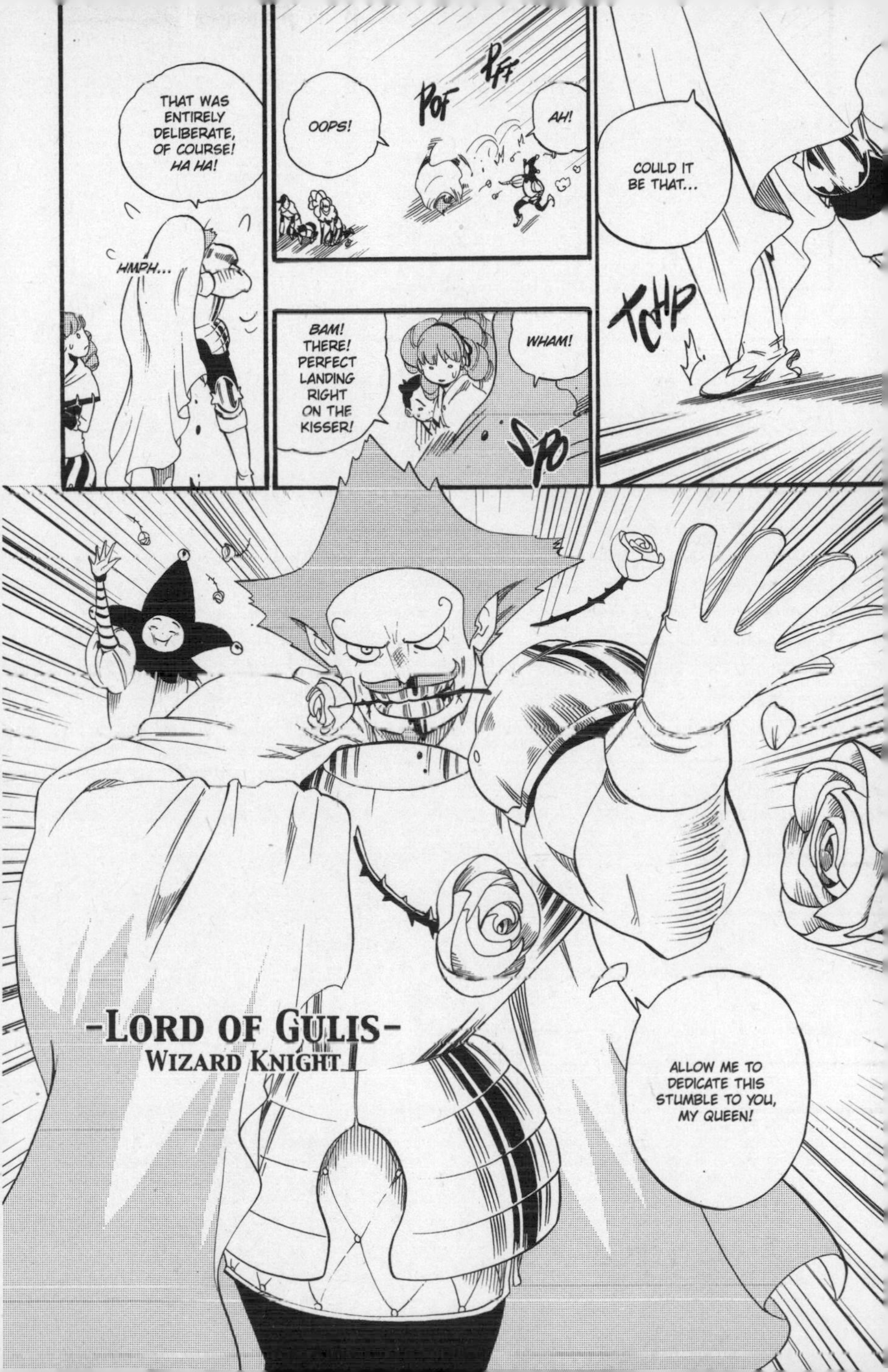
COULD IT BE THAT...
TCHP
PFF
AH!
POF
OOPS!
WHAM!
BAM! THERE! PERFECT LANDING RIGHT ON THE KISSER!
SPO
THAT WAS ENTIRELY DELIBERATE, OF COURSE! HA HA!
HMPH...
ALLOW ME TO DEDICATE THIS STUMBLE TO YOU, MY QUEEN!
-LORD OF GULIS-
WIZARD KNIGHT

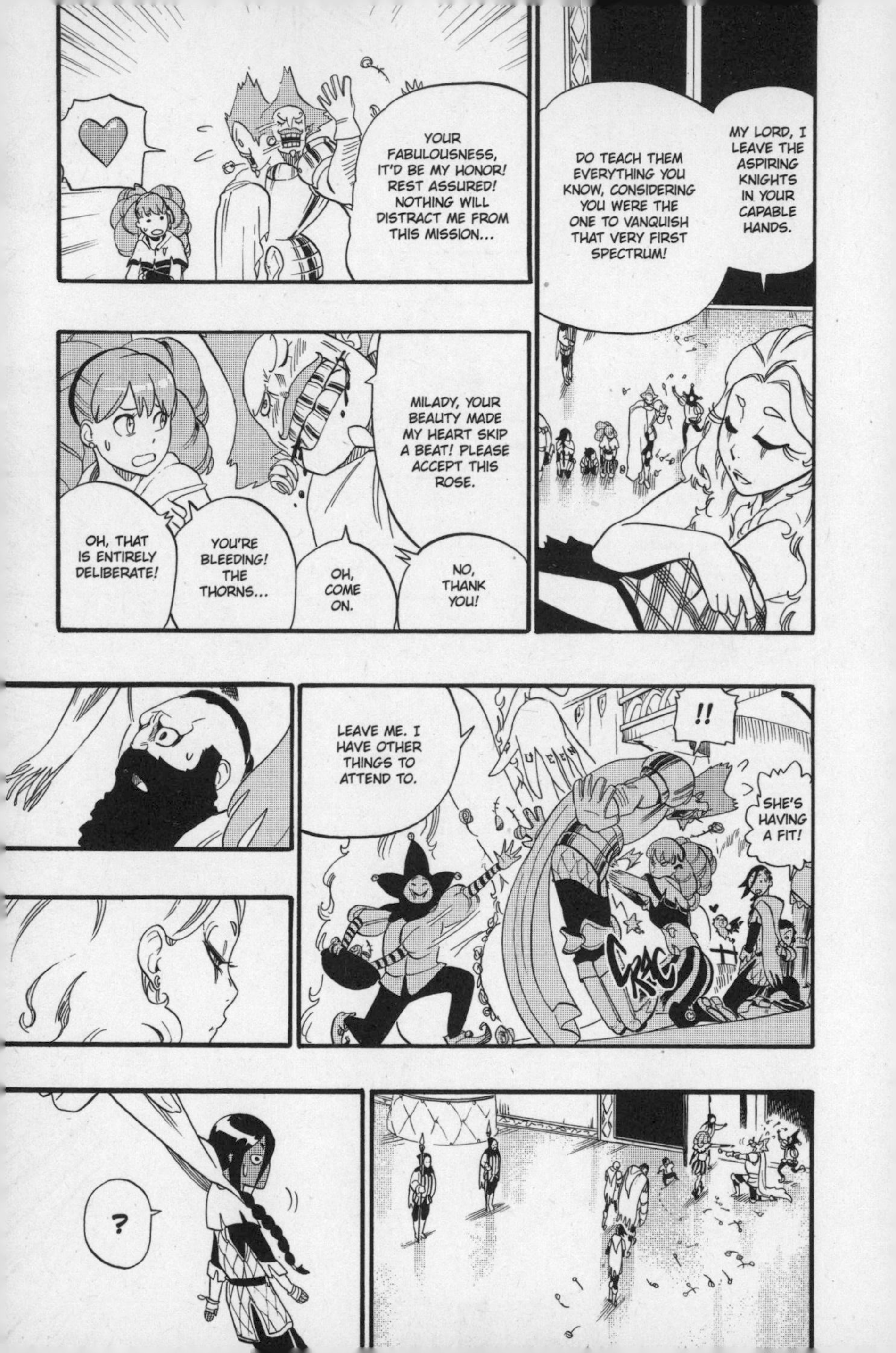
MY LORD, I LEAVE THE ASPIRING KNIGHTS IN YOUR CAPABLE HANDS.
DO TEACH THEM EVERYTHING YOU KNOW, CONSIDERING YOU WERE THE ONE TO VANQUISH THAT VERY FIRST SPECTRUM!
YOUR FABULOUSNESS, IT'D BE MY HONOR! REST ASSURED! NOTHING WILL DISTRACT ME FROM THIS MISSION...
MILADY, YOUR BEAUTY MADE MY HEART SKIP A BEAT! PLEASE ACCEPT THIS ROSE.
NO, THANK YOU!
OH, COME ON.
YOU'RE BLEEDING! THE THORNS...
OH, THAT IS ENTIRELY DELIBERATE!
!!
SHE'S HAVING A FIT!
LEAVE ME. I HAVE OTHER THINGS TO ATTEND TO.
CRAC
?

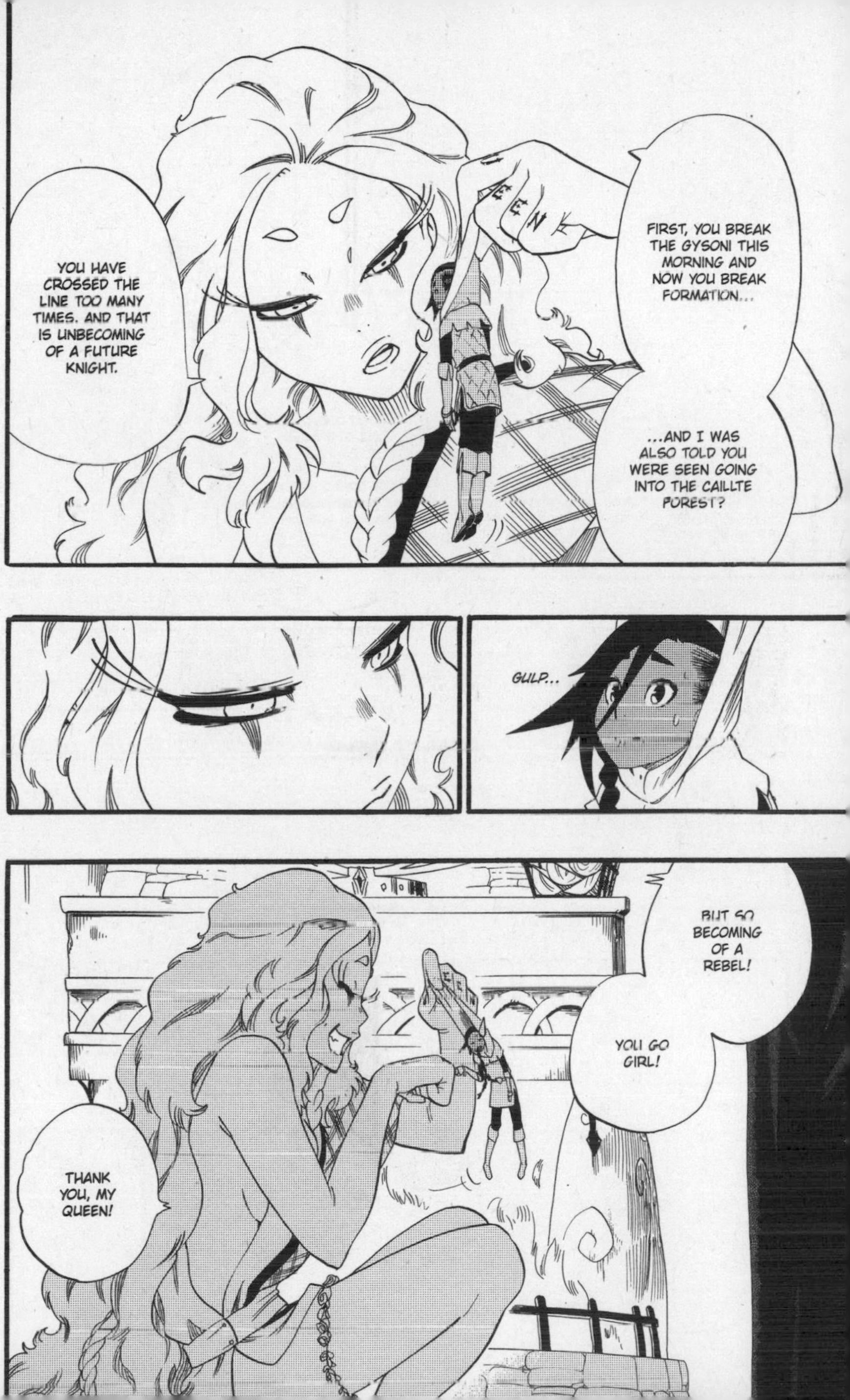
FIRST, YOU BREAK THE GYSONI THIS MORNING AND NOW YOU BREAK FORMATION...
...AND I WAS ALSO TOLD YOU WERE SEEN GOING INTO THE CAILLTE FOREST?
YOU HAVE CROSSED THE LINE TOO MANY TIMES. AND THAT IS UNBECOMING OF A FUTURE KNIGHT.
GULP...
BUT SO BECOMING OF A REBEL!
YOU GO GIRL!
THANK YOU, MY QUEEN!

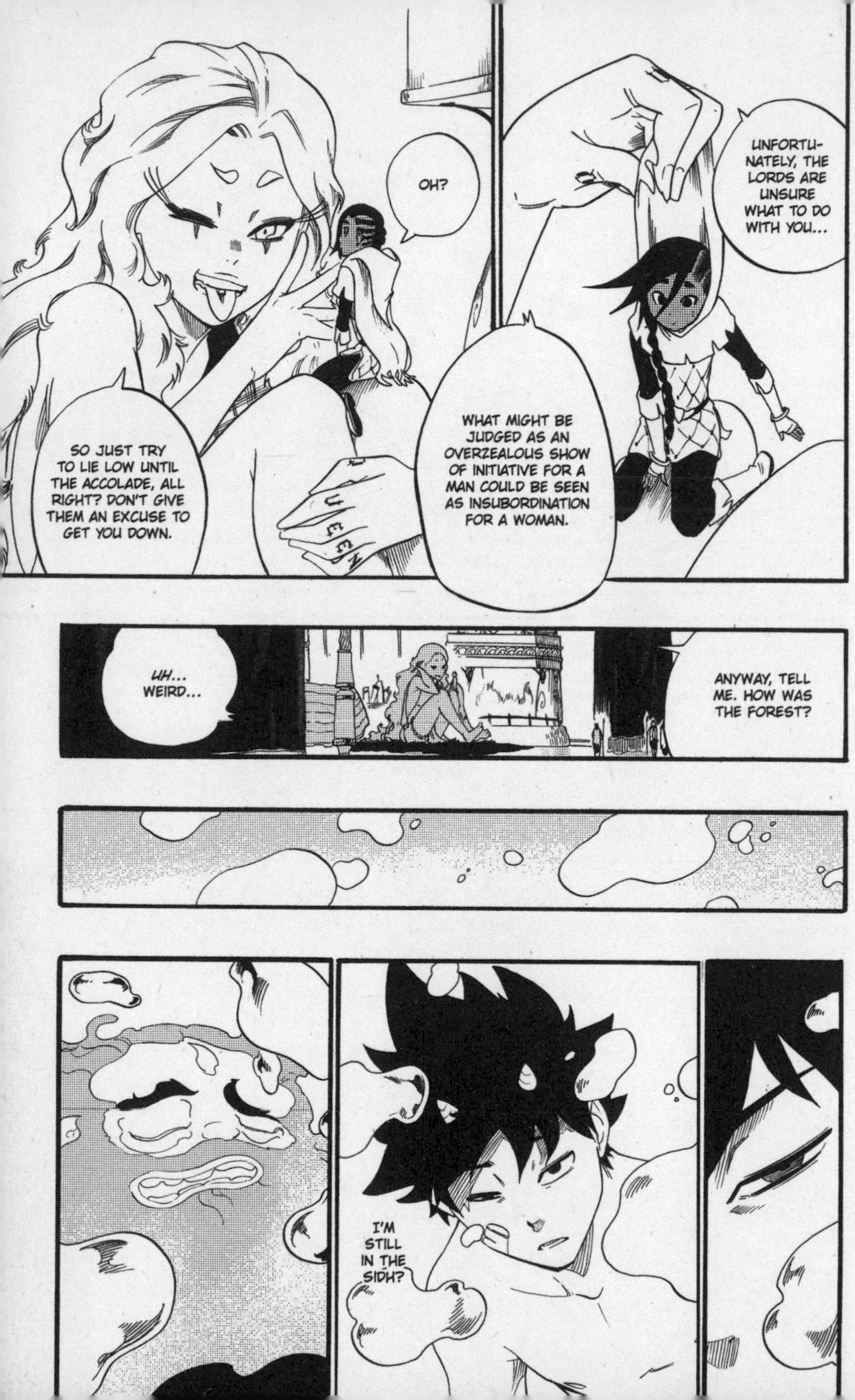
UNFORTUNATELY, THE LORDS ARE UNSURE WHAT TO DO WITH YOU...
WHAT MIGHT BE JUDGED AS AN OVERZEALOUS SHOW OF INITIATIVE FOR A MAN COULD BE SEEN AS INSUBORDINATION FOR A WOMAN.
OH?
SO JUST TRY TO LIE LOW UNTIL THE ACCOLADE, ALL RIGHT? DON'T GIVE THEM AN EXCUSE TO GET YOU DOWN.
QUEEN
ANYWAY, TELL ME. HOW WAS THE FOREST?
UH... WEIRD...
I'M STILL IN THE SIDH?

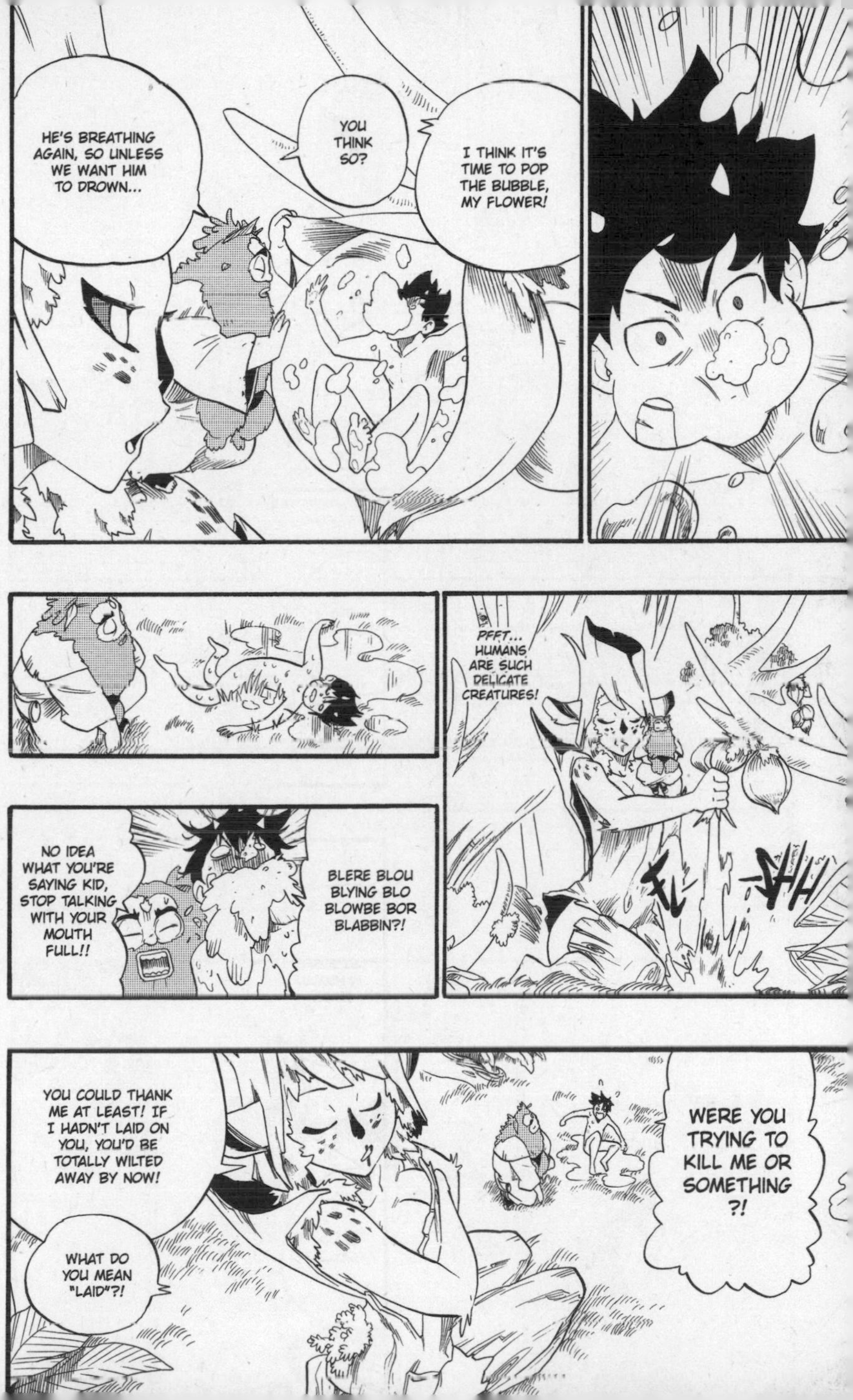
I THINK IT'S TIME TO POP THE BUBBLE, MY FLOWER!
YOU THINK SO?
HE'S BREATHING AGAIN, SO UNLESS WE WANT HIM TO DROWN...
PFFT... HUMANS ARE SUCH DELICATE CREATURES!
BLERE BLOU BLYING BLO BLOWBE BOR BLABBIN?!
NO IDEA WHAT YOU'RE SAYING KID, STOP TALKING WITH YOUR MOUTH FULL!!
WERE YOU TRYING TO KILL ME OR SOMETHING?!
YOU COULD THANK ME AT LEAST! IF I HADN'T LAID ON YOU, YOU'D BE TOTALLY WILTED AWAY BY NOW!
WHAT DO YOU MEAN "LAID"?!

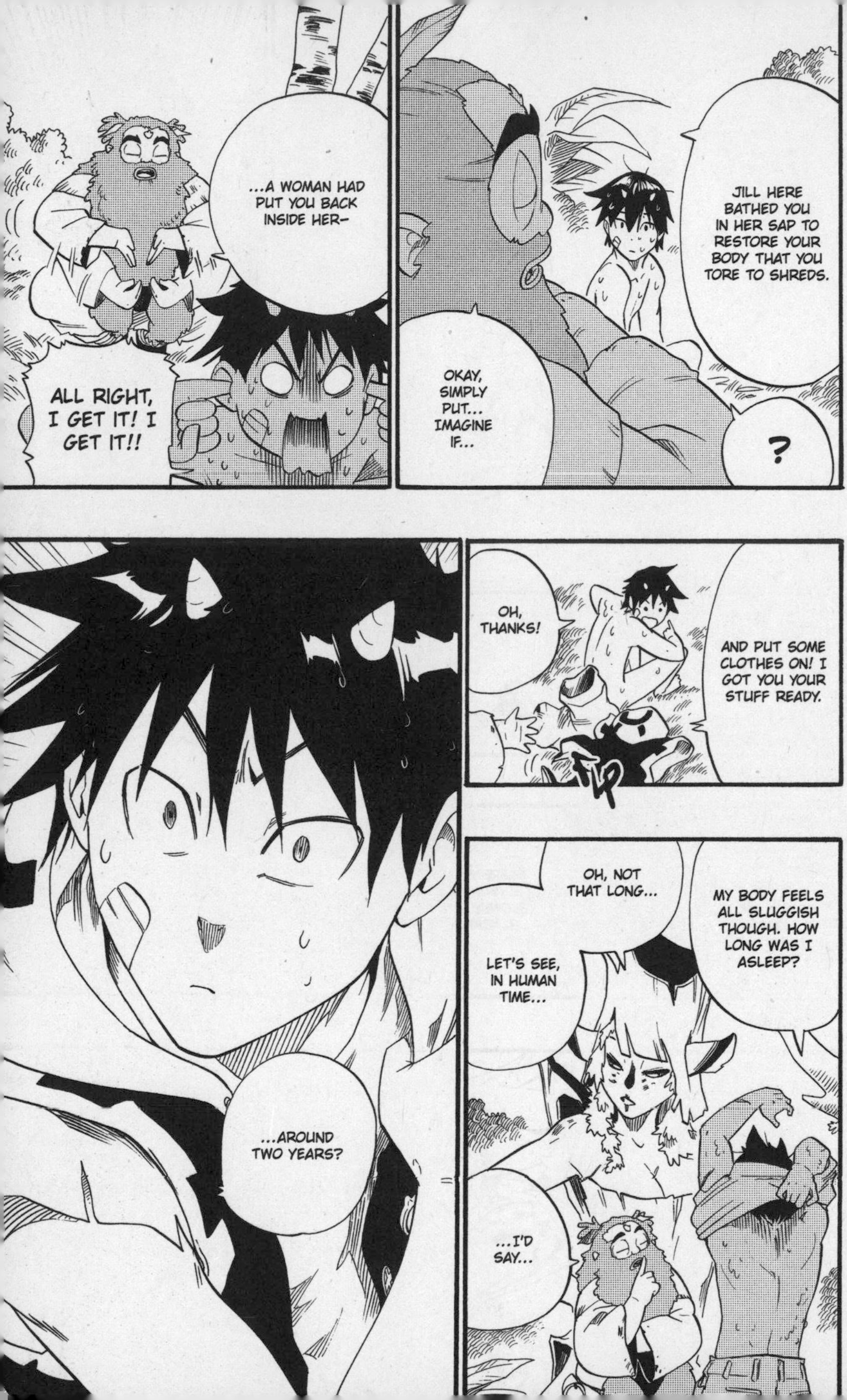
JILL HERE BATHED YOU IN HER SAP TO RESTORE YOUR BODY THAT YOU TORE TO SHREDS.
?
OKAY, SIMPLY PUT... IMAGINE IF...
...A WOMAN HAD PUT YOU BACK INSIDE HER-
ALL RIGHT, I GET IT! I GET IT!!
AND PUT SOME CLOTHES ON! I GOT YOU YOUR STUFF READY.
OH, THANKS!
MY BODY FEELS ALL SLUGGISH THOUGH. HOW LONG WAS I ASLEEP?
OH, NOT THAT LONG...
LET'S SEE, IN HUMAN TIME...
...I'D SAY...
...AROUND TWO YEARS?

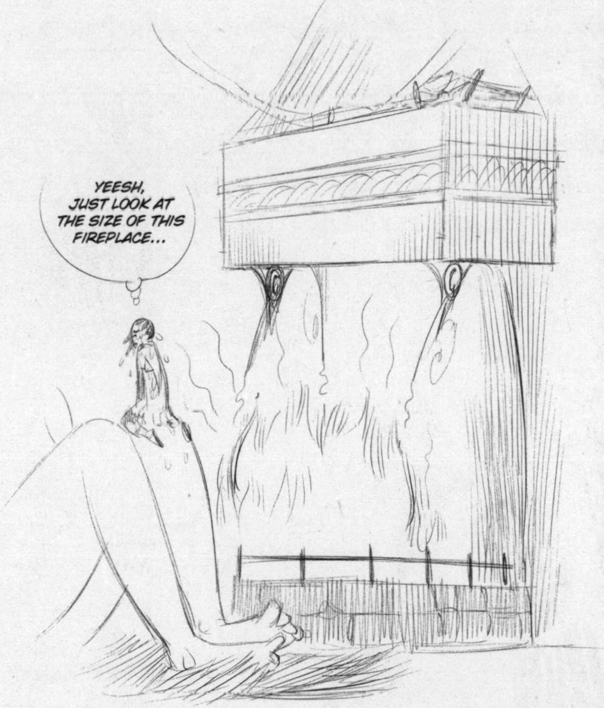
YEESH, JUST LOOK AT THE SIZE OF THIS FIREPLACE...

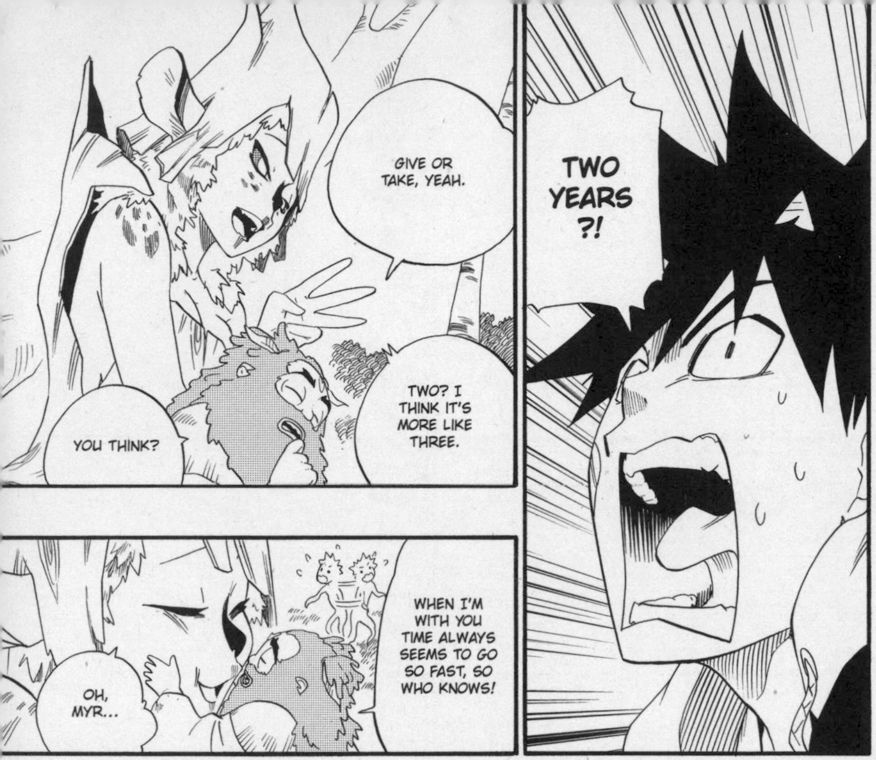
TWO YEARS ?!
GIVE OR TAKE, YEAH.
TWO? I THINK IT'S MORE LIKE THREE.
YOU THINK?
WHEN I'M WITH YOU TIME ALWAYS SEEMS TO GO SO FAST, SO WHO KNOWS!
OH, MYR...

CHAPTER 44 A WIZARD'S SENSES

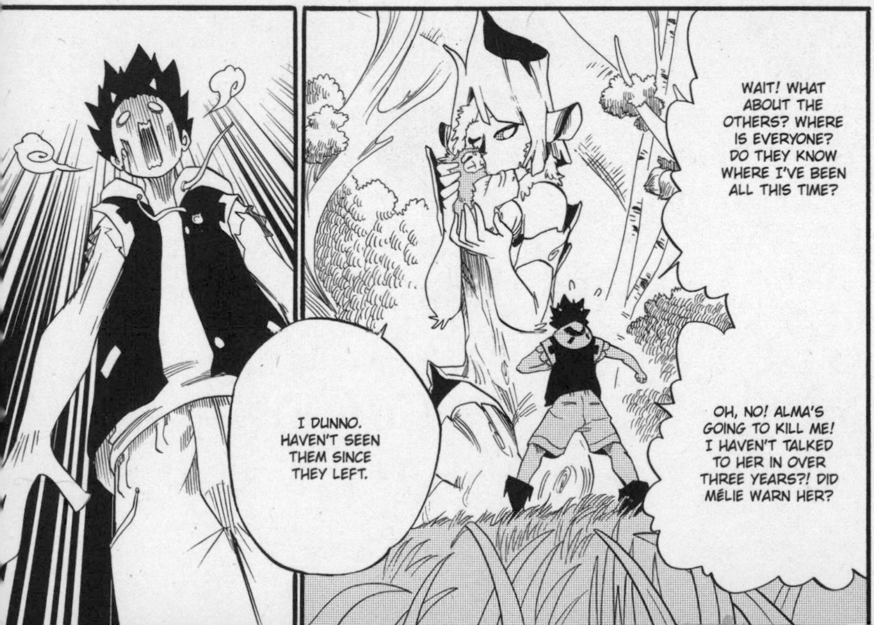
WAIT! WHAT ABOUT THE OTHERS? WHERE IS EVERYONE? DO THEY KNOW WHERE I'VE BEEN ALL THIS TIME?
I DUNNO. HAVEN'T SEEN THEM SINCE THEY LEFT.
OH, NO! ALMA'S GOING TO KILL ME! I HAVEN'T TALKED TO HER IN OVER THREE YEARS?! DID MÉLIE WARN HER?

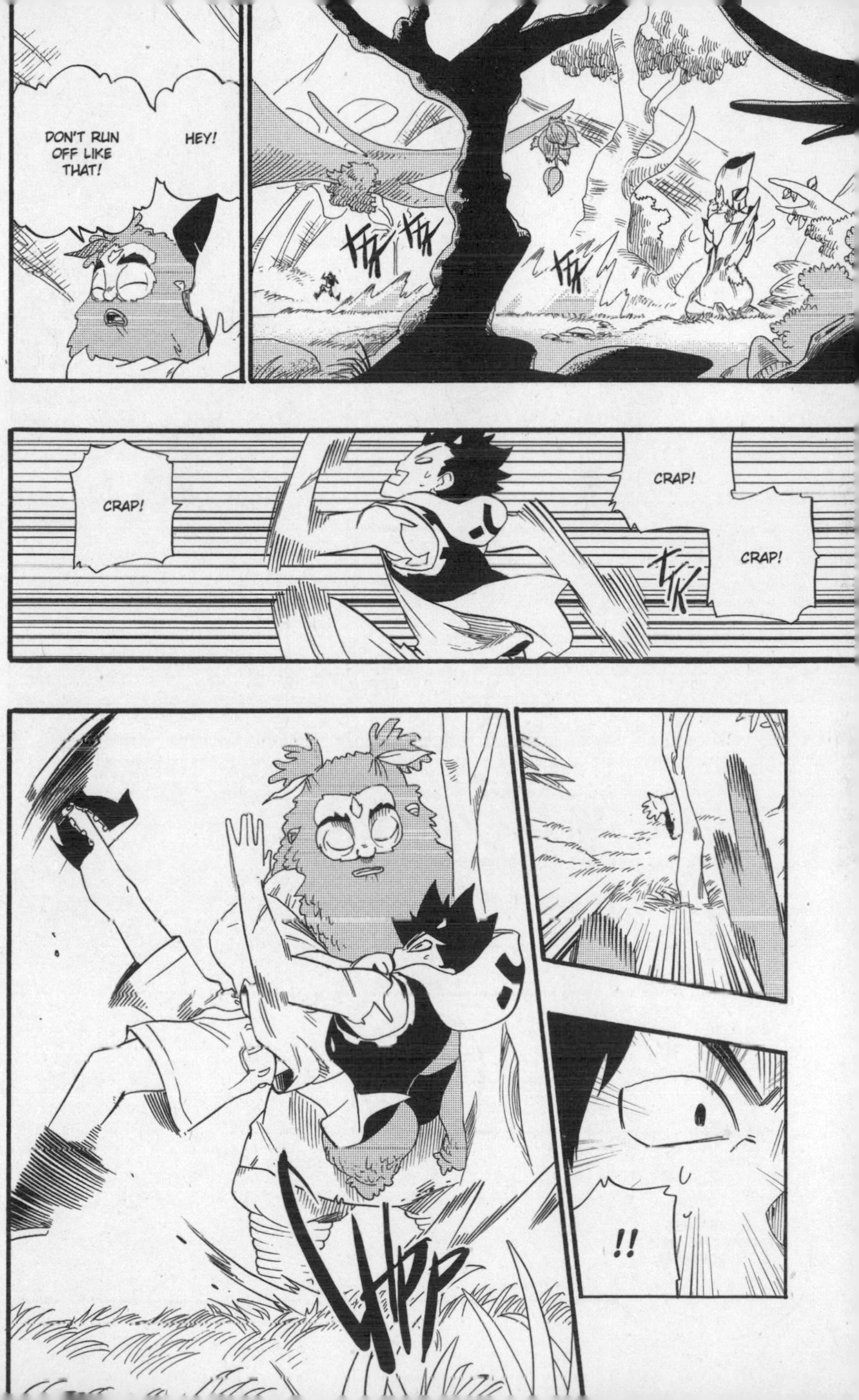
HEY!
DON'T RUN OFF LIKE THAT!
CRAP!
CRAP!
CRAP!
!!

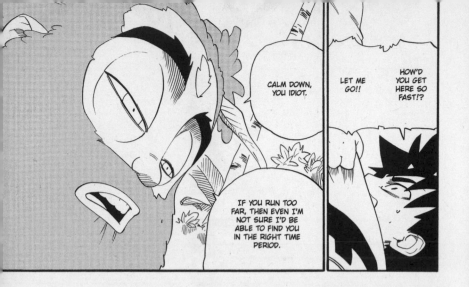

HOW'D YOU GET HERE SO FAST!?
LET ME GO!!
CALM DOWN, YOU IDIOT.
IF YOU RUN TOO FAR, THEN EVEN I'M NOT SURE I'D BE ABLE TO FIND YOU IN THE RIGHT TIME PERIOD.
WHAT?
LOOK... TIME GOES BY DIFFERENTLY HERE. IT'S NOT A LINEAR PROGRESSION.
IMAGINE IF TIME WERE A STRAIGHT LINE...
...THEN ENTERING THIS FOREST...
...WOULD BE LIKE ENTERING A BUBBLE THAT ISOLATES YOU FROM THAT.
CAILLTE FOREST
TIME
ENTERING THE FOREST
IF YOU'RE LIKE ME, AND YOU KNOW HOW TO NAVIGATE THIS FOREST, THEN YOU CAN GET OUT AT THE EXACT POINT YOU ENTERED AT.
OR EVEN A LOT LATER.
TIME
SO NOT BEFORE?
NO, BECAUSE HUMAN TIME ONLY GOES FORWARD.

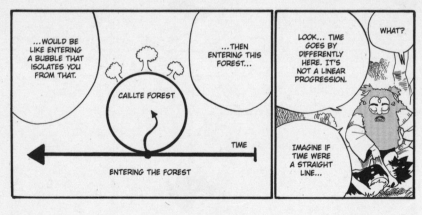

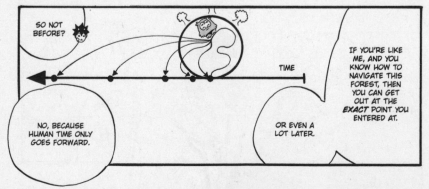

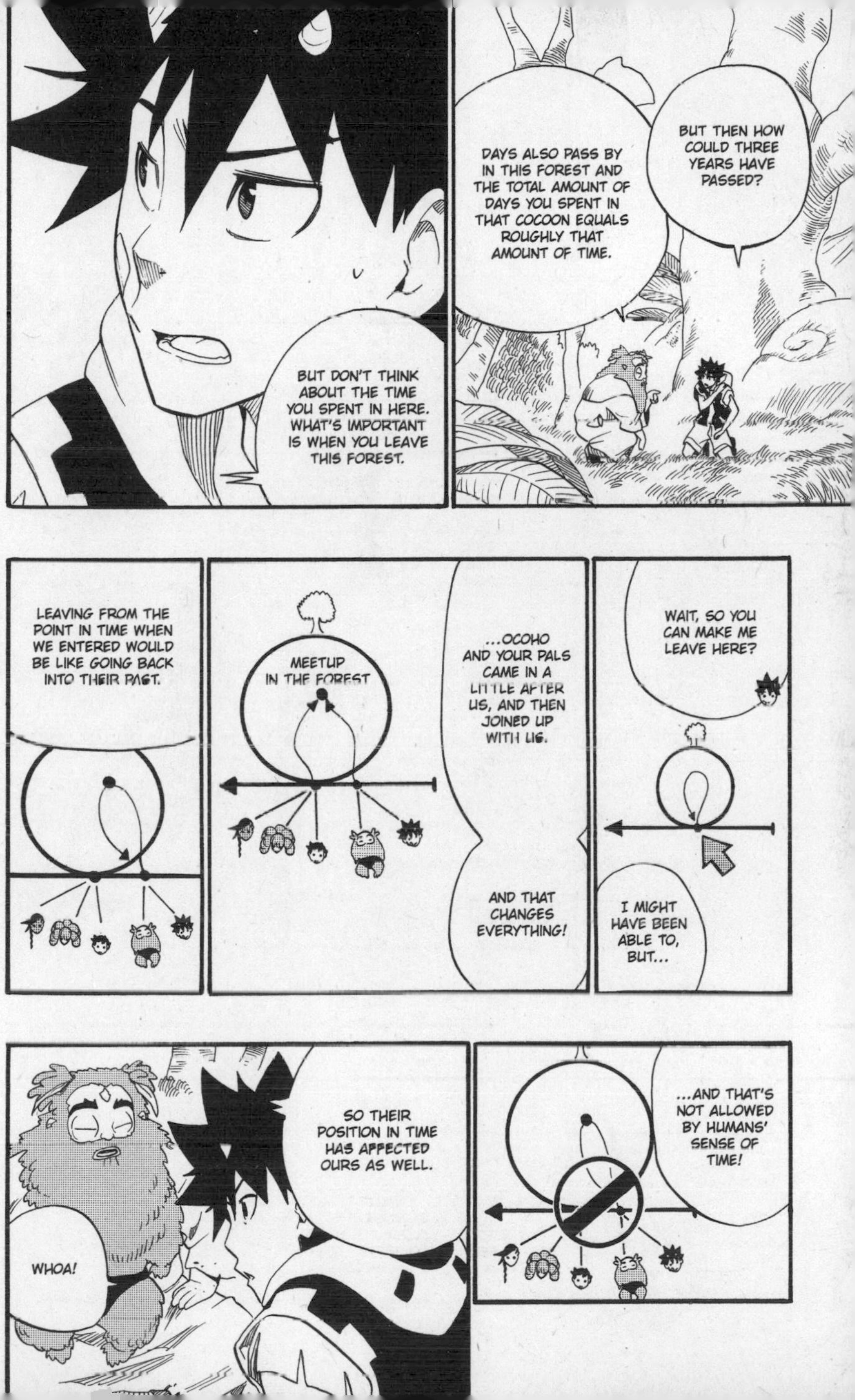
BUT THEN HOW COULD THREE YEARS HAVE PASSED?
DAYS ALSO PASS BY IN THIS FOREST AND THE TOTAL AMOUNT OF DAYS YOU SPENT IN THAT COCOON EQUALS ROUGHLY THAT AMOUNT OF TIME.
BUT DON'T THINK ABOUT THE TIME YOU SPENT IN HERE. WHAT'S IMPORTANT IS WHEN YOU LEAVE THIS FOREST.
WAIT, SO YOU CAN MAKE ME LEAVE HERE?
I MIGHT HAVE BEEN ABLE TO, BUT...
...OCOHO AND YOUR PALS CAME IN A LITTLE AFTER US, AND THEN JOINED UP WITH US.
MEETUP IN THE FOREST
AND THAT CHANGES EVERYTHING!
LEAVING FROM THE POINT IN TIME WHEN WE ENTERED WOULD BE LIKE GOING BACK INTO THEIR PAST.
...AND THAT'S NOT ALLOWED BY HUMANS' SENSE OF TIME!
SO THEIR POSITION IN TIME HAS AFFECTED OURS AS WELL.
WHOA!

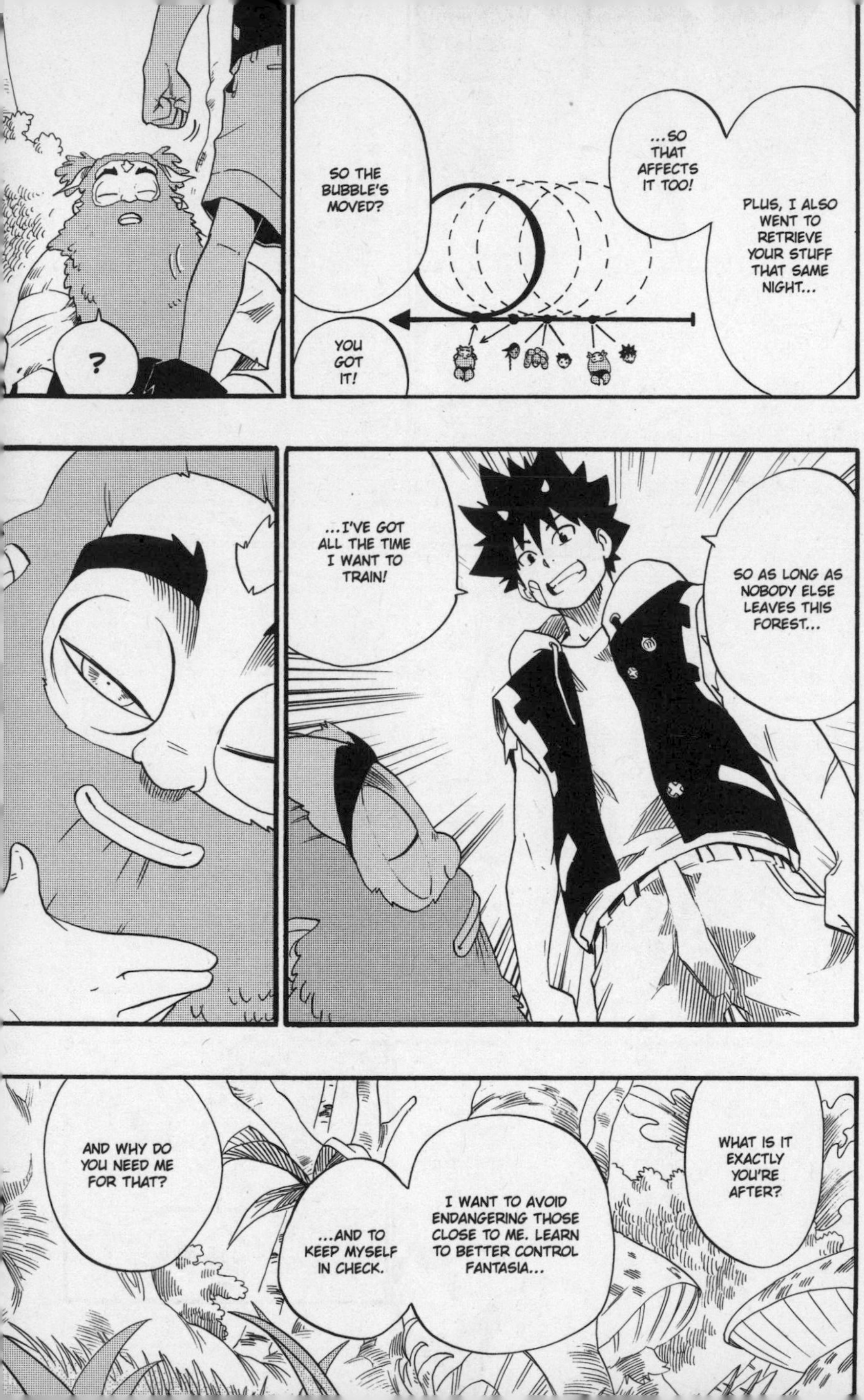
...SO THAT AFFECTS IT TOO!
PLUS, I ALSO WENT TO RETRIEVE YOUR STUFF THAT SAME NIGHT...
SO THE BUBBLE'S MOVED?
YOU GOT IT!
?
SO AS LONG AS NOBODY ELSE LEAVES THIS FOREST...
...I'VE GOT ALL THE TIME I WANT TO TRAIN!
WHAT IS IT EXACTLY YOU'RE AFTER?
I WANT TO AVOID ENDANGERING THOSE CLOSE TO ME. LEARN TO BETTER CONTROL FANTASIA...
...AND TO KEEP MYSELF IN CHECK.
AND WHY DO YOU NEED ME FOR THAT?

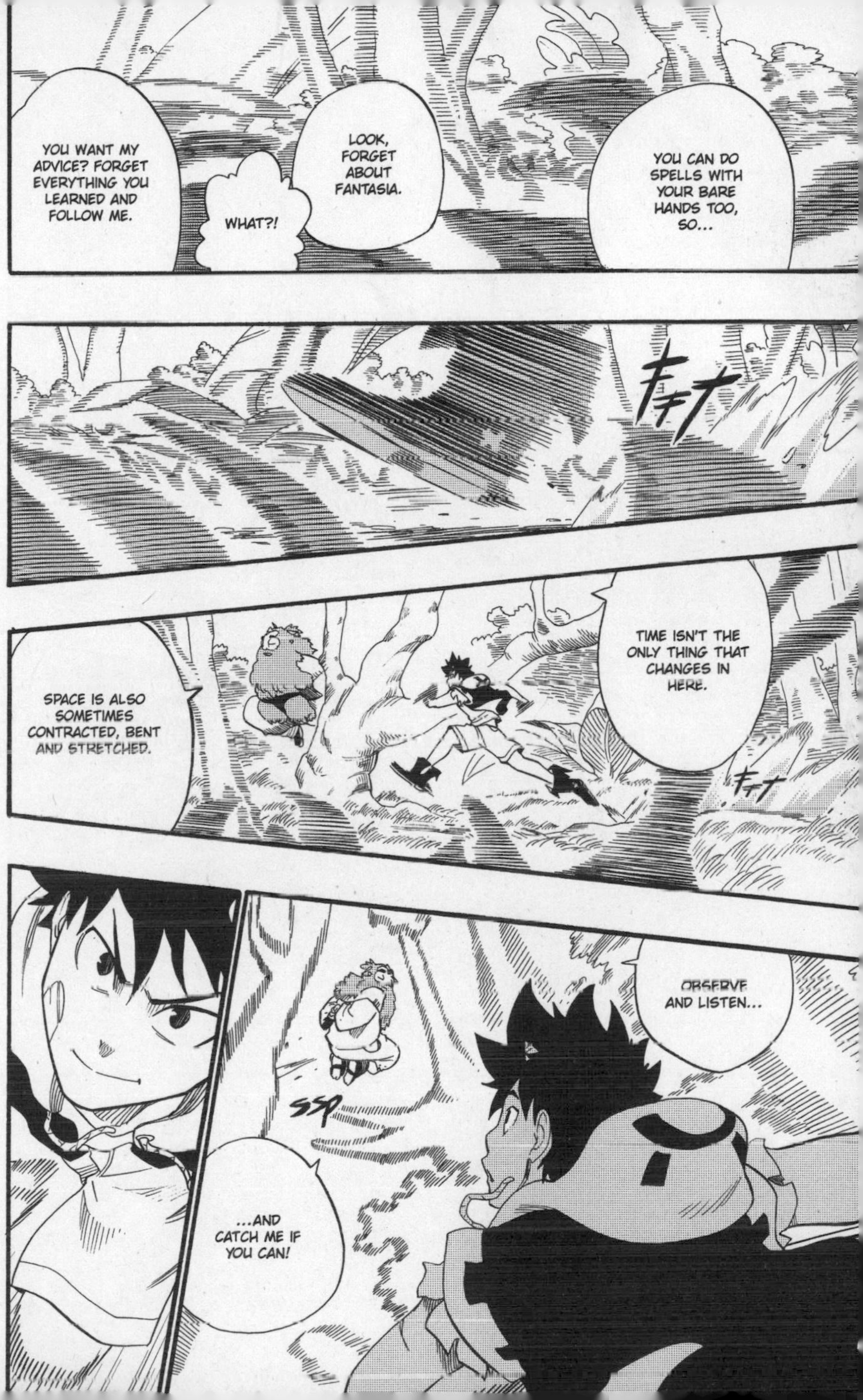
YOU CAN DO SPELLS WITH YOUR BARE HANDS TOO, SO...
LOOK, FORGET ABOUT FANTASIA.
WHAT?!
YOU WANT MY ADVICE? FORGET EVERYTHING YOU LEARNED AND FOLLOW ME.
TIME ISN'T THE ONLY THING THAT CHANGES IN HERE.
SPACE IS ALSO SOMETIMES CONTRACTED, BENT AND STRETCHED.
OBSERVE AND LISTEN...
SSP
...AND CATCH ME IF YOU CAN!

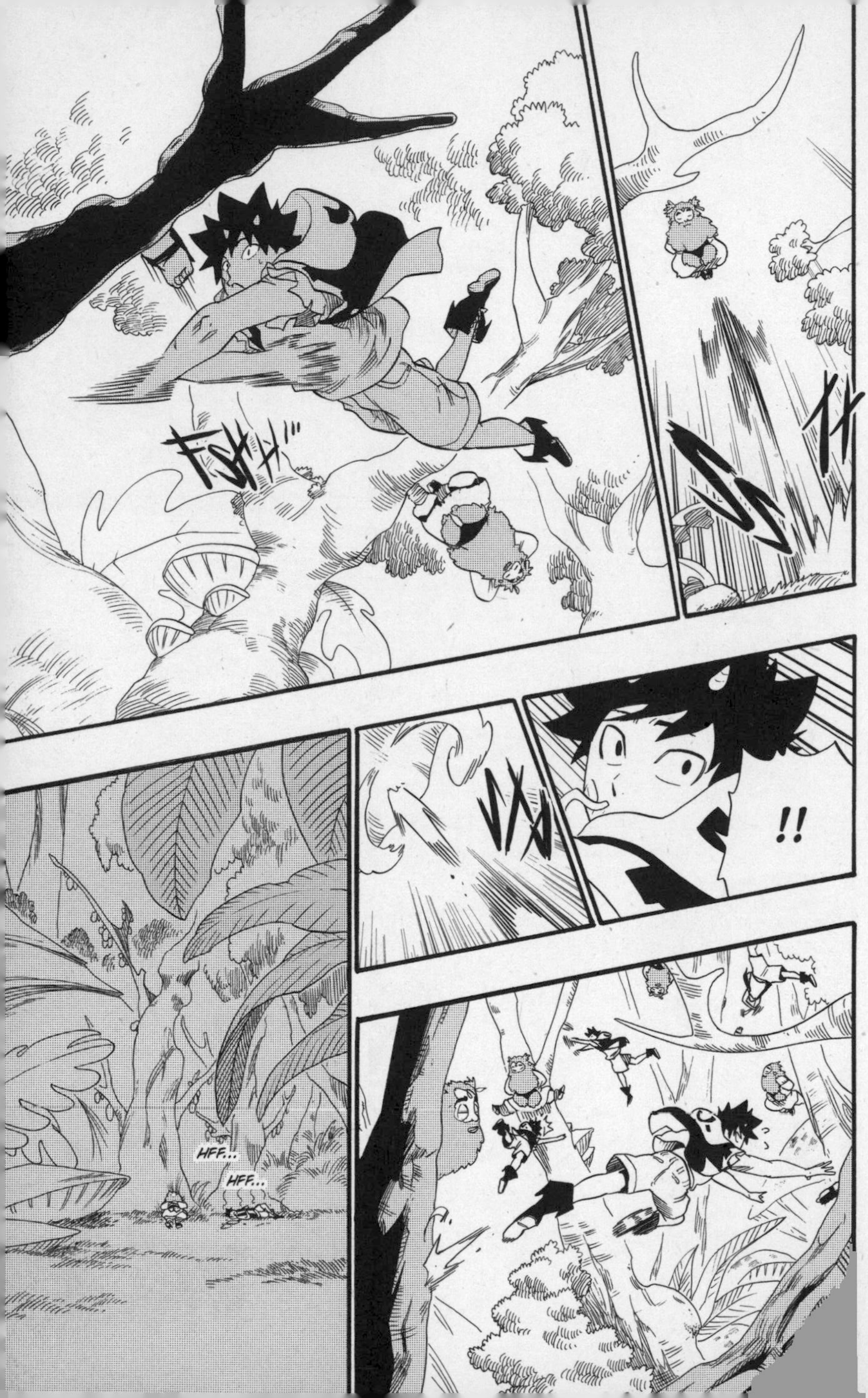
FSHH
!!
HFF...
HFF...

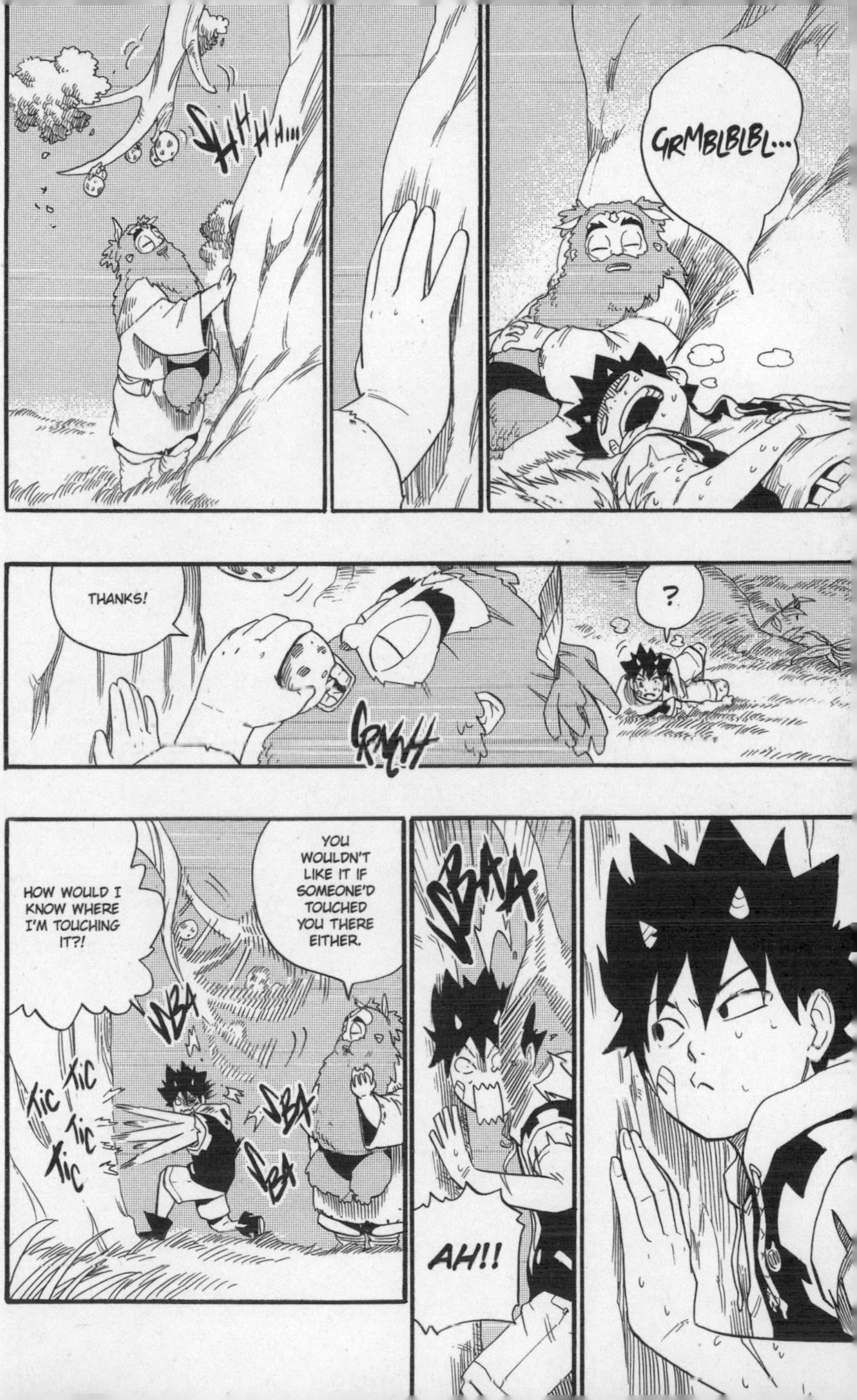
GRMBLBLBL...
SHHH...
?
THANKS!
CRNCH
SBRA
AH!!
YOU WOULDN'T LIKE IT IF SOMEONE'D TOUCHED YOU THERE EITHER.
HOW WOULD I KNOW WHERE I'M TOUCHING IT?!
SBA
TIC TIC TIC TIC
SBA
SBA

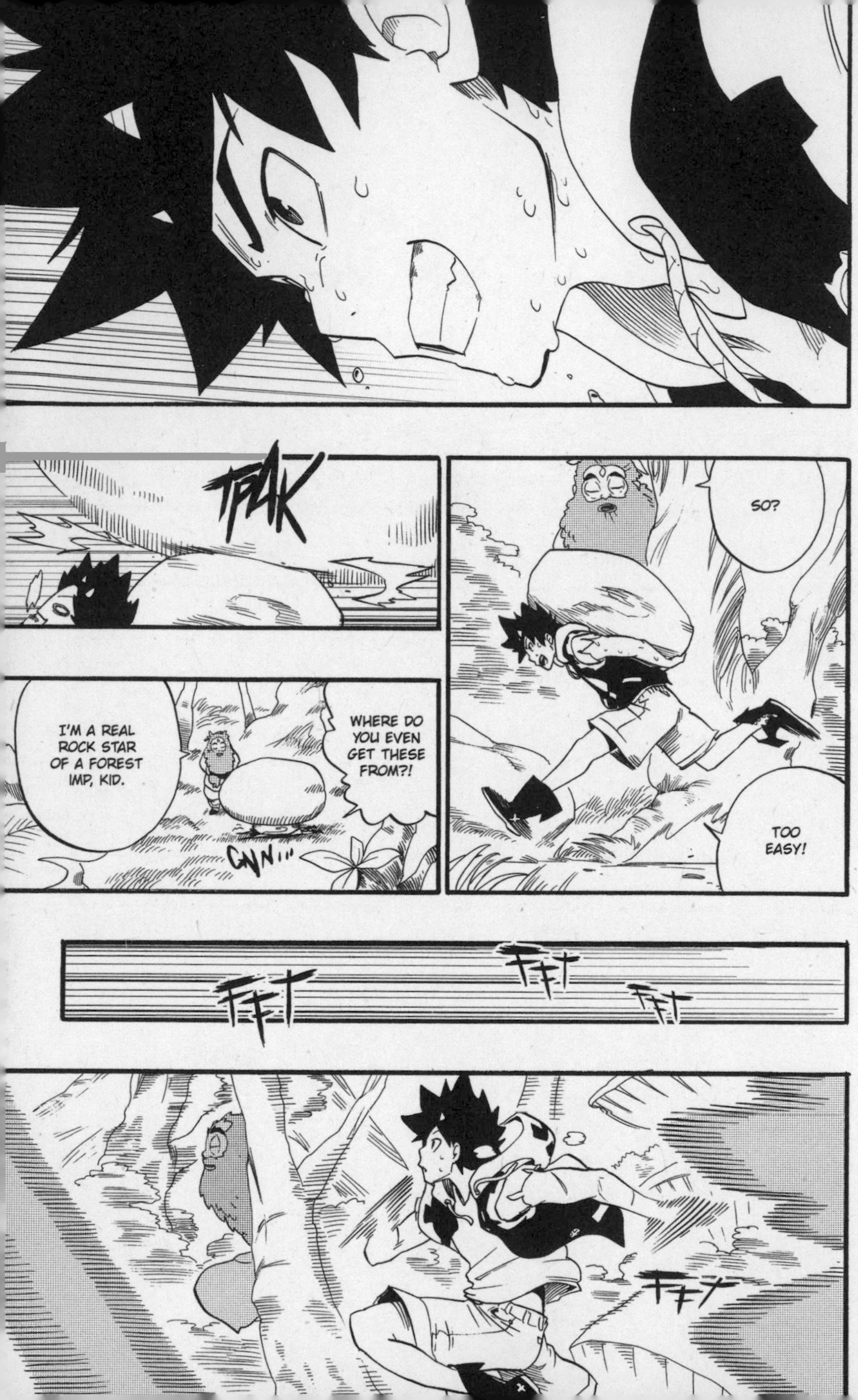
SO?
TOO EASY!
TRAK
WHERE DO YOU EVEN GET THESE FROM?!
I'M A REAL ROCK STAR OF A FOREST IMP, KID.
GNN...
FFT
FFT
FFT
FFT

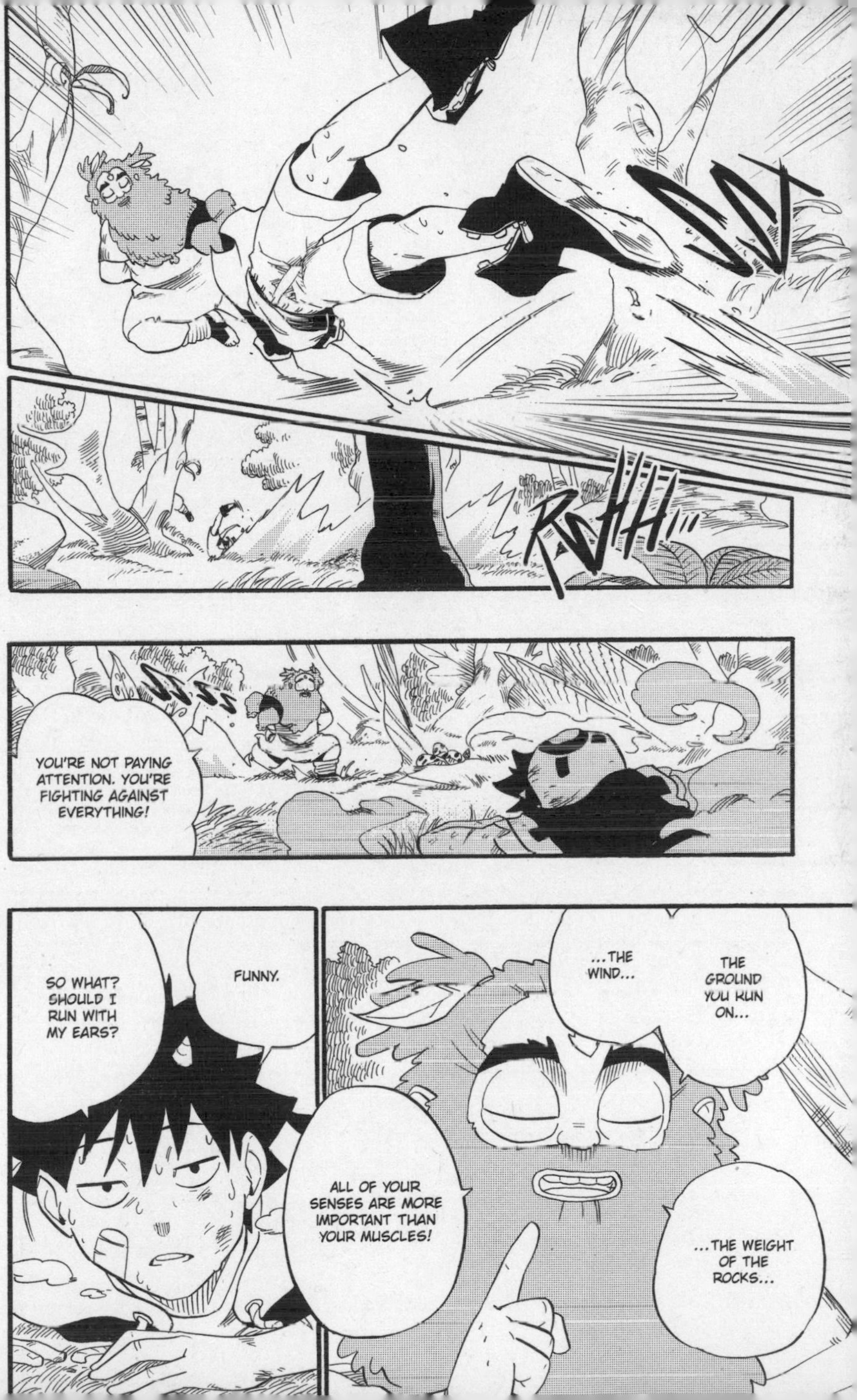
YOU'RE NOT PAYING ATTENTION. YOU'RE FIGHTING AGAINST EVERYTHING!
THE GROUND YOU RUN ON...
...THE WIND...
...THE WEIGHT OF THE ROCKS...
ALL OF YOUR SENSES ARE MORE IMPORTANT THAN YOUR MUSCLES!
FUNNY.
SO WHAT? SHOULD I RUN WITH MY EARS?

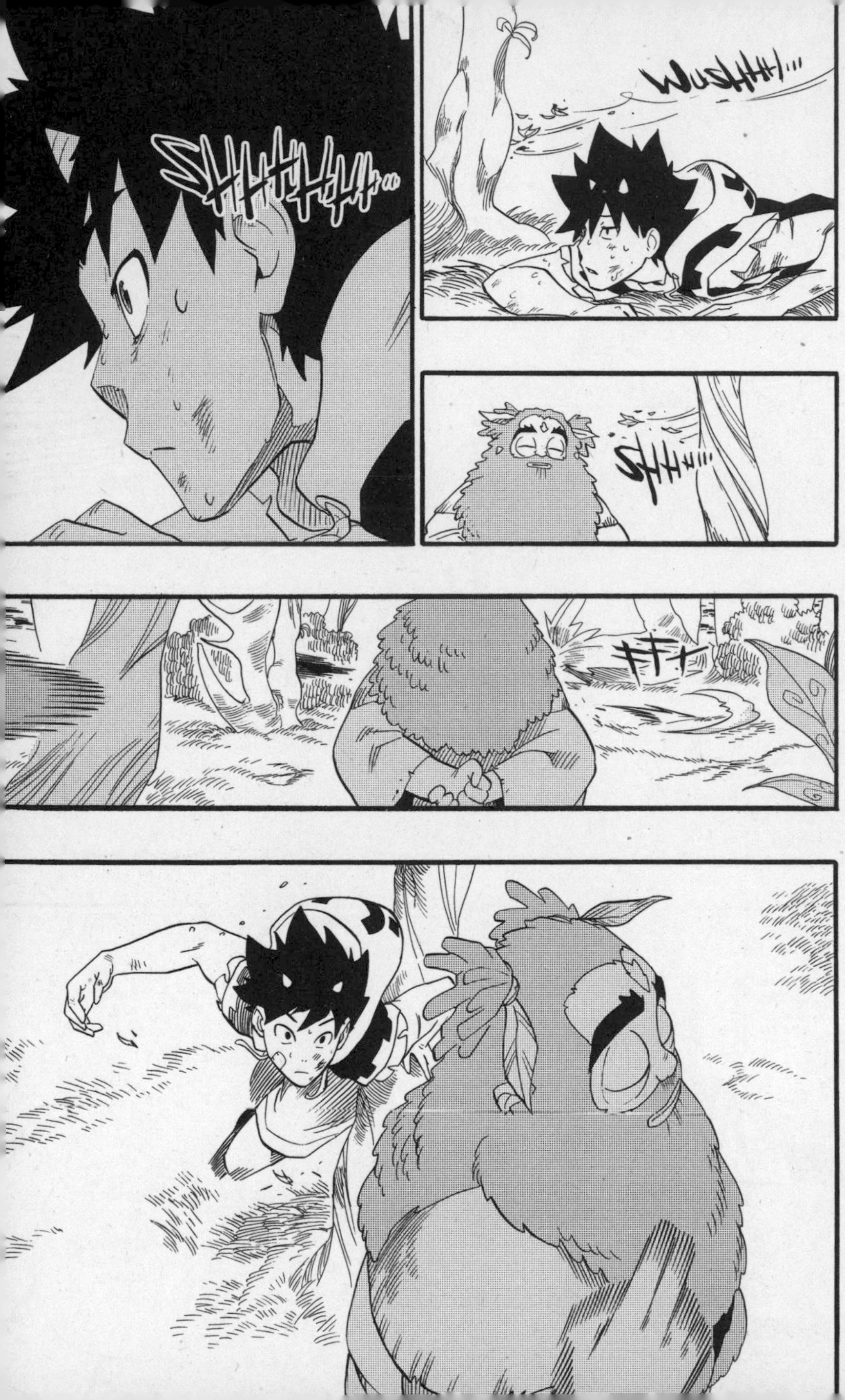
WUSHH!!...
SHHHHHH...
SHHH!!!
FFT

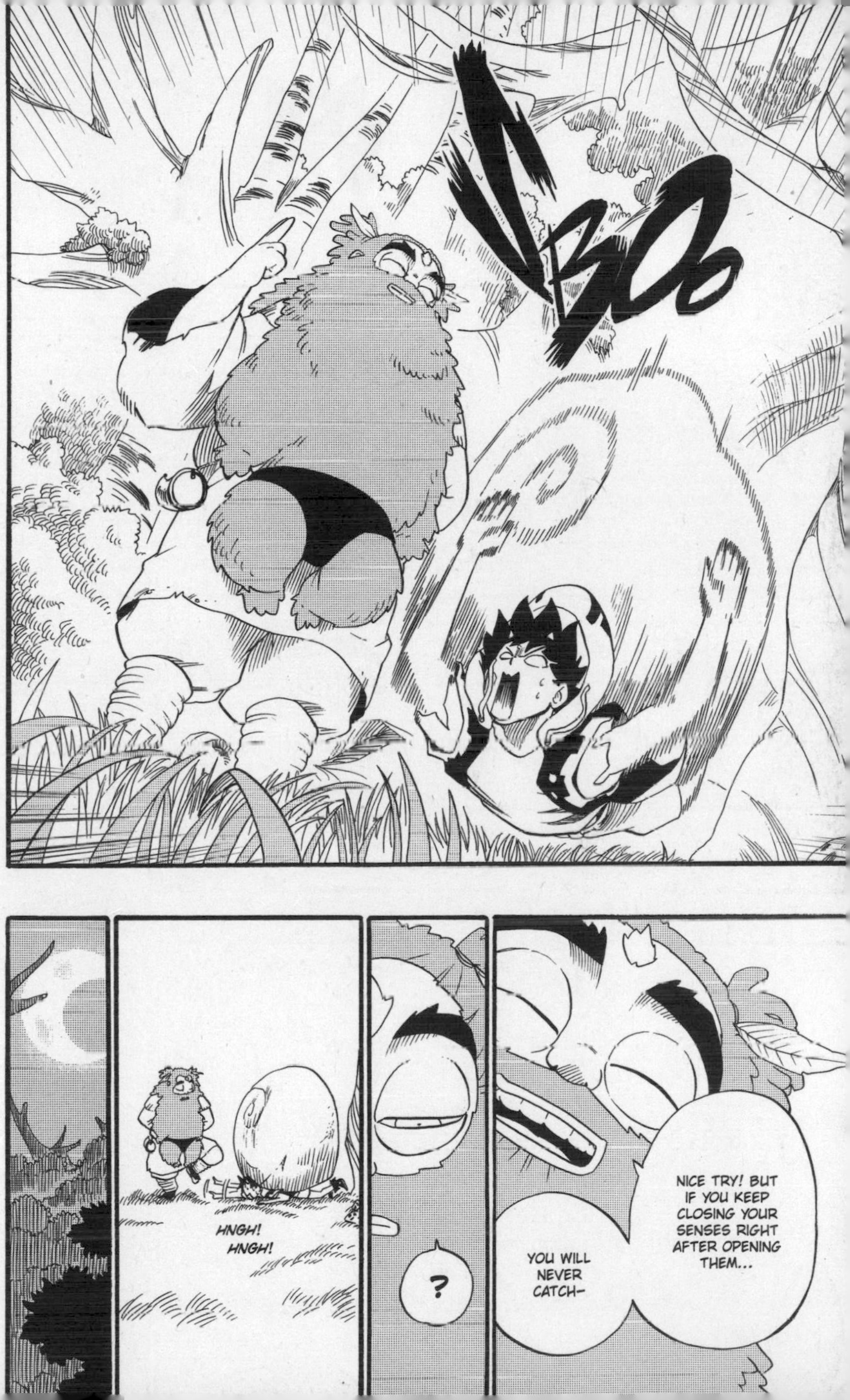
NICE TRY! BUT IF YOU KEEP CLOSING YOUR SENSES RIGHT AFTER OPENING THEM...
YOU WILL NEVER CATCH-
?
HNGH! HNGH!

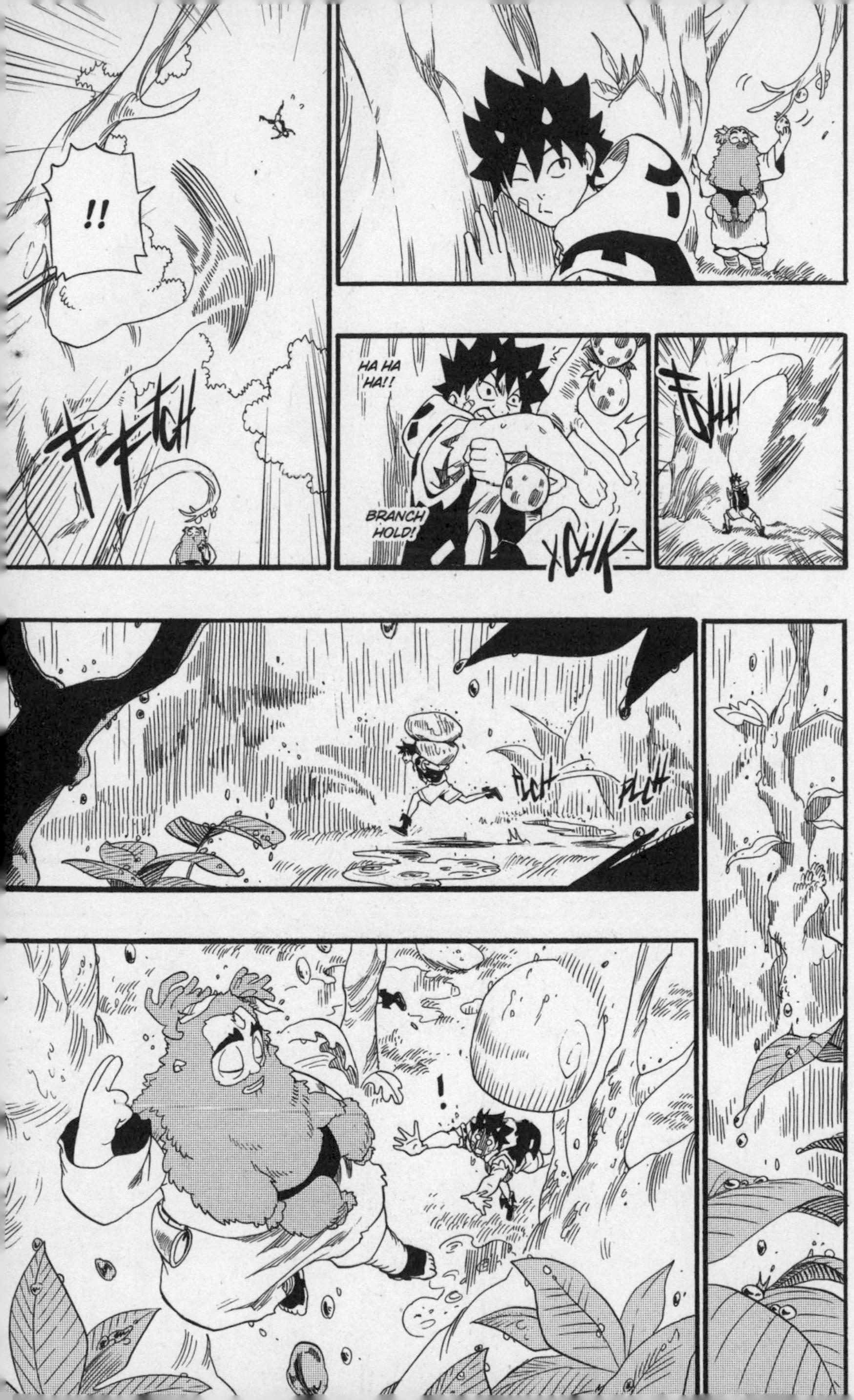
FSHH
HA HA HA!!
BRANCH HOLD!
XCHK
!!
TFFTCH
PLCH
PLCH
!

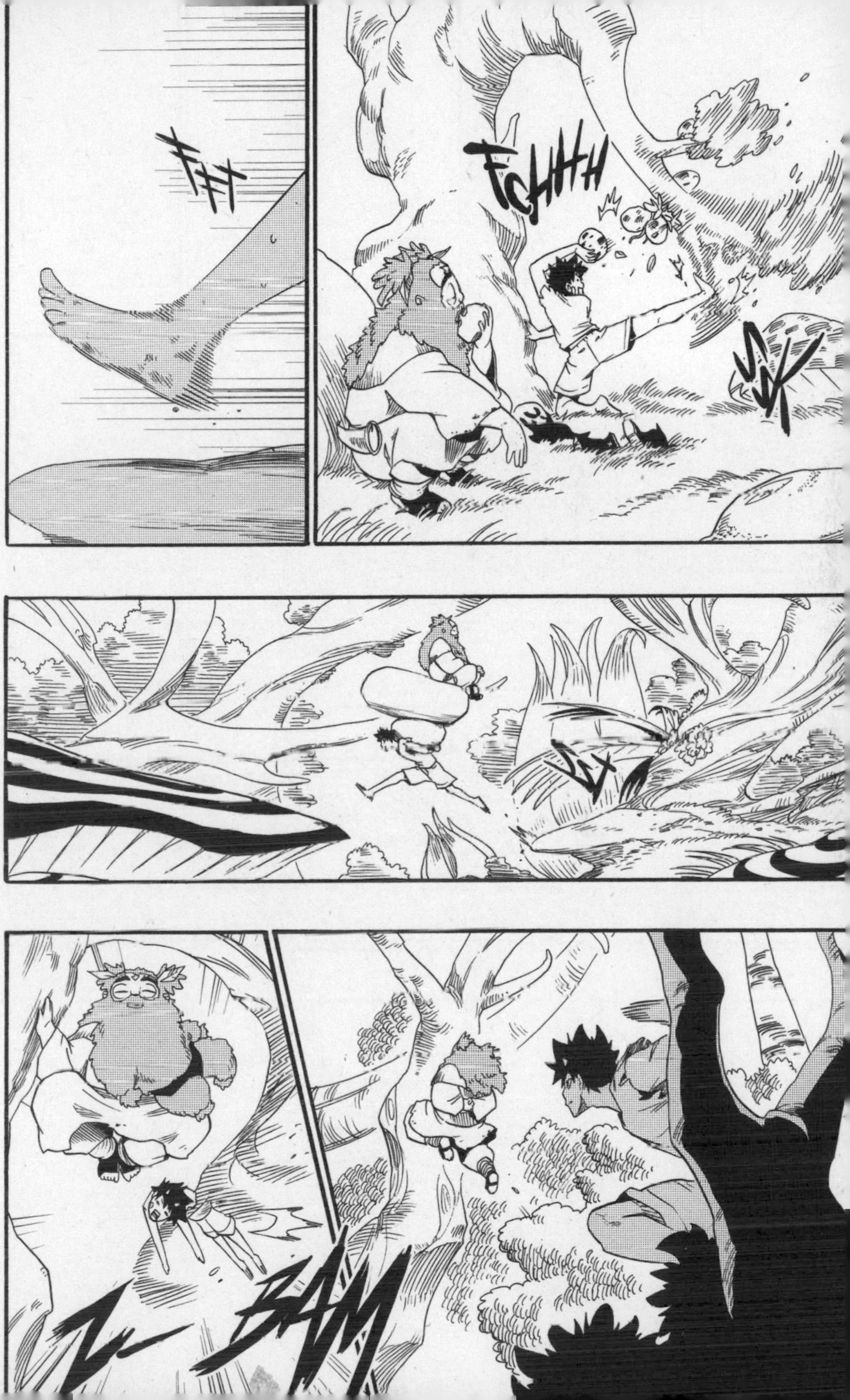
FCHHH
FFFT
BAM

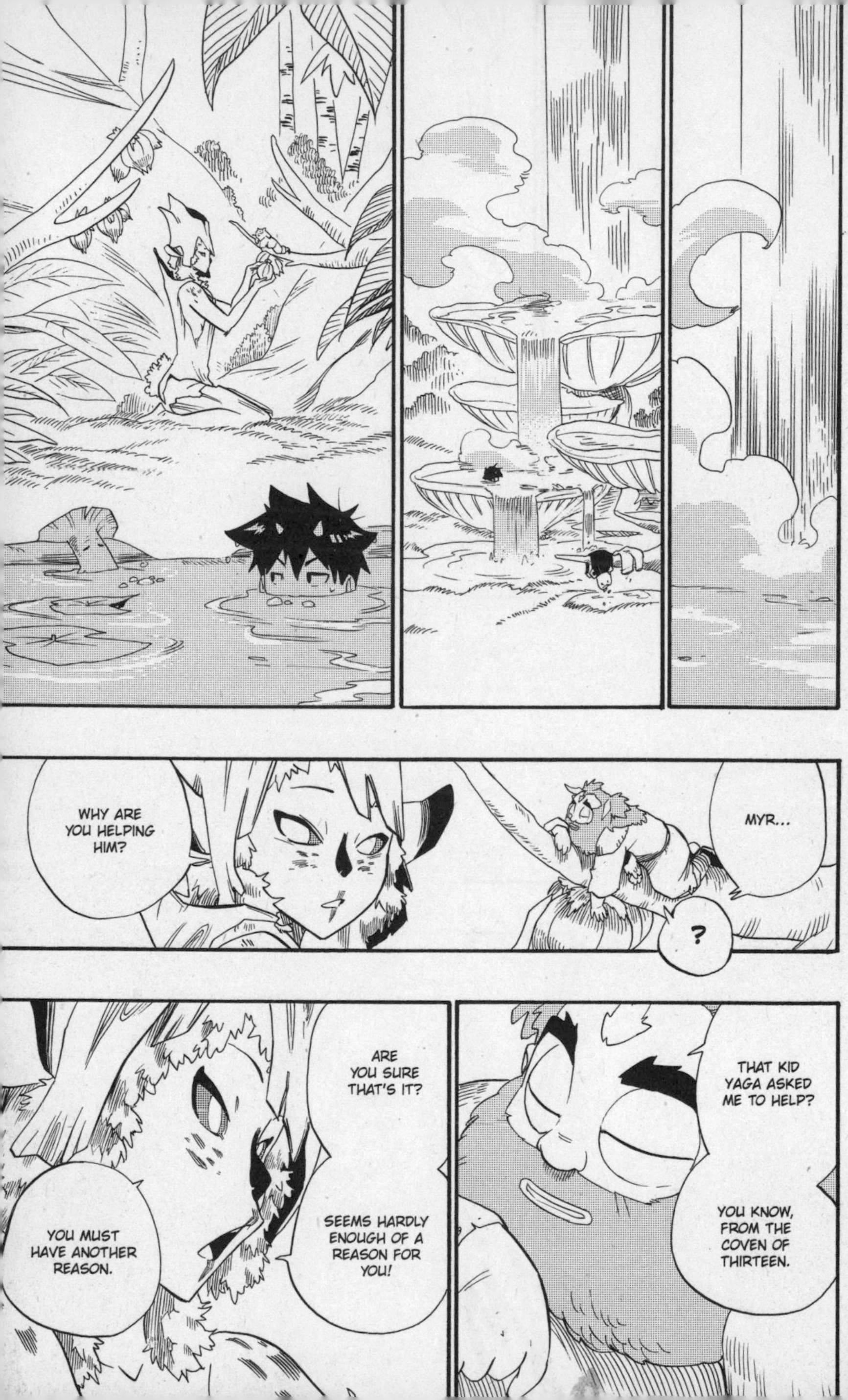
MYR...
?
WHY ARE YOU HELPING HIM?
THAT KID YAGA ASKED ME TO HELP?
YOU KNOW, FROM THE COVEN OF THIRTEEN.
ARE YOU SURE THAT'S IT?
SEEMS HARDLY ENOUGH OF A REASON FOR YOU!
YOU MUST HAVE ANOTHER REASON.

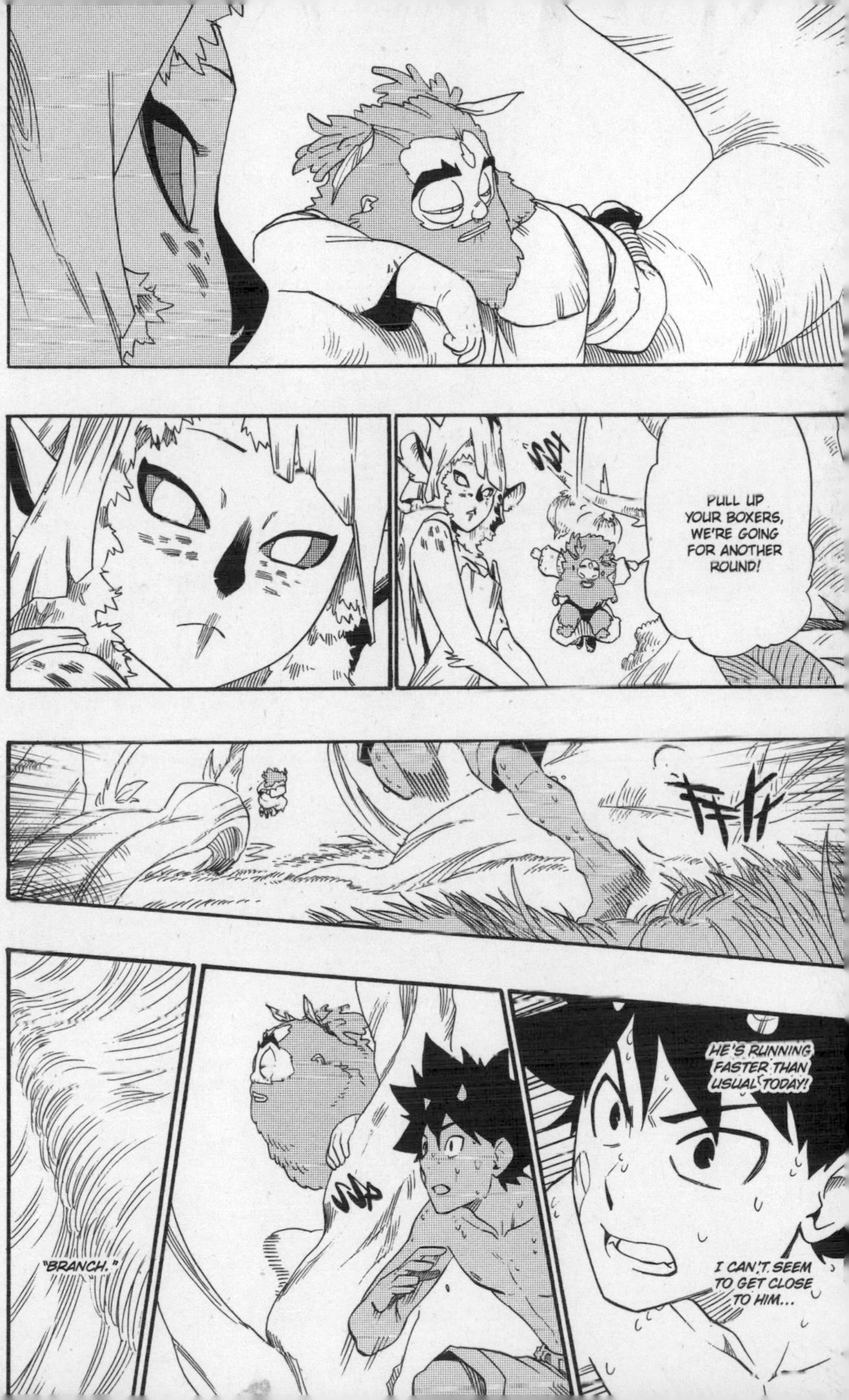
PULL UP YOUR BOXERS, WE'RE GOING FOR ANOTHER ROUND!
HE'S RUNNING FASTER THAN USUAL TODAY!
I CAN'T SEEM TO GET CLOSE TO HIM...
"BRANCH."

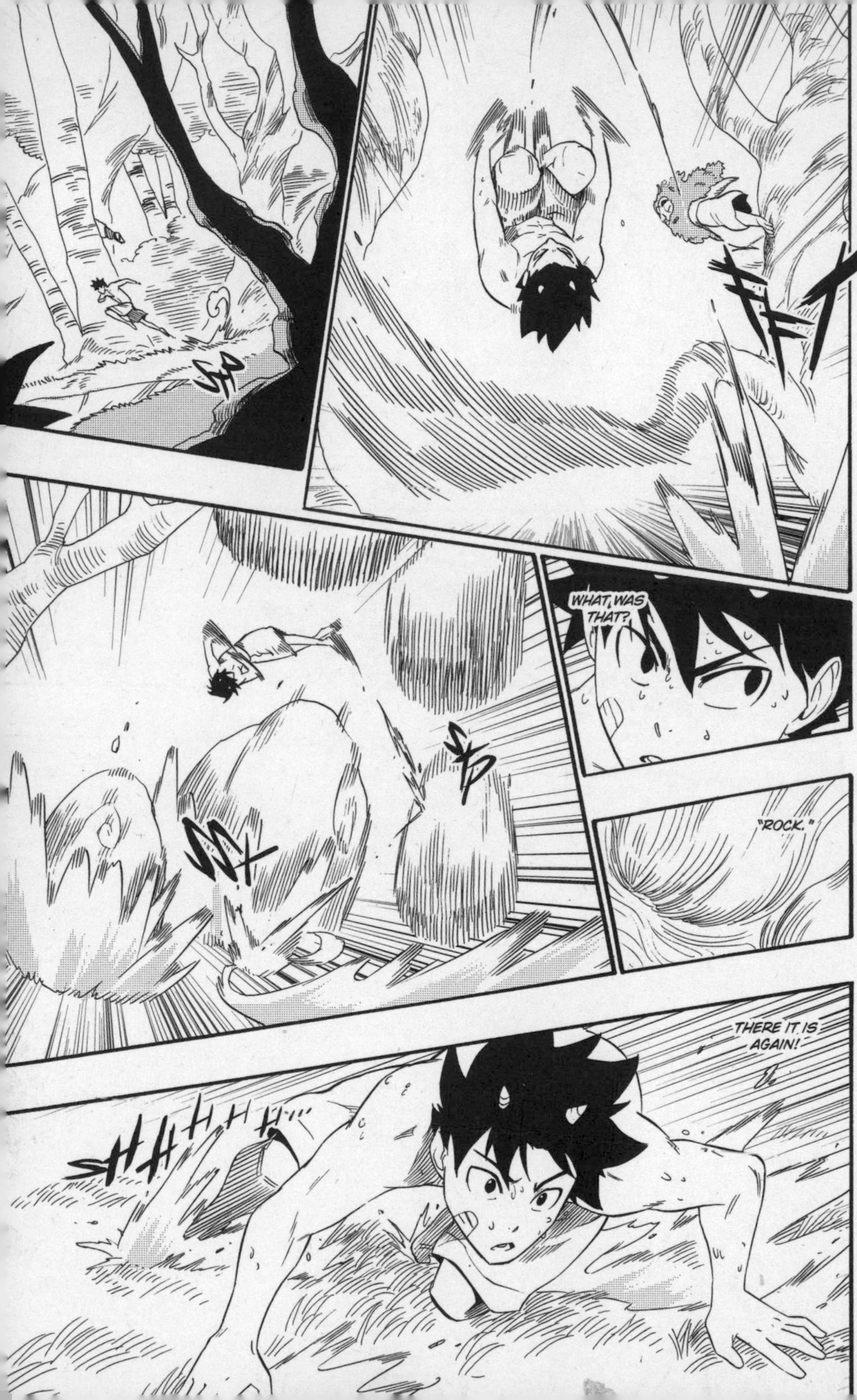
WHAT WAS THAT?
"ROCK."
THERE IT IS AGAIN!

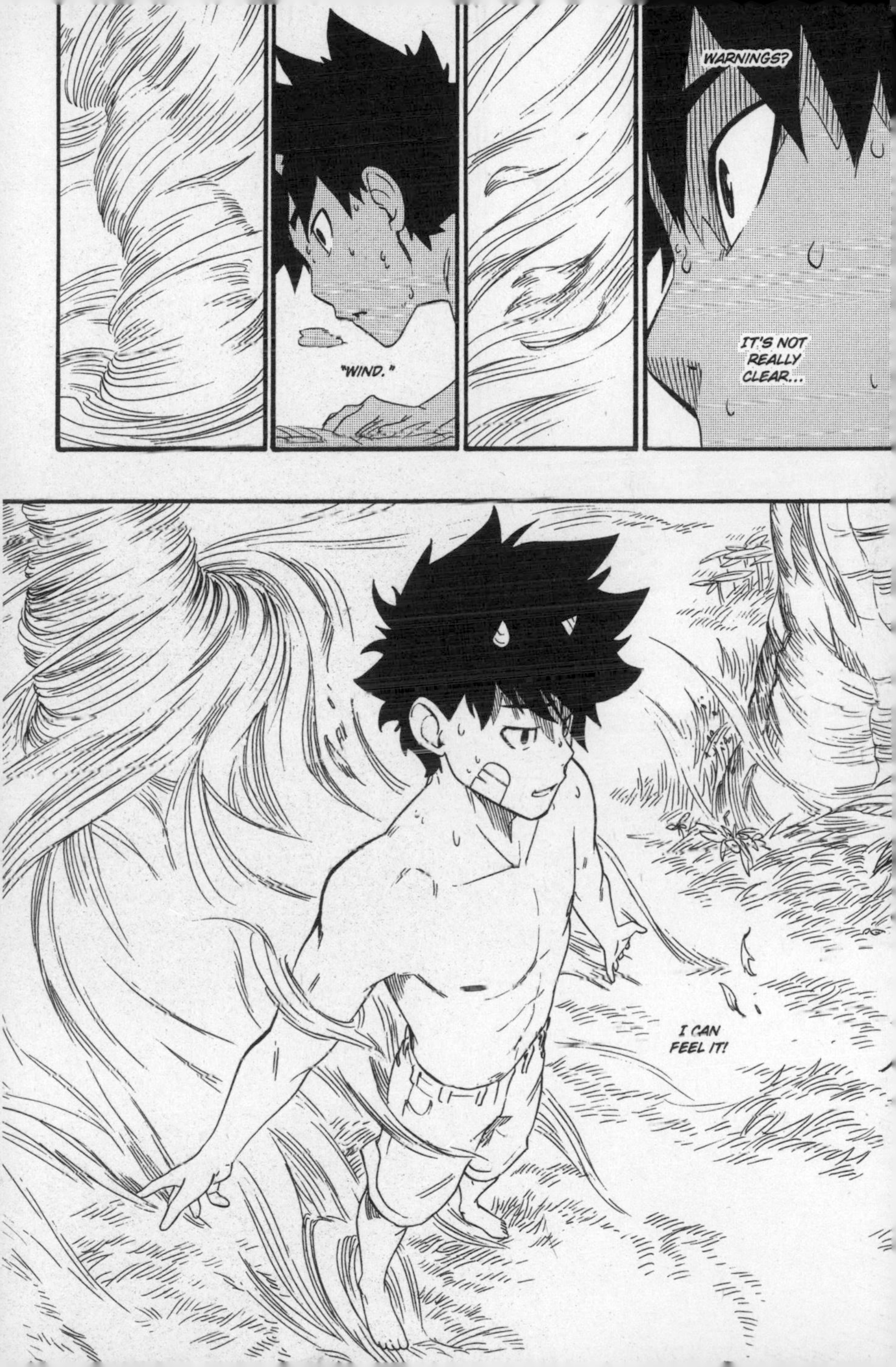
WARNINGS?
IT'S NOT REALLY CLEAR...
"WIND."
I CAN FEEL IT!

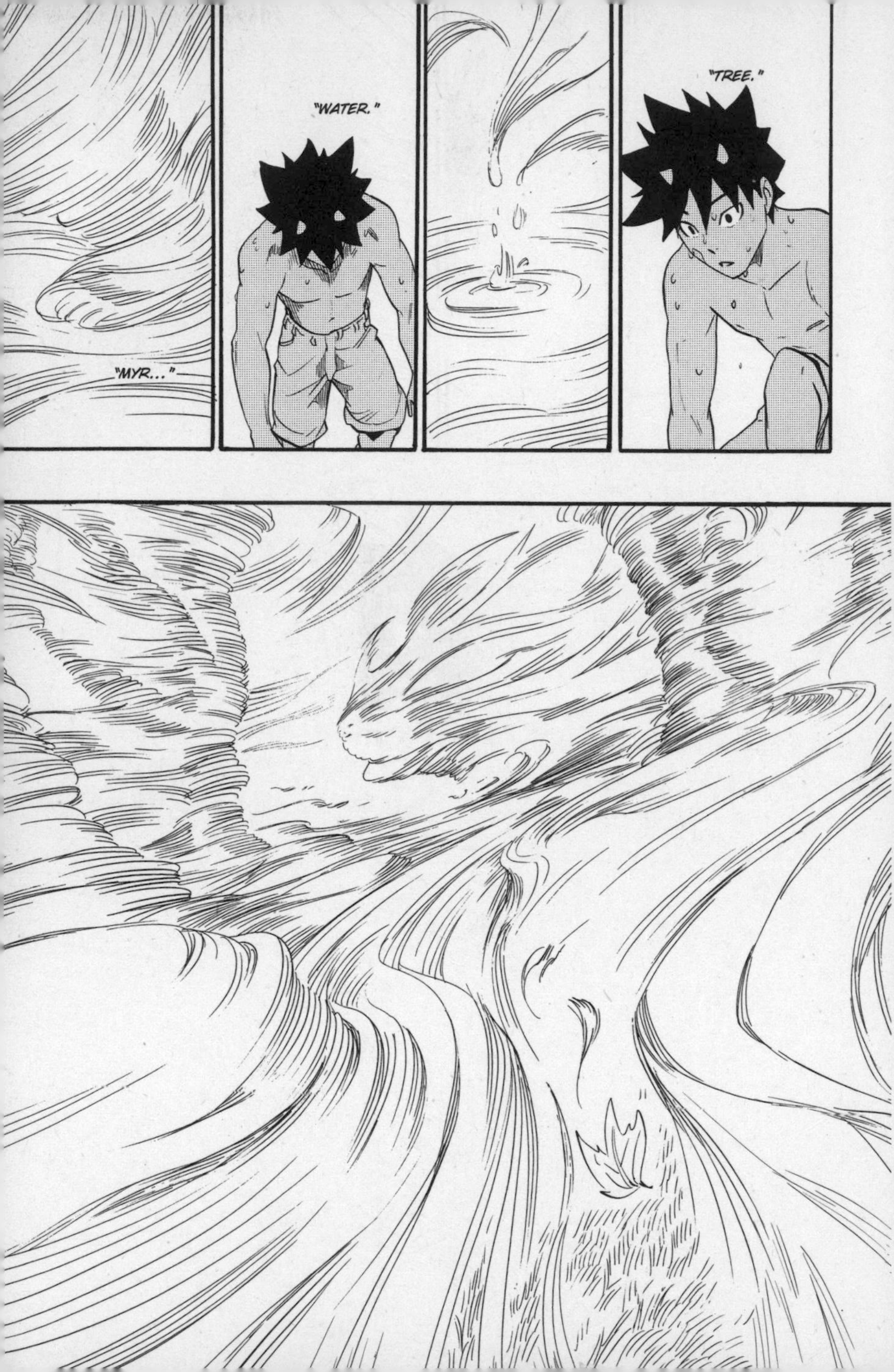
"TREE."
"WATER."
"MYR..."

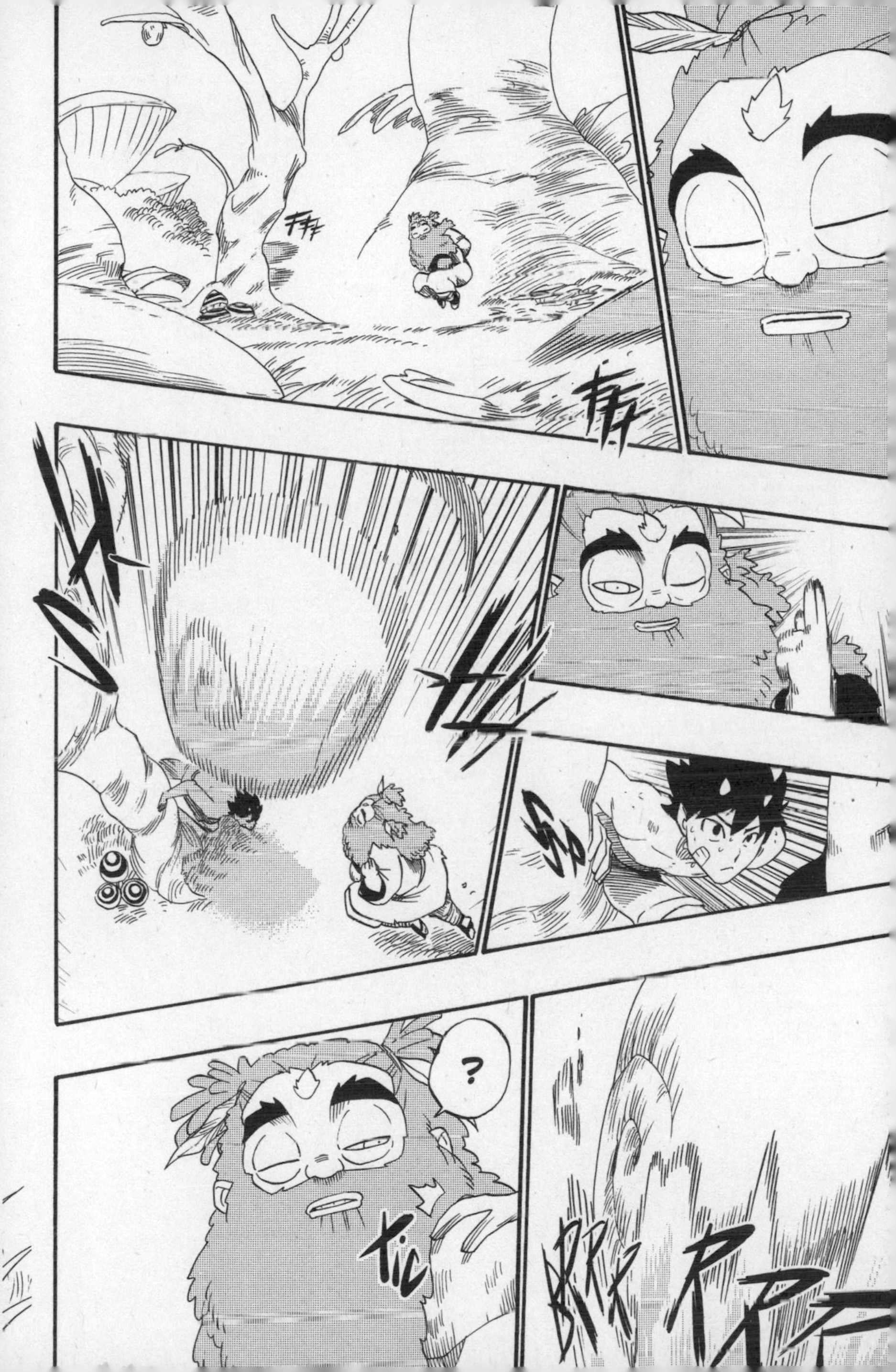
?
tic
BRRRRR

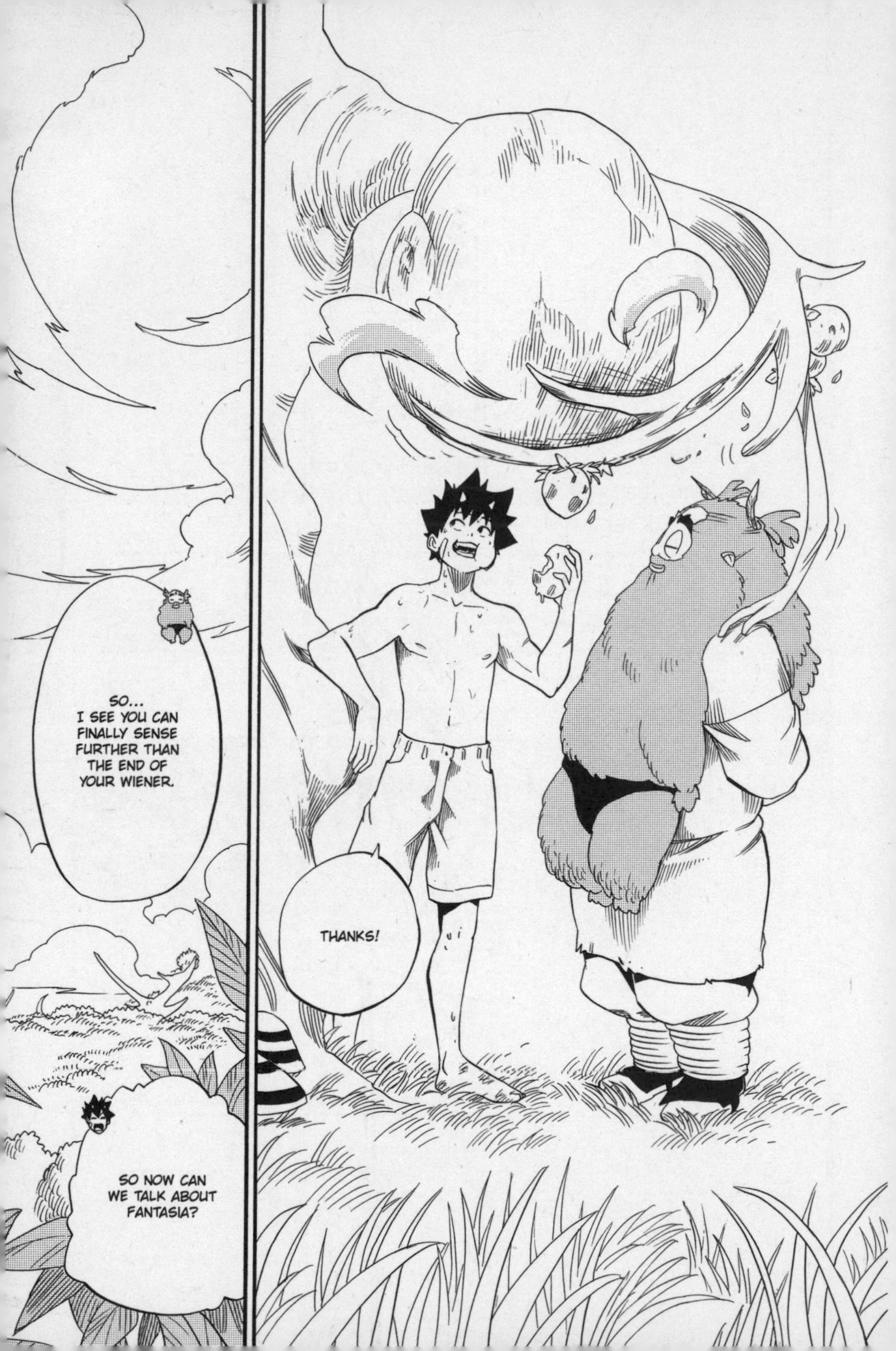
THANKS!
SO... I SEE YOU CAN FINALLY SENSE FURTHER THAN THE END OF YOUR WIENER.
SO NOW CAN WE TALK ABOUT FANTASIA?

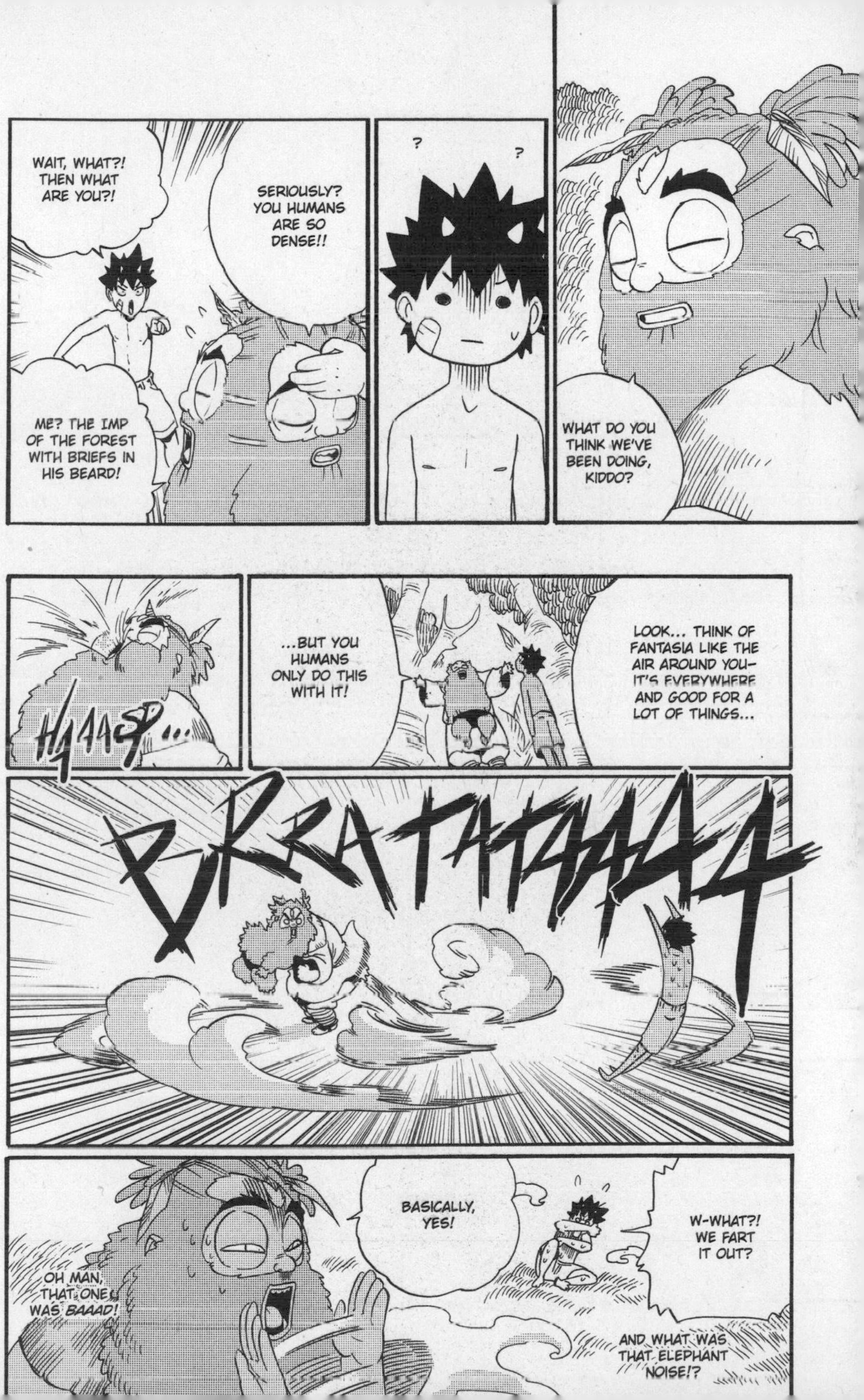
WHAT DO YOU THINK WE'VE BEEN DOING, KIDDO?
? ?
SERIOUSLY? YOU HUMANS ARE SO DENSE!!
WAIT, WHAT?! THEN WHAT ARE YOU?!
ME? THE IMP OF THE FOREST WITH BRIEFS IN HIS BEARD!
LOOK... THINK OF FANTASIA LIKE THE AIR AROUND YOU— IT'S EVERYWHERE AND GOOD FOR A LOT OF THINGS...
...BUT YOU HUMANS ONLY DO THIS WITH IT!
HYAASP...
PRRATATAAAA
W-WHAT?! WE FART IT OUT?
AND WHAT WAS THAT ELEPHANT NOISE!?
BASICALLY, YES!
OH MAN, THAT ONE WAS *BAAAD*!

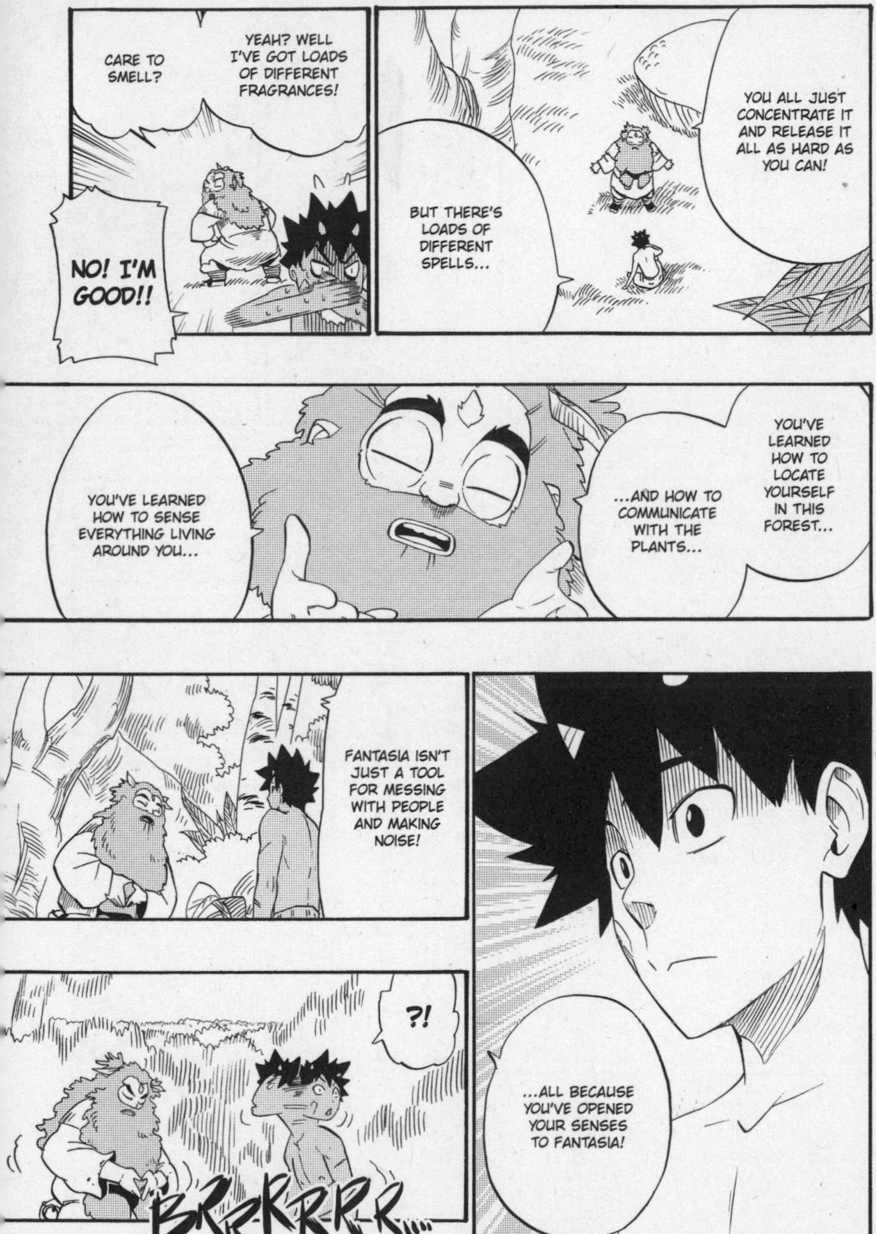
YOU ALL JUST CONCENTRATE IT AND RELEASE IT ALL AS HARD AS YOU CAN!
BUT THERE'S LOADS OF DIFFERENT SPELLS...
YEAH? WELL I'VE GOT LOADS OF DIFFERENT FRAGRANCES!
CARE TO SMELL?
NO! I'M GOOD!!
YOU'VE LEARNED HOW TO LOCATE YOURSELF IN THIS FOREST...
...AND HOW TO COMMUNICATE WITH THE PLANTS...
YOU'VE LEARNED HOW TO SENSE EVERYTHING LIVING AROUND YOU...
...ALL BECAUSE YOU'VE OPENED YOUR SENSES TO FANTASIA!
FANTASIA ISN'T JUST A TOOL FOR MESSING WITH PEOPLE AND MAKING NOISE!
?!
BRRRRRR...

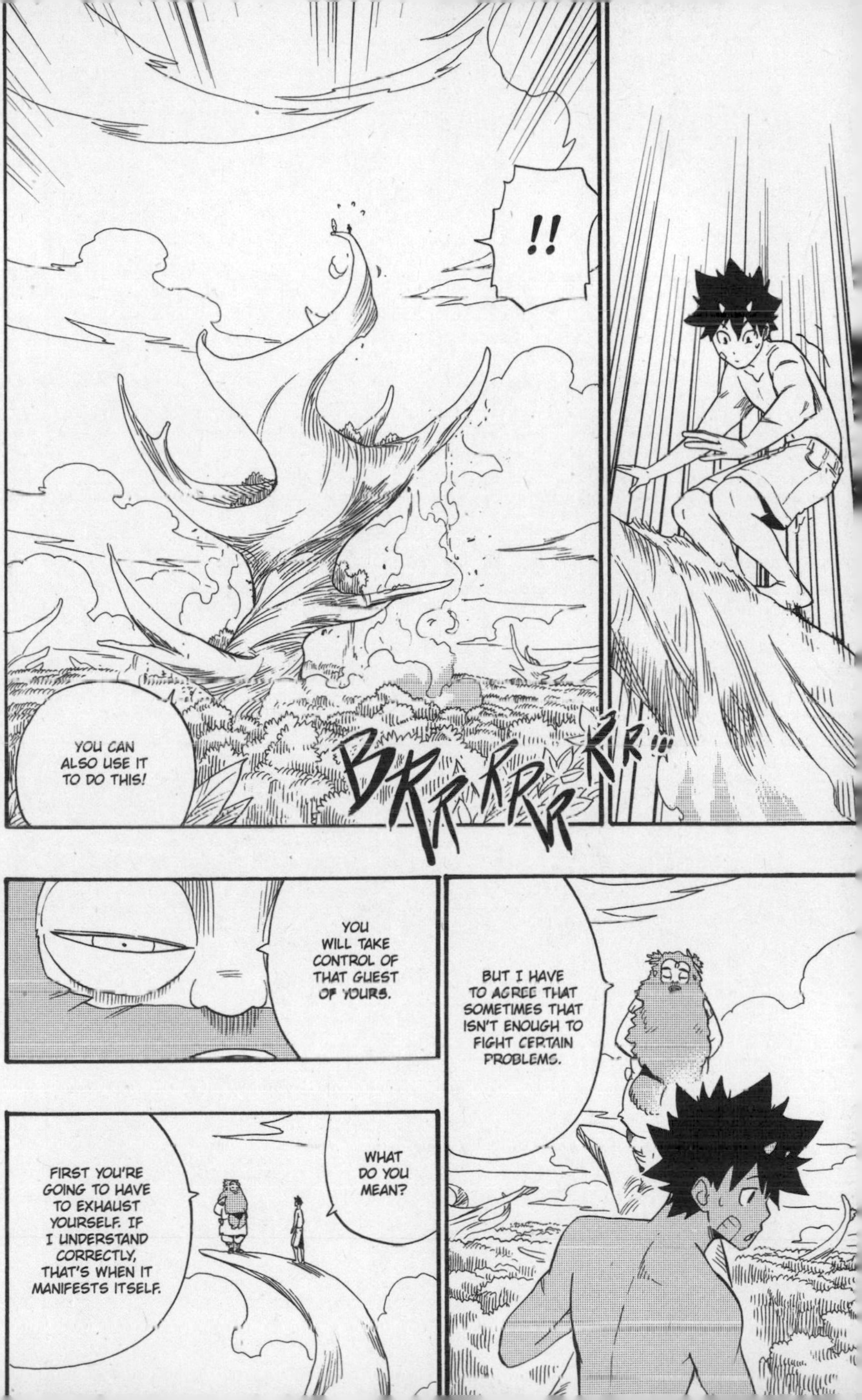
YOU CAN ALSO USE IT TO DO THIS!
BRRRRRRRRR...
!!
BUT I HAVE TO AGREE THAT SOMETIMES THAT ISN'T ENOUGH TO FIGHT CERTAIN PROBLEMS.
YOU WILL TAKE CONTROL OF THAT GUEST OF YOURS.
WHAT DO YOU MEAN?
FIRST YOU'RE GOING TO HAVE TO EXHAUST YOURSELF. IF I UNDERSTAND CORRECTLY, THAT'S WHEN IT MANIFESTS ITSELF.

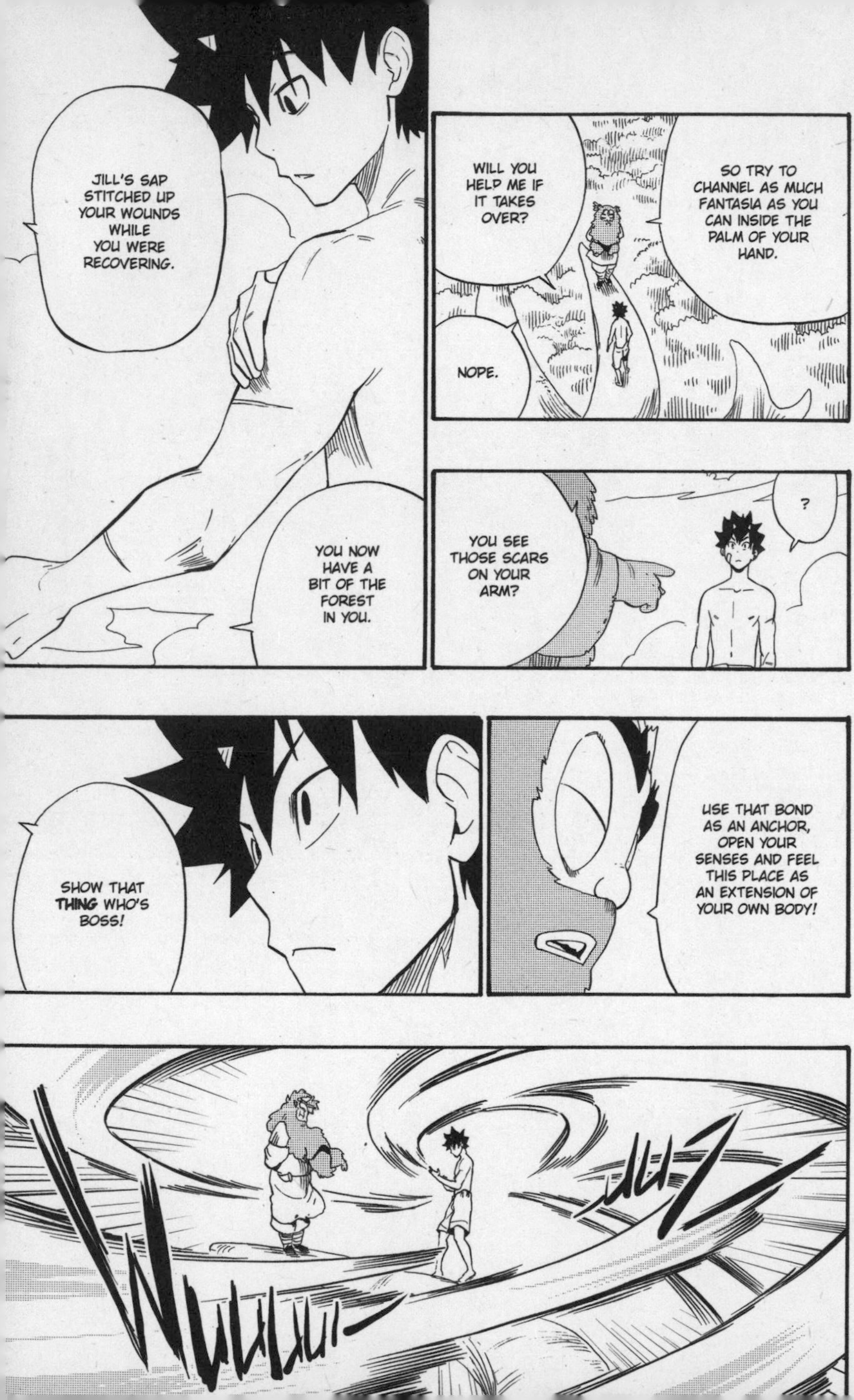
SO TRY TO CHANNEL AS MUCH FANTASIA AS YOU CAN INSIDE THE PALM OF YOUR HAND.
WILL YOU HELP ME IF IT TAKES OVER?
NOPE.
?
YOU SEE THOSE SCARS ON YOUR ARM?
JILL'S SAP STITCHED UP YOUR WOUNDS WHILE YOU WERE RECOVERING.
YOU NOW HAVE A BIT OF THE FOREST IN YOU.
USE THAT BOND AS AN ANCHOR, OPEN YOUR SENSES AND FEEL THIS PLACE AS AN EXTENSION OF YOUR OWN BODY!
SHOW THAT **THING** WHO'S BOSS!

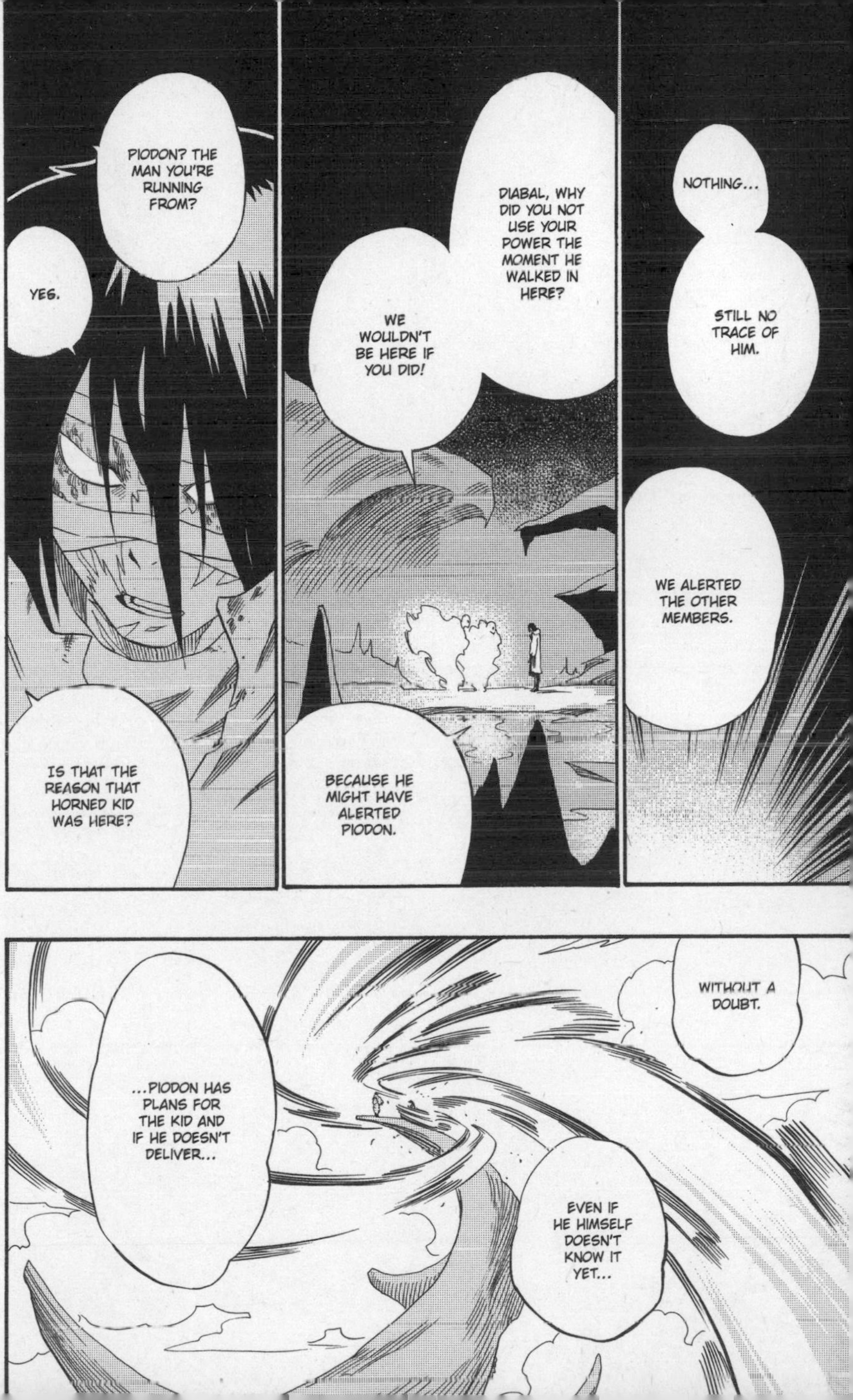
NOTHING...
STILL NO TRACE OF HIM.
WE ALERTED THE OTHER MEMBERS.
DIABAL, WHY DID YOU NOT USE YOUR POWER THE MOMENT HE WALKED IN HERE?
WE WOULDN'T BE HERE IF YOU DID!
BECAUSE HE MIGHT HAVE ALERTED PIODON.
PIODON? THE MAN YOU'RE RUNNING FROM?
YES.
IS THAT THE REASON THAT HORNED KID WAS HERE?
WITHOUT A DOUBT.
...PIODON HAS PLANS FOR THE KID AND IF HE DOESN'T DELIVER...
EVEN IF HE HIMSELF DOESN'T KNOW IT YET...

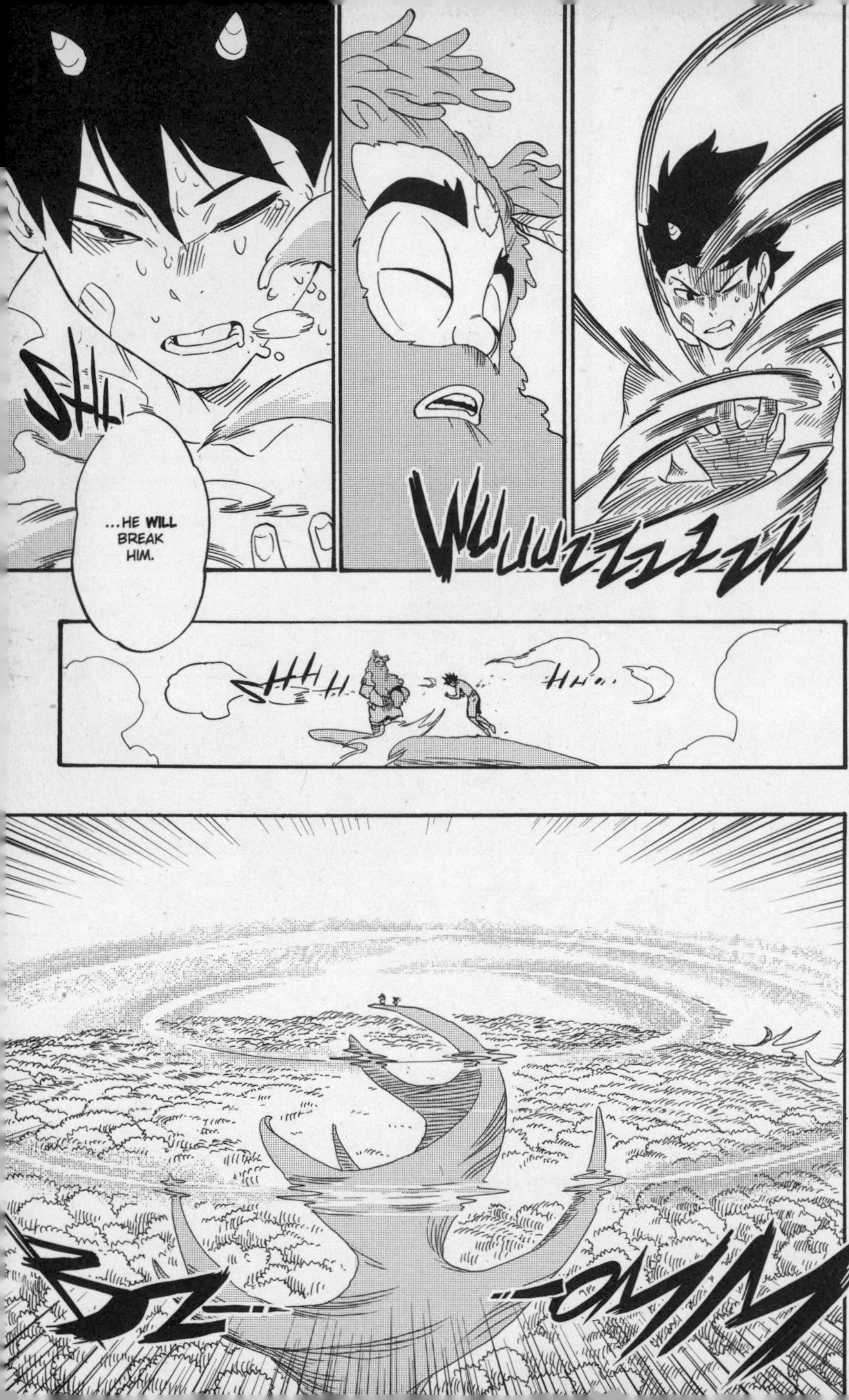
WUUUZZZZZU
SHH
...HE WILL BREAK HIM.
SHHHH
HH...
RZZ...OMM

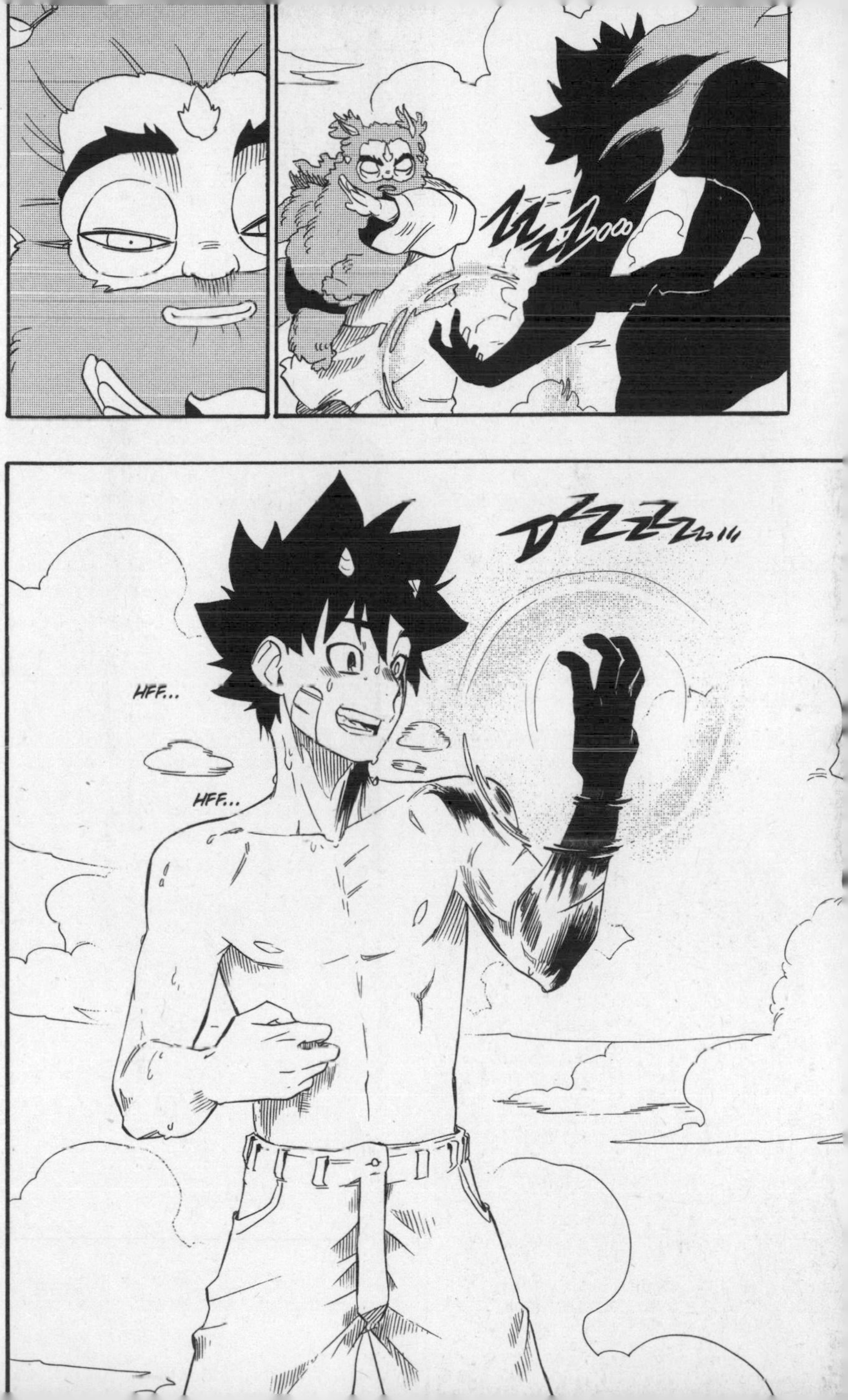
HFF...
HFF...

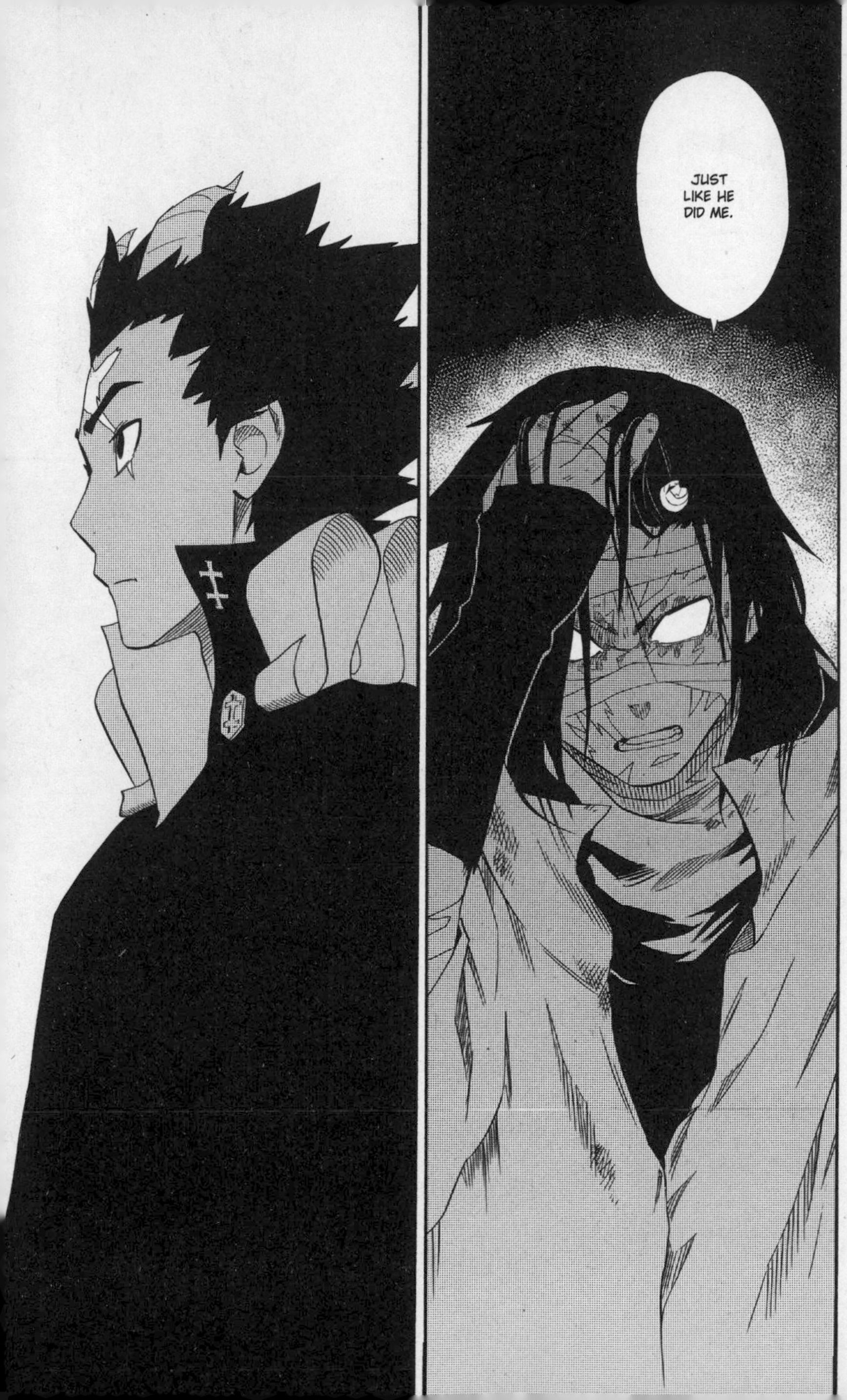
JUST LIKE HE DID ME.

TO BE CONTINUED...

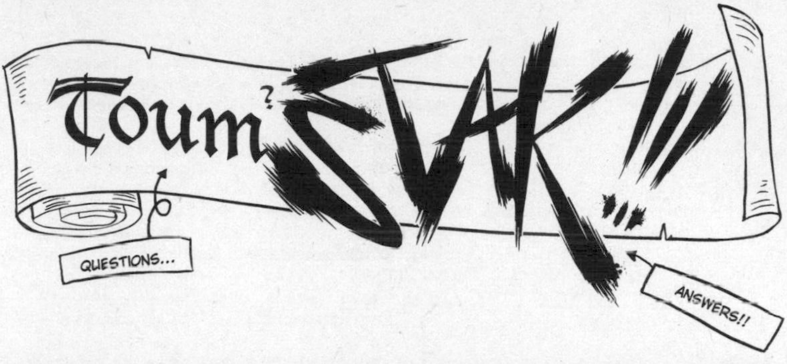
Toum? STAK!!!
QUESTIONS...
ANSWERS!!

Jules Martin: I'm a big fan of your manga. I've read it a couple of times and there are a few small details that I'm curious about. In volume 4, when Alma is down, we can see the Bravery Duet's emblem even though we're only told of them in volume 5. Are you a pro at foreshadowing like Oda (*One Piece*)? And the marking Doc mentions, will we be getting more information on small details like those? And Grimm. When will we finally know more about him?

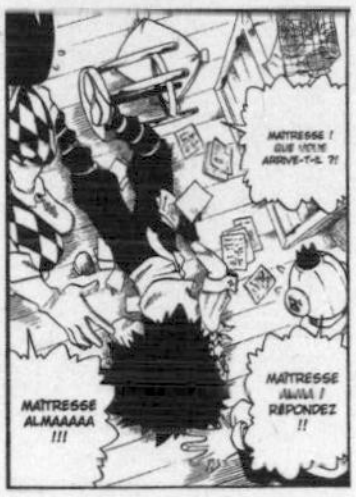
MAÎTRESSE ! QUE VOUS ARRIVE-T-IL ?!
MAÎTRESSE ALMA ! RÉPONDEZ !!
MAÎTRESSE ALMAAAAA !!!

Tony Valente: Nicely spotted! That is indeed the Bravery Duet we see back in volume 4!
As for the markings Doc mentioned, I think you're talking about the notebook he shows to Seth in volume 2, right? That's part of the mystery of the Nemeses. And that info will come in little by little! As for Grimm, this volume mentions a few new details and maybe caused just as many new questions too, but that wasn't on purpose. I swear! But, hey! Since it's just you and me here, let me in on a little secret: Grimm is actually... *Hmm*... No, actually, never mind. I'll tell you next time, I think we're being watched.

....

Cassandra. L: Hey, Tony! I have a couple of really important questions for you! Seth, Grimm and Hameline's Fantasia are clearly a different color. Does that have any specific meaning?
Tony Valente: It's similar to how voices change depending on the person talking.

Cassandra. L: Why did Grimm wrap his entire body and even his face in toilet paper—I mean bandages?
Tony Valente: Because he's suffering from turbo diar—I mean, a big infection.

Cassandra. L: Fantasia seems to come from the air and the world around the characters. But where do the Thaumaturges' Miracles come from?
Tony Valente: That is something I can't really go into further detail here...
Well, I **could** go into further details about it here, but I won't.

Cassandra. L: Will there be some romantic story elements? (The part between Hameline and Seth was kind of cute.)
Tony Valente: Sure! Not sure yet. We'll see. Maybe.

Cassandra. L: That's it. Good luck with everything and thanks again for showing that even French people can write great manga!
Tony Valente: Thank you! (^u°)/

....

Tommy: Hi! What software do you use on your computer to draw?

Tony Valente: To draw, nothing. I draw my storyboards by hand. But for the screen tones I use Manga Studio. And for coloring I use Clip Studio Paint. The basic versions (cheaper) are enough for me, so that's what I use!

Shango: Hi! Congratulations on *Radiant*'s big success! I wanted to know what inspired you for Ocoho's personality. I just really love her character and I don't know why, but I just hope we'll someday see a team made of Seth, Mélie, Doc, Grimm and Ocoho going on a *BIIIIIIG* adventure, but maybe I'm being too unrealistic. ^^
Tony Valente: *Aaah*! Thanks for liking my characters! ^^ I'm sorry to say that Ocoho wasn't really specifically inspired by anyone in particular. She's just a character I made around the same time I made Seth. Which was...a few years ago now. At first, *Radiant* was supposed to start with a trio composed of Seth, Ocoho (whose name was Méloko back then) and Grimm. But in the end, I had to make the character grow a little bit first, and when I was thinking of a story arc with the Wizard Knights, she fit right into that world. By the way, her name means "barn owl" in the native tongue of an indigenous North American people called the Huron.

Mathieu: Hi, Tony! I just bought volume 5 of your AMAZING manga (no, really, I mean it) and now I've got a couple of questions, but not specifically about this last volume. So in volume 4, chapter 27, page 10, when Torque speaks, there's an empty dialogue bubble! Why is that? A printing error? He had nothing to say? Anyway, I was just wondering...
Tony Valente: Oh! Yeah! No! He just didn't have anything smart to say. And things... No, that was just a mistake...

Mathieu: Also, will we see the bearded guy again in the future? Um...Santori? And what's his Miracle anyway? Is it linked to mister-I'm-so-broken-and-don't-have-pupils we see at the end of volume 5?
Tony Valente: Yes, we will see him again, but no they're not linked!

Mathieu: Does Baron Cristolom use any drugs (you know, the two bottles of "Vino Divino" that make his quads swell up)?
Tony Valente: The Vino Divino is a well-guarded secret of the Merchant Barons. It can make quads grows bigger, arms and other useful parts of your body you'd want to make bigger like the end of your...nose! Or your t...toes! But that's not just it...

Kelly Hidelock: Hi, I wanted to know if we'll have the opportunity to know more about Alma and her past? Goodbye!
Tony Valente: Hi. Yes. Thanks! xoxo..

Liebgott Nathan: Hi! First of all, I wanted to tell you I *adoooore* your manga!!!!!!!!! But I had a few technical questions regarding the parchment that wizards use to stock objects. Is there a limit to the amount of items a parchment can contain? Can we stock up on items of any size or weight or is there a maximum limit to how much you can get?
Tony Valente: The amount depends on the size of the parchment and the skill of the wizard doing the miniaturizing! But even a super skilled wizard wouldn't be able to miniaturize, say, a castle. Even with a big parchment. Unless it's like a really big parchment and a really small castle... That I don't know.

Liebgott Nathan: Lastly, is that the spell the wizard with all the bandages, Grimm (super cool), uses?
Tony Valente: Yes.

Diego Escobedo: We know that Seth possesses a huge amount of Fantasia, but does he have more than Merlin? And does a wizard's Fantasia increase with training or is it capped?

Tony Valente: Seth doesn't possess any Fantasia, just like any other character doesn't. Fantasia is an element that is everywhere! Wizards just learn how to manipulate it. The thing with Seth is that he can do that with his bare hands. And Merlin was super strong, but his legend dates from a couple of centuries ago. There's no mentioning of him using his bare hands though... Maybe his butt?

Send your questions to: radiant@ankama.com

I hear the universe is 13.8 billion years old and it's filled with energy and still growing... I don't know how it keeps its energy after all these years! Me, I'm in my thirties and I'm starting to feel the effects of time on my body. So I wonder how I'll be 13.8 billion years from now. I'll probably have used up my pension fund by then, so I'll have to get back to working again. Will I still be working on *Radiant*? Nah, I'll be done by then. I'm not counting on drawing more than a billion volumes.

—Tony Valente

Tony Valente began working as a comic artist with the series *The Four Princes of Ganahan*, written by Raphael Drommelschlager. He then launched a new three-volume project, *Hana Attori*, after which he produced *S.P.E.E.D. Angels*, a series written by Didier Tarquin and colored by Pop.

In preparation for *Radiant*, he relocated to Canada. Through confronting caribou and grizzlies, he gained the wherewithal to train in obscure manga techniques. Since then, his eating habits have changed, his lifestyle became completely different and even his singing voice has changed a bit!

RADIANT VOL. 6
VIZ MEDIA Manga Edition

STORY AND ART BY **TONY VALENTE**

Translation/(´･∀･`)ｻﾌﾟ?
Touch-Up Art & Lettering/**Erika Terriquez**
Design/**Julian [JR] Robinson**
Editor/**Marlene First**

Published by arrangement with MEDIATOON LICENSING/Ankama.
RADIANT T06
© ANKAMA EDITIONS 2016, by Tony Valente
All rights reserved

Printed in the U.S.A.

Published by VIZ Media, LLC
P.O. Box 77010
San Francisco, CA 94107

10 9 8 7 6 5 4 3 2 1
First printing, July 2019

viz.com

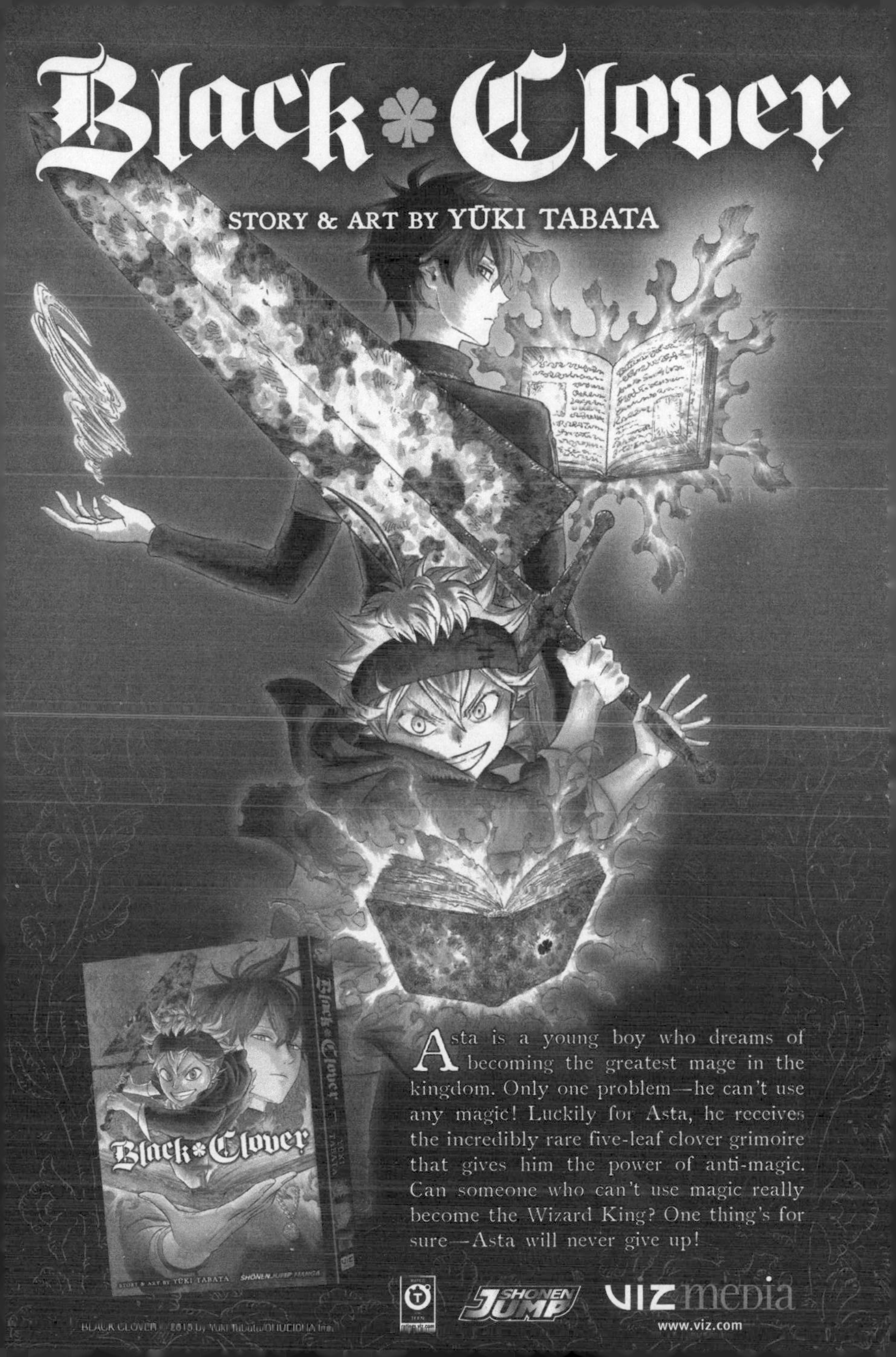
Black Clover
STORY & ART BY YŪKI TABATA
Asta is a young boy who dreams of becoming the greatest mage in the kingdom. Only one problem—he can't use any magic! Luckily for Asta, he receives the incredibly rare five-leaf clover grimoire that gives him the power of anti-magic. Can someone who can't use magic really become the Wizard King? One thing's for sure—Asta will never give up!
BLACK CLOVER © 2015 by Yuki Tabata/SHUEISHA Inc.
SHONEN JUMP
VIZ media
www.viz.com

DEMON SLAYER
KIMETSU NO YAIBA

Story and Art by
KOYOHARU GOTOUGE

In Taisho-era Japan, kindhearted Tanjiro Kamado makes a living selling charcoal. But his peaceful life is shattered when a demon slaughters his entire family. His little sister Nezuko is the only survivor, but she has been transformed into a demon herself! Tanjiro sets out on a dangerous journey to find a way to return his sister to normal and destroy the demon who ruined his life.

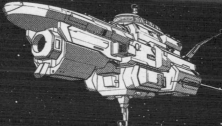

Dr. STONE

STORY BY
RIICHIRO INAGAKI

ART BY
BOICHI

One fateful day, all of humanity turned to stone. Many millennia later, Taiju frees himself from petrification and finds himself surrounded by statues. The situation looks grim—until he runs into his science-loving friend Senku! Together they plan to restart civilization with the power of science!

YOU'RE READING THE WRONG WAY

RADIANT reads from right to left, starting in the upper-right corner, meaning that action, sound effects, and word-balloon order are completely reversed from English order.

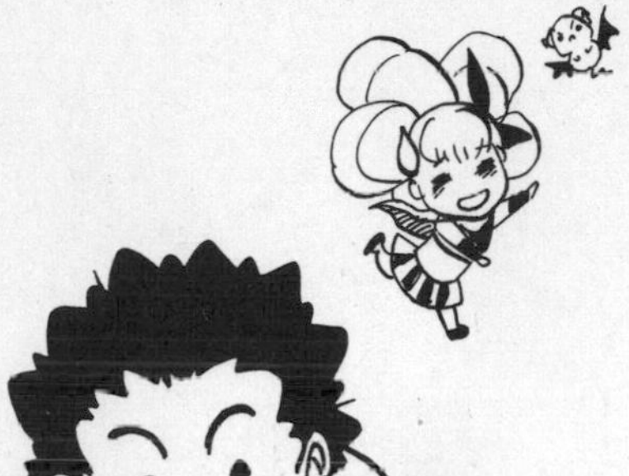

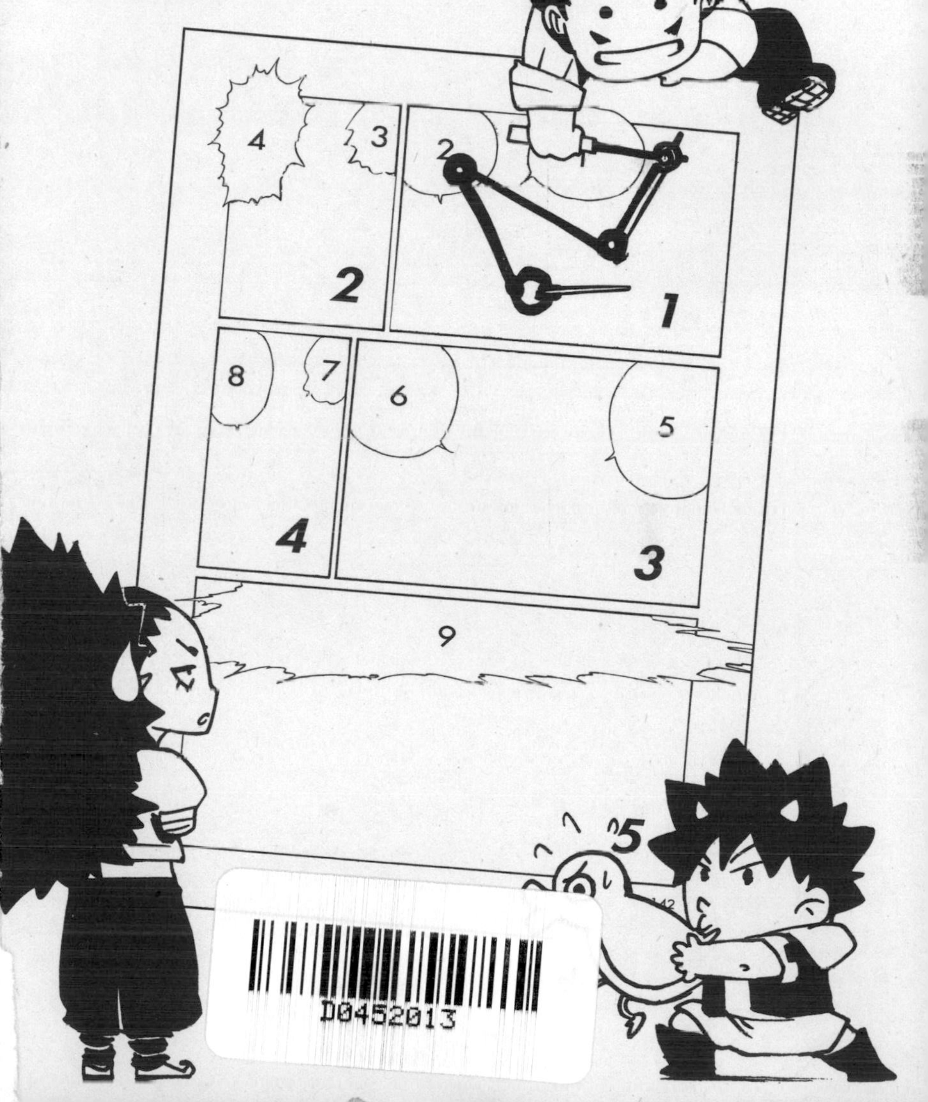

1
2
3
4
5
6
7
8
2
3
4
9
5